MOVING MONEY

MOVING
MOVING
MOVING
MOVING
MOVING
MOVING

**An Empirical Analysis
of Federal
Expenditure Patterns**

MONEY
MONEY

**Thomas J. Anton
Jerry P. Cawley
Kevin L. Kramer**

**University of
Michigan**

MONEY
MONEY
MONEY
MONEY

O G
& H

Oelgeschlager, Gunn & Hain,
Publishers, Inc.
Cambridge, Massachusetts

GARDNER WEBB COLLEGE LIBRARY

Copyright © 1980 by Oelgeschlager, Gunn & Hain, Publishers, Inc. All rights reserved. No part of this publication may be reproduced, stored in a retrieval system, or transmitted in any form or by any means—electronic mechanical photocopy, recording, or otherwise—without the prior written consent of the publisher.

International Standard Book Number: 0-89946-066-6

Library of Congress Catalog Card Number: 80-21700

Printed in the United States of America

Library of Congress Cataloging in Publication Data

Main entry under title:

Moving money.

   Bibliography: p.
   1. United States—Appropriations and expenditures. 2. Government spending policy—United States. 3. Intergovernmental fiscal relations—United States. I. Anton, Thomas Julius.
HJ2051.M68   353.0072   80-21700
ISBN 0-89946-066-6

This book is based on research funded by the Department of Housing and Urban Development under Research Grant H-2956, September 1978. All analyses and interpretations contained in the study, however, are the sole responsibility of the authors.

HJ
2051
.A78

Contents

List of Maps

List of Figures

List of Tables

Preface

This study was stimulated by curiosity over the distribution of federal government expenditures. Like many other observers, we began to notice the rapid increases in federal grants to state and local governments several years ago. We wondered whether there were any patterns to these increases, and how such patterns might be explained. Our search for information about these matters led fairly quickly to a realization that no one really knew very much about them. None of the "authoritative" data sources seemed detailed enough to answer any but the most superficial questions. Worse yet, when various data systems were compared, major inconsistencies were apparent. Almost accidentally we stumbled across a little-known data source that seemed to us more useful than the more conventional authoritative sources. As we began to work with this data system, the *Federal Outlays* series, our major question was gradually expanded from "where does the federal government spend its money?" to "why is there so little good information on where the federal government spends its money?" Exploring this issue led us to conclude that one important source of poor information was poor thought: concepts and theories essential for defining significance and ordering information are either poorly developed or analytically weak. This book is an effort to respond to this growing set of concerns. It is simultaneously an analysis of the distribution of federal dollars, an extended commentary on how and why federal data are weak, and an effort to develop a conceptual scheme capable of ordering data in ways that might help to explain, no less than describe, expenditure patterns.

One result that emerges clearly from the following analysis is that there are, in fact, established patterns of federal fund distribution. This conclusion would appear both trivial and transparent were it not for the multitude of current observers who assume or allege that federal government expenditures are somehow "chaotic" or "out of control."

Federal spending has grown enormously and is marvelously complex, but there is order in the growth and pattern to the complexity. A second clear result is that the structure of federal expenditures seems remarkably stable through time. Since most federal dollars are distributed to individuals, often through formulas, and since population patterns change slowly, states with the largest populations receive more federal dollars now, as they did ten, twenty, or fifty years ago. Because many more federal dollars are being distributed now than fifty years ago, however, the largest states are receiving much more, relative to the smallest states, than they did earlier: "them that has, gits." The system is not so much "redistributive" as it is "prodistributive." Third, there is considerable instability in the system when numbers are disaggregated to agency or program for grantors, or to counties and cities for recipients. Instability among distributions by grantors provides much of the dynamism of the system, allowing spending to be responsive to newly emerging funding needs. Among county and city recipients, on the other hand, funding instability is more problematic because it is less predictable. Overall, however, federal expenditures exhibit patterns of stability and dynamism that seem appropriate for a system with well-established commitments but constantly changing demands.

Trying to study this system through established data systems is difficult because the most comprehensive and authoritative information reports are designed to achieve purposes that may have little to do with research objectives. First and foremost, expenditure decisions are *political* decisions, which answer the question "who to support" more than they define what to do. Data systems operated by O.M.B., Treasury, or Census provide information to inform national budget and management decisions, or an aggregate record of government fiscal operations, but these data are not easily linked to the political processes that shape federal expenditures. *Outlays* data, on the other hand, provide expenditure information by specific *program,* which in turn can be aggregated to agency and department totals and thus link directly into the politics of spending processes. Observing program initiation and institutionalization suggests that much of what is relevant to those processes is missed by explanatory paradigms built on "rational choice" or "organizational processes" models. We suggest an alternative paradigm, "choice as experiment," whose operational principle is neither "pick the best (most rational) solution" nor "do what you did last time," but rather "spend some money and see what happens." This paradigm seems more faithful to processes of initiation and institutionalization that are built on advocacy by coalitions of interested beneficiaries. Program, choice, and coalition thus become the major elements of a conceptual scheme we believe to be useful in reaching for explanations of observed expenditure patterns.

Viewing expenditures as inherently political, observing program details in relationship to the larger expenditure system of which they are parts, and observing the system for a long enough period to sense the historical roots of system development together form a perspective on federal expenditures that differs rather considerably from other perspectives currently in vogue. We have found our perspective useful in helping to distinguish between questions to which there are answers and answers to which there are neither questions nor analytic ideas capable of raising meaningful questions. We believe that we have answered some important questions in this work. In answering them, we hope that we have raised others appropriate to investigating a system characterized by both stability and dynamism. To the extent that we have raised as well as answered meaningful questions, we have done some justice to a problem that is, by turns, important, interesting, and unending.

Acknowledgments

Perhaps more than most information-gathering excursions, this enterprise has been totally dependent on the goodwill, cooperation, and intelligence of the hundreds of federal officials who willingly gave us their time and advice—as well as their computer tapes. We owe a very special debt, however, to Assistant Secretary Donna Shalala, of the Department of Housing and Urban Development, who encouraged our work and ultimately funded it; to former Deputy Assistant Secretary David Puryear, who also encouraged our work and gave good advice at opportune moments; and to Dr. John Ross, our Technical Representative at H.U.D., who kept us in rein, often with well-deserved criticism, but more often with sensible and helpful advice. Walter Haase of the Office of Management and Budget provided a helpful memo at a very important time, while both Larry Hush of O.M.B. and J. Norman Reid of the Department of Agriculture provided useful criticism at many times. None of this work would have been possible at all without the dedicated, intelligent and continuing support provided by Luther Burgess of the Community Services Administration, who probably thinks he has taught us a lot about numbers, but who in fact has taught us even more about politics, commitment, responsibility, and friendship. (Thanks, Buck.)

Members of our team based in Ann Arbor were fewer in number but at least as important as our Washington colleagues. Kathryn Jones provided an unmatched level of administrative and research skill during the entire life of the project, in addition to managing the many "crises" the rest of us generated. Peter D. Ward made a major contribution to our data organization and processing work and helped us to think more clearly about the significance of these numbers. Samuel Evans, Alice Hayes, Carmine Scavo, Terryl Mairs, and Laura Urbanski made very different but essential contributions.

We hope the following materials reflect the quality and quantity of the assistance we have received. To the extent that they do not, the Principal Investigator assumes full responsibility.

Chapter 1

The Problem of Federal Government Expenditures

Few issues of domestic political concern have generated as much sustained interest during the past decade as the distribution of federal expenditures among state and local governmental jurisdictions. Depending on the perspective of the observer, the issue can have many "faces." To politicians, the size and growth rate of the federal budget is a prominent concern. For administrators charged with implementing large federal programs, program complexity and political accountability are major problems. Scholars who probe these matters, meanwhile, are confronted with still another "face" of the issue, namely, the absence of data to support unambiguous conclusions regarding who gets what from the federal treasury, or why. At the present time, no one really knows where federal money is spent; thus we are unable to even describe, let alone analyze, the causes or consequences of federal fund flows. To understand the "issue" posed by federal expenditures, therefore, it is essential that we sort out its most important dimensions and address the question of data availability.

THE AMERICAN POLITICAL ECONOMY

The size of the public sector has been a recurring source of controversy in American politics since the beginning of the republic. Ideologically committed to free enterprise, but pragmatically aware of the necessity for governmental action to cope with emerging social problems, American citizens and politicians have repeatedly argued over whether government action was desirable and, if desirable, which level of government should act. No final resolution of these disputes has ever been achieved. Instead, public sector action and arguments against such action have grown together, with all levels of government participating in cycles of expansion closely tied to eras of opportunity or crisis. Frontier and commercial development stimulated governmental growth in the nineteenth century, and a major depression sandwiched between two world wars led to considerably more rapid government growth in the twentieth century.[1] Opposition to public sector expansion has been constant, but government expansion has continued nonetheless. In the American polity, pragmatism has triumphed over principle.[2]

The pragmatic triumph has effectively undermined the major doctrines traditionally used to oppose federal government growth: states rights and property rights. Proposals for new federal activities in banking, commercial regulation, labor regulation, housing, welfare, and other program areas were all attacked on grounds that such activities were no business of the federal government. The Constitution, it was said, created a federal government of *limited* powers, enumerated in clear language, beyond which that government had no legal right to act. Powers not specifically enumerated were reserved to the states, it was argued, thus preventing federal action in areas such as corporate regulation or income security that were not stated in constitutional language. Although repeatedly argued, the states rights doctrine suffered from a major political liability: federal government participation in a large number of state and local programs not mentioned in the Constitution, from education to highways. Arguments against such actions thus threatened the beneficiaries of federal participation, undermining the possibilities for effective political opposition. When national courts invented the doctrine of *implied* powers to justify national action, the legal path toward federal expansion became clear. For more than a century, politics not law has been decisive in determining whether and how the federal government will act.[3] Today there are virtually no areas of governmental concern in which the federal government is not involved.[4]

Conceived as a boundary beyond which no government could penetrate, individual rights to own and dispose of property were ideas often used to oppose federal expansion. These, too, were ambiguous ideas, since enormous federal grants to individuals, corporations, and governments during the nineteenth century had made clear that federal action could be used to *grant* property wealth to individuals.[5] When an income tax was adopted by the federal government early in this century, the power to take away that form of property was established. Shortly after the second World War had come to a close, a series of federal court decisions expanded this power. If a higher "national purpose" required it, the national government could confiscate real property, could confiscate income, could confiscate individual contributions already made to pension funds, and could even take away an individual's rights to *earn* income by denying professional practice licenses. Furthermore, the federal urban renewal program made clear that this federal-state-local program could not only confiscate one individual's rights to property, but could also allocate those same rights to another individual (or corporation) if such action would serve a public purpose. Although arguments for private property as a limitation on government expansion continue to be made, after 1950 it was clear that no such limitation existed—provided that some "national purpose" could be found to justify encroachment on private property rights.[6] In property rights, as in states rights, political negotiation rather than legal disputation have come to define the expandable boundaries of federal government action.

None of this should be taken to mean that the rhetoric of free enterprise and individual freedom is without significance. That the public sector consumes far less of the gross national product in the United States than in other industrialized nations must be attributed, in part, to the braking effect of these ideas.[7] The braking effect, however, is more a matter of politics than of principle.[8] Individuals or groups that benefit from government programs often find these ideas useful in opposing programs for which they may be asked to pay but from which they will gain little benefit. Thus homeowner and realtor groups that are heavily subsidized ($25 billion in 1978) by federal mortgage and property tax write-offs consistently have opposed government-assisted housing programs for those who cannot afford to purchase their own homes. Agricultural producers, heavily subsidized through product payments, crop insurance, grants and low-interest loans, consistently have opposed programs to assist urban areas. Corporations, heavily subsidized by liberal depreciation and loan programs, consistently have opposed liberalized unemployment benefit or safety regulation programs. None of these groups succeed all the time, and benefit distributions can change dramatically from one period to another, but the principle of "I support government benefits for me but oppose them for you" is as old as American politics.

In the absence of operative legal or philosophical restraints against federal growth, the self-interested pursuit of federal benefits provides multiple opportunities to expand total benefits for groups capable of acting in concert. Between 1950 and 1978, when wars in Korea and Vietnam, a suburban population explosion, urban disruption followed by fiscal collapse, and a newly developed environmental consciousness, all provided opportunities for coalition-formation, federal budget outlays more than doubled each decade. New definitions of national political purpose, from the interstate highway program of the mid-1950s to the war on poverty of the 1960s to the fiscal assistance programs of the 1970s, mobilized coalitions powerful enough to cause budget outlays to grow considerably more rapidly than the gross national product, as Table 1.1 reveals.[9] An even more striking revelation in Table 1.1 is the extraordinary growth in federal grants-in-aid, which grew three times more rapidly than total budget outlays during this period. By 1978 federal grants of $80 billion accounted for nearly 22 percent of total domestic outlays and represented some 28.2 percent of state and local government own-source revenue.[10] Indeed, federal grants now constitute the single most important source of state-local revenue, surpassing property, sales and income taxes in significance. More than ever before, the federal government has become the chief banker for thousands of state and local governments.[11]

Apart from its obvious fiscal implications the recent growth of federal grants-in-aid has considerable political significance. Structurally, local governments have been brought into a direct and continuing relationship with the federal treasury—a relationship that, for most municipalities, is quite unprecedented.[12] Many larger and older American cities, in particular, now derive 50, 60 or as much as 70 percent of their revenues from federal programs.[13] Politically, sums as large as these have created powerful incentives for local and state officials to compete for federal program dollars. Acting as individual jurisdictions or through state, county or city associations, lower-level governments have become increasingly active in shaping federal expenditure programs.[14] More than 1,100 assistance programs are now listed in the *Catalog of Federal Domestic Assistance,* of which some 700 distribute money. Administrative coordination between these programs, or the lack of it, has become a matter of increasing concern, as has the multitude of different and often conflicting rules required for participation.[15] Agitation over these issues, fueled by concern over the fairness of grant distribution patterns, clearly has been the major source of renewed political interest in those patterns.[16]

Important as grants-in-aid have become, however, they represent no more than a portion of a much larger transformation in federal spending policies. Federal benefits are not confined solely to grants; they are also delivered in the form of direct payments to individuals, direct loans, loan guarantees, and tax expenditures, all of which have experi-

TABLE 1.1

Growth in Federal Grants-In-Aid and Non-Defense Domestic Outlays Compared to GNP, Budget Outlays, and State and Local Own Source General Revenue, FY 1950-1978 (Billions of Dollars)

Fiscal Year	GNP	Total Budget Outlays		Grants In Aid	Grants as % of Total Budget Outlays		Grants as % of State and Local Own Source General Revenue		
		Total	Non-Defense		Total Outlays	Domestic Outlays	State & Local	State	Local
1950	264.9	42.6	30.2	2.3	5.4	7.6	13.6	26.1	2.1
1955	380.0	68.5	28.7	3.2	4.7	11.1	11.1	21.2	2.7
1960	497.3	92.2	47.1	7.0	7.6	14.9	16.1	31.1	2.6
1965	657.1	118.4	71.0	10.9	9.2	15.4	17.5	32.4	3.7
1970	959.0	196.6	118.0	24.0	12.2	20.3	20.1	33.6	5.1
1975	1,457.3	334.2	248.7	49.8	14.9	20.0	26.0	37.3	12.9
1978	2,060.4	461.2	356.0	77.9	16.9	21.9	28.2	37.0	17.5
Increase 1950-1978	677%	983%	1079%	3287%					

Sources: Office of Management and Budget, Budget Review Division, Fiscal Analysis Branch, "Federal Government Finances, January 1980 Edition," (Washington, D.C.: Office of Management and Budget, 1980), and "Federal Grants-In-Aid to State and Local Governments, January 1980 Edition," (Washington, D.C.: Office of Management and Budget, 1980); and U.S. Department of Commerce, Bureau of the Census, Historical Statistics of the United States, Colonial Times to 1970, Part 2 (Washington, D.C.: U.S. Government Printing Office, 1975), pp. 1125-1126, 1129, 1133 and Governmental Finances in 1974-75 and 1977-78 (Washington, D.C.: U.S. Government Printing Office, 1976 and 1978), pp. 46. GNP figures are for fiscal year period. Budget figures are for total budget outlays.

enced more dramatic recent increases than have grants-in-aid.[17] Between 1970 and 1978, for example, expenditures for direct payments to individuals more than doubled (to $180.5 billion),[18] as did the amount of outstanding federal loans (to $440.2 billion).[19] Compared to FY 1970, the advancement of "new"[20] government-sponsored enterprise loans in FY 1978 increased by two-and-one half times (to $27.9 billion new activity, $126.8 billion outstanding), direct government loans quadrupled (to $19.8 billion new activity, $120.4 billion outstanding), and guaranteed loans increased by nearly five times (to $11.3 billion new activity, $193.1 billion outstanding).[21] By providing credit at more favorable terms than are available in private capital markets, these programs provide sizeable subsidies to increasing numbers of individual and corporate borrowers, as well as governments. Because federal credit is generally extended over a number of years, these subsidies link millions of homeowners, farmers, corporations, and governments into a semi-permanent relationship with the federal treasury.[22] The significance of this linkage is suggested by the $440 billion in federal loans outstanding in 1978—an amount roughly equivalent to total federal budget outlays in that year ($461 billion).[23] Moreover, these programs, together with federal borrowing in general, give the federal government a commanding presence in United States capital markets. As Table 1.2 reveals, federal government credit activity has accounted for as much as 40 percent of total annual credit market activity (funds raised) in the past decade, and has averaged some 25 percent during that period. Capital markets in the United States may in some sense be "private," but the major actor in those markets is now the federal government.

Tax expenditures, defined by Section 3(a)(3) of the Congressional Budget and Impoundment Control Act of 1974 as ". . . those revenue losses attributable to provisions of the federal tax laws which allow a special exclusion, exemption, or deduction from gross income or which provide a special credit, a preferential rate of tax, or a deferral of tax liability . . . ,"[24] provide federal benefits through tax reduction rather than direct grants or loans. Politically, tax expenditures are less visible than grant or loan programs, but in fact they are both larger and growing more rapidly than either.[25] In 1975, when grants were barely $50 billion and new federal credit activity just under $65 billion, tax expenditures amounted to some $93 billion.[26] Since that time, as a recent study by the Congressional Budget Office has pointed out, tax expenditures have ". . . grown at an average annual rate of 14 percent," compared to an average annual rate of 11 percent for direct federal spending.[27] By 1979 the $150 billion in legislated tax expenditures was nearly twice the $83 billion in grants and growing (Figure 1.1). Inflation appears to have accounted for some of the increase in these subsidies, but new legislation also has added beneficiaries. Under the 92 tax code provisions providing such subsidies in 1980, some $206 billion will be distributed in fiscal 1981, in addition to the $759 billion distributed in the period 1975–1980.[28] These clearly are huge sums, allocated to encourage a desired activity (i.e., home ownership) or simply to provide aid considered desirable (i.e., tax-exempt student loans). What activities to encourage, or which groups to benefit, of course, are inherently political decisions.

Taken together, rapid growth in direct federal expenditures, including grants to state and local governments, the even more rapid growth in federal tax expenditures, and the expansion of federal participation in national credit markets have given the federal government an unprecedented influence over the national economy. Indeed, in fiscal 1978, the sum total of federal budget outlays ($461 billion), outstanding loans and loan guarantees ($440 billion) and tax expenditures ($124 billion) amounted to just over $1.0 trillion, or roughly half of the 1978 GNP of $2.13 trillion.[29] Adding the $302 billion raised and spent by sub-national governments in that year[30] would only emphasize what federal

TABLE 1.2

Federal Fund-Raising Role in Domestic Credit Market (Billions of Dollars)

Item	Fiscal Year										
	1969	1970	1971	1972	1973	1974	1975	1976	T.Q.	1977	1978
Total funds raised in U.S. credit markets*	96.9	93.6	124.9	162.8	206.9	193.0	179.7	248.0	67.9	319.5	366.9
Raised under Federal auspices	11.3	16.4	32.2	39.7	46.5	24.0	64.8	97.5	19.1	79.0	94.5
Federal borrowing from public	-1.0	3.8	19.4	19.4	19.3	3.0	50.9	82.9	18.0	53.5	59.1
Guaranteed borrowing	7.8	2.3	12.2	15.6	14.0	6.2	5.7	10.3	-0.1	14.1	11.3
Government-sponsored enterprise borrowing	4.5	10.3	0.6	4.7	13.2	14.8	8.2	4.3	1.7	11.4	24.1
Federal participation rate (percent)	11.7	17.6	25.8	24.4	22.5	12.5	36.1	39.4	28.2	24.8	25.8

NOTE* Nonfinancial sectors; Federal Reserve Board Flow of Funds Accounts estimates.
SOURCE: Office of Management and Budget, "Special Analyses F: Federal Credit Programs," in Special Analyses, Budget of the United States Government, Fiscal Year 1980 (Washington, D.C.: U.S. Government Printing Office, 1979), Table F-1, p. 135.

FIGURE 1.1

COMPARISON OF OUTSTANDING LOANS, TAX EXPENDITURES, GRANTS-IN-AID,
NON-DEFENSE OUTLAYS, & TOTAL BUDGET OUTLAYS

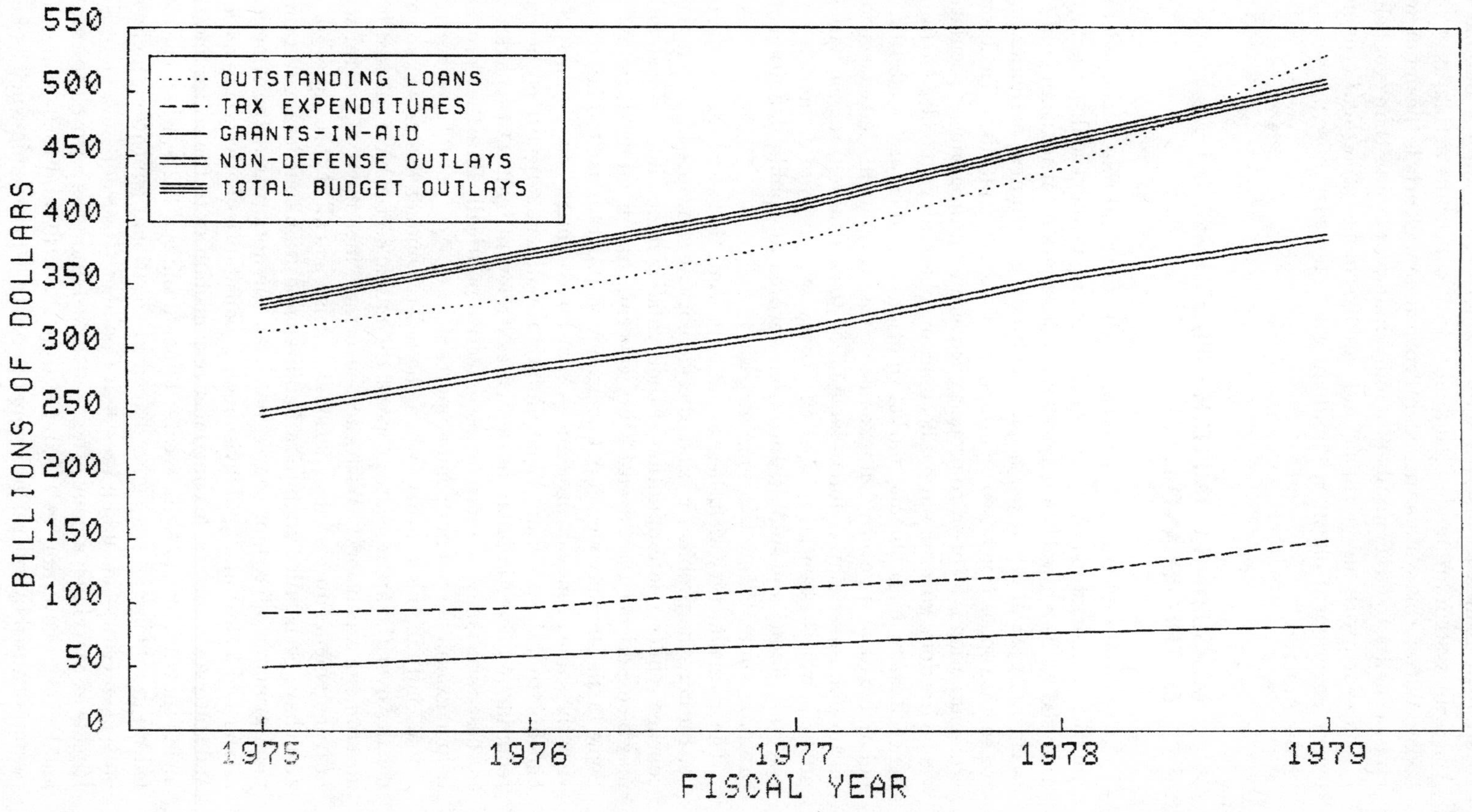

government figures themselves show, namely, that major economic decisions in the American system are made or influenced by politicians acting in or for governmental bodies. Within this system the federal government clearly is the major actor, distributing larger benefits, to larger numbers of individuals and groups than ever before. We are dealing, in short, with an enormous and rapidly-changing *political* economy in which the federal government plays the dominant role. The federal fisc has been transformed into "Bank America."

MEASURING COMPLEXITY: PROBLEMS OF THEORY AND DATA

Despite its growing significance, the financial role of the federal government is not clearly understood, in large measure because ideological disputes have overshadowed analysis.[31] Given a widespread preference for market rather than public sector solutions to emerging social problems, proposals for new government activities have seldom failed to generate opposition based on principles of market capitalism. Taxation to support government action is a threat to property; government programs or regulations violate individual freedom; government has become (or is becoming) too large to function efficiently; hence, if there are problems, market solutions are to be preferred. In recurring cycles of public debate over government expansion, these arguments have been countered by their mirror-opposites: market forces have failed (or are failing) to deal with social problems; public power is essential to deal effectively with private or market power; taxation is essential to fund and staff organizations devoted to a public definition of interest; hence, *this* program and *these* taxes are necessary.

The main difficulty with these arguments is not that they are invalid, though they may be. Rather, the problem is that the ideological concepts in which the arguments are couched render a determination of their validity impossible. "Freedom" to an employer may be experienced as "license" to a government official or "tyranny" to an employee. Some taxpayers may view a public agency or program as "too large," while others may view the same agency or program as "not large enough," particularly if the latter group benefits from the program. What ambitious politicians regard as "needs" or "problems" requiring public action may be viewed as irrelevant by most taxpayers. Debates framed in these terms may be more or less effective politically, but they provide little analytic help in examining public spending patterns.

Especially in this century, when the federal budget has grown so rapidly, recurrent debates over the appropriate scope of the public sector have focused largely on federal government expansion.[32] With each successive increment in federal spending, particularly increments unrelated to national defense, so-called "principles" of American federalism have been called upon to rationalize opposition to federal government growth. The main principle offered, of course, has been the notion that the American Constitution established a clear and final division of responsibilities between the national government and state governments, leaving most responsibilities to the states and the local governments they might choose to create. Thus during the 1920s, when the modern system of federal grants-in-aid was being shaped in vocational education, highways, and health, outspoken critics—including President Coolidge, Governor Lowden of Illinois, Governor Ritchie of Maryland, among others—attacked grants as a threat to state responsibilities and local self-government.[33] Later, during the 1940s and 1950s, concern over the threat to states caused by federal government growth led academics such as Leonard D. White to condemn the "march of power to Washington" [34] and politicians such as former President Hoover and President Eisenhower to initiate commissions to investigate methods of returning power to the states.[35] Ideological hostility to government growth in general was thus joined to a fear that power had become too centralized in Washington. Both themes were captured energetically in a December 1952 bulletin published by the National Association of Manufacturers, entitled *Bring the Government Back Home*:

> The Federal Government is too big. It is so big and so complex that it cannot be efficiently managed by any man or group of men.
>
> The burden of its cost is now a greater load than the economy can carry and remain prosperous.
>
> The steady pressure for more power to regulate and control is a growing menace to individual and civil liberty.
>
> The increasing concentration of political power and economic control in the federal government is destroying the economic and governmental environment which is essential to the survival of the American system of free enterprise and to the preservation of the American constitutional system of a union of states.
>
> Unless the trend toward ever bigger government is halted, and until it is reversed, the states and private business alike face the prospect of ultimate, complete domination by the federal government. And complete federal domination IS totalitarianism.[36]

As political ideology these ideas may be more or less attractive, but they offer no analytic help in determining the appropriate scope of either state or federal action. The brief and highly ambiguous U.S. Constitution provides no clear guidelines for the assignment of government functions, nor have American courts or politicians ever been able (or willing) to reach agreement on the matter. As Austin F. MacDonald wrote more than a half-century ago, "The concept of a function as national or local varies with time and place. Highway construction may properly have been a local obligation only three decades ago; the advent of the automobile may have transformed it overnight into a matter of national concern. Public health may properly be a national function in the United States and a local function in another country, because of widely varying conditions." [37] What MacDonald later refers to as ". . . metaphysical distinctions concerning local and national functions" [38] clearly have never been more than temporary barriers to American government action, whatever ideology American politicians have espoused. The recurrent cycles of public debate over the metaphysics of assignment, however, may well have obscured the dynamics of public sector growth by focusing so much attention on ". . . a principle that is impossible of application." [39]

Quite apart from ideological blinders, the complexity of the American public sector has itself been a major obstacle to clear understanding. A half century ago there were more than 155,000 governmental jurisdictions of various kinds in the United States, organized in 48 very different state systems, with a bewildering variety of organizations, accounting systems, taxes, and political processes. In the past several decades many of these "governments"—primarily school districts—have been eliminated, but we are still left with 50 very different states, 3,141 counties, 36,000 municipalities, and 41,000 special districts of varied form and purpose. Expansion of federal expenditures and federal programs, moreover, has vastly increased the complexity of federal government operations. The size and scale of federal agencies such as Defense or H.H.S. are enormous, federal statutes and regulations appear to multiply exponentially, and the 1,100 federal assistance programs, each with its own purposes and rules, have tied state and local units into the federal system in so many ways that no one seems able to comprehend what is taking place. Merely to imagine some strategy to grasp this huge and varied system is difficult; carrying out such a strategy has always seemed to border on the impossible.

Although hostility to federal government size, growth and complexity are old themes in American political debate, they appear to have achieved a higher level of popularity and significance in the late 1970s as signs of something called "government overload."[40] Public concern over criminal actions associated with the President, hostility to rapid growth in federal welfare programs, analyses of a number of federal programs that purported to demonstrate that such programs had failed to achieve their intended purposes, and pronouncements by eminent academics that American politics had become "too democratic" and therefore undisciplined all contributed to a growing sense that the American system as a whole was no longer capable of intelligent or effective public action.[41] Growth in federal programs and expenditures was increasingly viewed as mindless, rather than purposive, producing activities that were not only ineffective but beyond control.[42]

The largely negative images of federal government activities contained in discussions of "government overload" rely on concepts that pre-judge the conclusions to be reached— in that sense they have no analytic utility.[43] These images are also vastly overdrawn.[44] That government programs are often poorly planned, badly administered, ineffective and occasionally corrupt is of course true, as any number of careful studies attest. To elevate such examples to a universally valid principle is to ignore equally numerous examples of programs that do work, do achieve beneficial results and are effectively managed.[45] To suggest, furthermore, that the mix of variably effective federal programs is somehow beyond intelligent comprehension betrays an absence of theoretical imagination no less than a lack of familiarity with easily available information. Federal expenditures are large, growing, and enormously complicated, to be sure, but there are identifiable patterns to who gets what and how that are well within our grasp.

Consider, as an example, federal grants-in-aid, which are often said to have grown so large and become so numerous that they defy analysis. In fact it can be shown, however, that grant expenditures are highly concentrated in a modest number of programs. Figure 1.2, based on O.M.B.'s 1979 *Catalog of Federal Domestic Assistance,* reveals that 80 percent of federal grant expenditures are made by only 50 programs, and that the largest 100 programs account for some 95 percent of all grants-in-aid.[46] Learning enough about 50 to 100 programs to make sensible statements about origins, development, and distribution can hardly be regarded as an easy task, but surely it should not be seen as an impossible undertaking. Grants or other federal assistance may well be provided through 1,100 or so different programs, but only a fraction of those need be investigated to understand the basic contours of the grant system.

As federal allocations are patterned into a recognizable structure so, too, are recipients of those allocations. Indeed, despite enormous recent growth in federal grants, there is a striking *stability* in the recipient structure that dates back for decades. Since at least the mid-1920s most federal grants have been concentrated in a handful of states, typically those with the largest populations, and *these have generally been the same states* (see Appendix Table 1.1).[47] Thus when the distribution patterns of federal grants are correlated across years, the relationships show a powerful stability within periods of a single decade, and surprisingly powerful stability across a half century (Table 1.3). States receiving the largest amounts of federal aid decades ago, in short, are the states receiving the largest amounts today. Since total grant funds distributed have increased so much, one consequence of this stability is a much larger dispersion, in per capita dollars, around

Table 1.3. Correlations of Federal Grants Received by State, 1924–1978

Time Period	Correlation	Time Period	Correlation
1924–1930	.77	1924–1930	.77
1930–1940	.87	1924–1940	.65
1940–1950	.93	1924–1950	.72
1950–1960	.98	1924–1960	.76
1960–1970	.94	1924–1970	.55
1970–1978	.98	1924–1978	.55

the state average per capita grant. In 1924 the difference between the biggest state "winner" and biggest state "loser" was only $21 per person. By 1960 this difference had increased to $200, and it expanded further to $312 in 1970 and $759 in 1978. States that were "losers" decades ago are losing more relative to the mean and states that were "winners" decades ago are now winning *much* more relative to the mean per capita grant. Never a redistributive system, federal grants can more accurately be thought of as a "prodistributive" system following the principle, "winners win, losers lose." Accounting for such stability during a period of rapid social change is a major intellectual puzzle, to which we return below. We note it here primarily to emphasize the existence of intelligible patterns in federal spending, rather than the "incomprehensible chaos" that has often been alleged.

As barriers to understanding, ideology and alleged complexity must be regarded as trivial compared to the most significant barrier of all: lack of consistent and unambigu-

FIGURE 1.2

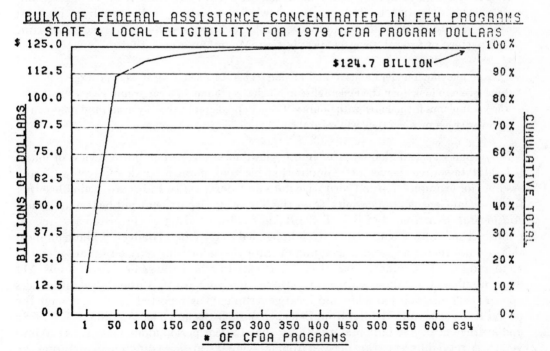

THIS CHART DEPICTS THE LARGE DOLLAR VALUE (CUMULATIVE) OF RELATIVELY FEW PROGRAMS. ADDING HUNDREDS OF PROGRAMS AFTER THE FIRST 10% HAS RELATIVELY LITTLE ADDITIONAL CUMULATIVE IMPACT.

Table 1.4. Comparison of Grants-in-Aid Totals for the 50 States and D.C. Reported by Treasury and Census, FY 1969–1978 (Millions of Dollars)

Fiscal Year	Grants-In-Aid Totals Reported By		
	Treasury	Census	Difference
1978	75,293	69,592	5,701
1977	66,084	62,610	3,474
1976	57,719	55,587	2,131
1975	48,570	46,994	1,576
1974	45,092	41,831	3,261
1973	43,057	39,256	3,801
1972	35,217	31,253	3,964
1971	29,272	26,146	3,126
1970	23,717	21,858	1,859
1969	19,742	19,153	589

Sources: Data calculated from The Department of the Treasury, *Federal Aid to States* (Washington, D.C.: U.S. Government Printing Office, 1969–1979; and Bureau of the Census, Department of Commerce, *Government Finances* (Washington, D.C.: U.S. Government Printing Office, 1970–1980)

ous data. Leaving aside the important but unmanageable question of how 50 states and thousands of local governments account for federal expenditures in their jurisdictions, the more important fact is that the federal government itself has no clear understanding of how much money it spends, where, or in what form. Senator Moynihan of New York, among others, has been repeatedly frustrated in his efforts to understand federal expenditure patterns and for several years has urged the federal government to ". . . give some concentrated attention to finding out just what it *is* doing." [48] Judging from his most recent report to his constituents, however, not much progress has been made. Referring to the pattern of federal resource distribution, Moynihan argues that

> . . . no one much understands it, and no one seems responsible for it. New Yorkers sometimes seem to look upon the Federal fisc in much the manner of a cargo cult. Every so often the great planes fly in, laden with bounty. Then, unpredictably, they fly away, and none can know whether or when they will return. [49]

Moynihan's typical eloquence is, in our view, an exaggeration, but a review of major federal data sources leaves little doubt that his main point is valid. Analysts typically assume, for example, that authoritative data on federal aid to states are available either from official Census publications, from the Treasury Department publication, *Federal Aid to States,* or from O.M.B.'s "Federal Aid to State and Local Governments" report, published annually as a special analysis appended to the federal budget. [50] These publications do not report all federal spending in state areas, focusing only on grants-in-aid to state and local governments, but they do purport to report the same flow of funds. Yet when numbers from these sources are arrayed for comparison, rather large differences appear. Federal grants to state and local governments as reported by Treasury for the period 1969 through 1978 differ from Census reports by as much as $5.7 billion (FY 1978), and average nearly $3 billion annually for that 10-year period alone (Table 1.4). Worse yet, these total differences are derived from individual state area differences of impressive magnitude. [51] For fiscal 1977, Treasury reports $7.45 billion in federal grants to New York; Census reports $6.52 billion. For fiscal 1976, Treasury reports $5.80 billion to California; Census reports $6.23 billion. For fiscal 1974, Treasury reports $2.13 billion to Texas; Census reports $1.90 billion, and so on. Although small from the perspective of national totals, differences that can exceed $1 billion for a single state in a single year (New York, FY 1972) clearly raise questions about how to interpret such data.

Year to year differences of this magnitude, furthermore, render it virtually impossible to judge whether Census or Treasury provide "better" numbers for cross-time analysis. Table 1.5 underlines this evaluative problem. From 1969 through 1978 the average annual *difference* between Census and Treasury figures for a single state was never less than $7.7 million, was often over $100 million, and reached as much as $631 million for the state of New York alone. Serious analyses of changes in the flow of funds into states clearly would require a judgment about the appropriateness of either data base for such analyses, but how would such a judgment be made? And if a choice were not made, what meaning or significance could be attached to the result?

Questions of interpretation become even more pointed when we compare Treasury and O.M.B. numbers (Table 1.6). Annual O.M.B. analyses provide national totals for programs and functions, without disaggregating these total figures into state or lower-level figures. Disaggregation by state is done by Treasury, whose officials work closely with O.M.B. staff to produce a *Federal Aid to States* document that is specifically designed to provide the financial detail absent from O.M.B. totals.[52] Close inter-agency cooperation appears to produce national totals that are reasonably close, portrayed in Columns A. Apart from the transition quarter, when accounting procedures were confused, and fiscal 1970, when a discrepancy of $240 million is shown, annual totals are quite similar or identical. A glance at reported spending by agency, however, reveals that close *national* totals are produced from *agency* spending totals that are vastly different (Columns B).[53] For fiscal 1978, when Treasury and O.M.B. differ by only $12 million nationally, O.M.B. reports $119 million more for Department of Agriculture expenditures than does Treasury, $84 million more for Labor, and $103 million more for Transportation. Treasury reports $98 million more than O.M.B. lists for H.E.W. and $222 million more than O.M.B. reports for H.U.D. in the same year. Table 1.6 makes clear that fiscal 1978 is no isolated case but is instead the normal pattern found in these reports. In fiscal 1972, for example, the negligible $1 million national difference conceals differences in reported agency spending of as much as $133 or $138 million.

Some of the differences between O.M.B. and Treasury numbers are almost certainly due to differences in accounting and reporting procedures. O.M.B. figures are based on reports of "expenditures" submitted by agency budget officers while Treasury figures are based on reports submitted by agency accounting division officers. Although both information channels utilize the same definition of "grants" (based on O.M.B. Circular A-11) they are nevertheless different channels, often producing very different sums for the same agency or program. O.M.B. and Treasury officials meet each year to attempt to reconcile such differences, but time and resource constraints often preclude reconciliation at the level of agency or program expenditure. Amounts that cannot be reconciled in detail are nevertheless reported, usually under the rubric "Adjustments undistributed to States," producing the similar national totals without affecting the different program or agency totals.[54] Similarity in national totals is thus largely an artificial accounting similarity, driven by the need to prepare these documents in time for submission with the federal budget. Both differences in detail and relative similarity of national sums are therefore understandable consequences of the processes through which these data are produced. Understanding the processes, however, does not eliminate discrepancies in the data.

Table 1.5. Cumulative Total and Yearly Differences in State-Area Grants-In-Aid Totals Reported by Treasury and Census, FY 1969–1978 (Thousands of Dollars)

Area	Absolute Differences	
	Cumulative	Yearly Average
Alabama	805,266	80,527
Alaska	188,268	18,827
Arizona	504,869	50,487
Arkansas	646,901	64,690
California	3,172,968	317,297
Colorado	258,731	25,873
Connecticut	978,798	97,880
Delaware	77,290	7,729
District of Columbia	888,975	88,897
Florida	1,024,150	102,415
Georgia	1,591,552	159,155
Hawaii	382,582	38,258
Idaho	185,220	18,522
Illinois	1,756,705	175,671
Indiana	665,656	66,566
Iowa	196,260	19,626
Kansas	221,313	22,131
Kentucky	821,527	82,153
Louisiana	958,642	95,864
Maine	335,759	33,576
Maryland	363,604	36,360
Massachusetts	1,452,611	145,261
Michigan	496,042	49,604
Minnesota	380,373	38,037
Mississippi	1,338,275	133,827
Missouri	749,681	74,968
Montana	225,007	22,501
Nebraska	209,563	20,956
Nevada	118,506	11,851
New Hampshire	193,253	19,325
New Jersey	1,810,787	181,079
New Mexico	369,657	36,966
New York	6,315,437	631,544
North Carolina	930,578	93,058
North Dakota	121,819	12,182
Ohio	1,756,669	175,667
Oklahoma	507,257	50,726
Oregon	301,996	30,200
Pennsylvania	2,887,722	288,772
Rhode Island	176,762	17,676
South Carolina	606,895	60,689
South Dakota	213,315	21,331
Tennessee	895,787	89,579
Texas	1,612,908	161,291
Utah	147,062	14,706
Vermont	77,629	7,763
Virginia	442,020	44,202
Washington	644,418	64,442
West Virginia	702,517	70,252
Wisconsin	573,289	57,329
Wyoming	101,446	10,145

TABLE 1.6

Comparison of Initial Grants-In-Aid Totals
Reported by O.M.B. and Treasury, FY 1969-1978

| | Columns-A | | | Columns-B | | | | |
| | Initial Grants-In-Aid Totals Reported by (millions of dollars) | | | Differences* In Agency Totals Reported by O.M.B. and Treasury (millions of dollars) | | | | |
Year	O.M.B.	Treasury	Difference*	D.O.A.	H.E.W.	H.U.D.	D.O.L.	D.O.T.
1978	77,889	77,901	-12	119	-98	-222	84	103
1977	68,396	68,437	-41	62	249	-166	87	-192
T.Q.	15,909	16,444	-535	75	-228	-235	6	-107
1976	59,037	59,112	-75	83	235	-12	1	-345
1975	49,723	49,723	0	-2	4	-1	1	5
1974	46,040	46,040	0	9	22	-13	-10	-4
1973	43,963	43,964	-1	13	209	-15	5	-6
1972	35,940	35,941	-1	6	133	-3	-138	10
1971	29,844	29,845	-1	-59	-51	-10	1	9
1970	23,955	24,194	-239	-152	86	52	0	-59
1969	20,255	20,287	-32	34	6		-93	-3

NOTE: "+" indicates O.M.B. number is greater; "-" indicates Treasury number is larger.
SOURCES: Office of Management and Budget, "Federal Aid to State and Local Governments," in Special Analyses, Budget of the U.S. Government for fiscal years 1971-1980 (Washington, D.C.: U.S. Government Printing Office, 1970-1979); Department of the Treasury, Federal Aid to States for fiscal years 1969-1978 (Washington, D.C.: U.S. Government Printing Office, 1969-1979).

15

TABLE 1.7 -- COMPARISON OF YEARLY GRANTS-IN-AID EXPENDITURES REPORTED IN THE ANNUAL AND HISTORICAL TABLES IN F.A.T.S.L.G.

FISCAL YEAR	YEARLY REPORTED ACTUAL EXPENDITURE	ACTUAL EXPENDITURES REPORTED IN HISTORICAL TABLES IN F.A.T.S.L.G. FOR FISCAL YEAR BUDGET						
		1980	1979	1978	1977	1976	1975	1974
1978	77,889	77,889						
1977	68,396	68,415	68,396					
T.Q.	15,909		15,909	15,909				
1976	59,037	59,094	59,037	59,037				
1975	49,723	48,832	49,723	49,723	49,723			
1974	46,040	43,354	43,308	43,308	43,308	46,040		
1973	43,963	41,832				43,963	43,963	
1972	35,940	34,372				35,940	35,940	35,940
1971	29,844	28,109				29,849	29,844	29,844
1970	23,955	24,018				23,954	23,954	23,954
1965		10,904	10,904	10,904	10,904	10,904	10,904	10,904
1960		7,020	7,020	7,020	7,020	7,040	7,040	7,040
1955		3,207	3,207	3,207	3,207			
1950		2,253	2,253	2,253	2,253			

SOURCES: "Federal Aid To States And Local Governments," in Office of Management And Budget (previously The Bureau Of The Budget), Special Analyses, Budget Of The United States Government, fiscal years 1972-1980, the annual detailed listing of grants-in-aid and the annual historical tables.

Table 1.8. Comparison of Revised National Totals for Grants-in-Aid to State and Local Governments Reported by O.M.B. and Treasury, FY 1969–1978 (Millions of Dollars)

	Grants-in-Aid Totals Reported By		
Fiscal Year	O.M.B.	Treasury	Difference
1978	77,889	77,901	12
1977	68,415	68,437	22
T.Q.	15,909	16,444	535
1976	59,094	59,112	18
1975	48,832	49,723	891
1974	43,354	46,040	2,686
1973	41,832	43,964	2,132
1972	34,372	35,941	1,569
1971	28,109	29,845	1,736
1970	24,018	24,194	176
1969	20,255	20,287	32

Sources: "Federal Aid to States and Local Governments," in Office of Management and Budget, *Special Analyses, Budget of the United States Government* (Washington, D.C.: U.S. Government Printing Office, 1971, 1978, 1979), Historical Trend of Federal Grant-In-Aid Outlay tables from 1980 budget report, 1971 budget report for the 1969 data and 1979 budget report for the T.Q. data; and The Department of the Treasury, *Federal Aid to States* (Washington, D.C.: U.S. Government Printing Office, 1969–1979)

An important additional complication arises from annual changes made by O.M.B. to improve the process of budget preparation. As such changes are introduced, O.M.B. updates its grants-in-aid figures to conform to the most recent reporting conventions. The result, depicted in Table 1.7, is that national grant totals for specific years are changed from one year to another. In 1976 "F.A.T.S.L.G." reported $46,040 billion in grants for fiscal 1974, but the historical table shown in the 1980 "F.A.T.S.L.G." analysis lists $43,354 billion for fiscal 1974. Differences between grant totals listed in the 1980 historical table and grant totals reported in previous annual reports vary from $63 million more in fiscal 1970 to $2,686 billion less in fiscal 1974. Depending on the table and report used, therefore, as many as three different totals can be obtained for the same year, from the same source. O.M.B. refers to this as a "living system."

These procedures, of course, further complicate comparisons between different data sources. Table 1.8 illustrates the point by contrasting O.M.B.'s "revised" grant-in-aid totals for fiscal years 1970–1978 with Treasury's *Federal Aid to States* year-end figures, as reported earlier in Table 1.6. Recall that Table 1.6 reported differences of no more than $1 million between Treasury and O.M.B. annual totals for fiscal years 1971 through 1975. The "revised" figures in Table 1.8, however, now show an average annual difference of more than $1 billion between O.M.B. and Treasury totals. Whereas Treasury and O.M.B. reported identical year-end sums for fiscal 1974 and 1975, the "revised" sums now show differences of $2.7 billion and $891 million, respectively. Unravelling the sources of these kinds of differences would itself be an undertaking of some magnitude.[55]

The data systems we have briefly reviewed—Census, O.M.B., Treasury—are typically regarded as "authoritative," yet it is apparent that conclusions regarding trends in nothing more than federal grants to states since 1969 would be vastly different, depending on which source were used, or indeed depending on which report from the same source were used. Because national totals mask state totals that are even more varied, furthermore, conclusions about grants to individual states are subject to even more confusion. Differences amounting to billions of dollars in national totals and hundreds of millions in state-by-state totals obviously are subject to interpretive hazards, particularly since there is no consistency in the *magnitude* of year-to-year reporting discrepancies. Readers interested in specific state discrepancies are invited to find their own examples in Appendix Table 1.2, which reports totals from Census and Treasury (thus O.M.B.) data for all states and the District of Columbia from 1969 through 1978. In no year, for no state, do any of the grant figures reported by these sources match. Census, Treasury and O.M.B. reports all show vast increases in federal aid to state and local governments over the past decade, but beyond that it is extraordinarily difficult to know how to draw reliable conclusions from these data.

Although analysts can only regard these varying numbers and the confusion they inevitably produce as perverse, the absence of a single, comprehensive and consistent record of federal spending seems to us quite understandable. No great insight is required to appreciate the enormous diversity of purposes pursued, and the heterogeneity of the agencies created to pursue them, by the entity referred to as "the federal government." It seems perfectly reasonable to suppose, therefore, that information needs will be as diverse as agency purposes require and that, absent a strong demonstration of need, there will be no consistent and comprehensive data base.[56] Data systems, in short, do not exist in a vacuum; data are "created" because someone wants or needs information. If federal expenditures are as important to the national economy as we have suggested, and if such expenditures are a product of political processes rather than "objective" social or economic forces, and if presently available data systems seem inadequate, we must answer the question, "What data do we want or need in order to better understand the American political economy?"

Posing this question forces us to confront conceptual and theoretical issues since, if "data" are not simply "out there" but are always "created," it follows that all data systems are based on some theory or theories that define what is or is not significant. From this perspective each of the major data systems we have reviewed suffers from an even more fundamental defect: lack of articulation between the "data" and a plausible image of the political processes through which such data are produced. Federal expenditures are organized by program, within agency. A considerable literature on national budgeting, furthermore, makes clear that federal resource allocation takes place through a fragmented process of program-by-program calculation, involving individual program managers, agency and department leaders, O.M.B. officials, relevant congressional committees, and often supportive clientele groups. The data required for such calculations typically include some record of historical accomplishment, a record of prior-year spending and service to clientele groups, and a proposal to improve program operations in the forthcoming year by expanding expenditures. These data are presented in great detail in agency budget proposals, and in somewhat less detail in the federal budget appendix— which is nonetheless a huge document. Use of such data makes clear that the politics of federal spending is very much a politics of individual federal programs.

In summarizing these activities, however, the major federal data systems aggregate these program data into department or functional totals that have little to do with program politics. O.M.B. summaries by function and agency provide useful information for decisions on national budget totals, but spending decisions are not made by "function." [57] The Treasury break-out of grants to states, apart from its other difficulties, aggregates hundreds of programs into fewer than 120 purposive categories, few of which form the bases of expenditure decisions. Even Census, which provides the most comprehensive record of federal spending *in* states and local jurisdictions, summarizes federal activity in no more than 12 categories, aggregating program decisions through techniques difficult to unravel.[58] These reporting systems are all useful enough for some purposes, despite their inconsistencies. But they are designed to provide statistics for national total calculations, or generally summarize state and local distribution of federal dollars, rather than provide information on program expenditures. If the most important component of the American political economy is federal expenditures, understanding that component clearly requires a data system capable of handling federal *program* decisions.

It is also important that such a data system be comprehensive in its coverage. As noted above, much of the recent public debate of federal spending has focused on federal grants to state and local governments, and much of our attention here has been drawn to information about grants. Yet, as we also have noted, alternative spending mechanisms such as loans or tax expenditures are increasing more rapidly than grants. Ideally we would like a system that would permit us to track such mechanisms, as well as direct expenditures for federal government operations, or federal purchases from the private sector. Is there a data system both comprehensive enough in its coverage and "political" enough in its conceptual focus to provide an adequate analytic tool? Or, short of canvassing each federal program for budget and expenditure information can such a system be created to provide a single source of reliable information? The answer to both questions is "yes." Such a system exists, and it can be improved. We refer, of course, to a fourth data source, known earlier as "Federal Outlays" and now published annually by the Community Services Administration as *Geographic Distribution of Federal Funds.*

DEVELOPING AN ALTERNATIVE DATA SYSTEM

The outlays data series is derived from O.M.B. Circular A-84, effective 1967, which requires all executive departments and establishments to submit annual reports of obligations incurred from federal funds in state and local areas.[59] Agency reports are summarized and published annually by C.S.A. in 53 volumes: one for each state, one for the trusts and territories, and one reporting national totals. Outlays data have several important advantages over other federal data systems.[60] First, outlays reports are *comprehensive*, including payments to individuals, salaries, loans and loan guarantees and procurements as well as grants. This creates the possibility of estimating the total fiscal impact of the federal government in a given area, no less than the impact of one kind of obligation, such as grants-in-aid. Second, outlays data have more *depth* than other data systems, which disaggregate only to the state level. Outlays are reported for all states, but they are also reported for all countries, and all cities of 25,000 or more population, creating major opportunities for substate analyses of various kinds.[61] Third, outlays reports have been published since 1968, opening up possibilities for observing changes in federal spending patterns. And finally, outlays are *program*-level data, permitting analyses that reflect the political terms in which spending decisions are made.

These advantages are real enough but, like other federal data sources, outlays data are afflicted with several problems that dictate caution in their use.[62] Because improvements in reporting procedures have been made more or less annually, there are difficulties in comparability from one year to the next and data quality seems significantly "harder" in the period since 1974. Outlays data also credit state and local jurisdictions with some funds that are never used *in* those jurisdictions. Outlays for foreign assistance payments or State Department foreign operations, for example, are credited to states such as New York because funds are channeled through banks located there. Or, outlays reports credit jurisdictions with receipts that are known to be expended elsewhere, in whole or in part. Defense Department procurements, for example, are obtained from prime contractors who are known to issue sub-contracts to suppliers often located elsewhere. Yet outlays are reported only to the location of the prime contractor. Similarly, interest payments on the national debt are credited primarily (52 percent in 1977) to New York, although an important fraction of these obligations are distributed across the country by large New York financial institutions. Or, some agencies simply do not report certain program expenditures to C.S.A. (e.g., selected U.M.T.A. programs). Clearly, outlays data require adjustment if they are to be used with confidence.

Solutions to many of these problems are possible but are not yet fully developed. In this study, therefore, we propose to simply adjust the outlays data to permit analyses that avoid the more perverse consequences of using unadjusted figures. Defense Department procurements, interest payments on the national debt, and other "non-influence" outlays (primarily foreign payments) are all reported separately. Because these obligations are either known to be inaccurate or known to be expended abroad, they are excluded from the calculation of a wholly new number, "net domestic outlays," made up of all other federal obligations.[63] For state-regional analysis, we also exclude the District of Columbia which, because of its heavy concentration of government employees and federal spending, causes outlays totals for the South Atlantic (division) or the South (region) to be artificially inflated.[64] Net Domestic Outlays are now available in total and per capita form for 1975, 1977 and 1978. In this analysis, however, we rely primarily on 1975 and 1978 calculations.

PLAN OF THE STUDY

The existence of a politically-relevant, comprehensive, recurrent and *improvable* data system, tracking federal expenditures through time, provides a unique opportunity to improve our understanding of the American political economy. As it stands, the outlays data system seems to us superior to other federal data systems in coverage and theoretical relevance. Annual improvements initiated by the Community Services Administration together with adjustments we have made, moreover, will produce data of higher quality with each successive year. Since these data will continue to be easily integrated with demographic data from Census, B.E.A., and other federal sources, to say nothing of considerable attitude, opinion, and political data coded by geographic area, it is clear that we stand on the threshold of extraordinarily powerful analyses of federal spending *impacts,* as well as more accurate estimates of expenditure patterns.

This volume does not attempt to cross that threshold yet. Instead, partly because essential quality improvements remain unfinished, and partly because improvements that have been made lead to conclusions that challenge many current images of federal expenditure patterns, we pursue here the more limited task of describing these patterns. Two themes are pursued simultaneously. Use of our new statistic, "net domestic outlay," will permit a more plausible analysis of "who gets what" from the federal treasury than other analyses now available, not only because the number is better but also because we apply it to counties and cities, as well as states. Further pursuit of the "who gets what" theme leads as well to a discussion of the distribution of various types of federal spending: formula grants, project grants, direct payments, loans, operating expenses, and so on. Since tax expenditures cannot now be distributed accurately, however, we are unable to include them in this study.

Our second theme is more political: "who gives what." Because federal agencies are crucial political and administrative actors in fund distributions, we analyze spending obligations incurred by the largest 15 agencies in states, counties, and cities. And because we view the politics of federal expenditure as predominantly a politics of programs, we review several important aspects of program outlays for the 46 largest federal grant programs. Taken together these programs account for more than 70 percent of domestic spending. We propose to ask whether program outlays differ by state, whether such outlays are stable through time, whether urban areas are provided more or less than rural areas, whether "hard" dollars are allocated differently from "soft" dollars, and whether federal program managers seem more or less responsive to various measures of "need." We will not achieve a full explanation of individual program outlays in answering such questions, but we may move toward better understanding of the major parameters of program-level decisions.

Pursuit of these two themes for states, counties, and cities for a period that spans two presidential administrations (1975–1978)[65] allows us to develop preliminary estimates of patterns of stability and change in federal expenditure patterns. Since these estimates will be more accurate than any others currently available, they should provide a useful set of images of the current state of the American political economy. They are also intended to provide a bench-mark set of measurements for comparison with later extension of these analyses through time. Finally, they provide a basis for consideration of conceptual tools appropriate to explanations as well as descriptions of federal expenditure patterns.

NOTES

1. Overviews of the history of government growth in the United States may be found in Mosher and Poland, 1954; Fabricant, 1952; and Kendrick, 1955.
2. Despite considerable evidence to the contrary, the fiction that the United States had a laissez-faire political economy prior to the twentieth century has been perpetuated either in the form of a political ideology, employed to criticize selected governmental activities, or as a "strawman" argument, against which to evaluate the changing nature of twentieth-century governmental activities. For introductions to the sizable (and mounting) body of research on federal, state, and local governmental policies that clearly demonstrates the vital nature of governmental activities in helping to shape the American political economy since the founding of the republic, see Handlin, 1943; Handlin and Handlin, 1947, 1969; Hartz, 1943, 1968; Heath, 1943, 1954; Goodrich, 1948, 1956, 1960, 1961; Gates, 1934, 1954; Hurst, 1964; Nash, 1964; Johnson, 1962; and Scheiber, 1969, 1972, and 1975 (and the citations therein).
3. For a flavor of early twentieth-century arguments against the federal grants-in-aid system on the basis of legal grounds, see Burdick, 1923; and Corwin, 1923.
4. Indeed, a common-place charge against "the federal government" is that it is too involved in everything. See, Anderson, 1980; D. Walker 1978b, 1979.
5. On the importance of federal land grants in influencing state and local politics, for instance, see Gates, 1934, 1954; and Goodrich, 1960.
6. Fifteen years ago Charles A. Reich surveyed the changing nature of "property" rights in relation to the post-World War II expansion of federal government activities in the U.S. in a series of excellent articles in the *Yale Law Review* (1964—a popular version of this piece later appeared in *The Public Interest* (1966b); 1965, 1966a).
7. Anthony King (1973a, 1973b), for instance, has argued that ". . . *the State plays a more limited role in America than elsewhere because Americans, more than other people, want it to play a limited role.* In other words, the most satisfactory explanation is one in terms of Americans' beliefs and assumptions, especially their beliefs and assumptions about government" (1973b, p. 418). Recent cross-national survey data on mass public attitudes (i.e., Almond and Verba, 1963) and a number of works on public views on equity

and the proper role of government in the U.S. can be read as supporting King's thesis. It should be noted, however, that King equates "state" activity with "direct operating responsibilities," thereby downplaying the hardly neutral role of government at all levels in the U.S. through tax, credit, and regulatory activities. A fuller appreciation of the range of governmental activities (federal, state, and local) in the U.S. might very well lead to a different comparative view of the role of the "state" in the U.S. relative to other nations than the perspective presented by King.

8. Oscar Handlin forcefully presented this view in 1943 (p. 65), when, after reviewing the evidence concerning the thesis that a body of laissez-faire ideas existed and were an important source of the perceived limited role of government, he concluded that this thesis is ". . . not worth talking about . . . . Discussion of the development of economic policy in terms of laissez-faire is hardly meaningful. The issues in the determination of American economic policy through most of the nineteenth century were not whether the government had or had not a role in the economy, but, what was to be the character of its role, what agencies were to exercise it, who was to control it, and in whose interests it was to operate. As for theory, ideas phrased in terms of laissez-faire were so rare and so thoroughly divorced from reality and practice that they remained almost completely sterile." Thus, in the nineteenth century (the widely perceived heyday of laissez-faire), like in more recent times, calls for a laissez-faire economy were more matters of interest than principle, with the determination of what role government would play depending on the relative balance of political influence among interests within the context of specific issues and times.

9. A great deal of discussion has focused on the dimensions, causes, and consequences of the growth of federal expenditures in recent decades. With some important exceptions (i.e., Sundquist, 1968), however, the debate has revolved around the merits of general interpretations of changing federal expenditure patterns, without appreciably advancing our understanding of the political processes that have generated federal expenditure commitments through time. For critiques of the literature, see Anton, 1980c; and Anton, with Cawley, 1980.

10. The figures in Table 1.1 on federal grants-in-aid to state and local governments systematically overstate federal aid to states, while understating federal aid to localities, because of Census's practice of counting federal aid to localities passed through the states as federal aid to states, instead of as federal aid to localities.

11. Many articles have commented on the expanded level of federal funds flowing into state and local governmental jurisdictions in recent years, but few works have attempted to systematically assess the implications of this "federal largess"—to use Reich's term. Useful initial analyses of this topic, which point to distinctively different images and explanations of the kinds of changes that are occurring, include Anton, 1980c; Anton, with Cawley, 1980; Reich, 1964, 1966; Hamilton, 1978; Lowi, 1974, 1978, 1979; Stenberg, 1980; and D. Walker, 1979.

12. Anton, 1979a.

13. Nathan, 1978.

14. Beer, 1976; Haider, 1974; Farkus, 1971.

15. Clark (1980) and Heclo (1979), for example, present useful summary tables and figures showing the recent growth in federal regulations, as measured by the number of pages in the *Federal Register* and the *Code of Federal Regulations*. The relationship between such summary measures of increased federal regulatory activities and the "desirability" and the "utility" of particular federal regulations is, of course, dependent on one's perspective.

16. Popular concern over the regional distribution of federal expenditures in recent years is one manifestation of this renewed concern, as is the more recent attention to the large city versus small town and rural community geographic distribution of federal funds. For empirical assessments of federal expenditure patterns by regions and community sizes, see Chapters 2 and 3 of this volume.

17. This point merits emphasis because most of the recent discussions about changing federal expenditure patterns have focused solely on federal grants-in-aid, especially direct federal-local programs. Clearly, a fuller appreciation of the full range of federal expenditures (as well as regulatory activities) is needed if we are to develop a more sophisticated understanding of the changing federal presence in the American political economy and its causes and consequences.

18. Office of Management and Budget, "Payments for Individuals, January 1980 Edition," (Washington, D.C.: Office of Management and Budget, 1980), p. 4

19. Office of Management and Budget, *The Budget of the United States Government, Fiscal Year 1980* (Washington, D.C.: U.S. Government Printing Office, 1979), p. 26.

20. The Office of Management and Budget reports what we term "new," current year federal credit activities as "net" funds advanced—the difference between the amount of loans outstanding at the beginning and at the end of the year.

21. Loan data are from Office of Management and Budget's *The Budget of the United States Government, Fiscal Year 1980* (Washington, D.C.: U.S. Government Printing Office, 1979), p. 26 and "Special Analysis F:

Federal Credit Programs," in the *Special Analyses, The Budget of the United States Government, Fiscal Year 1980* (Washington, D.C.: U.S. Government Printing Office, 1979), Table F-1, p. 135.

22. Very little attention has been paid to the politics of federal credit support; most analyses focus on the economics of loan policies. Huitt (1963) provides an overview of Congressional organization for handling credit activities; the volume on the Banking and Currency Committees from the Ralph Nader Study of Congress provides useful information (Salamon, 1975); Lowi (1974, 1978, 1979) offers some provocative speculations on the political importance of recent changes in federal credit policies; Henry Aaron's *Shelter and Subsidies* (1972) provides a good discussion of housing loan programs; and volumes in the yearly Brookings Institution's *Setting National Priorities* series in the federal budget provide useful information. O.M.B.'s yearly chapter on "Federal Credit Programs" in the *Special Analyses* volume of the U.S. Budget report provides detailed financial data on federal credit programs, as do the *Treasury Bulletin* and the *Annual Report of the Secretary of the Treasury on the State of the Finances* reports by the Department of the Treasury.

23. According to the latest figures, in FY 1979 total outstanding federal loans slightly exceeded total budget outlays; see Figure 1.1.

24. United States Senate, 1976, p. 1

25. Despite the magnitude of tax expenditures, very little systematic research appears to have been done on either the politics of tax expenditures or the relative merits of tax expenditures versus direct expenditures and loan assistance in pursuing federal activities. Excellent discussions of tax expenditures may be found in a number of works by Stanley Surrey (for instance, 1957, 1970, 1973, 1976), who first defined the concept of tax expenditures in 1967 when he was Assistant Secretary for Tax Policy in the Treasury Department. His book *Pathways to Tax Reform* (1973) provides both a superb review of tax expenditure policies and politics and an introduction to relevant research. Henry Aaron's *Shelter and Subsidies* (1972) contains a good discussion of housing policies. Surrey's book and later *Policy Science's* article (1976) and a chapter in Joseph A. Pechman's *Federal Tax Policy* (1977, Chapter 3) overview the tax legislation policymaking process. Additional insights into the politics of tax legislation can be culled from the literature on Congress; see especially, Huitt, 1963; Manley, 1968, 1970a; Rudder, 1977 and two volumes in the Ralph Nader Study of Congress—Spohn and McCollum, 1975; and Salamon, 1975. Useful reviews of tax expenditure policies in recent years include: Pechman, 1978a, 1979a; Hartman and Pechman, 1977; and Bleckman, Gramlich, Hartman, 1975, pp. 184–189. Since budget year 1976, pursuant to the Congressional Control and Impoundment Act of 1974, O.M.B. has published an annual listing of individual tax expenditure "programs" as part of the *Special Analyses* volume of the budget. The Congressional Budget Office has published similar analyses, as has the House Ways and Means committee. The Committee on the Budget, United States Senate (1976) has published a compendium of background material on tax expenditure provisions.

26. For sources of grant and loan data, see Tables 1.1 and 1.2; tax expenditure figures are from the Congressional Budget Office, *Tax Expenditures* (1980), Table 1.2, p. 12.

27. Congressional Budget Office, 1980, p. ix.

28. Congressional Budget Office, 1980, p. ix and Table 2, pp. 12–13.

29. We suggest this comparison of outlays, outstanding loans and tax expenditures relative to GNP merely as a crude indicator of the financial scope of the federal role in the American political economy. In our view, ratios of governmental financial activities to GNP provide nothing more than first approximations of the relative importance of public sector activities. They provide no meaningful yardsticks by which to measure the "desirability" or "dangerousness" of government activities; such judgments turn on the value placed on individual federal expenditure program efforts. In this regard, it is instructive to note, as Rose and Peters have (1978, p. 265), that disaster was once predicted if public sector (federal, state, and local) expenditures (*just* outlays) consumed more than 25% of the national product (Clark, 1945). Over the years, as government expenditures have increased, the threshold that *must* not be crossed lest liberty, freedom and democracy be lost and political bankruptcy occur has been raised. Taken together in FY 78 federal budget outlays, outstanding loans and tax expenditures, and state and local government own-source expenditures *exceed* 60% of the United States GNP, marking the arrival of the U.S.A. at the threshold Milton Friedman has argued represents a loss of liberty (Friedman, 1976). Yet no one would seriously argue that liberty was lost in the United States in FY 1978.

Data on federal outlays and outstanding loans are from the Office of Management and Budget, *The Budget of the United States Government, Fiscal Year 1980* (Washington D.C.: U.S. Government Printing Office, 1979), pp. 577 and 26 respectively. Tax expenditure data are from the Congressional Budget Office (Mark Steitz, main author), *Tax Expenditures: Current Issues and Five Year Budget Projections for Fiscal Years 1981–1985* (Washington, D.C.: U.S. Government Printing Office, 1980), Table 1.2, p. 12. GNP data are from the Council of Economic Advisors, *Economic Report of the President (January 1980)* (Washington, D.C.: U.S. Government Printing Office, 1980), Table B-1, p. 203.

30. U.S. Department of Commerce, Bureau of the Census, *Governmental Finances in 1977–78* (Washington, D.C.: U.S. Government Printing Office, 1980), p. 16.

31. More generally, our understanding of the dimensions, causes, and consequences of intergovernmental change in the United States has been impeded because of the eclipse of systematic, empirical investigation by value-infused, "global" assessments of "change" in intergovernmental interactions; for an elaboration of this argument, see Anton, with Cawley, 1980.

32. For a discussion of the often-overlooked "dynamism" of state and local public sector change, see Anton, with Cawley, 1980. In addition, there is a large body of historical and contemporary research bearing on this topic that has seldom been considered in the framing of current discussions about the size, complexity, rate of change, and consequences of government growth (usually meaning just federal government growth) in the U.S.

33. For assessments of criticisms of the grants system in the 1920s, see MacDonald, 1928a, and Harris, 1940. It is interesting to note that despite the popular criticisms of the grants system in the 1920s for usurping state and local responsibilities, detailed analyses of federal-state-local relations in administering the grants system done in the 1920s by both scholars (Arneson, 1922) and public sector interest groups (MacDonald, 1928b—the report of the Committee on Federal Aid to the States of the National Municipal League) repeatedly found scant evidence of federal usurpation of state and local responsibilities. During the 1930s concern over the centralization of power in federal hands expanded (for a sampling of this literature, see Graves 1934, 1936a, 1936b, 1938). However, as V. O. Key noted in 1940, in reference to Graves' work, most of this concern focused on ". . . the fact of Federal influence—a matter of general significance in the evolution of federalism—rather than with the differentiation of situations in which that influence occurs" (1940, p. 7). And empirical studies of federal-state-local administrative relations in the 1930s, such as Key's *The Administration Of Federal Grants To States* (1937), documented no "march of power" to the banks of the Potomac. Nevertheless, in the late thirties and early forties, the image of growing federal power appears to have gained wider currency, despite the absence of what could reasonably be called systematic, empirical evidence, because of the changing values analysts employed in assessing the grants system. The increased levels of federal expenditures were criticized because they resulted more from "political advocacy" than "conscious planning" and because such "magnitudes" of "uncoordinated" federal program dollars (with matching rates) flowing into state and local governmental jurisdictions were assumed to be causing serious distortions in state and local "spending priorities" in various "functional areas." We mention this set of ideas because they clearly reflect lines of criticism of federal expenditure policies, which were popular in the 1950s and which have resurfaced today, despite the continued absence of systematic, empirical evidence documenting this perspective. Indeed, as in the 1920s and 1930s, a sizable body of recent empirical research exists that calls into question this line of interpretation (for a summary-assessment of this work, see Anton, with Cawley, 1980). MacDonald (1940) is an example of an early call for better coordination and planning of the grants system, and Harris (1940) contains a good discussion of contemporary assessments of the grants system in the late 1930s.

34. White, 1953.

35. Graves (1964) provides a useful review of the activities of the Commission on Intergovernmental Relations (commonly known as the Kestnbaum Commission) and the later Joint Federal-State Action Committee. On the Kestnbaum Commission, see also the Commission reports (1955) and Anderson, 1955a, 1956a; on the Joint Federal-State Action Committee, see the Committee's reports (1957, 1958, 1960) and Grodzins, 1960a, pp. 267–268. In addition, see the earlier report of the Council of State Governments (1949).

36. As cited in Anderson, 1955a, pp. 5–6.

37. MacDonald, 1928, pp. 253–254.

38. MacDonald, 1928, p. 254.

39. MacDonald, 1928, p. 254. For a similar assessment of the English case, see Sidney Webb, 1920, pp. 89–94.

40. For an extended critique of this body of literature, see Anton, with Cawley, 1980. See also McKay, 1979. Heclo (1977) provides a useful summary presentation of the "governmental overload" argument. In recent years the "governmental overload" thesis has become widely used as a framework for assessing the politics of advanced industrial nations; see, for example, Rose and Peters, 1978; King, 1975; Crozier, 1975; Schmitter, 1977b; and Douglas, 1976; in addition to the works cited below.

41. At least two distinct lines of argument are evident on the "governmental overload" thesis: here termed the "system" and the "institutional/leadership" perspectives. The best serious presentation of the "system" perspective in terms of the U.S. case and other advanced industrial nations is Rose and Peters' *Can Government Go Bankrupt?* (1978), which puts forth the thesis that, in the face of economic pressures greater than those of the 1930s' depression, government can no longer continue on a "business-as-usual" basis because "past commitments to future spending threaten to overload government, requiring it to spend more money than can be provided by the fruits of economic growth" (p. 9). Citizens are losing confidence in government,

apathy is spreading, and governmental authority is increasingly being undermined—political bankruptcy is at hand! Thus, "*If* past trends continue, American politicians have upwards of a decade in which to act before political bankruptcy becomes an immediate threat. The same is true of the governments of Germany and France. By contrast, in Italy, Sweden, and Britain, the threat of bankruptcy is near at hand" (p. 9). See also Peters and Rose, 1980.

As applied to just the U.S. case, the central element of the "system" perspective is the notion that demands on the government are outracing the capacity of the government to respond to such demands effectively. Too many "groups" (in increasing numbers) are (free) lunching at federal expense and, because of the political clout of these groups, governmental leaders have been unable to or unwilling to limit their access to the federal fisc. Instead, ad hoc, hyper-responsive reactions to powerful vested interests ratchets up federal expenditures through a maze of uncoordinated federal programs, thereby producing inefficient and ineffective policy responses. Excesses of "democracy" and "pluralism" are producing political immobility. For applications of the "system" perspective to the U.S. case, see Beer, 1977a; Huntington, 1975a, 1975b; and Bell, 1975. See also Bell, 1978; and Wildavsky, 1973.

In contrast to the "system" perspective, the "institutional/leadership" perspective stresses the lack of leadership, an especially crucial problem given the division of powers in the U.S., the particularistic nature of Congress, the lack of responsible parties (worse still, the decline of parties since the 1960s), and recent failings in presidential competence. In many ways this argument is a modern version of the "responsible party" argument. Excellent presentations of this view are Sundquist, 1976, 1980; see also Sundquist, 1979, 1968; Seidman, 1972; and Hardin, 1974. See in addition the exchange between Patrick Caddell (1979a, 1979b) and Warren E. Miller (1979) concerning whether President Carter is really caught in a downward spiral of public confidence or may be helping to create it, and the exchange between Arthur Miller (1974a, 1974b) and Jack Citrin (1974) concerning the interpretation of public opinion survey measures of public trust in government.

42. The best presentation of this position is found in a number of U.S. Advisory Commission On Intergovernmental Relations (A.C.I.R.) reports. See Anderson, 1980; Beam, 1979a; Colella, 1979. More generally, see D. Walker, 1978b, 1979; and Beam and Colella, 1979.

43. This vision of recent trends in American politics has become so widespread that some writers no longer ask if government in the U.S. is overloaded and seek to investigate the question empirically; instead they assume that government is overloaded and they ask why—see, for example, Thomas, 1980. See also Beer, 1977a; and Huntington, 1975a, 1975b.

44. For instance, a recent Advisory Commission On Intergovernmental Relations (A.C.I.R.) bulletin summarizes what is said to be a popular view as follows: ". . . growing numbers of people contend that government has become a monster of excessively pervasive and inordinately complex proportions. In this view, the proliferation of regulations and programs and the extreme *intergovernmentalization* of implementation have created a largely uncontrolled and unaccountable system—'Leviathan' run amuck" (Colella, 1979, p. 6).

Another analysis in this same bulletin judges this Leviathan to be "in good part a mistake," and asserts the "Evidence of systemic overload is everywhere in Washington (and across the nation)," including ". . . state houses, municipal buildings, and polling places throughout the land." According to this analysis, "Local and state officials find it nearly impossible to exercise coherent policy or administrative control over the array of federal programs in which they participate" (Beam, 1979a, p. 19). It should be noted that the Anderson, Beam, and Colella overviews of this theme are summary presentations of A.C.I.R.'s recent five-year, ten-volume study of the changing role of the federal government. Although the A.C.I.R. study included case studies of program evolution in seven major functional areas, the systematic, empirical investigation of the range of possible effects of the evolving federal presence on state houses, municipal buildings, and polling places across the land was beyond the scope of A.C.I.R.'s review.

45. Contrast, for instance, the differing assessments of the Great Society programs set forth in Ginzberg and Solow, 1974; Glazer and Kristol, 1976; *Commentary*, 1973; and Levitan and Taggart, 1976, 1976–1977. For an insightful comparative assessment of the U.S. welfare "crisis," see Rein and Heclo, 1973. Evaluations of federal programs are often rooted more in commitments to different political values than in systematic, empirical research yielding "clear-cut" interpretations. On the impact of values on interpretations of recent federal activities, see Aaron's excellent book, *Politics and the Professors* (1978), as well as Wirt, 1979; McKay, 1979; Etzioni, 1976–1977; and Anton, with Cawley, 1980.

46. It is also worth noting that of the 92 provisions in the tax laws which are estimated to yield $206 billion tax expenditures in FY 1981, just 12 provisions will account for 69% of the $206 billion tax expenditures.

47. These grants data are for what Treasury reports as grants to states, termed direct payments to states in earlier years. The grants data for the earlier years include small amounts for (what were later called) grants for payments to individuals and Emergency Assistance Relief, which we made no attempt to separate out

for the purposes of this initial analysis. A preliminary investigation of the distribution patterns for both just grants for payments to individuals, and just the Emergency Assistance Relief of the 1930s turned up similar state concentration patterns. From 1930 on the data are from Treasury's *Federal Aid To States* report; the 1924 data are taken from MacDonald, 1928a, p. 244.

48. Moynihan, 1978, p. 12.

49. Moynihan, 1979, p. 1.

50. Since 1969 Treasury has published the annual *Federal Aid to States* report as a separate volume; earlier (from 1930) it was published as an appendix table to the *Annual Report of the Secretary of the Treasury on the State of the Finances.* Since the 1960s, the "Federal Aid to State and Local Governments" has been included in O.M.B.'s annual *Special Analyses, Budget of the United States Government* volume. The Census data referred to here are from the *Governmental Finances* series, collected in conjunction with Census' '2' and '7' year *Census of Governments* and *Annual Survey of Governments.* Census has published national-level grants-in-aid data for the period 1902 to the present; detailed state and sub-state level data are available for the period since the 1950s, with more fragmentary data stretching back to the early years of the twentieth century.

51. Needless to say, there are also significant differences at the regional and divisional levels.

52. Pursuant to O.M.B. Circular No. A-11, Treasury Circular No. 1014 and Part 2, Chapter 7000, *Treasury Fiscal Requirements Manual,* the grants-in-aid expenditure data reported by Treasury and O.M.B. are supposed to be consistent with each other. Indeed, since the late 1960's the O.M.B. report has employed the Treasury data in constructing a table on the regional distribution of federal grants. Previously O.M.B. had drawn on Census data in presenting a similar table. For discussions of the O.M.B. and Treasury data collection processes, see Cawley and Kramer, 1979 and Lilla, 1978.

53. O.M.B. agency grants-in-aid totals are from the annual agency table in the F.A.T.S.L.G. report. Treasury agency totals were calculated by summing up for each agency the individual column totals reported in F.A.T.S.; no attempt was made, however, to dig out the small amounts of grant expenditures for these agencies reported by Treasury in a "Miscellaneous" column in the F.A.T.S. document and add them to the agency totals reported in Table 1.6.

54. Treasury's practice of simply listing various program expenditures in the "Adjustments Undistributed to States" category, rather than showing their actual distribution across states, causes confusion concerning which states get how much of grant expenditures reported in the *Federal Aid to States* document. For example, we have attempted to allocate the $562 million of "undistributed" funds in the "Human Development" category in the FY 1977 F.A.T.S. report, using *Catalog of Federal Domestic Assistance* codes to identify programs and outlays data reported by Community Services Administration's Federal Information Exchange System (F.I.X.S.) to derive expenditure figures for state areas. Comparing these F.I.X.S. and F.A.T.S. based state-area figures for Human Development program expenditures we found:

> Expenditures increase by $86 million to New York, by $38 million to Illinois, and by $32 million to California. Only three states (Michigan, Nevada, and New Hampshire) experience a dollar decline in "Human Development" spending in F.I.X.S. However, in percentage and rank order terms, there is considerable variance between the two patterns. Minnesota may alternatively be viewed as well-off in F.I.X.S. (ranked 20th) or very unfortunate in F.A.T.S. (ranked 50th). Tennessee and Wisconsin experience similar, if less spectacular rises in rank from F.A.T.S. to F.I.X.S. (Cawley and Kramer, 1979, p. 12; see Appendix Tables 6.4–6.6 in the Epilogue of this report for a tabular documentation of these points.)

> Because the programs identified in F.I.X.S. as "Human Development" programs report outlays for FY 1977 that achieve a total ($1,804 million) nearly identical to the total reported by Treasury for "Human Development" ($1,820), it is therefore clear that we were dealing with the same sets of federal activities. And, because the distribution of dollars reported as undistributed by Treasury through the C.S.A. data adds significant amounts of federal assistance to some states, and changes the pattern of assistance *among* states in a quite noticeable way, it is therefore also clear that a more comprehensive effort to reconcile Treasury data with other data sources, focusing on more than a single account might well lead to a substantial adjustment in current perceptions of federal assistance trends. For extended discussions of this and related points, see Anton, 1979a and Anton, 1980a.

55. It should be noted that Census, O.M.B. and Treasury provide detailed discussions of the scope and limitations of the expenditure data they report. O.M.B.'s yearly "Federal Aid to State and Local Governments" report, for instance, contains a very informative comparison of O.M.B.'s grants-in-aid figures with Census, national income and product accounts (N.I.A.), Treasury, C.S.A. and *Catalog of Federal Domestic Assistance* figures. Unfortunately, "consumers" (governmental, journalistic and academic) of these federal data systems very rarely heed the data quality cautions accompanying these reports.

56. A useful guide into the labyrinth of available federal information systems is the General Accounting Office's *Federal Information Sources and Systems* (1977). A recent survey of federal information sources conducted by the Office of Management and Budget (Doyle, 1979) provides even more detailed and timely information on available federal data bases. In addition, the two volume review of government statistics published by the Office of Federal Statistical Policy and Standards, the Department of Commerce, provides a wealth of information on sources, history and quality of federal information bases, as well as an overview of potential directions in which government statistical collection procedures may evolve; see Joseph W. Duncan and William C. Shelton, *Revolution in United States Government Statistics, 1926–1976* (1978) and *A Framework for Planning U.S. Federal Statistics for the 1980's* (1978). See also the Statistical Policy Division, Executive Office of the President, Office of Management and Budget (now headquartered in the Commerce Department), *Statistical Services of the United States Government* (1975) and *Federal Statistical Directory* (1976).

57. Since the 1974 reforms of the congressional budget process, functional reviews of federal expenditure and tax policies gained additional importance through the creation of new Senate and House budget committees, designed to establish functionally defined caps on total federal program spending. Nevertheless, within the broad guidelines of aggregate functional limits on federal program expenditures, the politics of federal spending still revolves around individual federal program activities. Not only are expenditures for individual programs adjusted within functional areas to meet initial functional spending caps, but in addition, changes in individual program expenditures during the course of the budget year process lead to readjustments in initial functional and total budget spending limit estimates. Interactions with congressional, administrative, and various interest group officials during the course of research on the FY 1981 budget and budgetary process has clearly demonstrated to us the central importance of program politics.

58. Census reports federal intergovernmental revenue in seven major functions (broken down to subfunctions in various reports) and a residual all "other" federal revenue category. Because the basic Census functional scheme was designed prior to the recent expansion in federal programs, over the years Census has reported more and more federal aid in the "other" category, making it even more difficult to determine which functional classifications contain precisely which federal programs.

59. The F.I.X.S. information system does not cover judicial, Congressional and certain classified expenditures. For details on F.I.X.S. agency reporting requirements, see the Community Services Administration's annual reporting instructions (for example, C.S.A., 1976).

60. Appendix Figures 1.1–1.3 to this chapter provide detailed comparisons of the collection procedures, purposes, coverage, accounting systems, and timeliness of eight of the major "government-wide" federal data bases. These charts demonstrate the advantages of using the Community Services Administration F.I.X.S. data system, as well as illustrate the opportunities for merging other data bases (both those provided in the charts and others) with the C.S.A. data—research opportunities made possible by C.S.A.'s employment in F.I.X.S. of the same basic account system for tracking federal expenditures used by O.M.B. and Treasury and common geographic place codes. For further elaboration on this point, see the Epilogue to this volume.

61. Only Census data possess comparable geographic depth. Census intergovernmental transfer data, however, systematically under-report federal aid to cities, while systematically overstating the magnitude of state aid to cities. This is due to the way Census treats federal grants-in-aid to lower level governmental jurisdictions that are passed through state governments. Census counts all such assistance as "state" aid while restricting "federal" aid only to direct federal-local payments. For details, see Anton, 1979a.

62. For more detailed assessments of C.S.A.'s F.I.X.S. information system, see Anton, 1978 and 1980a; the O.M.B. established *Interagency Task Team Report on Improvements to the Federal Outlays Report by Geographic Region, OMB Circular A-84 Policy and Associated Process,* 1974; Congressional Budget Office (Peggy L. Cuciti, main author), *Troubled Local Economies and the Distribution of Federal Dollars,* 1977; Nathan, Jaffe, Dommel, and Fossett, 1977; Hines and Reid, 1978, 1977a, 1977b; Reid, 1979; and A.C.I.R., 1977a, pp. 134–135.

63. The net domestic outlay figure encompasses 81%, 82% and 83% of the total federal outlays reported in C.S.A. for fiscal years 1975, 1977 and 1978. Defense procurements, interest on the public debt and "noninfluence" activities respectively constituted 12%, 11%, 12%; 6%, 6.5%, 4.5%; and .5%, .4%, .5% of the total federal outlays.

64. Readers interested in seeing what difference the inclusion of D.C. in regional and division analyses makes are referred to the data presented in Thomas J. Anton, Jerry P. Cawley, and Kevin L. Kramer, *I.F.A.P. National Summary Data Tables,* this volume.

65. Technically, the period 1975–1978 spans three presidential administrations and three Congresses (94th–96th), since the FY 1975 budget was first proposed by the Nixon administration and later amended by the Ford administration.

Chapter 2

Federal Spending in States and Regions: Patterns of Stability and Change

One consequence of large-scale increases in federal spending is a renewed interest in state and regional distributions of these federal benefits. Higher stakes, of course, are bound to attract more players with stronger interests in the federal spending game, but there are two further sources of the new concern. One is the classic issue of equity, given a fresh costume in debates over "sunbelt" or "snowbelt" biases in the federal aid system. Taking money from declining states of the North to give to developing states of the South and West is alleged to be taking place and to be unfair. A second source of concern arises from the widely shared sense that these transfers represent something "new"—that some major "change" has taken or is taking place in federal fiscal activities. Although the "equity" issue is too confused conceptually and empirically to be given extended treatment here, we can offer far better estimates of which states receive how many federal dollars. In doing so we will also be in a position to assess the extent to which major shifts in state or regional distributions of federal funds have occurred.[1]

PATTERNS OF SPENDING

Total federal outlays grew from $350.4 billion in fiscal 1975 to $507 billion in fiscal 1978.[2] When Defense procurements, interest, and foreign outlays are removed, these totals are reduced to $284 billion and $421 billion, respectively. These very substantial reductions from the data base, amounting to more than $395 per person in 1978. As might be expected, removing these sums from total outlay figures has a noticeably different impact on regional totals. The strongest impact is experienced in the East where significant interest and foreign assistance payments are channeled through large banks in

Table 2.1.   Differences Between Total and Net Domestic Per Capita Outlays, by Region: 1975, 1978

Region	1975	1978
Northeast	$550.18	$582.70
North Central	175.24	278.78
South	204.44	333.27
West	369.18	526.98

New York, New Jersey, and Connecticut (Table 2.1). Removing these data from the total removes a substantial portion of reported spending in the Northeast. But the West region, too, loses large sums due to the unusual significance of Defense procurements in that region. Per capita Defense procurements to the West region in 1975, 1977, and 1978 are the highest of any region. The North Central region, which appears to receive relatively little in either defense or interest outlays, shows the smallest impact from removal of these data. The South also shows a somewhat less impressive reduction than might have been expected, in view of repeated claims that defense spending is unusually concentrated in the South. Excluding these reported outlays from the calculation of a "Net Domestic" total obviously reduces the significance of these data somewhat, but in return we are able to provide a far more accurate estimate of where the bulk of federal outlays go. Let us begin by observing the structure of federal outlays.

Given the rapid recent increases in federal grant outlays and the frequently asserted proliferation of different types of grant programs, it is easy enough to believe that some fundamental change in the structure of intergovernmental fiscal relationships has taken, or is taking place. At first glance, however, these data appear to contradict the "fundamental change" hypothesis. Whether measured in total dollars received or per capita dollars received, there are very powerful correlations between state outlays in 1975 and state-level outlays in 1978: $r = .9987$ for total dollars and $r = .9068$ for per capita dollars, using the adjusted "net domestic" data base. Both scatter plots and rank order correlations (Tau$_\beta$ = .76) make clear, furthermore, that relative state position is also fairly stable from 1975 to 1978. Table 2.2 displays one aspect of this stability by showing state "winners and losers" in per capita rank order. Among the top fifteen "winners" in 1978, only Nebraska and Georgia were not included at the top in 1975. Among the bottom fifteen "losers" in 1978, only Delaware, Indiana, and Connecticut are not (quite) as badly off in 1975. There are some dramatic changes in ranks across years, to be sure: Nebraska jumps from 27 to 11, or West Virginia drops from 22 to 41. Most of the moves are moderate, however, reflecting a basic stability in these fiscal interactions during the 1975–1978 period. (Maps 2.1 and 2.2)

Stability also characterizes the distribution of outlays by Census Division or region. Table 2.3 compares per capita outlays by division and region with the national per capita amount for both years. At the regional level rank orders are the same for both years, with the West and South not only above the national mean, but moving further away from it. Similarly the North Central and Northeast regions are not only below the national mean in both years, but also moving further below the mean from 1975 to 1978. Divisional rankings are not precisely the same in both years. The Mountain and South Atlantic Divisions increase their lead over other areas through time, while the East North Central, New England, West South Central, and Mid Atlantic Divisions continue to lag behind the national average, by increasing per capita amounts. The only striking shift is the West North Central Division, which moves from a position below the national mean in

TABLE 2.2

The Distribution of Winners and Losers in Federal Expenditures in FY 1975 and 1978

STATE	PER CAPITA OUTLAYS		DIFFERENCE OF STATE PER-CAPITA OUTLAYS FROM NATIONAL PER-CAPITA TOTAL		RANKING	
	1975	1978	1975	1978	1975	1978
TOP EIGHTEEN STATES						
ALASKA	3405.	4107.	2085.	2194.	1.	1.
NORTH DAKOTA	1638.	3285.	318.	1372.	9.	2.
NEVADA	1700.	2852.	380.	939.	6.	3.
NEW MEXICO	1968.	2817.	648.	904.	3.	4.
SOUTH DAKOTA	1620.	2714.	300.	801.	10.	5.
HAWAII	2016.	2664.	696.	751.	2.	6.
MONTANA	1603.	2552.	283.	639.	11.	7.
COLORADO	1749.	2480.	429.	566.	5.	8.
WYOMING	1662.	2446.	342.	532.	7.	9.
IDAHO	1545.	2435.	225.	521.	14.	10.
NEBRASKA	1307.	2394.	-13.	480.	27.	11.
MARYLAND	1785.	2392.	465.	478.	4.	12.
VIRGINIA	1654.	2344.	334.	431.	8.	13.
ARIZONA	1555.	2340.	235.	427.	13.	14.
GEORGIA	1473.	2313.	153.	400.	16.	15.
BOTTOM EIGHTEEN STATES						
DELAWARE	1229.	1769.	-91.	-145.	38.	36.
TEXAS	1250.	1757.	-70.	-156.	35.	37.
ILLINOIS	1241.	1756.	-79.	-158.	36.	38.
NEW HAMPSHIRE	1255.	1712.	-65.	-201.	32.	39.
VERMONT	1203.	1681.	-117.	-232.	39.	40.
WEST VIRGINIA	1344.	1663.	24.	-251.	22.	41.
LOUISIANA	1150.	1643.	-170.	-271.	41.	42.
NORTH CAROLINA	1136.	1609.	-184.	-304.	43.	43.
PENNSYLVANIA	1142.	1589.	-178.	-325.	42.	44.
NEW JERSEY	1072.	1535.	-248.	-378.	44.	45.
INDIANA	945.	1472.	-375.	-441.	50.	46.
WISCONSIN	1007.	1425.	-313.	-488.	46.	47.
CONNECTICUT	961.	1424.	-359.	-490.	49.	48.
OHIO	962.	1403.	-358.	-510.	48.	49.
MICHIGAN	976.	1365.	-344.	-549.	47.	50.

MAP 2.1
1975 NET DOMESTIC PER-CAPITA OUTLAY

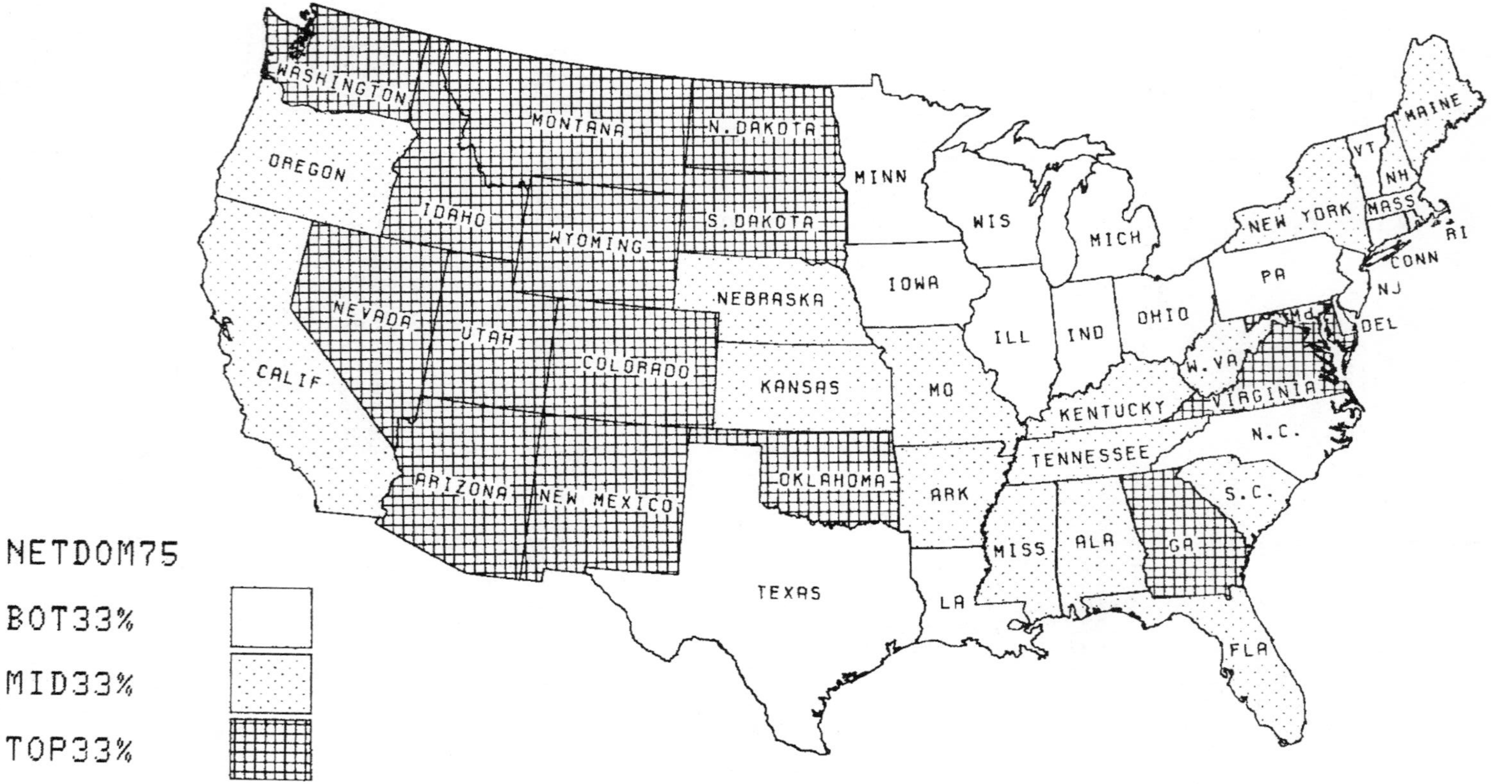

NETDOM75

BOT33%

MID33%

TOP33%

MAP 2.2
1978 NET DOMESTIC PER-CAPITA OUTLAY

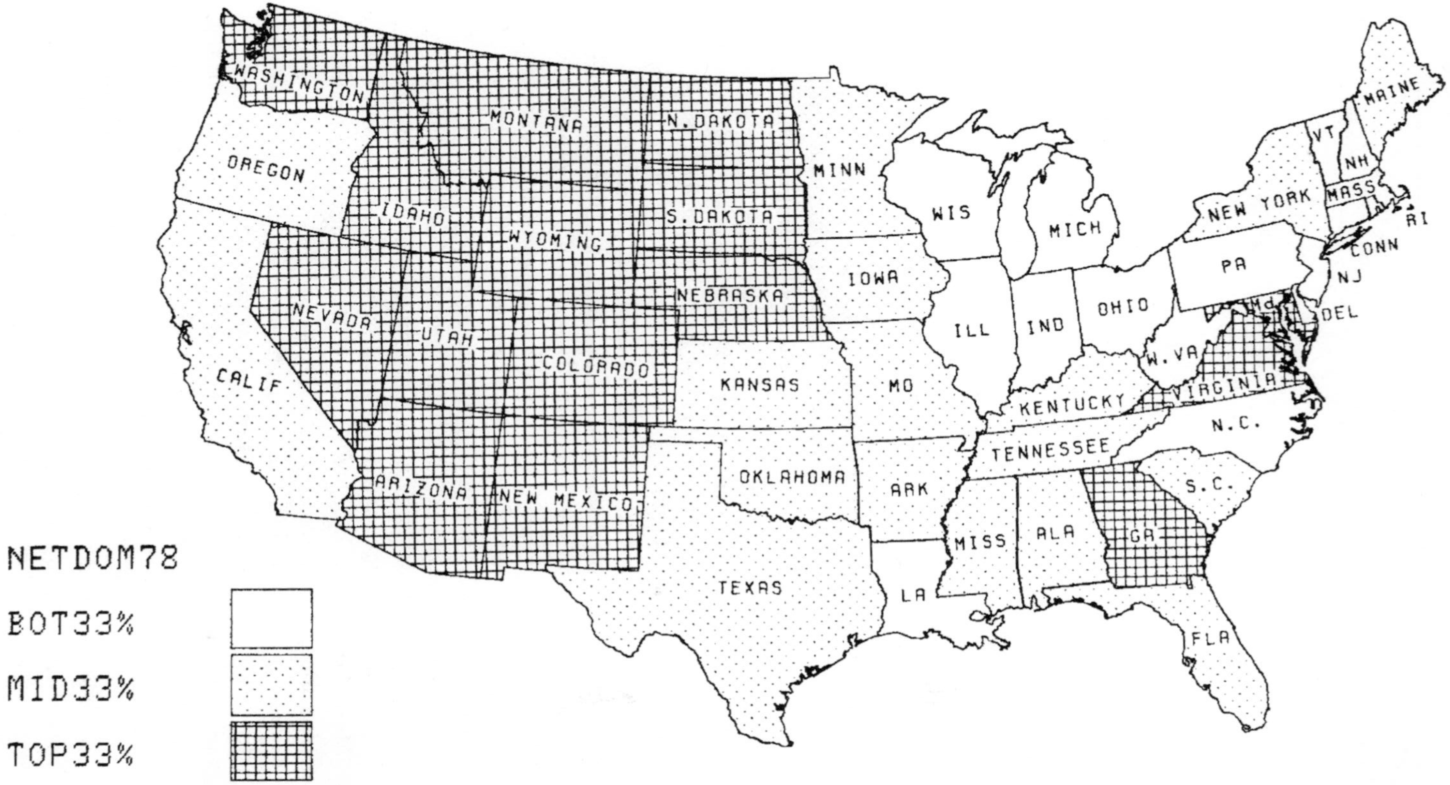

NETDOM78

BOT33%

MID33%

TOP33%

Table 2.3. Dollar Differences from National Per Capita Domestic Outlays, by Census Divisions and Regions, 1975 and 1978

Region/Division	1975 Per Capita	Rank	1978 Per Capita	Rank
New England	−164.86	8.	−227.14	8.
Middle Atlantic	−137.22	7.	−206.89	7.
East North Central	−275.83	9.	−411.26	9.
West North Central	−57.91	5.	127.54	4.
South Atlantic	369.36	1.	507.18	2.
East South Central	22.42	4.	66.70	5.
West South Central	−58.63	6.	−129.87	6.
Mountain	341.73	2.	559.56	1.
Pacific	169.87	3.	136.80	3.
Northeast	−144.03	3.	−211.95	3.
North Central	−212.73	4.	−253.72	4.
South	167.06	2.	218.68	2.
West	213.56	1.	245.70	1.
Total U.S.	1,320.02		1,913.42	

1975 to a position far above the mean in 1978. These data, with defense procurements *excluded,* thus confirm the widely-discussed conclusion that western states, and to a lesser extent southern states, continue to maintain a commanding lead over other areas in receipt of federal disbursements.[3]

Although these numbers appear to suggest an impressive system stability and, within stability, a continuing domination of western and southern states, we are not inclined to attach a great deal of significance to them. For one thing, regional and divisional aggregations are both arbitrary and highly artificial, masking the considerable state-by-state variation that exists *within* regions or divisions. Demographically, Vermont has more in common with Wyoming than with Massachusetts, or Rhode Island, with whom Vermont shares a common regional and divisional assignment. Connecticut and New Jersey, alike in so many ways, nevertheless are assigned to different divisions. Within the same region (west) differences in per capita income by state can exceed $2,200, and differences in per capita outlays can exceed $2,200. Disparities of this magnitude are masked when data are aggregated by region or division, confounding efforts to find regionally based "patterns" in, for example, relationships between personal income and outlays.

More fundamentally, it is not at all clear that dividing total outlays by total state population produces a very meaningful number. Per capita calculations are obviously convenient to use and they do provide an easily-understood estimate of federal spending activities across state boundaries. The practical and theoretical significance of such rough estimates, however, is not easily discerned. In fiscal 1978, for example, South Carolina ($1,853.26) and Missouri ($1,862.44) both recorded per capita outlay amounts within about $10 of the New York per capita outlay of $1,855.53. The New York per capita figure was based on total outlays of some $32.9 billion, while total outlays in South Carolina were $9 billion, and Missouri outlays reached $5.4 billion. One might use these numbers to argue that South Carolina received "less" and Missouri "more" than New York in per capita terms. Although technically accurate, the assertion would also be misleading, given the outlays actually distributed. Unless more information were available regarding the kinds of outlays made in each state, it would be impossible to know what other conclusions to draw. Payments to individuals are known to have very different impacts from payments to governments, for example, just as capital (or "hard") outlays are known to have different impacts from outlays for government administration, or social services activities. Statements about more or less, in short, are necessarily ambiguous when based on calculations of per capita totals.

The problem, of course, is that per capita calculations have no clear relationship to either allocation processes or programmatic purposes for which federal outlays are made. Although state population is commonly used in the design of federal outlays programs, very few programs rely on total population alone. Instead, programs are typically designated for some portion of the total state population: the number or proportion of persons over 65, or under 18, or below a designated income level, or some combination of these proportions with other data elements. Federal outlays, moreover, are not made "as a whole," but through the separate and largely uncoordinated actions of program managers, within agencies, that are related to other agencies in departments, which typically expect and receive annual increments in authorized spending levels, through a complex but highly routinized budget process. Total per capita calculations do not reflect allocation processes or political purposes because they cannot. Before accepting images of stability or change based on such calculations, therefore, it is clearly essential to observe outlay patterns in finer detail.

TYPES OF FEDERAL OUTLAYS

Outlays data permit the analysis of eleven different types of federal obligation. Although distinctions between these types are not always as clear as they might be, the "type" designations come much closer to conceptions of purpose and process than overall per capita figures, and thus offer a useful opportunity for more detailed examination. For this report we have selected five of the most important types and collapsed the remainder into a single category as follows:

1. *Formula Grants.* This category includes all grant funds distributed according to some specific formula. As noted earlier, formula elements often include population, the proportion of a jurisdiction's population that falls within some specified class, physical or economic characteristics of the jurisdiction, or combinations of various formula elements. Distribution of formula grant funds is relatively automatic, once the formula algorithm has been determined. Understandably, then, recent dramatic increases in dollars allocated for such grants have been accompanied by considerable conflict over the terms to be included in various formulas. Dramatic as these increases have been, formula grants *as a proportion* of net domestic outlays declined from 18.6 percent in 1975 to 16 percent in fiscal 1978.[4]

2. *Project Grants.* Project grants are made available for specified purposes or projects, defined by legislation and interpreted by federal regulations. Since nationally defined purposes are the criteria for awarding such grants, state and local jurisdictions typically are required to submit applications for evaluation by federal program managers. Jurisdictions selected as recipients of project grants typically are required to submit a variety of interim and final reports to the granting agency, showing what was accomplished with federal funds and how those accomplishments contribute to the achievement of national purpose. Compared to formula grants, project grants assign considerably more discretion to federal program managers in deciding which units should receive grant funds. The distribution of project grant funds thus can be taken to reflect both national political

priorities and the discretionary judgment of national administrators as well as local "grantsmanship." Project grants increased from 5.2 percent of net domestic outlays in 1975 to 6.1 percent in 1978.[5]

3. *Direct Payments.* Although somewhat ambiguous in concept, this category includes payments that are primarily made to individuals or non-governmental organizations. Various social security, welfare, and unemployment insurance programs are included here. Medicaid, however, is not included as a direct payment, since federal funds are distributed to state governments for distribution to suppliers of medical services to needy populations. (Medicaid is treated as a formula grant.) Not surprisingly, direct payments represent the bulk of domestic outlays, rising from 33.1 percent in 1975 to 38 percent in 1978.[6]

4. *Direct Loans.* Various programs loan federal funds directly to individuals or organizations for purposes such as the creation of business enterprise, support of agricultural activities, or disaster relief. While not large relative to total federal obligations, direct loan outlays increased by just over 478 percent between 1975 and 1978, from $1.67 to $9.66 billion. As a proportion of total domestic outlays, direct loans increased from .6 percent in 1975 to 2.3 percent in 1978. Increases of this magnitude in a single type of federal obligation clearly seem both interesting and potentially significant.

5. *Guaranteed Loans.* For nearly a half century the federal government has guaranteed banks and other financial institutions against losses on loans made to individuals for a variety of purposes. Agencies such as H.U.D., V.A. or the Department of Agriculture administer large mortgage programs to encourage home purchase, Commerce and Agriculture Department programs offer loan guarantees for business or agricultural enterprise, and H.E.W. guarantees loans for purposes such as financing the costs of higher education. These programs, too, have increased dramatically, nearly doubling between 1975 and 1978. Guaranteed loans represented some 11 percent of total outlays in 1978, up from 8.2 percent in 1975.[7]

6. *Other Domestic Outlays.* This category, which groups together the remaining classes of federal outlays, is dominated by salaries and expenses paid to federal employees. Other obligations, such as non-defense procurements or commodity distribution, are less significant in total dollars but included in order to provide a comprehensive report of remaining types of federal financial activity. Outlays included in this category fell from 34.3 percent of total outlays in 1975 to 26.8 percent in 1978.[8]

A more comprehensive view of the forms in which federal obligations are incurred permits a more accurate assessment of what is, and what is not, changing. Table 2.4, which displays per capita allocations for the various types of assistance in 1975 and 1978, makes clear that, while total outlays are increasing over all, some types of outlay have far greater rates of increase than others. The quite dramatic increase in direct loans (+465%), coupled with the very substantial increment in guaranteed loans (+94%), seem interesting because neither type of assistance represents an "expenditure" but rather a commitment that, if made, will ultimately be recovered by the federal treasury (less underwriting costs). Should this pattern persist, it would suggest a change in federal outlay policy of some significance. Formula grants, said by many to represent the cornerstone of a shift to a "new federalism," are increasing far less rapidly (+26%) than many have supposed and in fact constituted a smaller fraction of total outlays in 1978 than they did in 1975. Project grants, whose reduction was a major goal of advocates of the "new federalism," actually increase in significance in 1978 (+71%) totaling $25.8 billion, $11 billion higher than the 1975 spending level. Far and away the largest dollar increases, if not percentage increase, have occurred in direct payments, spurred on by medical, welfare

Table 2.4. Per Capita Types of Federal Outlay, 1975 and 1978

	Formula Grants	Project Grants	Direct Payments	Direct Loans	Guaranteed Loans	Other
1975	230.74	69.50	443.34	7.87	109.99	458.59
1978	290.40	118.79	728.37	44.42	212.87	518.57
% change	+25.86	+70.93	+64.29	+464.67	+93.53	+13.08

and social security increases. Rankings of states by total federal receipts may not have changed very much, but these figures suggest that *what* the states are receiving may indeed have changed.

When these outlay types are broken down by region, interesting patterns emerge. In Table 2.5 we show these patterns by comparing differences between national and regional per capita types of outlay. The West, we can now see, achieves its relatively favored position by exceeding the national per capita allocation in formula grants and guaranteed loans. The South achieves its advantage primarily through project grants and guaranteed loans. Although considerably below the national mean in net outlays, the Northeast is further above the mean than any other region in formula grants, project grants, and direct payments. Apart from the very dramatic shift in the direct loans category, the North Central region continues to lag behind other regions in both years.

These patterns become more sharply defined when divisions, rather than regions, are observed. The very large increase in direct loans between 1975 and 1978 clearly benefited the West North Central states of North and South Dakota, Minnesota, Iowa, Kansas, Nebraska, and Missouri more than other states, although states in the West South Central and Mountain areas were also considerably above the national mean. Legislation enacted in 1976, which expanded both eligibility criteria and funding for rural electrification and development loans, rural housing loans and emergency disaster loans, appears to be the source of much of this outlay expansion, and for the equally noticeable expansion in guaranteed loans as well. In the Northeast, New England states moved from a position below the national per capita mean for direct payments in 1975 to a position considerably above the mean for direct payments in 1978. Although the per capita increment was similar for the heavily populated Mid Atlantic states of New York, New Jersey and Pennsylvania, the per capita difference from the national mean was much greater in these states than in New England. New England states, however, increased their lead over other divisions in the receipt of project grants.

Analyzing types of outlays rather than total outlays shifts our perspective from what states get to what federal programs give. From the latter perspective, federal outlays assume a more dynamic quality through time. Programs and funding levels change, sometimes in response to economic and demographic change, sometimes in response to new program initiatives on the part of Congress or the Executive Branch. The result, within states and regions, appears as a constant shifting in types of outlay receipts. Under conditions of economic decline, direct payments for welfare assistance, medical costs or unemployment insurance increase more-or-less automatically in industrial states, as do formula grants tied to economic indicators. Population movements from one state to another have a similar effect on federal transfer payments or formula grants tied in some way to population. As new programmatic concerns make their way onto the national political agenda—environmental protection, energy or mass transportation are prominent recent examples—outlays addressing such issues begin to be made, often in the form

TABLE 2.5

Dollar Differences from National Per-Capita, By Type of Assistance
Expenditure by Division and Region, FY 1975 and 1978

AREA	NET DOMESTIC TOTAL		FORMULA GRANTS		PROJECT GRANTS		DIRECT PAYMENTS		DIRECT LOANS		GUARANTEED LOANS		OTHER TYPES OF ASSISTANCE	
	FY 75	FY 78	FY 75	FY 78	FY 75	FY 78	FY 75	FY 78	FY 75	FY 78	FY 75	FY 78	FY 75	FY 78
REGION														
N.E...	-144.03	-211.95	10.96	43.58	10.98	15.41	17.86	66.15	-4.37	-31.51	-54.48	-110.49	-124.99	-195.08
N.CT..	-212.73	-253.72	-27.17	-38.16	-9.75	-11.81	-20.15	-28.05	-2.60	32.78	-12.87	-18.11	-140.19	-190.38
SOUTH.	167.06	218.68	1.84	-14.07	-.52	4.09	9.67	-8.30	4.70	2.67	27.14	41.42	124.21	192.87
WEST..	213.56	245.70	23.54	26.55	1.36	-8.80	-10.19	-25.67	1.28	-13.63	42.36	89.02	155.20	178.24
DIVISION														
N.ENG.	-164.86	-227.14	6.56	31.60	16.61	46.93	-9.94	27.75	-2.46	-26.96	-48.04	-112.11	-127.60	-194.35
M.A...	-137.22	-206.89	12.40	47.58	9.13	4.91	26.95	78.94	-5.00	-33.03	-56.58	-109.96	-124.14	-195.33
E.N.C.	-275.83	-411.26	-27.98	-35.46	-8.85	-7.10	-42.48	-68.36	-4.45	-23.04	-34.14	-68.63	-157.94	-208.67
W.N.C.	-57.91	127.54	-25.17	-44.67	-11.97	-23.18	34.63	69.54	1.93	167.85	39.31	104.12	-96.65	-146.11
S.A...	369.36	507.18	3.77	-7.24	21.65	37.95	33.71	43.55	3.91	-5.82	31.41	37.79	274.89	400.95
E.S.C.	22.42	66.70	14.45	5.82	-15.79	-17.23	4.45	-28.20	2.80	3.37	20.39	29.51	-3.88	73.43
W.S.C.	-58.63	-129.87	-9.38	-37.20	-25.63	-34.59	-24.89	-75.65	7.19	15.31	24.76	54.54	-30.71	-52.27
MOUNT.	341.73	559.56	38.13	16.55	6.16	-6.90	-27.52	-51.70	4.45	10.11	106.73	289.97	213.76	301.52
PAC...	169.87	136.80	18.57	30.02	-.28	-9.46	-4.28	-16.64	.21	-21.88	20.41	19.30	135.23	135.47

38

of project grants or the recent explosion of direct and guaranteed loan programs. Observing outlay types moves us closer to understanding these patterns than analysis of per capita totals by exposing variety in the type and quantity of federal response to social and political change. We can move still closer by observing patterns of outlay by agency.

AGENCY OUTLAY PATTERNS

Federal departments are far more than administrative agencies. Like all organizations, individual departments represent a particular "mobilization of bias," [9] in favor of some purposes or activities, opposed to others. Departmental biases, however, are supported by constituencies that are represented in Congress and protected by strong alliances between constituency groups, Congress, and agency bureaucrats. These alliances create a powerful political claim on a share of each year's national budget that is extremely difficult to adjust in the short run. Because agency biases are shaped by constituencies that are spread unevenly across the country, it is to be expected that federal departments will have closer fiscal relationships to some states than to others.

In general, Departmental outlays are highly correlated with state population, particularly for agencies such H.E.W., whose programs are dominated (76 percent in 1978) by direct payments, or Labor, whose programs are dominated (74 percent in 1978) by formula grants. The correlations shown in Table 2.6, however, reveal that the population-outlay relationship is not universally strong, and hardly exists at all for the Department of Interior, whose programs seem directed toward more sparsely-populated areas. Among the less robust correlations, Agriculture might appear surprisingly high, in view of that agency's presumptive bias toward less-populated farm areas. It must be remembered, however, that Agriculture in fact operates several programs with a decidedly urban focus, among them the very large school lunch and food stamp programs. The rather high 1975 correlation for Agriculture is thus understandable, as is the moderate decline in 1978, when the large new direct and guaranteed loan programs concentrated in agricultural states came into place. A weaker population-outlay relationship for the Small Business Administration in 1978 suggests a "spreading effect" in S.B.A. outlays, away from the more populous states. NASA and Commerce outlays, too, appear to be less concentrated in highly populated states than are outlays for other large agencies. [10]

State concentration of agency outlays can be measured by the proportion of each agency's annual outlay total that is allocated to a given state (see Maps 2.3–2.5). These calculations (see Appendix Table 2.1) make clear that agency outlays are indeed highly concentrated: in no case are more than six states required to accumulate a third of agency outlay totals; only three are required to reach that level for E.P.A. disbursements. For NASA, California alone accounts for nearly 40 percent of agency outlays and nearly 67 percent of the total is achieved by adding Texas, Maryland and Florida. It is also clear that agencies often concentrate their outlays in different states. Michigan, low in Agriculture, heads the list for E.P.A. obligations. Georgia, low in H.E.W. payments, stands first in outlays from the Small Business Administration.

Concentration of agency outlays therefore seems as much a characteristic of recent intergovernmental fiscal relations as is agency specialization in the type of outlay distributed. Outlays are more concentrated for some agencies than others, to be sure, and some agencies—Agriculture, or H.E.W., for example—distribute several types of outlay rather than one or two. But specialization in outlay form and geographic focus seems a common characteristic among the deliverers of federal funds to states and regions. Depending on

Table 2.6. Correlations Between State Population and Agency Spending, 1975 and 1978

Agency	1975	1978
Agriculture	.772	.676
Commerce	.668	.581
Defense	.697	.721
E.P.A.	.909	.700
G.S.A.	.878	.855
H.E.W.	.979	.985
H.U.D.	.921	.912
Interior	.188	.271
Justice	.968	.955
Labor	.957	.950
NASA	.636	.650
S.B.A.	.854	.597
D.O.T.	.883	.889
Treasury	.954	.782
V.A.	.924	.900

the interaction between state characteristics and the mix of programs administered within Departments, different states, at different times, will benefit more or less from agency disbursements.

This conclusion may seem rather too bland. We offer it primarily to call attention to the variability in both federal government activities and the enormously varied characteristics referred to by the words "state" or "region." Variability at the receiving end of the outlays pipeline is captured poorly, if at all, by aggregating data at the state or regional level. Thus, while richer and more populous states seems to do better than their opposites in the receipt of federal funds, there is enough within- and between-state variability to undermine the significance of this observation, particularly when outlays are broken down by form or agency. Similarly, aggregating federal outlays by form or agency may have more political and programmatic meaning than total sums, but the increment in our understanding is hardly satisfying. Understanding *what is being delivered* clearly requires a deeper appreciation of federal funding purposes.

PROGRAM OUTLAYS

In creating an improved outlays data system, we have included separate reports for 46 of the largest federal programs, selected according to *Catalog of Federal Domestic Assistance* codes. Apart from capturing as large a proportion of total assistance as possible (70 percent of net domestic outlays in 1978), programs were selected to represent a broad mix of agencies and a mix of established and new program activities. Thus well-established programs such as Aid to Families with Dependent Children (H.E.W.) or Highway Trust Fund disbursements (Transportation) are included, as are more recently initiated programs such as General Revenue Sharing (Treasury), C.E.T.A. (Labor), or the Emergency Public Works program (Commerce). Since a number of these programs by-pass the states or are targeted on lower-level jurisdictions, county or city analysis seems a more appropriate vehicle for detailed examination of program distributions. Our focus here on state-level analysis nevertheless permits a brief commentary on three aspects of program outlays that seem both interesting and important.

The first represents a modification of our earlier conclusion that agency outlays are highly concentrated because, we suggested, agency "bias" is directed toward differentially concentrated constituency groups. This formulation overlooks the multiple constituencies serviced by many large agencies; hence the probability that a single agency may have or develop a number of distinctively different funding biases. A clear, if simple, example is the Department of Transportation, which for years has distributed highway planning and construction grants to states with extensive hard-surfaced highway systems. Observing the distribution of such grants in 1975, states such as Texas, California, Michigan, or Pennsylvania emerge as the largest beneficiaries (Map 2.6). Creation of an Urban Mass Transportation Authority within the Department of Transportation, however, established a different bias, with a different geographic focus. Observing U.M.T.A. distributions for 1975 (Map 2.7) reveals a heavy concentration in New York, New Jersey, and Georgia, while states such as Michigan, Texas, or Pennsylvania drop to positions closer to the bottom of the funding list. Multiple biases are of course even more noticeable in larger and more complex agencies whose constituencies sometimes do, and sometimes do not, overlap. Thus Maps 2.8 and 2.9 showing outlay distributions for two Department of Agriculture programs, Waste and Water Disposal and Low and Moderate Income Housing, look very different indeed.

Multiple objectives in large agencies, coupled with the obvious but easily overlooked fact that many different agencies often pursue the same (or very similar) objective, create conditions for competition or cooperation that have scarcely been explored. Agriculture and H.U.D., for example, both operate large housing assistance programs for low-to-moderate income families, with largest outlay amounts concentrated in the same groups of states. Similarly, Agriculture and E.P.A. both operate water and waste disposal programs that show (Maps 2.10 and 2.11) overlapping patterns in the midwest, south and west. Agency interest in constituency expansion, in order to broaden support for program appropriations, would suggest patterns of competition in the delivery of these program outlays. Within Michigan, however, Agriculture's waste and water program is concentrated in largely rural counties, while the E.P.A. wastewater treatment program distributes larger amounts to urban counties. In this state, a "high" beneficiary from both programs, there may well be some form of cooperation between agencies in deciding where to allocate funds.

A second aspect of state-level program outlays that is worth a brief comment is the relative proportion of "hard" and "soft" outlays within states. Relying primarily on *Catalog of Federal Domestic Assistance* descriptions, we made an effort to code each of the 46 reported programs as "hard" or "soft," depending on whether they appeared to be designed primarily to deliver services or funds to individuals, or to support capital investment activity. These judgments were not always easy to make: many programs mix "hard" and "soft" purposes, many program descriptions are quite difficult to interpret, and unrestricted programs such as General Revenue Sharing provide no basis at all for discrimination (using the best available information of GRS uses, we coded it "soft"). The results are therefore no more than judgmental, but the effort seemed worthwhile largely because "hard" and "soft" monies are thought to be distributed quite differently, and to have quite different impacts on state and local economies.[11]

Nation-wide, some three-quarters of these program dollars turn out to be "soft" and, in contrast to widely held expectations, to be distributed about the same way as "hard" outlays are distributed. As our scatter-plot reveals (Figure 2.1), states that do well in the receipt of soft dollars also tend to do well in the receipt of hard dollars (1975: $r = .88$; 1978: $r = .87$), probably for similar reasons: they are large states, with large populations

MAP 2.3
DISTRIBUTION OF AGRICULTURE OUTLAYS—1978

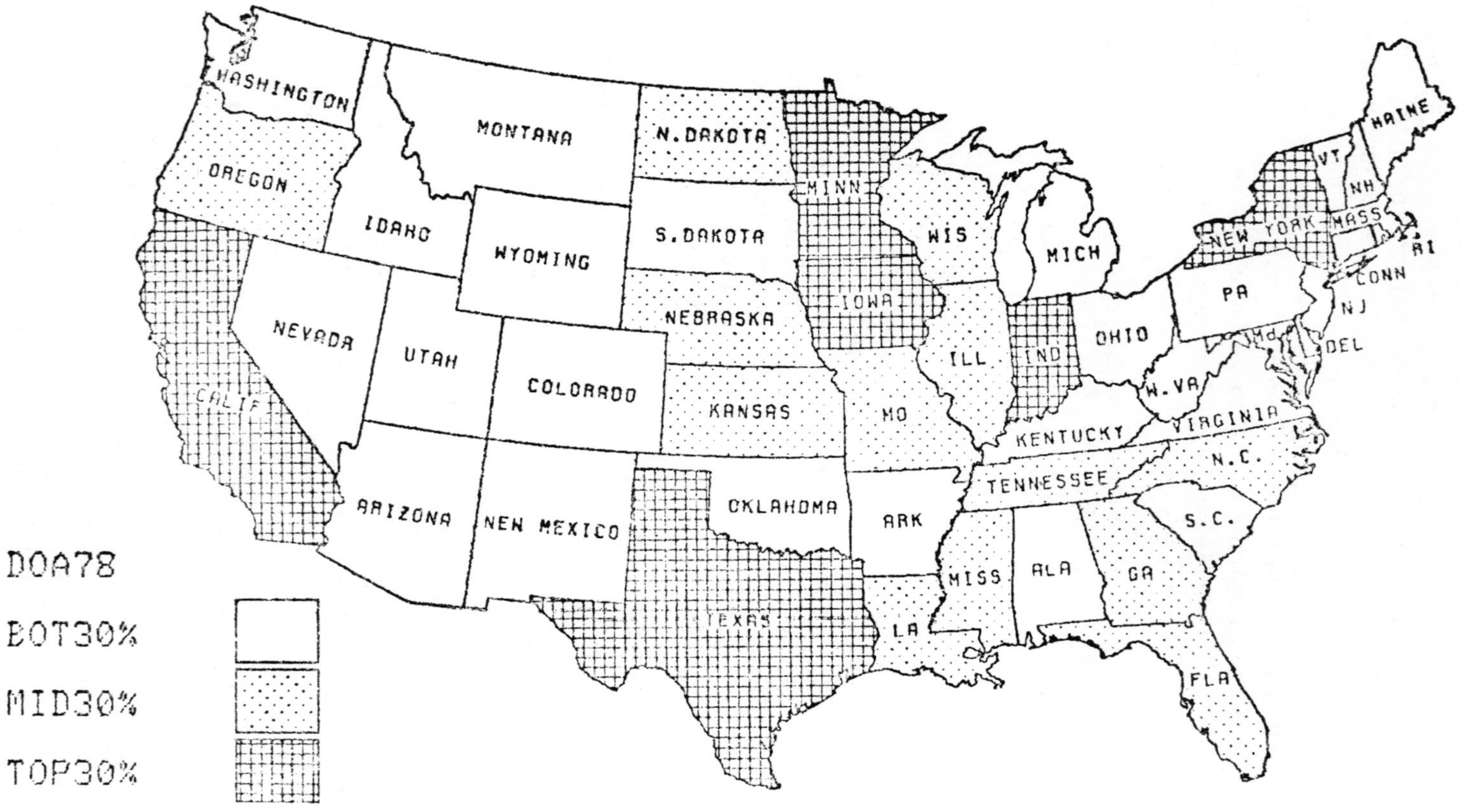

DOA78
BOT30%
MID30%
TOP30%

MAP 2.4
DISTRIBUTION OF E.P.A. OUTLAYS—1978

EPA78
BOT30%
MID30%
TOP30%

43

MAP 2.5
DISTRIBUTION OF S.B.A. OUTLAYS—1978

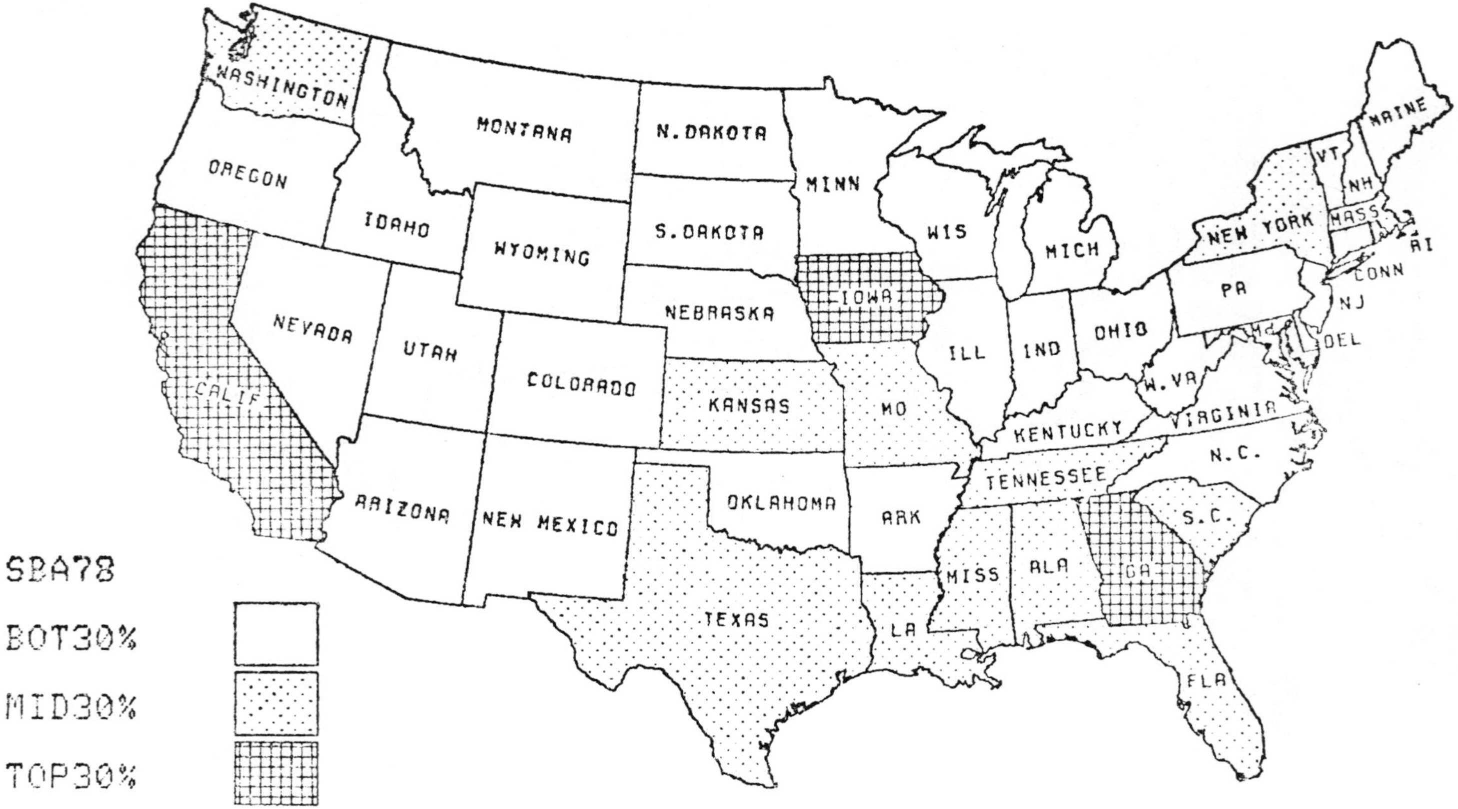

SBA78

BOT30%

MID30%

TOP30%

44

MAP 2.6
DOT: HIGHWAY PLANNING AND CONSTRUCTION—1975

DOTHIGHS
BOT33%
MID33%
TOP33%

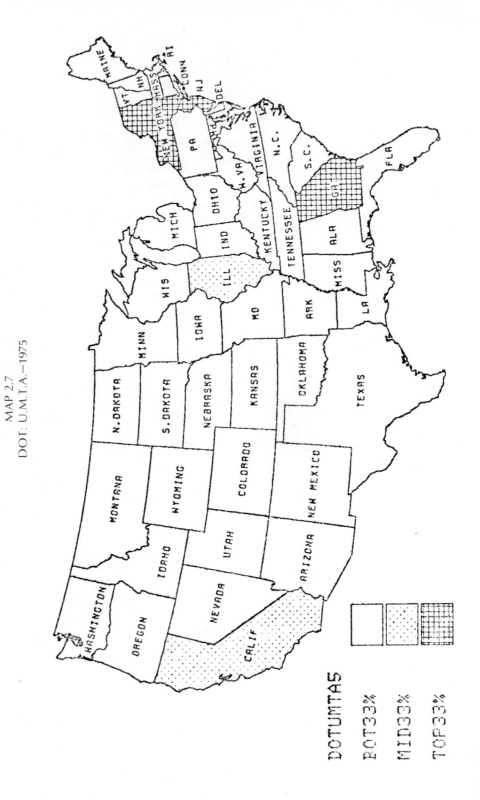

MAP 2.7
DOT: U.M.T.A.—1975

DOTUMTAS
BOT33%
MID33%
TOP33%

46

MAP 2.8
AGRICULTURE: LOW/MOD INCOME HOUSING—1978

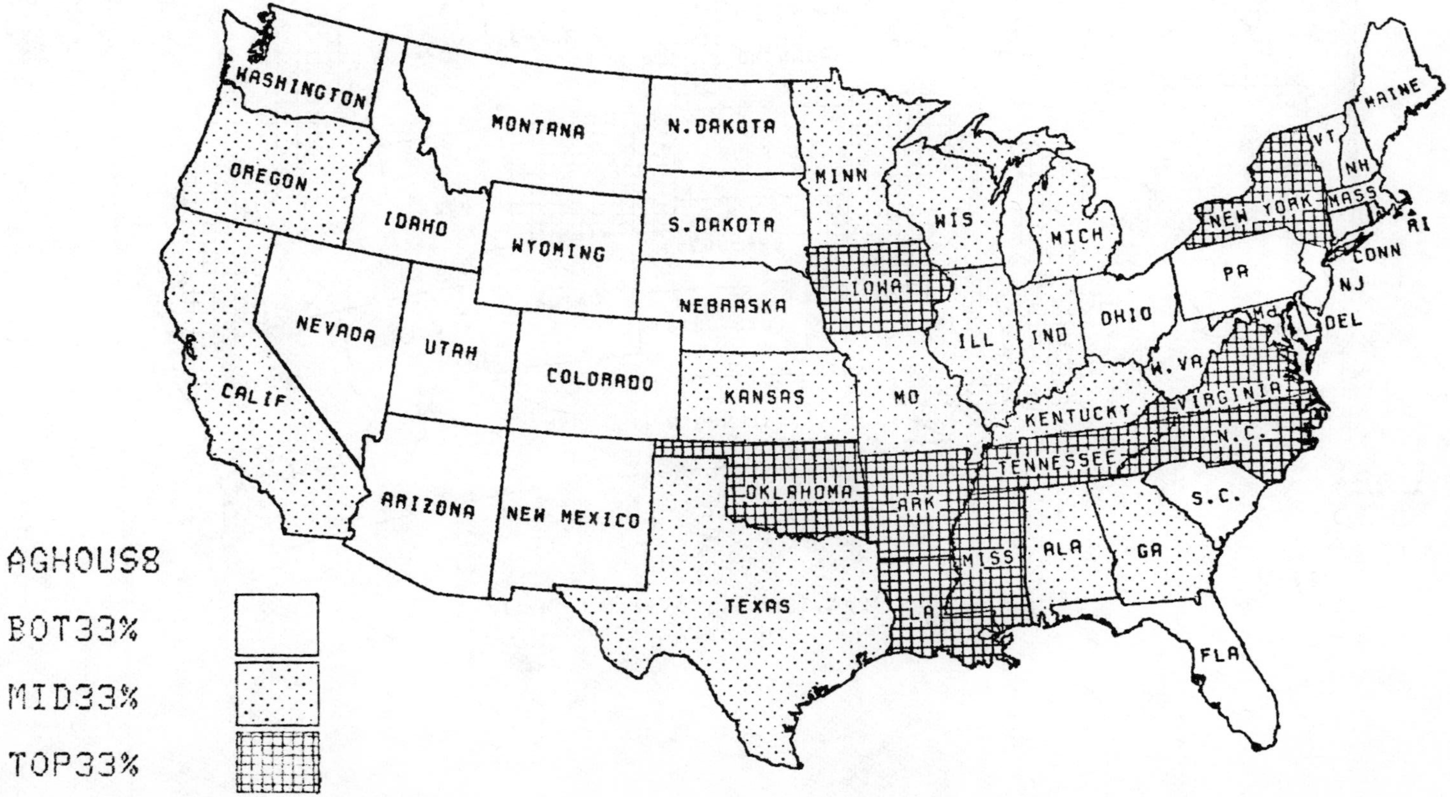

AGHOUS8
BOT33%
MID33%
TOP33%

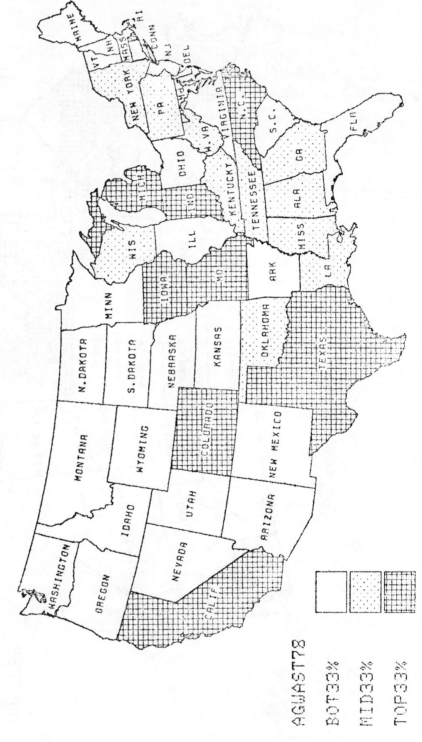

MAP 2.9
AGRICULTURE WASTE AND WATER–1978

AGWAST78
BOT33%
MID33%
TOP33%

48

MAP 2.10
HUD: LOW/MODERATE HOUSING–1978
BY CONCENTRATION OF PROGRAM DOLLARS

HUDHOUS8
BOT33%
MID33%
TOP33%

GARDNER WEBB COLLEGE LIBRARY

MAP 2.11
EPA: WASTEWATER TREATMENT—1978
BY CONCENTRATION OF PROGRAM DOLLARS

EPAWAS8
BOT33%
MID33%
TOP33%

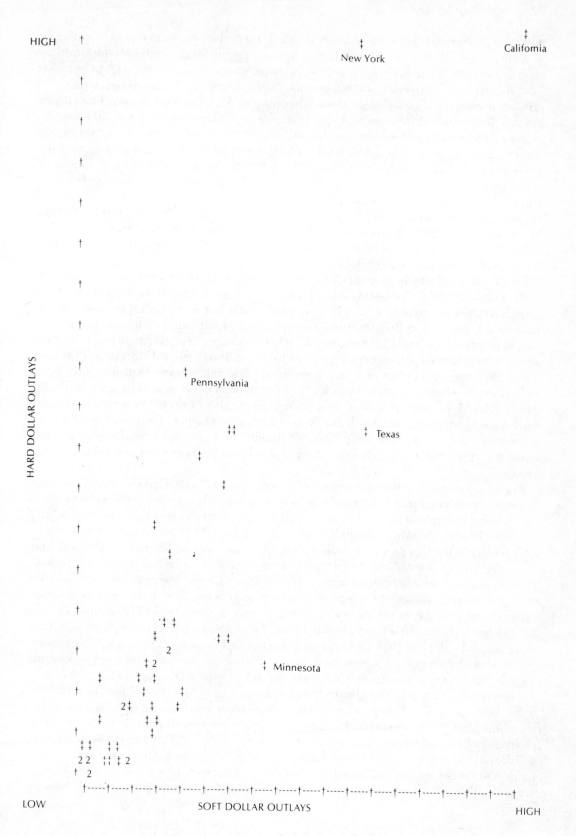

FIGURE 2.1
SCATTERPLOT OF DISTRIBUTION OF HARD AND SOFT DOLLAR OUTLAYS BY STATE

51

and thus likely to attract more of whatever program dollars are available in Washington at a given time. States whose hard-money receipts are unusually high—Mountain states such as Idaho or Wyoming, for example—are states whose total receipts tend to be rather low. At the other extreme, states such as Pennsylvania or Massachusetts receive a greater proportion of soft dollars than other states. Whether hard or soft, federal program dollars tend to flow more to people than places, although some divisional biases are evident. While soft dollars increased by 39% from 1975 to 1978 and at relatively equal rates of increase across divisions, hard dollars increased by 85% with pronounced differences in rates of increase by division. West North Central ($+131\%$) and Mountain states ($+113\%$) received the largest increased in hard dollars while New England ($+59\%$) and South Atlantic ($+66\%$) states experience much smaller rates of increase. Divisonal biases also appear in per capita comparisons: In 1978, West North Central ($602.63) and Mountain states ($620.98) receive almost twice the national average amounts of hard dollars. By contrast, the Middle Atlantic ($201.08) and New England states ($219.67) rank lowest in per capita hard dollars.

Finally, it is extremely important to note the lack of stability in the flow of program dollars through time. We began this discussion by noting an apparent stability in the intergovernmental fiscal system when national totals or per capita totals were used as measures. From 1975 to 1978 total outlays increased dramatically, with some variation in rate of increase from state to state, but with little change in relative position among the states. States that were high beneficiaries in 1975 remained high in 1978; states that were low in 1975 remained low in 1978. The appearance of stability began to disintegrate, however, when we observed outlay flows by type of financial assistance or by agency. States whose relative position remained low or high in total outlays often were states that experienced shifts from one dominant type of outlay to another. Thus while position remained relatively stable, the components of stability often changed. Similarly, stable position was often maintained despite shifts of dominant support from one agency to another.

At the program level, the appearance of stability virtually disappears, except for large direct payment programs or formula grants tied to population or population characteristics. A clear example of instability is the S.B.A.'s physical disaster loan program, which presumably *should* change rapidly (Maps 2.12 and 2.13). Comparing outlay patterns in 1977 and 1978 for this program reveals that from one year to the next, California and Iowa move from low to high in program outlays, Kentucky moves from high to low, Georgia moves from medium to high, and New York moves from high to medium. Although a program designed to respond to unpredictable physical disasters may seem an extreme case, the pattern is quite similar for a range of more typical programs that deliver either hard or soft money. In Michigan, for example, programs such as C.E.T.A. move dramatically up, then down, from one year to the next, E.P.A. water treatment moves down, then up, from one year to another, or vocational education moves up slightly, then down, then up sharply, from one year to the next (Figures 2.2 to 2.4).

These examples typify the classic "good news-bad news" quality of federal disbursement. Because national program priorities change from year to year, and because many programs permit administrators to exercise considerable discretion in their allocation of program dollars, federal outlays can and do respond rather quickly to new needs or new political commitments. That is the good news. The bad news is that such variable responses are often unpredictable, particularly in discretionary programs, thus undermining the ability of state officials to either plan or manage federal receipts very well. Assum-

MAP 2.12
SBA: PHYSICAL DISASTER LOANS—1977

SBAEMG7
BOT33%
MID33%
TOP33%

MAP 2.13

SBA: PHYSICAL DISASTER LOANS—1978

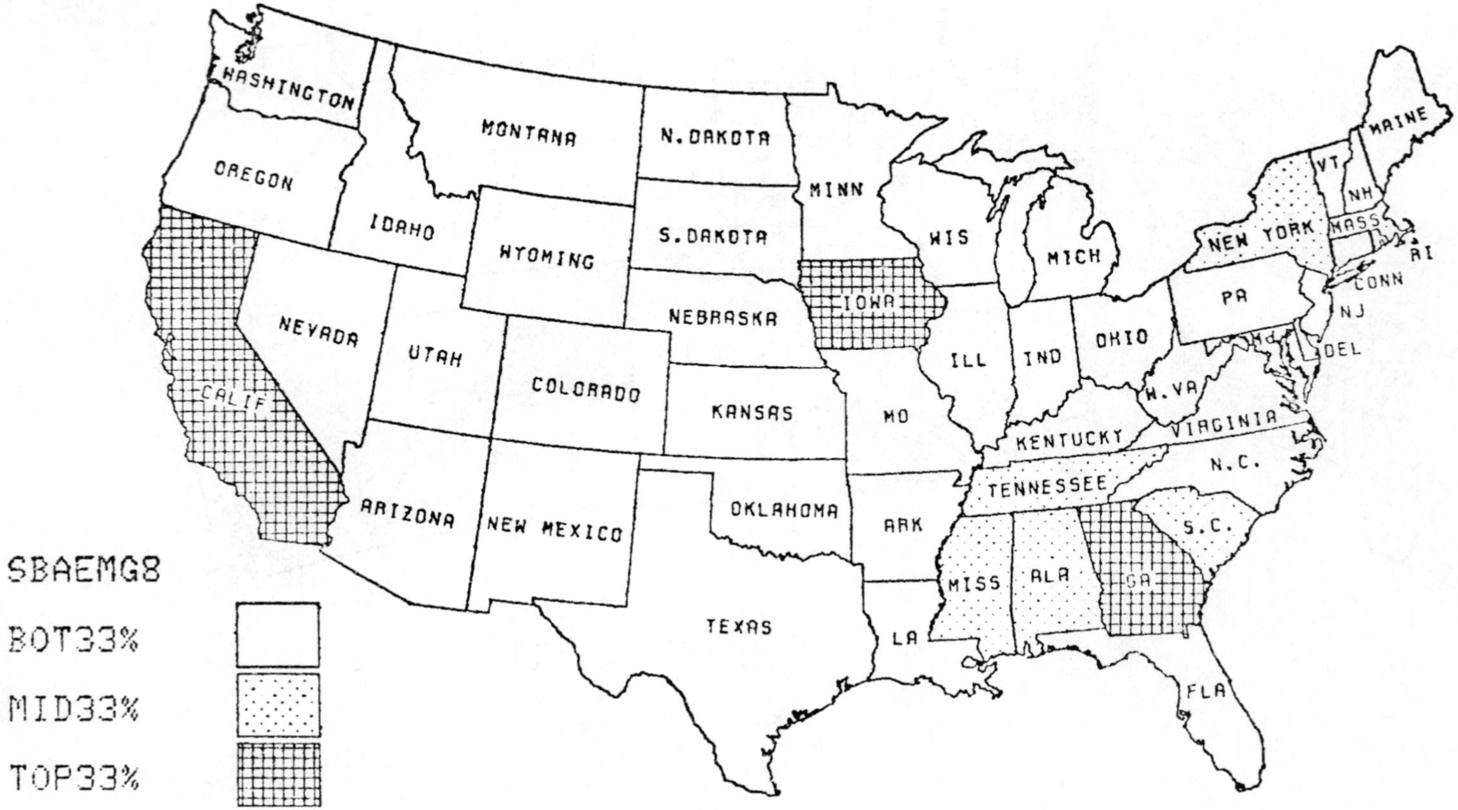

SBAEMG8

BOT33%

MID33%

TOP33%

FIGURE 2.2

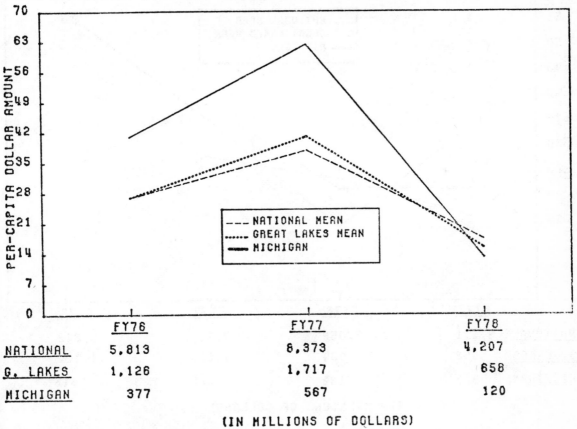

COMPREHENSIVE EMPLOYMENT & TRAINING ASSISTANCE
LABOR (CFDA # 17232)

	FY76	FY77	FY78
NATIONAL	5,813	8,373	4,207
G. LAKES	1,126	1,717	658
MICHIGAN	377	567	120

(IN MILLIONS OF DOLLARS)

Comprehensive Employment and Training Assistance is intended to provide job training and employment opportunities for the economically disadvantaged. Given the high levels of unemployment which characterized the Michigan labor force during the 1973–1976 recessionary period, it is not surprising to find Michigan ranked 6th in per-capita C.E.T.A. outlays in 1976 and as high as 3rd in 1977. This position changed radically in 1978, however, as per-capita outlays went from $62.25 in 1977 to $13.17 in 1978 for a reduction in national ranking to 26th.

ing continued growth in federal outlays, the dilemma posed by useful but unpredictable funding flows seems certain to require continued attention.

Several conclusions emerge from the preceding analysis:

1. Although federal outlays continue to grow, there appears to be no major shift in the state or regional distribution of total outlays. Indeed, there appears to be considerable stability in state and regional distributions, when measured by per capita totals. The West and South continue to lead the rest of the nation in total per capita receipts, the Northeast benefits more than the rest of the country from project grants, the West benefits most from formula grants, and the North Central region benefits most from the recent expansion of direct and indirect loans.

FIGURE 2.3

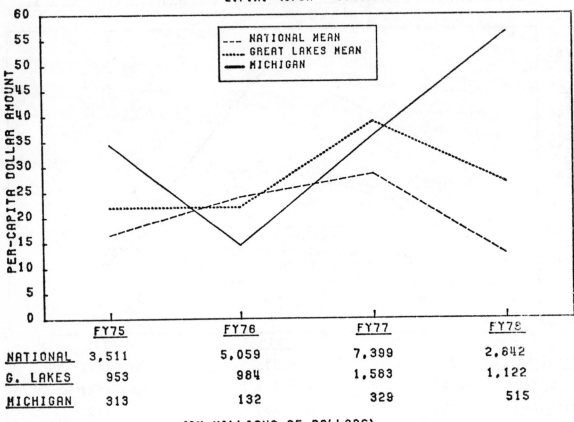

WASTE WATER TREATMENT
E.P.A. (CFDA # 66418)

	FY75	FY76	FY77	FY78
NATIONAL	3,511	5,059	7,399	2,842
G. LAKES	953	984	1,583	1,122
MICHIGAN	313	132	329	515

(IN MILLIONS OF DOLLARS)

The Construction (Project) Grants for Wastewater Treatment Works are intended to assist and serve as an incentive in the construction of adequate municipal sewage treatment works and are administered by the Environmental Protection Agency. In contrast to Michigan's rank of 29th (1978) nationally in per-capita agriculture waste disposal grants, Michigan ranks 1st in 1978 per-capita E.P.A. construction grant spending ($56 per-capita), at a time when national spending for this program has decreased markedly (−19%) as well as within the Great Lakes states. E.P.A. construction grants to Michigan have increased by 64.5% with all but twenty counties receiving grant assistance.

Figure 2.4 compares per-capita Agriculture and E.P.A. Waste Water program outlays, with E.P.A. activities clearly more dominant.

2. Project grants are more significant in 1978 than they were in 1975; formula grants, however, decline as a proportion of total outlays.

3. Major federal departments tend to concentrate most of their expenditures in a very few states but, because many departments serve multiple constituencies, the concentration of agency spending among states varies from year to year.

4. Disaggregated by program, federal outlays are often quite unstable through time, both because new programs are created and because existing allocations are made ac-

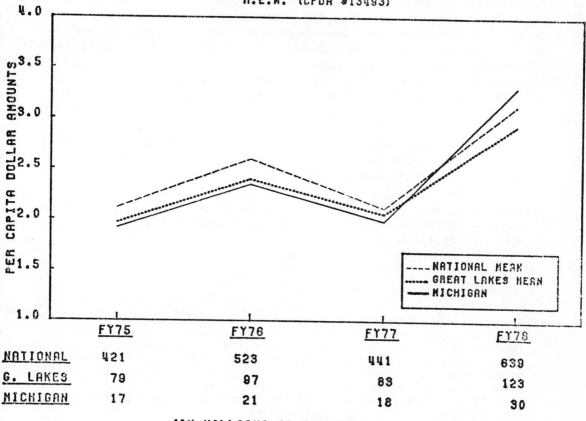

VOCATIONAL EDUCATION
H.E.W. (CFDA #13493)

	FY75	FY76	FY77	FY78
NATIONAL	421	523	441	639
G. LAKES	79	87	83	123
MICHIGAN	17	21	18	30

(IN MILLIONS OF DOLLARS)

Whereas federal Vocational Education program spending has increased by almost 52% since 1975, Vocational Education spending in Michigan has increased by almost 73% from $17 million in 1975 to $30 million in 1978. This dramatic increase in spending has shifted Michigan's national per-capita position from 38th in 1975 to 29th in 1978, although still below Ohio (26th in 1978) and Wisconsin (20th in 1978).

cording to changing patterns of administrative discretion. At the program level, therefore, outlays by state tend to be difficult to predict.

5. There is a strong relationship between federal outlays and state population and this relationship remains strong for agency and program outlays. Patterns of distribution for "hard" and "soft" monies are quite similar.

6. Although it is convenient to summarize outlay distribution by region, there is little support in these data for a distinctively "regional" bias in program, agency or functional outlays. When state-level figures are used, per capita income has only a moderate relationship to federal outlays.

7. Agency, functional, and program spending all appear to change dramatically from year to year in their respective patterns of state distribution. We take this to indicate an impressive degree of federal responsiveness to changing conditions and political demands.

These conclusions both reveal and help us understand the central paradox of federal spending patterns: component variability within overall system stability. Viewed from the perspective of state recipients, a high level of stability across time is apparent in state and regional rankings, with Southern and Western states benefiting most when a total per capita measure is used. These patterns are neither new nor strange; they arise from the allocation of most types of federal spending—formula grants, payments to individuals of salary and expense payments—on the basis of population or population-based criteria. Since population changes slowly, federal outlays based on population are bound to reflect that underlying stability. As new problems or new actors emerge in the political system, however, new programs are adopted or old programs are reshaped to deal with emergent conditions. Viewed from the perspective of federal agency or program spenders, therefore, there is considerable fluctuation from year to year in the distribution of funds among the states. Because new or altered expenditures typically are additions to an existing program mix, the pre-existing pattern of distribution is only marginally affected by program instability. General stability in the pattern of recipients *and* program instability are thus equally characteristic of federal expenditures among the states. Understanding this apparent paradox requires both highly aggregated data and data that are disaggregated to the level of agency and program.

NOTES

1. For a selection of rather different conclusions regarding the regional distribution of federal monies, based on different measures of "federal-regional presence," and examining different time periods, compare Anton, 1980a; Anton, Cawley, Kramer, forthcoming; MacDonald, 1928a, pp. 242–252; Harris, 1956; Jusenius and Ledebur, 1976; Havemann, Stanfield, Pierce, *et al.,* 1976; Havemann and Stanfield, 1977; General Accounting Office, 1977a; Hines and Reid, 1977a, 1977b; Reid, Godsey, and Hines, 1978; Vehorn, 1977; Moynihan, 1978; Lilla, 1978; The Academy for Contemporary Problems, 1978; Gifford, 1978; Labovitz, 1978; Catsambas, 1978; Pack with Folkman, 1978; Markusen and Fastrup, 1978; Markusen, Saxeniam, Weiss, 1979; and Rafuse's (1977) review of the recent debate as of early 1977.
2. All subsequent outlay figures cited are calculated from the C.S.A. data.
3. The first and second place rankings of the West and South is maintained when defense civilian and military payrolls are removed from the calculation.
4. Expressed in dollar amounts, formula grants increased from $52.8 billion to $67.5 billion from FY 1975 to FY 1978.
5. Project grants were $14.8 billion in FY 1975 and $25.8 billion in FY 1979.
6. Direct payments were $94.1 billion in FY 1975 and $158.5 billion in FY 1978.
7. Guaranteed loans were $23.4 billion in FY 1975 and $46.3 billion in FY 1978.
8. Other domestic assistance totaled $97.4 billion in FY 1975 and $112.8 billion in FY 1978.
9. The phrase is from Schattschneider, 1960.
10. NASA outlay patterns reflect, to a degree, subcontracting practices not geographically tracked by the F.I.X.S. data.
11. For a listing of programs coded as "hard" or "soft," see the National Summary Tables, this volume.

Chapter 3

_____

Federal Outlays in Counties

INTRODUCTION

In their present form, outlays data provide opportunities for more powerful analysis at the county level than at the state level.[1] States are so heterogeneous that state-level descriptive statistics confuse more than they reveal: Arizona, for example, is more "urban" (79.5 percent) than Connecticut (77.3 percent) or Pennsylvania (71.5 percent) according to Census statistics. Within-state heterogeneity also implies that summary outlay statistics are similarly confusing. Per capita calculations, in particular, often mask very significant outlay disparities between heavily populated and rural areas within a single state.

County-level data does not suffer from this problem. With 3,145 units to work with it becomes possible to organize counties into groups that are far more homogeneous, and thus more easily observe patterns in the data. Summary statistics for such groupings should therefore be less ambiguous and considerably more meaningful than state-level statistics. Of the forty-six selected programs, only Vocational Education does not report below the state level. This should permit a comprehensive and detailed treatment of program outlays. We propose, accordingly, to extend our previous analyses of agency, functional, and program outlays by paying special attention to two related issues that have been the subject of considerable recent debate: the impact of county size on outlay patterns and the relationship between federal outlays and counties that exhibit various dimensions of social need.

Table 3.1.   Average Number of C.F.D.A. Programs, by County Size Class, 1975

County Size	Average Number of Programs
Under 25,000	61
25,000–49,999	75
50,000–99,999	91
100,000–249,999	111
250,000–999,999	152
Over 1,000,000	262

THE FEDERAL PRESENCE

At the outset it is important to realize how thoroughly saturated American counties are with federal dollars. We can see this federal presence clearly by observing the number of federal programs, as identified in the *Catalog of Federal Domestic Assistance,* that are active within county jurisdictions.[2] Apart from the unusual case of Yellowstone National Park, treated as a county in these data, there is no county in the United States, regardless of population, that does not benefit from a substantial number of federal programs. Even Loving County, Texas, with an estimated 1975 population of 114 persons, had 22 operating federal programs in 1978. At the other extreme, Los Angeles County, California and Cook County, Illinois, benefited from 377 and 368 separate programs, respectively, in 1978. As these numbers suggest, and Table 3.1 verifies, more populous counties tend to have a larger number of federal programs. But no county lacks federal programs and, apart from a hundred or so counties that failed to receive guaranteed loans in 1978, virtually no county lacks federal outlays of all types. At the county level, the federal presence is comprehensive and pervasive.

AGENCY EXPANSION

Agency "presence" in counties is not uniform, however. Table 3.2 reports the number of counties in which outlays for 15 major agencies were reported in 1975 and 1978, using a data base that excludes counties in which state capitols are located and the District of Columbia, thus reducing the total number of counties from 3,145 to 3,085.[3] These data reveal that the Department of Agriculture, H.E.W., Labor, Transportation and the Veterans' Administration spread their outlays into virtually all counties, while NASA and Commerce reach only a fraction of all counties. Other agencies reach the majority of counties, but show contrasting trends. G.S.A.'s reach remains stable, while E.P.A. and Justice reach many fewer counties in 1978 than they did in 1975. H.U.D., Interior and the Small Business Administration, however, all provide outlays to substantially more counties in 1978 than they did in 1975. For these three agencies, a "spread" into more and more counties is evident. Examination reveals that this drive toward agency "spreading" is focused almost exclusively on the smallest counties. In 1978, H.U.D., Interior and S.B.A. added 246,278, and 270 additional counties of under 25,000, respectively.[4]

Table 3.2. Number of Counties Served by 15 Agencies, 1975 and 1978

Agency	1975	1978
Agriculture	3,081	3,082
Commerce	1,554	1,756
Defense	3,014	3,064
E.P.A.	2,316	1,905
G.S.A.	1,764	1,752
H.E.W.	3,081	3,084
H.U.D.	2,768	3,025
Interior	2,073	2,487
Justice	2,209	1,647
Labor	3,079	3,084
NASA	369	383
S.B.A.	2,473	2,799
D.O.T.	3,032	3,057
Treasury	3,081	3,084
V.A.	3,080	3,083

COUNTY DEMOGRAPHIC VARIETY

County jurisdictions, of course, vary enormously in land area, density, wealth and other socio-economic dimensions, no less than size. Table 3.3 gives some idea of county diversity by reporting selected county characteristics by population size class—roughly from least to most urban—and by region. Since we intend to ask whether federal outlays have any relationship to these characteristics, the data shown in Table 3.3 are worth some preliminary consideration.

Measured by per capita income, county wealth is clearly related to population: as population increases, so too does income, presumably reflecting the larger concentrations of manufacturing and retail (rather than farm) employment found in the larger counties. The least wealthy counties are concentrated in the East and West South Central states, which, along with the South Atlantic Region, also have the largest concentrations of black people, and rather high concentrations of people over 65. Although blacks and the elderly appear to be similarly concentrated in the smallest and largest counties, they seem to be concentrated in different places. Rather high concentrations of persons over 65 are found in eastern and north central states, where per capita income is relatively high, and where larger non-black populations tend to overshadow the large number of blacks found in the larger cities of those regions. In the south there are heavy concentrations of elderly people in counties such as Dade or Sarasota in Florida, where retirement and social security benefits push up income levels for predominantly white populations. Across the nation, therefore, there is a weak but negative correlation ($r = -.108$) between percent black and percent over 65, and a similarly weak but negative correlation ($r = -.107$) between per capita income and percent over 65.[5] A fairly strong ($r = -.377$) negative relationship exists, however, between per capita income and percent black. Compared to the elderly, blacks are more likely to be concentrated, far more likely to have low income levels and, apart from the largest counties, likely to be distributed in different places than are the elderly.

Table 3.3 also helps to clarify the significance of recent population movements. While counties in all size classes gained population between 1970 and 1975, the largest gains

TABLE 3.3

County Demographic Characteristics,
By Population Size and Division

	Number of Counties	Per Capita Income	Percent Over 65	Percent Black	Percent Urban	Population Change, 1970-1975	Percent Manufacturing	Percent Retail
Population Size								
Under 25,000	1,817	3,669.95	13.41	10.09	26.49	5.82	18.47	17.74
25,000-49,999	594	3,654.13	11.67	9.90	40.49	8.42	26.64	18.49
50,000-99,999	331	3,978.04	9.81	8.80	51.35	9.10	27.10	19.17
100,000-249,999	211	4,418.03	9.59	7.11	70.07	9.14	26.98	20.06
250,000-499,999	64	4,670.45	9.58	8.06	81.55	7.70	26.60	20.82
500,000-999,999	45	5,314.84	10.69	11.32	93.35	2.68	25.42	21.12
Over 1,000,000	23	5,167.35	10.33	14.97	97.76	1.57	25.23	20.94
Census Division								
New England	61	4,165.89	11.12	2.18	72.52	7.97	30.24	18.18
Middle Atlantic	147	4,148.49	11.20	10.18	80.77	4.36	31.97	17.62
East North Central	430	4,054.53	10.04	9.15	72.82	5.41	30.66	18.70
West North Central	611	4,289.50	12.36	3.98	60.65	2.26	12.51	19.88
South Atlantic	581	3,512.31	10.90	18.62	60.77	9.84	29.04	16.64
East South Central	360	3,004.62	10.71	19.05	47.19	6.43	30.41	15.78
West South Central	464	3,332.97	10.24	15.10	71.76	5.65	15.82	19.58
Mountain	271	4,090.28	8.24	1.58	66.01	13.40	8.43	19.27
Pacific	160	4,620.38	9.84	5.65	85.04	12.78	16.65	18.89

were made in counties of 50,000 to 250,000, suggesting both a continued suburbanization and recently observed increases in counties outside metropolitan areas. Population gains in counties larger than 500,000 were very slight. As the regional figures demonstrate, the greatest population increases took place in the Mountain and Pacific counties, while North Central and Mid Atlantic counties—many of which have large populations—grew less rapidly than counties in any other region. Indeed, counties of 500,000 or more people actually lost population in the Mid Atlantic, East and West North Central regions, largely because of declines in the large cities of those regions. At the county level, population shifts away from the largest and oldest urban areas into suburbs and non-metropolitan counties is suggested by fairly strong negative correlations between population change and per capita income for all but the smallest counties. Small-to-medium-sized counties, particularly in the Mountain and Pacific states, are gaining people, retail employment and income, while older and larger counties appear to be losing both people and jobs.

COUNTY CHARACTERISTICS AND FEDERAL OUTLAYS

However brief, these demographic summaries suggest at least something of the diversity and dynamism that characterize American county jurisdictions. In seeking to discover whether federal outlays have any relationship to these patterns of diversity, we think it reasonable to use per capita statistics. Although often misleading when calculated for state-level data, the very diversity of counties make it possible to group them into reasonably homogeneous population classes that reduce the ambiguity of per capita calculations.[6] Table 3.4 reports such grouped calculations for selected forms of assistance and for selected agency outlays. Over all, the county size–per capita outlay relationship is U-shaped, with both the smallest and largest counties receiving higher per capita amounts than the medium-sized counties, in both 1975 and 1978. Note, however, that the per capita distance between the smallest and largest counties increases substantially from 1975 to 1978: only $35 separates the low and high county per capita amounts in 1975 while the per capita difference in 1978 reaches $520. Clearly the smallest counties, as the change rates displayed in the last column show, have experienced a far more rapid expansion in outlays (+84.7%) received than the largest units (+41.2%).

Table 3.4 permits us to observe some of the important sources of small-county gain. Formula grants obviously were not a major source. Although the smallest counties do very well indeed in per capita formula outlays, such outlays hardly increased at all in those counties from 1975 to 1978, while counties in the large size categories gained a good deal. The real gains made by the smallest counties were derived from project grants, which more than doubled, and direct loans, which increased more than ten-fold from 1975 to 1978. Virtually all of this increment—eight of nine billion direct loan dollars in 1978—was accounted for by two programs: emergency disaster loans administered by the Department of Agriculture and loans provided by the Small Business Administration. As we see in Table 3.4, both these agencies show their highest per capita outlays and their highest rates of outlay increase in the smallest counties. Although per capita H.U.D. outlays are far higher in the larger county units, such outlays experience a five-fold increase to the smallest counties. As seems true for the Department of Interior and the Small Business Administration, H.U.D. appears to have made a determination to "reach out" to provide program services to counties outside of its traditional urban constituency.

TABLE 3.4

County Level Per Capita Outlays,
1975 and 1978

Size Class	Net Domestic Per Capita		Formula Grants		Project		Direct Loans		Agriculture		H.U.D.		S.B.A.		%Change 75-78 Net Domestic Total
	1975	1978	1975	1978	1975	1978	1975	1978	1975	1978	1975	1978	1975	1978	
Under 25,000	1,382	2,393	269	271	38	92	31	323	350	911	10	51	20	97	84.71
25,000-49,999	1,068	1,715	184	212	35	77	13	86	159	321	13	50	9	43	64.17
50,000-99,999	1,146	1,697	180	202	45	81	9	42	113	207	21	68	8	27	51.84
100,000-249,999	1,220	1,774	175	214	53	86	5	20	68	109	34	96	8	18	49.07
250,000-499,999	1,158	1,680	165	201	48	71	6	18	47	72	46	118	7	18	46.10
500,000-999,999	1,302	1,861	182	231	64	101	3	7	59	82	45	118	6	14	44.79
Over 1,000,000	1,347	1,873	250	301	94	159	3	9	53	90	45	114	7	16	41.21

Table 3.5. Per Capita Outlays in SMSA and Non-SMSA Counties, 1978

	N	Per Capita Dollars 1978		Percent Change 1975–1978	
		SMSA	*Non-SMSA*	*SMSA*	*Non-SMSA*
Under 25,000	(1,817)	$1,971.95	$2,413.20	48.15	74.36
25,000–49,999	(594)	1,431.19	1,783.92	63.67	59.92
50,000–99,999	(331)	1,704.68	1,693.44	52.55	45.72
100,000–249,999	(211)	1,806.68	1,661.75	45.14	46.54
250,000–499,999	(64)	1,677.83	1,787.52	45.46	22.46

Note: By definition, there are no non-SMSA counties with a population of 500,000 or larger.

OUTLAYS IN URBAN COUNTIES

One observable consequence of this federal effort to reach out is that per capita outlays are higher in counties outside of metropolitan areas than in SMSA counties (see Table 3.5). Non-SMSA counties in the two smallest size classes received $441 and $353 more per person in 1978 than SMSA counties in the same size categories received. However, rates of increase from 1975 outlays appear higher for SMSA counties than non-SMSA counties. In particular, SMSA counties in the 250,000–499,999 category experienced a much higher rate of increase in per capita receipts ($+45\%$), than non-SMSA counties of the same size ($+22\%$) which may well reflect a trend toward higher outlays for suburban counties. Although non-SMSA counties do not exist among counties larger than 500,000, it is important to note that rates of outlay increase for such counties (42.9 percent for counties of 500,000 to 999,999 and 39 percent for counties over 1,000,000) were considerably lower than rates of increase for the smaller non-SMSA counties.

Because Standard Metropolitan Statistical Areas often include counties that are not densely populated, SMSA designation does not always provide a good indicator of the "urban" qualities of a particular county. There should nevertheless be considerable SMSA-urban correspondence and, to the extent that there is, we would expect to find a similar pattern among counties designated as more or less "urban." As Table 3.6 reveals, that expectation is fulfilled. Grouping counties from least to most urban makes clear that non-SMSA counties do better than SMSA counties in both per capita outlays and rate of increase in per capita outlays within every "urban" grouping, but especially within the counties designated as least urban. Whether measured by the number of counties

Table 3.6. Per Capita Outlays in SMSA and Non-SMSA Counties, by Urban Percent

Percent Urban	Per Capita Dollars 1978		Percent Change, 1975–1978	
	SMSA	*Non-SMSA*	*SMSA*	*Non-SMSA*
0–19	$1,335.17	$2,520.01	57.45	76.39
20–39	1,374.79	1,894.79	58.01	67.45
40–59	1,574.45	1,937.37	59.16	59.59
60–79	1,859.94	2,344.55	45.57	66.31
80–100	2,055.52	2,432.79	43.20	49.30

Table 3.7.   Per Capita Outlays in SMSA and Non-SMSA Counties, by Division

Census Division	Per Capita Dollars 1978		Percent Change 1975–1978	
	SMSA	Non-SMSA	SMSA	Non-SMSA
New England	$1,359.24	$1,649.16	45.42	39.94
Mid Atlantic	1,445.29	1,407.65	44.65	48.42
E. North Central	1,280.86	1,630.26	52.42	55.55
W. North Central	1,702.89	2,682.88	58.44	108.08
South Atlantic	2,063.82	1,804.20	41.79	53.44
E. South Central	1,809.04	1,821.19	53.30	55.26
W. South Central	1,715.28	2,103.33	54.14	64.16
Mountain	2,440.61	3,097.31	62.79	61.54
Pacific	2,233.90	3,194.04	46.98	64.15

reached or outlay dollars received, the less urban and non-metropolitan counties of the United States appear to have significantly expanded their interactions with the federal outlay system.

Viewed regionally, small-county expansion has been most noticeable in the West North Central, West South Central and Pacific areas of the country. Spurred by the very rapid increases in direct loan programs noted earlier, per capita outlays to counties in the West North Central states more than doubled from 1975 to 1978, primarily through large outlay increments to non-SMSA counties (Table 3.7). Non-SMSA counties also appear to have captured a disproportionate share of the Pacific-area increment. Only in the New England states and, to a much smaller extent the Mountain states, have outlays to SMSA counties increased more rapidly than outlays to non-SMSA units. But even in these two divisions, per capita outlays to non-SMSA counties exceed per capita outlays to SMSA counties, by $290 in the New England states and $556 in the Mountain states.

SMALL-COUNTY GAIN—URBAN COUNTY LOSS?

These observations of relationships between federal outlays and county size appear to lead to different evaluative conclusions. On one hand, many more small counties have begun to take advantage of federal programs and large outlay increments have been directed to smaller Mountain and Pacific area counties which, as we have seen, have experienced substantial population increases. These observations would suggest that our national fiscal system is becoming more integrated and is allocating money to places in which people are choosing to settle—both outcomes may reasonably be thought of as "good." Yet, on the other hand, these "goods" appear to have come at the expense of more urbanized metropolitan counties, known to have serious social problems, which receive fewer dollars and smaller increments in dollars than their smaller and less urban counterparts. If we assume that urban fiscal as well as social problems continue to be severe, surely these outcomes would have to be regarded as unfortunate.

Neither of these conclusions can be regarded as firm, however, since to some extent they are both artifacts of the statistics we have chosen to use. Total outlays delivered to large counties are much larger than outlays in small counties but, because even a relatively small sum divided by a small population can seem large, smaller counties often appear more advantaged than large units. It is also true that many counties are so large

Table 3.8.   Correlations Between Urban Population and 1978 Outlays, by Size Class

	Net Domestic Total	Formula Grants	Project Grants	Direct Payments
Under 25,000	.42	.26	.12	.61
25,000–49,999	.25	.07	.19	.41
50,000–99,999	.34	.15	.20	.31
100,000–249,999	.49	.34	.25	.52
250,000–499,999	.51	.62	.40	.57
500,000–999,999	.36	.39	.26	.57
Over 1,000,000	.85	.66	.54	.94

that diversity of either social condition or outlay pattern within county boundaries can be masked by using per capita or proportion data aggregated at the county level. Before judging the adequacy of federal outlay patterns, therefore, we need a closer analysis of outlay patterns within counties of various size classes.

If urban counties are as disadvantaged as our initial analysis seems to suggest, we would expect to find negative relationships between various kinds of federal outlay and the number of "urban" residents in county populations. But, as Table 3.8 reveals, these relationships are uniformly positive for total outlays, formula and project grants and direct payments, the major components of domestic spending. Within each population group, in other words, federal outlays tend to increase as urban population increases. These correlations are not uniformly strong; one or two are weak, bordering on non-existent. They are quite strong enough, however, to make clear that urban jurisdictions are benefited rather than disadvantaged by the flow of federal outlays, and that these benefits tend to grow as county size increases. Correlations for 1975 outlays, not shown here, reveal a similar pattern except for project grants to counties in the 250,000–499,999 size class, which were only weakly associated with urban population in 1975, but shifted to a stronger positive ($r = .40$) relationship for fiscal 1978. Since project grants often reflect the discretionary judgments of federal officials this change, too, can be taken as a sign that federal program managers are sensitive to urban needs.

Another insight into these patterns emerges from the data shown in Table 3.9, which reports relationships between the number of blacks in county populations and the same outlay indicators. We know that strong negative relationships exist between percent black and per capita income or, from the opposite perspective, strong positive relationships exist between percent black and percent of county families whose income falls below the defined poverty level ($r = .765$ and .761 for counties of 500,000 to 999,999 and 1,000,000 or more, respectively). We also know that black concentrations are highest in small southern counties, but that large numbers of black people live in our largest urban areas. Table 3.9 reflects these different patterns by showing very slight relationships between urban and black populations in the smallest counties, but fairly strong positive relationships in the larger size classes. The black poor are largely rural in small southern counties, but predominantly urban elsewhere. Outlays generally follow these distributions, with weak-to-negative relationships between black population and outlays in smaller counties, but fairly strong relationships in the larger counties. Both formula grants and project grants have moderately strong associations to black population in large counties, reflecting outlay programs designed to distribute funds to disadvantaged groups and discretionary program decisions. Formula grants and percent black are also positively associated in the smallest counties, which seems understandable, given the

TABLE 3.9

Correlations Between
Black Population Percent Urban
and 1978 Outlays By Size Class

	Percent Urban	Net Domestic	Formula Grants	Project Grants	Direct Payments
Under 25,000	.09	.09	.28	.00	.16
25,000-49,999	.04	.06	.07	.02	.08
50,000-99,999	.00	.08	.03	.03	-.01
100,000-249,999	.36	.37	.30	.16	.15
250,000-499,999	.25	.18	.24	.19	.18
500,000-999,999	.31	.49	.71	.65	.34
Over 1,000,000	.79	.74	.66	.66	.78

Table 3.10. Population Change (1970–1975) and 1978 Federal Outlays, by Size Class

	Net Domestic	Formula Grants	Project Grants	Direct Payments
Under 25,000	−.04	.12	.05	−.04
25,000–49,999	−.05	.02	.06	.08
50,000–99,999	−.04	.04	.04	−.07
100,000–249,999	−.07	−.13	−.09	−.06
250,000–499,999	.29	−.16	−.12	.18
500,000–999,999	−.01	−.39	−.32	.16
Over 1,000,000	−.19	−.33	−.30	−.29

black population distribution. To the extent that concentrations of black people represent concentrations of social needs, these figures suggest that federal outlays are in fact responsive to such needs.

Having observed earlier that many large urban counties, in which social needs tend to be concentrated, are either essentially stagnant or losing population relative to smaller counties, it becomes important to ask whether federal outlays are also declining in such areas. On a per capita basis, non-metropolitan and less urban counties appear to do better in federal receipts. When outlays are related to population change, however, a rather different picture emerges (Table 3.10). Net 1978 outlays are barely related, usually negatively, to population change, and the negative association is strongest in the largest counties. A positive correlation between outlays and population change is clearly apparent only for counties in the 250,000–499,999 size class, which achieve that correlation largely from types of spending not separately reported in Table 3.10. Formula Grants, Project Grants and, to a less decisive extent Direct Payments, all shift from positive to negative relationships as county size increases. This suggests that, while people may indeed be leaving urban counties, federal dollars are not. Formula provisions that target needy individuals, judgments made by federal program managers, and political commitments to maintain federal support for declining areas all appear to work toward maintaining at least current levels of support in large counties.

MANY WINNERS, FEW LOSERS

In general, then, federal outlays to counties seem both more complex and more interesting than our initial analysis suggested. Per capita outlays in smaller, non-metropolitan counties have indeed expanded, with substantial increments flowing to areas of rapid population growth. But strong *relationships* between federal outlays and urban or needy areas continue, and federal funds continue to flow in large amounts to areas of weak population growth, or even population decline. Since large and small, wealthy and poor, growing and declining, northern and southern counties all gain (only 100 counties experienced a decline in domestic outlays between 1975 and 1978), judgments about these patterns based on analogies to zero-sum games, in which one group gains *at the expense of* another, seem inappropriate. Viewed as a whole, federal outlays to counties reflect a system driven by interest and constituency accommodation, rather than centralized fiscal policy trade-offs.

Table 3.11. Selected Program Growth

	Percent Change, 1975–1978		
Program	All Counties	SMSA Counties	Non-SMSA Counties
Community health (H.E.W.)	+187.41	+83.33	+329.82
Low/moderate income housing loans (H.U.D.)	+379.45	+261.11	+715.76
Physical disaster loans (S.B.A.)	+113.62	+21.09	+169.83
Section 8 housing assistance (H.U.D.)	+669.52	+321.31	+959.18

FEDERAL PROGRAM OUTLAYS

We reported earlier that several federal agencies, including H.U.D., Interior and S.B.A., appear to have "spread" their outlays into more counties in 1978 than were serviced in 1975. Further confirmation of the direction of this "spreading effect" is illustrated in Table 3.11. Of the four programs which experience the greatest overall program growth in counties served from 1975–1978, the emphasis in growth is clearly toward rural areas. By listing the number of counties into which several major federal programs distributed funds in both years, we can observe the same "spreading effect" at a more specific level (Table 3.12). Emergency disaster loans obviously expanded a great deal but these probably reflect temporary adjustments. The more interesting adjustments occur in programs that reflect recently-recognized national priorities (U.M.T.A., Community Health), adjustments in older program purposes (School Aid to Federally Impacted Areas), or implementation of new priorities (Water and Waste Treatment). In some cases, as in the water treatment or mortgage insurance programs, expansion into new counties by several agencies pursuing very similar purposes suggests the possibility of agency competition in constituency expansion. Alternatively, expansion of a program within an agency that already has an extensive and well-developed network of local contacts (i.e., Agriculture) may simply reflect new services to an existing constituency. Note, too, that some programs reduce the number of counties serviced from 1975 to 1978, because of declining political support for program activities (i.e., L.E.A.A. and C.E.T.A.). In a rough sense, then, these changes reflect the distinction offered in our Chapter 5 analysis between "core" and "barometer" programs.

These kinds of changes, for whatever reasons, imply that funding instability should be as noticeable at the county level as at the state level. In Table 3.13 we report rates of change in Net Domestic Outlays from 1975 to 1978 by size class and region. Although the total figures hide the extreme variation in domestic outlay change among all counties—from −77 percent to a 4,668 percent increase—they nevertheless reveal substantial rates of change that appear to be patterned. Outlays to smaller counties have increased far more rapidly than outlays in larger counties, and Western counties clearly have gained far more rapidly than counties in New England or in the Mid Atlantic states. When total outlays are broken down by component types, the extreme variability in county outlays becomes more evident. Project grants and direct loans both increased by several hundred

Table 3.12. Federal Program Outlays

	Agency	*1975*	*1978*
SSA—disability	H.E.W.	3,081	3,081
SSA—retirement	H.E.W.	3,081	3,081
SSA—survivors	H.E.W.	3,081	3,081
Disability compensation	V.A.	3,080	3,083
Title I	H.E.W.	3,077	3,078
SSI	H.E.W.	3,068	3,078
Rehabilitation training	V.A.	3,065	3,089
Medicare—hospitals	H.E.W.	3,064	3,065
Medicare—supplemental	H.E.W.	3,064	3,065
Food distribution	AGR.	3,061	3,060
Food stamps	AGR.	3,056	3,071
School lunch	AGR.	3,054	3,047
Unemployment insurance	LABOR	3,050	1,126
Public assistance	H.E.W.	3,040	3,030
Medicaid	H.E.W.	3,029	3,039
Low/moderate housing loans	AGR.	2,874	2,871
Highway	D.O.T.	2,539	2,812
Property improvement loans	H.U.D.	2,509	2,686
Rural electric loans	AGR.	2,250	2,053
Commodity loans	AGR.	2,212	2,478
Block grants	L.E.A.A.	2,157	1,422
Mortgage insurance	H.U.D.	1,695	1,970
Wastewater treatment	E.P.A.	1,587	1,867
Emergency loans	AGR.	1,132	2,111
SAFA	H.E.W.	942	1,537
Community action	C.S.A.	788	816
Physical disasters	S.B.A.	778	1,662
C.D.B.G. entitlement	H.U.D.	707	702
Water & waste disposal	AGR.	667	955
C.E.T.A.	LABOR	496	368
Section 8	H.U.D.	269	2,070
Project grants	L.E.A.A.	248	255
Local public works	COMM.	246	182
U.M.T.A.	D.O.T.	223	326
Community health	H.E.W.	135	388
Mortgage insurance, low/moderate	H.U.D.	73	350

percent, in counties of different size class, in different regions, and other forms of outlay also increased at variable rates. Since the figures for component types of outlay represent only rates of increase, and not amount of dollars, their significance should not be exaggerated. We report them, however, to underline the extreme variability that can occur from one year to the next in county receipts of federal program dollars. Virtually all counties can count on next year's federal outlays being higher than this year's allocation, but both the amount and form of that increment are inherently uncertain.

HARD AND SOFT PROGRAM DOLLARS

When federal outlays are classified into "hard" and "soft" categories for the programs reported here, our previous state-level analysis showed very similar patterns of

TABLE 3.13

Percent Outlay Change, 1975-1978,
By Size Class and Division

	Net Domestic Total	Formula Grants	Project Grants	Direct Payments	Direct Loans	Guaranteed Loans
Size-Class						
Under 25,000	67.67	4.04	142.58	74.40	774.69	94.31
25,000-49,999	62.07	14.26	117.05	69.65	568.89	109.03
50,000-99,999	48.41	13.16	76.77	67.10	365.93	124.48
100,000-249,999	44.89	23.21	61.82	67.46	292.68	101.88
250,000-499,999	45.16	21.72	50.69	69.88	209.22	104.99
500,000-999,999	42.84	27.14	57.78	68.48	176.21	95.93
Over 1,000,000	39.14	22.57	78.44	67.97	178.45	63.87
Census-Division						
New England	43.66	25.98	50.06	80.82	259.49	60.45
Mid Atlantic	41.37	28.54	64.04	69.63	274.79	93.80
E. North Central	43.73	15.28	90.56	65.81	513.67	92.81
W. North Central	65.56	8.38	80.69	71.15	2081.94	116.88
South Atlantic	47.84	14.26	52.57	68.43	301.36	76.57
E. South Central	52.76	20.59	103.82	62.40	364.38	88.54
W. South Central	48.19	9.01	119.30	65.70	293.72	109.28
Mountain	59.35	6.75	66.60	74.97	356.12	151.21
Pacific	44.78	27.69	86.34	70.90	164.75	79.00

Table 3.14.   Distribution of Soft and Hard Dollars, 1975 and 1978, by Size Class and Division

	1975		1978	
	Soft	Hard	Soft	Hard
Size Class				
Under 25,000	63.69	36.31	55.39	44.61
25,000–49,999	74.05	25.95	68.12	31.88
50,000–99,999	75.12	24.88	70.63	29.37
100,000–249,999	77.48	22.52	72.89	27.11
250,000–499,999	78.62	21.38	73.61	26.39
500,000–999,999	81.26	18.74	76.10	23.90
Over 1,000,000	83.37	16.63	78.39	21.61
Census Division				
New England	81.59	18.41	82.59	17.41
Mid Atlantic	86.63	13.37	82.12	17.88
E. North Central	78.89	21.11	75.26	24.74
W. North Central	67.75	32.25	54.54	45.46
South Atlantic	73.62	26.38	71.29	28.71
E. South Central	73.48	26.52	68.10	31.90
W. South Central	74.82	25.18	66.48	33.52
Mountain	59.64	40.36	50.78	49.22
Pacific	77.86	22.14	71.98	28.02

distribution, except for a moderate bias toward "hard" outlays in the West North Central and Mountain regions. County-level analysis of these same programs (Table 3.14) reveals similar biases, but adds useful further points of clarification. It is clear, for example, that hard dollars represent a larger portion of outlays in small counties than in larger counties and that this pattern is maintained through time. Within each size class, hard dollars appear to increase in significance from 1975 to 1978, reflecting the large increments in physical improvement or disaster loan programs, classified as "hard," that occurred in 1978. But large counties, with more people and more people-oriented programs, continue to be the prime beneficiaries of soft outlay programs. Counties in New England, the Mid Atlantic and East North Central areas thus consistently show the highest concentrations of "soft" outlays.

FEDERAL OUTLAYS AND COUNTY "NEED"

One might expect that these patterns of "hard" and "soft" distribution could be explained in large measure by provisions in federal programs that direct funds to persons or families in "need," i.e., the aged, the poor, the dependent. Interestingly enough, and significantly enough, such expectations appear to be contradicted by measures of association between commonly used indicators. When the proportion of county population over 65 is correlated with social security program outlays, for example, a barely noticeable but *negative* relationship ($r = -.07$, 1978) is shown. Or, when the black proportion of county population is correlated with AFDC program outlays, a similarly slight relationship ($r = .03$, 1978) emerges. When a composite "need" index is constructed, composed of per capita

Table 3.15. Correlations Between "Need" Measures and Program Outlays

	Number over 65	Number Black	Number Poverty	Number Overcrowding Housing Units
SSA–1975	.9949	.8704	.9442	.9542
SSA–1978	.9956	.8590	.9356	.9462
AFDC–1975	.6588	.6341	.6795	.6939
AFDC–1978	.7020	.6776	.7254	.7361
Medicaid–1975	.5612	.5549	.5842	.5955
Medicaid–1978	.8424	.8058	.8639	.8737
C.D.B.G.–1975	.8221	.7990	.8179	.7845
C.D.B.G.–1978	.6175	.5697	.6982	.6501

income, percent over 65, percent of inadequate housing units and percent of families in poverty,[7] this index, too, correlates poorly with various outlay measures: .23 and .24 with net domestic assistance in 1975 and 1978; .14 and .16 with formula grants in 1975 and 1978; .23 and .24 with direct payments in 1975 and 1978.

These surprising results, which fly in the face of easily available information about the beneficiaries of these programs, emphasize a point made earlier, namely, that the form in which a variable is expressed can make a major difference in results achieved.[8] Too frequently efforts to model federal responsiveness to "need" are misspecified because they are insensitive to how programs actually allocate funds. When the *number* rather than the proportion of persons over 65 or the *number* rather than the proportion of black persons in a county are correlated with social security or AFDC outlays, the resulting measures change to $r = .99$ and $r = .68$, respectively. Proportions mask these relationships by giving undue weight to other population groups that may reside in a county where large numbers of aged or black people reside, or by giving undue weight to low outlays in smaller counties. Since federal programs typically focus on numbers rather than proportions, or on proportions of national rather than county populations, estimates of federal program output should rely on such figures whenever possible.

With these considerations in mind we have selected four large and important programs, from among the hundreds available, to illustrate the relationship between county-level measures of need and federal outlays. Social security outlays can be conveniently related to the number of persons over 65; AFDC outlays to the number of black or the number of families below the poverty line, Medicaid outlays to the same indicators, and C.D.B.G. outlays to these indicators plus the number of occupied housing units that are overcrowded (i.e., more than one person per room). These indicators are not entirely adequate. Black population and overcrowded housing indicators are derived from the 1970 Census, and families in poverty dates back to 1969—thus most are close to ten years old. Inadequate as they may be, we should learn something about federal program outlays from examining outlay-indicator relationships.

County-level correlations for the nation as a whole are displayed in Table 3.15, which generally shows rather strong relationships between all variables, suggesting the extent to which social needs are both concentrated and cumulative, and the extent to which programs designed to address those needs in fact to do so. Social Security outlays *do* go to counties in which large elderly concentrations exist, AFDC and Medicaid outlays *are* channeled into areas containing poor and black families, the Community Development Block Grant program does provide funds in areas of overcrowded housing. For these programs, at least, national purpose and national outlay seem very closely related indeed.

Only a few of these measures weaken very much when counties are grouped by region or size class. The association between C.D.B.G. outlays and overcrowded housing in 1978 falls to .49 in the East North Central area and to .41 in the West South Central states. Otherwise SSA-aged, AFDC-black, Medicaid-poverty and C.D.B.G.-crowded housing measures never fall below .58 and most are in excess of .80. AFDC-black and C.D.B.G.-crowded housing measures are weak in the smaller counties but again powerful in large counties—otherwise the regional measures are impressive. The results, in per capita terms, are shown in Table 3.16. Larger counties tend to do better in AFDC outlays while the now-familiar U-shape characterizes other program distributions by size class. Regional distributions seem unsurprising except for C.D.B.G. outlays in states of the West North and West South Central areas, which are considerably higher in per capita amounts than other regions. However limited these indicators may be, it is difficult to avoid the conclusion that federal programs designed to address certain measurable needs do in fact reach counties in which those needs exist.

MODELS OF UNDERSTANDING

What kinds of intellectual models might help us to explain these patterns? Efforts to impose a geographic model on these results by attributing significance to "region" or location seem unpersuasive to us. Federal outlays of various kinds produce different patterns of geographic distribution, to be sure. As we noted in our previous analysis of state-level outlays, however, there is little evidence that regional considerations *cause* different distributional patterns, although sensitivity to such considerations appears to be growing. Instead, outlays and the distributional patterns they produce appear to be driven far more by purposive interests, institutionalized in programs, managed by officials in agencies with strong ties to both affected constituencies and their representatives in Congress. Since these constituencies and interests often cut across regional lines, rather than being reinforced by such lines, we were driven to a closer examination of programs in our effort to understand state-level outlays. For county-level analysis we are similarly driven back to programs when we seek to understand, and not merely describe, outlay distributions. The "explanation" for rapid increases in small-county per capita outlays is found in new or expanded disaster and agricultural loan programs, not in the location of major recipient counties in the Plains or Mountain states.

Other efforts to impose a more sophisticated "ecological" model on these results seem to us to be similarly unpersuasive.[9] Although the idea that federal spending and social condition are related seems to make intuitive sense, explanations built on that idea are seldom better than ambiguous. Using population, percent black, percent over 65, per capita income and population change as predictors in multiple regression analyses, for example, we were able to generate rather impressive "explanations" of county-level domestic outlays: the 1978 outlay "explained" fell below 90 percent in only 15 states and below 80 percent in only five. When regressions were run by region or size class, however, the same model produced very different results and in fact "explained" very little of the variation in outlays to smaller counties. Nor did this model explain very much of the variation in formula grants, project grants, or other types of financial activity in medium-to-small counties. The powerful impact of demographic variables on aggregate spending *in general* simply disappeared when data were disaggregated by outlay type or size.

Other demographic variables might have been used, of course, or the forms of the variables might have been altered, or the units chosen differently, or a different statistical

TABLE 3.16

Per Capita Outlay, for Selected Programs,
1975 and 1978, By Size Class and Division

	AFDC		MEDICAID		SSA		CDBG	
	1975	1978	1975	1978	1975	1978	1975	1978
Size Class								
Under 25,000	15.12	16.19	36.57	57.87	76.14	129.83	25.73	16.93
25,000-49,999	14.72	17.80	30.99	51.73	64.20	109.91	14.98	10.49
50,000-99,999	15.03	17.82	25.37	41.16	55.61	94.24	12.23	14.06
100,000-249,999	19.22	22.18	25.50	38.99	57.14	97.43	12.85	12.90
250,000-499,999	22.53	27.36	25.51	40.09	58.01	101.63	12.24	13.99
500,000-999,999	23.88	29.38	27.25	40.51	70.69	125.56	13.75	18.33
Over 1,000,000	51.34	62.91	72.22	73.01	78.45	129.89	10.56	23.52
Division								
New England	26.16	30.78	39.73	63.01	71.98	114.54	11.70	9.43
Middle Atlantic	21.11	29.01	33.12	55.60	80.61	132.15	12.12	13.11
East North Central	16.91	20.28	33.29	48.74	74.80	128.62	10.28	10.80
West North Central	11.44	13.62	25.82	44.40	82.40	136.58	19.54	17.90
South Atlantic	17.14	17.55	34.28	52.40	57.62	91.86	14.51	13.05
East South Central	16.80	19.68	38.14	61.63	57.07	104.41	14.35	10.80
West South Central	14.83	19.82	42.79	68.86	75.13	133.79	20.77	24.99
Mountain	12.74	12.95	26.70	39.73	57.00	101.23	18.23	12.33
Pacific	23.72	34.94	29.36	50.25	77.53	139.38	9.44	11.68

model chosen. Had such changes produced much more powerful explanations, however, we would still be faced with the problem of knowing how to interpret the meaning of these "explanations." Population contributed far more to our powerful explanations than any other variable, but how does "population" produce "outlay"? The answer may be that formula grants or direct payments are specifically tied to population categories, but how are such ties achieved? And how do we begin to account for outlays to small counties, which are influenced by none of the variables in this model? Ecological variables that "explain" outlays, in short, must themselves be explained, and other variables taken into account for distributions that appear to have no obvious ecological explanation.

Although some of these "other" variables may occasionally be idiosyncratic—as in the case of natural disasters that motivate national emergency loan programs—we believe that the more important sources of explanation are well-structured. For county, as well as state-level outlay patterns, they consist of the programs established within federal agencies to achieve national purpose, the coalitions of groups, political representatives and administrators who generate outlay priorities, and the interactions between these coalitions and federal-state-local decision processes that translate outlay priorities into actual county-level distributions. Not all of these political and process variables are amenable to precise measurement. They can, however, be observed and analyzed in ways that move our understanding beyond what can be derived from less appropriate or ambiguous intellectual conventions.[10]

CONCLUSIONS

In considering the significance of this analysis, it is important to begin by recognizing the enormous diversity of conditions that characterize the 3,143 American county jurisdictions. Neither poverty nor prosperity is entirely concentrated in a single region, or counties of a single size class. Images based on limited analyses of large counties, or western counties, or predominantly agricultural counties are therefore bound to be misleading if applied to all counties. Capturing this diversity in ways that are intelligible is not easy to do, but it must be done if analytical work is to be taken seriously. Classifying counties by size within region, while hardly more than a first step, nevertheless leads us to a range of useful conclusions:

1. Many more counties were recipients of federal outlays in 1978 than in 1975. Agencies such as the Department of Housing and Urban Development, the Department of Interior and the Small Business Administration clearly "spread" their programs into more counties, and it is probable that other agencies, by adopting new programs in previously-serviced areas, also spread their activities.
2. With the exception of only 100 counties, all counties gained federal outlay dollars from 1975 to 1978. Rates of gain, however, exhibit extreme variation, in total outlays, in types of outlay, and in program outlays.
3. In both numbers served and per capita dollars received, counties in the smallest size classes made the largest gains between 1975 and 1978. Counties of 25,000 or fewer people are now more comprehensively integrated into the federal funding system than ever before.
4. Small counties in the West North Central area and rapidly growing counties in the Mountain and Pacific states made the largest per capita outlay gains between 1975

and 1978. A good deal of federal money is thus flowing to areas of population growth.

5. Very substantial outlay gains were also made by the largest counties, in all regions. Over all, total domestic outlays continue to be strongly associated with measures of county population size, but slightly negatively associated with measures of population *change* in the most populous counties. People may be leaving the largest and most urban counties, but federal dollars remain.

6. Program expansion or decline, hence funding instability from one year to the next, both exhibit more extreme fluctuation at the county than at the state level.

7. As a percentage of total county outlays, "soft" money is most significant in the larger counties of the East and North Central areas; "hard" monies are most significant in smaller counties of the West North Central and Mountain states.

8. Federal program outlays are closely associated with measures of "need" in programs designed to address those "needs."

9. Program expansion, increased allocations to growing and declining counties alike, and close association between "need" and outlay all suggest that federal outlays are quite responsive to both problems and opportunities. Selective program-by-program responses build a "system" by accretion that appears designed to satisfy as many interests as possible.

NOTES

1. Examples of the types of research that can be done include: Congressional Budget Office (Peggy L. Cuciti, main author), *Troubled Local Economies and the Distribution of Federal Dollars* (Washington, D.C.: U.S. Government Printing Office, 1977); Hines and Reid's (1977b) article in the *American Journal of Agricultural Economics,* which is an abridged version of an unpublished D.O.A. working paper (1977a) where Hines and Reid devote considerably more attention to data quality considerations.

2. The figures cited below understate the federal presence in counties because individual programs listed in the *Catalog of Federal Domestic Assistance* are not always reported separately to C.S.A. by the grantor agencies, who report one expenditure figure for a number of programs. For instance, Transportation reports one figure for its Urban Mass Transportation Assistance programs in fiscal 1978, while the 1978 O.M.B. *Catalog of Federal Domestic Assistance* lists *nine* separate programs as being active and funded in that year.

3. Because so many programs report their outlays *only* to the state capitol county, such counties are reported to receive many outlay dollars that are in fact distributed elsewhere. Including capitol counties in distributive analysis would thus artificially inflate their significance. The District of Columbia, also reported to receive large amounts of outlay dollars because of its concentration of government agencies, is excluded for similar analytic reasons.

4. In 1978, 96%, 67%, and 83% of the new counties served by H.U.D., Interior and S.B.A., respectively, were to counties under 25,000 in population.

5. We use per capita and percentage calculations here only to suggest different *distributions* of concentration of these population groups. See below for a different calculation of their joint concentration.

6. A good deal of ambiguity remains, of course, particularly when such calculations are made for very large counties, containing very diverse populations.

7. Construction of this index took the form

$$\frac{\text{P.C. Income (Nat. Mean)}}{\text{P.C. Income (Kty)}} + \frac{\% \text{ Population} > 65(\text{Kty})}{\% \text{ Population} > 65(\text{Nat. Mean})}$$

$$+ \frac{\% \text{ Households w/o Plumbing (Kty)}}{\substack{\% \text{ Households w/o Plumbing} \\ \text{(Nat. Mean)}}} + \frac{\% \text{ Poor Families (Kty)}}{\substack{\% \text{ Poor Families} \\ \text{(Nat. Mean)}}}$$

$$= \frac{(\text{SUM X})}{\text{MEAN X}} * 100 = \text{Need Index}$$

8. For a more extended discussion of this point and related measurement concerns, see Ward, 1979.
9. An expanded discussion of this point may be found in Thomas J. Anton, 1975.
10. More generally, we believe these criticisms to be applicable to the large body of research on the determinants of state and local expenditures. Over 30 years of research since V. O. Key's *Southern Politics* (Key with Heard, 1949) has produced meager advancement in our understanding of state and local policy processes because of a continuing commitment to simple ecological explanations, treating state and local political systems as closed systems that need not be probed into in detail. For a sampling of the "determinants" literature, see the research reviewed in Jacob and Lipsky, 1968; Lockhard, 1968a, 1968b; Dawson and Robinson, 1963; Fenton and Chamberlayne, 1969; Hofferbert, 1972; Jones, 1973; and Fried, 1975.

Chapter 4

The Federal City Connection

Of all the issues associated with recent trends in federal expenditures, federal aid to cities may be the most discussed, but the least understood.[1] Although the near bankruptcy of New York City in 1975 stimulated a new national awareness of that city's precarious fiscal condition, it has gradually become clear that New York is not alone. Hundreds of other cities, primarily but not exclusively in the Northeast and North Central regions of the country, appear to have entered a period in which local resources are no longer sufficient to support municipal services. More ominously, population migration coupled with dramatic losses of industrial and commercial jobs in many of these cities imply that local self-sufficiency may have been permanently lost. In some ways the federal response to these conditions has been impressive: new federal programs have poured billions of dollars into cities and "urban policy" has become a matter of serious concern at the highest levels of government. Despite the magnitude of both the problem and the federal response, however, the federal government knows less about its fiscal interactions with cities than about its interactions with virtually any other level of American government. An apparently simple number such as "total federal spending" is now impossible to obtain for a single city in a single year, let alone many cities for a period of years.[2] Before discussing federal expenditures in cities, therefore, we must distinguish between what we think we know and what we can know.

ESTIMATING THE FEDERAL PRESENCE

That federal assistance to cities has increased to very large amounts seems quite beyond doubt. Census figures show that since 1964 federal aid has increased by an annual

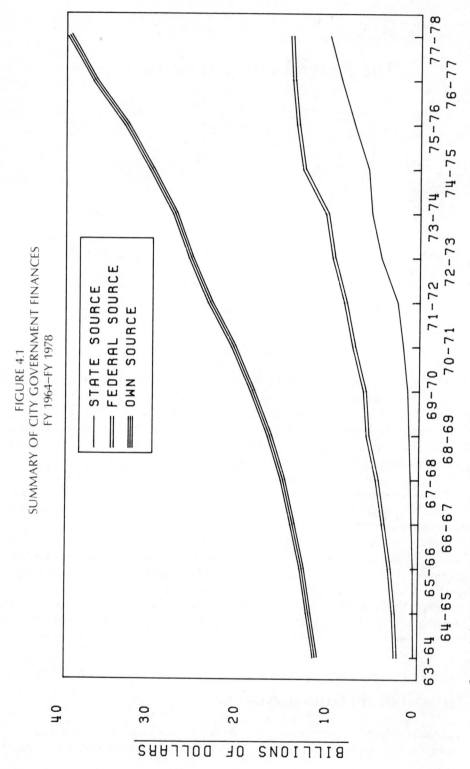

FIGURE 4.1
SUMMARY OF CITY GOVERNMENT FINANCES
FY 1964–FY 1978

STATE SOURCE
FEDERAL SOURCE
OWN SOURCE

Source: U.S. Department of Commerce, Bureau of the Census, *City Government Finances,* for fiscal years 1977–1978 and 1964–1965.

average rate of 32%, from $2.475 million in 1963–1964 to $14,482 million in 1978 (see Figure 4.1). One way to appreciate this expansion of federal largess is to note that only eight of the nation's largest thirty-nine cities received five percent or more of their total general revenues from the federal government in fiscal 1965. By 1978, more than half (25 or 39) of those cities were receiving twenty percent or more of total general revenue from the federal treasury, and cities such as Omaha, Cleveland, or San Antonio were receiving thirty percent or more of their general revenues from Washington (Table 4.1). These fractions would be much higher were it not for the inability of the U.S. Census to disentangle federal and state aid to local government—about which more will be said below. In fact, 1978 A.C.I.R. and Brookings estimates report levels of dependence on federal financial assistance to be as high as 69.6% for Detroit, 69.2% for Buffalo, and 68.8% for Cleveland.[3] Even New York City, apparently the least benefited by federal assistance in fiscal 1977, would show a much higher level of federal aid if federal dollars could be separated out from the 38 percent share contributed by "state" aid. Many observers have expressed concern that cities have become increasingly "dependent" on federal assistance. Whether these kinds of figures demonstrate "dependence"—in itself a complicated concept—or something else remains debatable. There is little room for debate, however, over the impressive fiscal presence of federal dollars in big-city revenues.

What can be debated—indeed, *should* be debated—is whether numbers from our most authoritative federal source can take us very much further in understanding federal spending in cities. Apart from the decennial enumeration, a government census is taken every fifth year, in years ending in "2" and "7," and annual surveys are conducted for all larger (above 50,000) cities and counties (above 100,000) as well as a sample of smaller governments. A *County and City Data Book* groups the most relevant portions of these data together in a volume published every fifth year, and the various groupings of the data are also available on tape. Census data are collected directly from source documents for all states and the largest cities and counties (over 300,000 and 500,000, respectively), but are largely based on the return of mailed questionnaires for smaller units. Use of mail surveys, coupled with the difficulty of devising adequate reporting categories for a system so large and so complex, give Census data at least as much ambiguity as can be found in O.M.B. and Treasury documents. Nowhere is this more true than in Census categories for the reporting of intergovernmental revenue to cities.

Notwithstanding the enormous increase in federal aid in recent years, Census continues to rely primarily on seven, necessarily abstract, categories to report intergovernmental revenue: education, employment security administration, health and hospitals, highways, housing and urban renewal, public welfare, and all other.[4] Since programs no less than assistance dollars have proliferated, the most obvious question to raise about these categories is "what goes into them?" A brief exercise will demonstrate how difficult it is to contemplate the use of Census data to understand intergovernmental finance.

Perhaps the most authoritative published source of information regarding Census aggregation procedures is the *Classification Manual, Governmental Finances*. Page 27 of the current version of that manual reports that the revenue category "education" includes "Federal grants for vocational education and rehabilitation, school lunch and milk programs, and grants and contractual amounts to institutions of higher education and for research and development programs." Part of this definition seems clear enough, despite the absence of specification for "grants" and "contractual amounts" designated for higher education. Even the minimal level of clarity suggested by these words is unraveled when we compare different reports of the same function, as is done in Table 4.2. For

PERCENTAGE DISTRIBUTION OF GENERAL REVENUE SOURCES FOR SELECTED LARGE CITIES
FY 1964-65 and 1977-78

TABLE 4.1

PERCENT OF TOTAL GENERAL REVENUE BY SOURCE

CITIES	% FEDERAL		% STATE		% LOCAL		% OWN	
	1977-78	1964-65	1977-78	1964-65	1977-78	1964-65	1977-78	1964-65
NEW YORK	7.75	1.25	38.36	24.81	.15	.10	53.74	73.84
DALLAS	11.56	0	1.32	.92	.20	1.47	86.91	97.62
NEWARK	11.88	.09	48.56	8.79	.52	1.71	39.04	89.41
HOUSTON	12.97	2.29	1.88	.23	.58	3.65	84.57	93.83
BOSTON	13.45	9.29	21.82	28.38	.13		64.60	61.69
ATLANTA	13.61	14.27	14.40	.79	3.04	3.64	68.96	80.20
LONG BEACH	15.61	.08	8.76	10.69	1.48	4.74	74.15	85.83
MEMPHIS	15.74	.54	26.17	25.48	18.27	3.40	39.82	54.59
DENVER	17.26	1.45	16.55	27.75	.19	19.39	66.14	70.17
SAN FRANCISCO	17.26	1.12	22.57	28.05	.85	.64	59.98	70.74
MILWAUKEE	17.60	1.77	30.77	35.92	2.21	.09	50.78	61.84
SEATTLE	19.44	.15	10.96	14.26	.96	.47	67.40	83.50
PHILADELPHIA	19.80	4.34	12.52	8.16	.66	2.08	66.71	87.15
BALTIMORE	20.02	2.96	42.06	41.06	.59	.34	37.26	55.19
PHOENIX	21.19	2.05	37.36	19.77	.91	.79	40.86	73.73
MINNEAPOLIS	21.22	.54	24.38	9.42	.53	4.45	53.50	86.32
LOS ANGELES	21.41	1.26	9.61	11.18	.01	3.72	68.44	85.75
ST LOUIS	22.89	.32	9.96	5.39	.01	1.82	67.14	94.15
DETROIT	23.20	4.67	21.67	15.36	2.50	.14	52.62	73.78
INDIANAPOLIS	23.76	1.18	23.17	11.36	.19	6.19	52.88	87.37
PITTSBURGH	23.96	13.75	15.48	6.73	2.14	.09	57.93	77.41
CINCINNATI	23.97	9.69	8.37	7.63	8.10	2.11	59.56	79.57
KANSAS CITY	24.91	4.70	3.93	4.50	.11	3.11	71.05	90.34
COLUMBUS	25.31	4.00	8.46	14.99	2.22	.46	64.01	78.96
BUFFALO	25.65	1.61	32.62	25.37	8.40	2.05	33.14	62.88
TOLEDO	26.75	2.56	8.06	11.54	1.29	10.14	63.90	84.61
CHICAGO	27.44	3.13	10.25	9.22	3.16	.52	59.15	87.13
FORT WORTH	27.66	4.25	1.42	1.50	3.28	1.33	67.65	93.92
SAN DIEGO	28.65	1.71	16.86	14.31	3.42	1.25	51.26	82.73
OKLAHOMA CITY	28.65	16.92	12.30	5.84	.05		69.00	77.24
NEW ORLEANS	30.35	4.77	11.83	14.88	.02	.66	57.80	79.69
OAKLAND	30.42	2.84	8.17	11.13	.88	1.58	60.53	84.45
PORTLAND	31.26	.73	6.92	8.27	.81	.80	60.70	90.21
SAN ANTONIO	31.87	2.36	2.58	.98	1.12		56.08	95.96
CLEVELAND	32.49	3.87	10.31	13.34	.81	.95	53.74	81.84
OMAHA	33.21	.37	11.07	4.09	1.98	5.54	50.49	90.00
LOUISVILLE	33.31	12.97	2.37	1.42	13.83	2.83	57.01	82.79
HONOLULU	38.62	4.12	4.35	17.22	1.03		56.87	78.66
DISTRICT OF COLUMBIA	41.36	26.29	0	0	1.78	.12		73.60

SOURCE: U.S. Department of Commerce, Bureau of the Census, City Government Finances, for fiscal years 1977-78 and 1964-65.

Table 4.2. Federal "Education" Aid to Michigan, Fiscal 1977, Michigan, Census and C.S.A. Data Sources

Data Sources	Dollar Amount
State of Michigan Budget[a]	246,812,836
Bureau of the Census[b]	388,021,000
Federal Information Exchange System[c]	416,251,259

[a] State of Michigan, *Executive Budget, Fiscal Year 1980* (np.:nd.) p. 27
[b] *State Government Finances in 1977* (Washington, D.C.: U.S. Government Printing Office, 1978), p. 18
[c] Calculated from the F.I.X.S. data tapes.

fiscal 1977 the State of Michigan Budget reports actual receipts by the Department of Education at a level more than $140 million *below* the sum reported by the Census. From another perspective, the C.S.A. data system reports $28 million *more* than Census for the 152 separate C.F.D.A. programs identified for functions 500–503 (education) and the school lunch and milk programs. Although it would be satisfying to know which of these numbers was most accurate, the more relevant point is that, so far as Census data are concerned, there is no way to tell.[5] The definition quoted above for "education" revenue is the only available published definition, but the definition tells us very little about the actual accounts used to reach the reported total. So far as we can see, the only way to find out where the Census number comes from is to attempt a reconstruction from Census work sheets—a task that might be conceivable for a single function for a single year, but hardly for all functions or for many years. For the moment at least, our rather limited understanding of what Census means by "education" or any other source of federal money is all we can expect to have.

From a city point of view, the problem of confused functional categories is overshadowed by the Census practice of *systematic under-reporting of federal aid to cities.* Census does use a category of "Federal" intergovernmental revenue but, as the *Classification Manual* tells us, for cities this category ". . . includes only direct receipts from the Federal government. *Federal grants channeled through the States are classified as local intergovernmental revenue from State governments* (code C)." [6] Thus, except for a few direct federal-local programs such as General Revenue Sharing or Anti-Recession Fiscal Assistance, all other federal dollars that reach local environments, including the large sums for health, social service or criminal justice programs, are classified as "state" aid.[7] Presumably this procedure is pleasing to state officials, but it has pernicious analytic and policy implications. Because federal and state dollar flows cannot be separated in Census data, accurate reports of the locational distribution of federal, thus state, dollars are impossible. Because accurate federal grant data for municipalities cannot be obtained, estimates of the interaction between local and non-local sources of funds in fiscal decision-making become impossible. Finally, estimates of either federal or state "impact" on the governmental program mix or the local economic environment are quite thoroughly subverted. Some efforts have been made to deal with this "pass through" problem, but no solution has emerged as yet.[8]

A good example of the difficulties presented by Census data is the contrast between those data and the information reported by New York City's Temporary Commission on City Finances. Using detailed information published annually by the New York City Comptroller, the Temporary Commission was able to show that federal aid as a proportion of total city revenue increased from 6.6 percent in fiscal 1965 to 20.6 percent in fiscal

Table 4.3. Federal Aid to New York City as Percentage of Total City Revenue: A Comparison of Census and TCCF

Fiscal Year	Census	TCCF
1965	1.3	6.6
1966	1.2	8.3
1967	2.6	12.6
1968	2.5	14.1
1969	1.7	14.6
1970	2.4	16.1
1971	1.8	17.3
1972	2.7	17.9
1973	4.7	21.6
1974	4.8	20.6
1975	4.8	20.6

Source: TCCF, *The Final Report of the Temporary Commission on City Finances,* Appendix III, Table 6, and U.S. Department of Commerce, Bureau of the Census, *City Government Finances,* various years. Total general revenue is the denominator used for the Census data.

1975 (Table 4.3). Census data for the same period, however, report only a fraction of the federal assistance shown by the Comptroller to have actually been received by the City. Clearly enough, use of the Census data to derive conclusions about the significance of federal aid in New York during the past decade would be seriously misleading.

Given this range of problems with presumably authoritative data sources, C.S.A. outlays data seem at first glance to provide a more promising source of city information. Whereas Census' *Government Finances* reports data for cities of 50,000 or more people, *Outlays* cover all cities of 25,000 or more population. Whereas Census reports only grants-in-aid, *Outlays* reports all types of federal fund activity, including loans, salaries, procurements, and direct expenditures. And unlike the "function" reporting format of Census data, *Outlays* data are specific down to the program level.

Despite these advantages *Outlays* data suffer from defects that seriously inhibit their use in city-level analyses. To begin with, outlays data have pass through problems comparable to those found in Census data. Outlays for a number of federal programs, including some rather large H.E.W. programs, are not reported in cities or counties at all, because state agencies do not report such information to Washington, or because federal officials make no effort to obtain such information, or both. Instead, C.S.A. reports outlays for such programs to the county and city in which the state capitol is located. Thus, while we know that spending for vocational education programs or L.E.A.A. programs is spread across the entire state of Michigan, there are *no* reported expenditures for these programs in Detroit, or Grand Rapids, or Flint; *all* of the money, is according to C.S.A. *Outlays,* expended in Ingham County, where Lansing is located.[9] Nationwide, outlays in state capital counties and cities are systematically inflated, while outlays in all other counties and cities are systematically understated. Moreover, a number of other large programs such as medical assistance or highway grants, are reported *only* to the county. Most of the reported expenditures for these programs probably occur in cities, but there are *no* recorded outlays for city units.

The systematic understatement of federal outlays to cities *in general* in the Outlays system is further aggravated by under-reporting of expenditures by some agencies. H.U.D. is a good example. Largely because of reporting difficulties internal to H.U.D., one of the agency's two largest expenditure programs, Section 8, has not been reported in Outlays at all, below market interest payments are not reported, rent supplements are not reported, leased housing payments are not reported, operating subsidies for public housing authorities are not reported, and basic home mortgage insurance programs are reported only in counties, with no reports at all for cities.[10] In short, Outlays reports of H.U.D. expenditures represent only a fraction of total H.U.D. obligations for any given year, further weakening the current usefulness of Outlays data for analyzing federal aid to cities.

The other major problem in the Outlays system is the considerable use made of statistical estimates to report sub-state allocations. O.M.B. Circular A-84 authorizes agencies to use proration techniques for city and county allocations whenever actual expenditure records are unavailable, so long as the techniques used are reported.[11] Reports of the techniques used make clear that there is considerable room for improvement. Some grants are still being distributed according to 1970 population figures, despite well-known changes in population, particularly in big cities. Others are being distributed according to population group fractions (i.e., percent between ages 5 and 14, etc.) that also are known to have changed. Actual outlay distributions based on outdated information present no problem: funds may not be going to appropriate locations but at least we know where they are going. It is the use of outdated figures to *report* outlays that are actually distributed on other, presumably more adequate, statistical grounds that causes problems. Since only 30 percent of the F.I.X.S. data are derived from actual records,[12] these problems clearly need attention.

The significance of these difficulties can be seen in Table 4.4, which reports available levels of information for the 46 programs we report separately in this study. These programs include most major federal expenditures and account for 56 percent of net domestic outlays in 1978. Yet, while more than 98 percent of these program dollars are reported to counties, less than 32 percent are available at the city level. It is worth noting that even this low level of reporting to cities represents an "improvement" over what is reported in the outlays system. We were able to obtain data from H.U.D. and from L.E.A.A. that permit us to report both Section 8 housing assistance and L.E.A.A. grants for cities; neither of these programs are reported at the city level in outlays reports. Incorporating more specific data from individual agencies is, of course, a promising long-run strategy for improving the outlays data system as a whole.[13]

Although public officials and many journalists have become sensitized to data quality problems as grants have increased,[14] academics typically have ignored or overlooked data deficiencies in producing their analyses. Thus several recent publications and dissertations have utilized C.S.A. data with no recognition at all of their limitations, including a recent paper that attempts to construct a "city" measure for which no "city" data exist in C.S.A.[15] The authors of another recent study that purported to find little correlation between certain agency outlays and measure of city need seemed quite unaware of the fact that many programs in the agencies selected do not report outlays in cities at all. Nor were these authors aware of either the *systematic under-reporting* of city-level data in C.S.A. or of the *systematic over-reporting* of state aid in Census data.[16] The problem they chose to address simply could not be addressed with the data they used (C.S.A. and Census), but they either did not understand the limitations of their data, or they preferred to disregard those limitations in favor of conclusions known to be both inaccurate and misleading.

We do not propose to either ignore or disregard the limitations of available data. A serious federal interest in cities, after all, is a relatively recent development, which may

TABLE 4.4—BREAKOUT OF SELECTED PROGRAMS BY LEVEL OF GEOGRAPHIC REPORTING, FY 1978

PROGRAM NAME	CFDA CODE	DOLLAR OUTLAYS (IN MILLIONS)	LEVEL OF GEOGRAPHIC REPORTING		
			STATE	COUNTY	CITY
FOOD DISTRIBUTION	10550	1,023	YES	YES	YES
FOOD STAMPS	10551	4,421	YES	YES	YES
NATIONAL SCHOOL LUNCH PROGRAM	10555	1,727	YES	YES	YES
EMERGENCY DISASTER LOANS	10404	3,411	YES	YES	NO
LOW/MODERATE INCOME HOUSING LOANS	10410	2,565	YES	YES	NO
RURAL ELECTRIC LOANS	10850	3,189	YES	YES	NO
COMMODITY LOANS	10051	6,365	YES	YES	YES
OTHER AGRICULTURAL LOANS	**	3,690	YES	YES	NO
WATER AND WASTE DISPOSAL	10418	303	YES	YES	NO
LOCAL PUBLIC WORKS	11300	161	YES	YES	YES
COMMUNITY ACTION	49002	357	YES	YES	YES
WATER AND WASTE TREATMENT	66418	2,842	YES	YES	YES
TITLE I EDUCATION	13428	2,258	YES	YES	NO
SAFA	13478	720	YES	YES	YES
VOCATIONAL EDUCATION	13493	639	YES	YES	NO
REHABILITATION SERVICES AND FACILITIES	13624	734	YES	NO	NO
SOCIAL SERVICES LOW INCOME	13642	2,846	YES	NO	NO
PUBLIC ASSISTANCE	13808	6,400	YES	YES	NO
SUPPLEMENTAL SECURITY INCOME	13807	5,303	YES	YES	NO
MEDICAID	13714	10,748	YES	YES	NO
MEDICARE-HOSPITAL	13773	17,740	YES	YES	NO
MEDICARE-SUPPLEMENTAL	13774	6,828	YES	YES	NO
SSA-DISABILITY	13802	11,963	YES	YES	NO
SSA-RETIREMENT	13803	57,083	YES	YES	YES
SSA-SURVIVORS	13805	20,772	YES	YES	YES
COMMUNITY HEALTH	13224	248	YES	YES	YES
CDBG-ENTITLEMENT	14218	2,536	YES	YES	YES
CDBG-DISCRETIONARY	14219	261	YES	YES	YES
SECTION 8 HOUSING	14156	2,879	YES	YES	YES
MORTGAGE INSURANCE REGULAR HOMES	14117	7,969	YES	YES	NO
MORTGAGE INSURANCE LOW/MOD INCOME	14137	1,846	YES	YES	NO
PROPERTY IMPROVEMENT	14142	1,199	YES	YES	NO
OTHER H.U.D. LOANS	**	14,020	YES	YES	NO
LAW ENFORCEMENT BLOCK GRANTS	16501	250	YES	YES	YES
LAW ENFORCEMENT DISCRETIONARY GRANTS	16502	408	YES	YES	YES
CETA	17232	4,207	YES	YES	YES
UNEMPLOYMENT INSURANCE	17225	889	YES	YES	YES
PHYSICAL DISASTER LOANS	59008	2,339	YES	YES	YES
SMALL BUSINESS LOANS	59012	2,665	YES	YES	NO
HIGHWAY PLANNING & CONSTRUCTION ASSISTANCE	20205	7,913	YES	YES	YES
URBAN MASS TRANSIT	20500	4,330	YES	YES	YES
GENERAL REVENUE SHARING	**	6,830	YES	YES	YES
ANTI-RECESSION FISCAL ASSISTANCE		1,316	YES	YES	YES
DISABILITY COMPENSATION	64109	4,957	YES	YES	YES
VETERANS HOSPITALIZATION	64009	4,699	YES	YES	YES
READJUSTMENT TRAINING	64111	2,977	YES	YES	YES
TOTAL $ REPORTED TO RESPECTIVE GEO UNITS			232,826	228,607	73,720
PERCENT OF PROGRAM DOLLAR TOTAL			100.00	98.19	31.66

*THESE 46 PROGRAM OUTLAYS REPRESENT 56% OF NET DOMESTIC OUTLAYS IN 1978.
**FOR SPECIFIC PROGRAMS UNDER THESE CATEGORIES, SEE APPENDIX TO ANTON, REPORT TO H.U.D., 1980.

well explain not only the absence of good federal expenditure data, but also the poor state of federal data on cities in general. In a recent paper, Fossett and Nathan have dramatized the present situation by showing how much more the federal government knows about counties than cities. Using standard census reports, they show that some 130 economic indicators are available for Washington County, Tennessee (population 80,000) but only 23 of those items are available for the city of Chicago.[17] Federal data, in short, can be used to address very few questions about cities, fiscal or otherwise. At best, we can address limited questions in a limited way, taking advantage of a data system that includes city information for at least some federal programs. As it happens, the programs for which we have information permit us to ask how well these programs deliver funds to their intended beneficiaries—a limited but hardly trivial question. Our answer to this question permits us to offer a further commentary on the uses of various data formulations to assess the relationship between city "need" and federal program spending.

TARGETING ON TARGETING

For the most part, federal expenditures are directed to people, not to cities. Recent growth of grant programs to government jurisdictions should not obscure the overwhelming significance of individual benefit programs as a fraction of total federal spending. For such programs—social security, welfare, aid to veterans, the handicapped, students, homeowners, businessmen, etc.—cities are technically irrelevant; they are simply the geo-political units in which such categories of individuals reside. Cities receive different "mixes" of programs because they contain different "mixes" of people.[18] Unfortunately, attempts to model this process tend to become distorted through use of aggregate statistics or non-precise "functional categories" which mask the underlying complexity of programs and recipients either within or across cities. Because outlays data can be disaggregated to the level of program activity, distributional processes may be summarized with some precision rather than estimated, and in terms related to intended recipients. Who, then, might intended recipients be, and how are they "mixed" in various cities?

Table 4.5 presents a number of city demographic characteristics arrayed by population size class, rate of population change (1970–1975), and by Census Division. When stratified by population size class, this sample of 909 cities confirms some familiar images: larger cities tend to have a higher percentage of blacks, older people, poverty and crowded housing than smaller cities, particularly those below 200,000 in population. Larger cities also tend to be declining in population with thirty-two of the forty-nine cities over 200,000 population (65%) losing residents from 1970–1975. It should be noted that considerable population decline is also experienced by cities smaller than 200,000 in population. From 1970–1975, 48% of the 730 cities less than 200,000 in population size lost residents. In fact, of the 83.7 million people represented in this sample of cities, 51.6 million or 61.7% live in cities with declining populations. Declining cities have higher concentrations of black, elderly, poverty families, crowded families, and lower per capita income levels than growing cities (Table 4.5, Part B). The majority of cities which conform to these characteristics are located in the North Eastern and North Central states and include such familiar examples as Newark, Cleveland, St. Louis, Detroit, Buffalo, Pittsburgh and East St. Louis, Illinois.[19] The most rapidly growing cities are least burdened by the problems that plague declining cities.

Finally, the spatial distribution of these city-level demographics may be viewed in

SELECTED CITY DEMOGRAPHIC CHARACTERISTICS
TABLE 4.5
BY POPULATION SIZE, POPULATION CHANGE, AND CENSUS DIVISION

CATEGORY	% OF TOTAL CITY POPULATION	AVG. POP CHANGE (1970-1975)	AVERAGE PERCENT BLACK	AVG. % 65 & OLDER	AVERAGE PERCENT MANUFACTURING	AVERAGE PER-CAPITA INCOME	AVERAGE PERCENT POVERTY	AVG. % CROWDED HOUSING
A) BY POPULATION SIZE								
25,000-49,999	22.14	2.81	8.11	9.54	26.43	4871.81	8.20	6.87
50,000-99,999	20.64	3.51	8.33	9.59	26.90	4840.08	8.23	7.12
100,000-199,999	13.74	3.89	12.84	9.47	25.93	4818.72	9.05	7.17
200,000-499,999	12.60	-2.45	17.75	11.43	22.00	4567.29	11.23	7.95
500,000-999,999	9.62	-1.05	24.98	9.86	21.86	4569.33	12.88	9.52
1,000,000 OR MORE	21.26	-4.83	29.02	10.42	26.52	4801.33	10.87	8.50
B) BY POPULATION CHANGE (1970-1975)								
> 10% DECREASE	7.28	-12.84	20.24	10.84	34.37	4259.81	11.27	8.56
0 TO -10% DECREASE	54.43	-4.26	10.58	10.63	29.53	4852.69	7.99	6.74
0 TO 10% INCREASE	25.49	4.71	8.24	9.09	23.90	4887.78	8.62	7.07
10 TO 20% INCREASE	7.66	14.35	7.88	7.96	20.46	4748.57	9.29	7.36
20% INCREASE OR MORE	5.14	31.00	4.32	7.59	19.98	5042.52	8.32	7.75
C) BY CENSUS DIVISION								
NEW ENGLAND	6.62	-1.85	3.03	11.61	34.05	4570.89	6.81	6.01
MID ATLANTIC	20.59	-2.96	11.13	11.80	32.14	4840.84	7.63	5.71
E. NORTH CENTRAL	19.89	-.75	9.20	9.21	33.84	5081.41	6.00	6.42
W. NORTH CENTRAL	6.13	.69	3.38	9.21	21.07	4949.08	6.18	6.52
SOUTH ATLANTIC	10.37	5.87	21.40	11.50	19.92	4749.41	12.83	7.78
E. SOUTH CENTRAL	3.87	1.20	23.63	9.77	24.08	3978.14	17.19	9.35
W. SOUTH CENTRAL	10.42	7.54	12.96	8.06	17.85	4186.78	13.55	9.99
MOUNTAIN	3.31	16.43	2.63	6.97	12.99	4627.42	8.60	7.67
PACIFIC	18.81	6.80	3.84	8.49	23.74	5260.34	6.84	6.88

Table 4.5, Part C. The migration of population from frostbelt cities to sunbelt cities is evident with cities in the New England, Mid Atlantic, and East North Central states experiencing population decline, while cities in the South Atlantic, West South Central, Mountain, and Pacific states report significant population increases. The highest concentrations of blacks are found in the South Atlantic, East and West South Central divisions, where poverty and crowded housing are higher than elsewhere and where per capita income tends to be the lowest. Large concentrations of the elderly are found in the South Atlantic division, particularly in Florida where many retirement communities are located. The percent of city population 65 and older is as high as 29% for Clearwater, 31% for St. Petersburg, and 49% for Miami Beach. Actually the New England and Mid Atlantic states have a somewhat higher concentration of elderly due to the smaller standard deviation among percent elderly in northern cities.

In order to examine the responsiveness of federal programs to these city characteristics, Census demographic and C.S.A. outlays data were merged to create a single data base.[20] Although C.S.A. reports outlays to *all* cities 25,000 or larger, the Census reports data only for "incorporated" places 25,000 and above, thus missing more than 160 municipal units that have the requisite population but not legal status—including very large "towns" in New York and metropolitan suburbs in Maryland.[21] The resultant data set for which we evaluate federal expenditure activity between 1975 and 1978 contained 909 cities.

If federal assistance targets to "needy" categories of people and if the large urban areas are as disadvantaged as the demographic data suggest, we would expect to find a greater federal presence in larger cities. This relationship is confirmed in Table 4.6.[22] From a program perspective, per capita food stamps, Section 8 housing assistance, C.D.B.G., C.E.T.A. and U.M.T.A. program dollars increase with city size. C.E.T.A. dollars average $11.47 per capita in cities 100,000 and less, while rising as high as $29.78 per capita for cities greater than one million in population. An even more dramatic example of this large city bias is U.M.T.A., which spends as little as $2.27 per person in cities less than 50,000 and as much as $56 per person for mass transportation in the largest cities. This is not to say that large cities always secure a major share of program dollars. Small Business Loans made to cities clearly are distributed with a preference for smaller units, and Commerce's Local Public Works program displays a similar tendency. Finally, we may observe that some programs such as H.U.D.'s Section 8 housing assistance channel similar levels of funds to cities, of all sizes with only $3.06 separating high and low 1978 per capita Section 8 recipients.[23]

At the more aggregate level, net domestic outlays to cities tend to increase with city size. In 1975, per capita outlays to cities less than 50,000 in population is $1,327, in contrast to cities 200,000 and larger which average per capita outlays of over $2,100. Direct payments also increase with size, reflecting both the higher concentrations of dependent populations in larger cities and the higher cost of city life. While larger cities may receive more federal dollars, their rate of increase in federal funds is lower than that of their smaller counterparts. Medium sized cities of the 100,000 to 200,000 population size range, report the highest rate of increase in net domestic federal spending (+45%), with federal assistance to larger cities growing more slowly (+38% average). Note that these findings understate the large-city bias in the flow of federal funds, since programs such as welfare, that distribute large amounts to city populations, are not reported at the city level in these data.

Large cities, then, do not appear to be disadvantaged in the flow of federal dollars. But it is not only the large cities which are experiencing distress. Recall that 382 of the sam-

SELECTED PROGRAM OUTLAYS STATISTICS BY POPULATION SIZE

TABLE 4-6

CITY CATEGORY	OUTLAYS (THOUSANDS OF DOLLARS)		PERCENT OF OUTLAYS TOTAL TO CITIES		PER-CAPITA		% CHANGE (1975-1978)
	1975	1978	1975	1978	1975	1978	
A) NET DOMESTIC OUTLAYS							
25,000-49,999	17322954.	24586509.	16.69	16.91	935.17	1327.29	41.93
50,000-99,999	16864752.	23748688.	16.25	16.33	976.98	1375.77	40.82
100,000-199,999	15076098.	21877761.	14.53	15.05	1313.31	1902.92	45.12
200,000-499,999	16684509.	22905316.	16.08	15.75	1583.02	2173.25	37.28
500,000-999,999	12714648.	17478736.	12.25	12.02	1580.46	2172.65	37.47
>1,000,000	25102888.	34812563.	24.19	23.94	1141.38	1957.29	38.68
B) DIRECT PAYMENTS							
25,000-49,999	6867998.	9476681.	17.65	17.38	370.77	511.59	37.98
50,000-99,999	7278295.	9938855.	18.71	18.23	421.64	575.73	36.55
100,000-199,999	5344684.	7597131.	13.74	13.94	464.88	660.80	42.14
200,000-499,999	6617113.	8752207.	17.01	16.06	627.83	830.42	32.27
500,000-999,999	4143384.	5953740.	10.65	10.92	515.03	739.99	43.68
>1,000,000	8652237.	12793845.	22.24	23.47	486.46	719.32	47.87
C) FOOD STAMPS (AGRICULTURE)							
25,000-49,999	294641.	333488.	17.33	17.12	15.91	18.00	13.16
50,000-99,999	270930.	301442.	15.90	15.48	15.66	17.46	11.51
100,000-199,999	186306.	204545.	10.96	10.50	16.20	17.79	9.79
200,000-499,999	231062.	229403.	13.59	11.78	21.92	21.77	-.72
500,000-999,999	294895.	289974.	17.34	14.88	36.66	36.02	-1.74
>1,000,000	423340.	589094.	24.89	30.25	23.80	33.12	39.15
D) LOCAL PUBLIC WORKS (COMMERCE)							
25,000-49,999	9428.	24242.	22.38	37.04	.51	1.31	157.11
50,000-99,999	8601.	8182.	20.41	12.50	.50	.47	-4.87
100,000-199,999	9639.	9320.	22.88	14.24	.84	.81	-3.31
200,000-499,999	4431.	10171.	10.52	15.54	.42	.97	129.52
500,000-999,999	3564.	-0.	8.46	-0.	.44	-0.	-0.
>1,000,000	6469.	13540.	15.35	20.69	.36	.76	109.30

(cont.)

TABLE 4.6
SELECTED PROGRAM OUTLAYS STATISTICS BY POPULATION SIZE

CITY CATEGORY	OUTLAYS (THOUSANDS OF DOLLARS) 1975	1978	PERCENT OF OUTLAYS TOTAL TO CITIES 1975	1978	PER-CAPITA 1975	1978	% CHANGE (1975-1978)
E) SECTION 8 HOUSING ASSISTANCE (H.U.D.)							
25,000-49,999	10416.	285174.	20.69	20.88	.56	15.39	2637.91
50,000-99,999	15229.	285455.	30.26	20.90	.88	16.54	1774.38
100,000-199,999	9482.	176654.	18.84	12.93	.82	15.37	1763.07
200,000-499,999	6010.	194424.	11.94	14.24	.57	18.45	3135.24
500,000-999,999	6306.	144650.	12.53	10.59	.78	17.98	2193.81
>1,000,000	2891.	279420.	5.74	20.46	.16	15.71	9563.87
F) C.D.B.G. (H.U.D.)							
25,000-49,999	235787.	194551.	17.19	11.55	12.73	10.50	-17.49
50,000-99,999	219634.	319636.	16.01	18.97	12.72	18.52	45.53
100,000-199,999	233479.	242167.	17.09	14.37	20.39	21.06	3.28
200,000-499,999	260670.	301906.	19.00	17.92	24.73	28.64	15.82
500,000-999,999	159928.	233650.	11.62	13.87	19.80	29.04	46.65
>1,000,000	261742.	392226.	19.08	23.32	14.72	22.09	50.08
G) C.E.T.A. (LABOR)							
25,000-49,999	151548.	271914.	8.20	11.51	8.18	14.68	79.42
50,000-99,999	226470.	270015.	12.26	11.43	13.12	15.64	19.23
100,000-199,999	346381.	429812.	18.74	18.19	30.13	37.38	24.09
200,000-499,999	345745.	408220.	18.71	17.28	32.80	38.73	18.07
500,000-999,999	234849.	279360.	12.71	11.82	29.19	34.73	18.95
>1,000,000	542953.	703760.	29.38	29.78	30.53	39.56	29.61
H) SMALL BUSINESS LOANS (SMALL BUSINESS ADMINISTRATION)							
25,000-49,999	122264.	249612.	19.43	25.35	6.60	13.48	104.16
50,000-99,999	121720.	199829.	19.35	20.29	7.05	11.58	64.41
100,000-199,999	108656.	165846.	17.27	16.84	9.45	14.43	52.63
200,000-499,999	96541.	155107.	15.35	15.75	9.16	14.72	60.66
500,000-999,999	50886.	84489.	8.09	8.58	6.33	10.50	66.04
>1,000,000	129034.	129865.	20.51	13.19	7.25	7.30	.64
I) U.M.T.A. (TRANSPORTATION)							
25,000-49,999	21634.	63221.	2.84	2.27	1.17	3.41	192.23
50,000-99,999	45191.	95894.	5.93	3.45	2.62	5.56	112.29
100,000-199,999	55693.	148304.	7.31	5.34	4.84	12.90	166.29
200,000-499,999	93268.	451983.	12.24	16.26	8.85	42.88	384.61
500,000-999,999	196009.	463557.	25.72	16.68	24.36	57.62	136.50
>1,000,000	350199.	1556335.	45.96	56.00	19.69	87.50	344.41

93

TABLE 4.2

Selected Program Statistics by Rate of Population Change

CITY CATEGORY	OUTLAYS (THOUSANDS OF DOLLARS)		PERCENT OF OUTLAYS TOTAL TO CITIES		PER-CAPITA		% CHANGE (1975-1978)
	1975	1978	1975	1978	1975	1978	
A) NET DOMESTIC							
> 10% DECREASE	9331366.	12296938.	9.29	8.75	1644.39	2166.99	31.78
0 TO -10% DECREASE	57475178.	80814542.	57.20	57.53	1355.64	1906.14	40.61
0 TO 10% INCREASE	22070379.	30826083.	21.96	21.94	1111.69	1552.72	39.67
10 TO 20% INCREASE	8187518.	11236857.	8.15	8.00	1371.79	1882.69	37.24
> 20% INCREASE	3422786.	5309306.	3.41	3.78	854.71	1325.80	55.12
B) DIRECT PAYMENTS							
> 10% DECREASE	3831642.	5019363.	9.97	9.35	675.22	884.52	31.00
0 TO -10% DECREASE	22806550.	32469676.	59.34	60.49	537.93	765.85	42.37
0 TO 10% INCREASE	8563008.	11698160.	22.28	21.79	431.32	589.24	36.61
10 TO 20% INCREASE	2325538.	3197725.	6.05	5.96	389.63	535.77	37.50
> 20% INCREASE	905756.	1293611.	2.36	2.41	226.18	323.03	42.82
C) FOOD STAMPS (AGRICULTURE)							
> 10% DECREASE	159960.	150239.	9.66	8.02	28.19	26.48	-6.08
0 TO -10% DECREASE	926457.	1131796.	55.94	60.41	21.85	26.70	22.16
0 TO 10% INCREASE	391250.	418820.	23.63	22.35	19.71	21.10	7.05
10 TO 20% INCREASE	116335.	118523.	7.02	6.33	19.49	19.86	1.88
> 20% INCREASE	62078.	54289.	3.75	2.90	15.50	13.56	-12.55
D) LOCAL PUBLIC WORKS (COMMERCE)							
> 10% DECREASE	7571.	7060.	17.97	10.96	1.33	1.24	-6.75
0 TO -10% DECREASE	25286.	38898.	60.02	60.37	.60	.92	53.83
0 TO 10% INCREASE	7137.	13334.	16.94	20.69	.36	.67	86.83
10 TO 20% INCREASE	2049.	3810.	4.86	5.91	.34	.64	85.93
> 20% INCREASE	89.	1335.	.21	2.07	.02	.33	1393.32
E) SECTION 8 HOUSING ASSISTANCE (H.U.D.)							
> 10% DECREASE	4657.	118609.	9.77	9.08	.82	20.90	2447.00
0 TO -10% DECREASE	21072.	758592.	44.23	58.05	.50	17.89	3500.06
0 TO 10% INCREASE	16442.	298964.	34.51	22.88	.83	15.06	1718.26
10 TO 20% INCREASE	2865.	86019.	6.01	6.58	.48	14.41	2902.48
> 20% INCREASE	2605.	44542.	5.47	3.41	.65	11.12	1609.77

TABLE 4-2

SELECTED PROGRAM STATISTICS BY RATE OF POPULATION CHANGE

(cont.)

CITY CATEGORY	OUTLAYS (THOUSANDS OF DOLLARS)		PERCENT OF OUTLAYS TOTAL TO CITIES		PER-CAPITA		% CHANGE (1975-1978)
	1975	1978	1975	1978	1975	1978	
F) C.D.B.G. (H.U.D.)							
> 10% DECREASE	163114.	285647.	12.00	17.13	28.74	50.34	75.12
0 TO -10% DECREASE	856226.	980356.	62.99	58.80	20.20	23.12	14.50
0 TO 10% INCREASE	259594.	283265.	19.10	16.99	13.08	14.27	9.12
10 TO 20% INCREASE	57883.	79786.	4.26	4.79	9.70	13.37	37.84
> 20% INCREASE	22482.	38084.	1.65	2.28	5.61	9.51	69.40
G) C.E.T.A. (LABOR)							
> 10% DECREASE	274543.	253960.	15.01	11.11	48.38	44.75	-7.50
0 TO -10% DECREASE	1062474.	1364009.	58.08	59.70	25.06	32.17	28.38
0 TO 10% INCREASE	299516.	381540.	16.37	16.70	15.09	19.22	27.39
10 TO 20% INCREASE	138652.	222713.	7.58	9.75	23.23	37.31	60.63
> 20% INCREASE	54018.	62654.	2.95	2.74	13.49	15.65	15.99
H) SMALL BUSINESS LOANS (SMALL BUSINESS ADMINISTRATION)							
> 10% DECREASE	35027.	50043.	5.69	5.26	6.17	8.82	42.87
0 TO -10% DECREASE	303738.	383950.	49.34	40.35	7.16	9.06	26.41
0 TO 10% INCREASE	184340.	350983.	29.95	36.89	9.29	17.68	90.40
10 TO 20% INCREASE	56208.	106002.	9.13	11.14	9.42	17.76	88.59
> 20% INCREASE	36271.	60556.	5.89	16.36	9.06	15.12	66.95
I) U.M.T.A. (TRANSPORTATION)							
> 10% DECREASE	74870.	269123.	9.85	9.80	13.19	47.43	259.45
0 TO -10% DECREASE	585614.	2089545.	77.02	76.13	13.81	49.29	256.81
0 TO 10% INCREASE	73085.	290423.	9.61	10.58	3.68	14.63	297.38
10 TO 20% INCREASE	18392.	57537.	2.42	2.10	3.08	9.64	212.84
> 20% INCREASE	8342.	38233.	1.10	1.39	2.08	9.55	358.29

pled cities (49%) are facing conditions of population decline. How responsive are federal programs to the difficulties of both growth and decline? Table 4.7 reveals a consistent pattern of targeting federal dollars to declining cities. Over 66% of total reported federal outlays to cities, $93 billion, goes to declining urban centers. Per capita outlays in 1975 were $2,167 to cities with the highest rate of population decrease, $841 more than the $1,326 received by the fastest growing cities from 1975 to 1978. Outlays to these "boomtowns," however, increased at a rate (55.12%) almost twice that of cities most in population decline. Direct payments display highly similar distribution patterns and, as would be expected, those cities most in decline received the highest per capita level of benefits.

Table 4.7 permits us to observe the effect of rate of population change at the program level. All of these programs, with the exception of Small Business Loans, demonstrate an impressive concentration of federal funds in declining cities. In 1978, as much as 86% of U.M.T.A. ($2,359 million), 76% of C.D.B.G. ($1,266 million), 71% of Local Public Works ($46 million), and 70% of C.E.T.A. ($1,746 million) funds are in declining cities. Per capita statistics also reflect this pattern of federal fund flows to declining areas. Per capita C.D.B.G. outlays are almost $29 for cities most in decline, but only $5.60 for "boomtown" cities. Section 8 housing assistance also shows a significant emphasis on declining cities, expending $21 per capita in contrast to $11 to cities expanding most rapidly. A clear exception to this pattern is the Small Business Loan program, which displays the opposite tendency. Small Business Loans to growing cities are almost twice as high ($17 vs. $9 per capita) and have expanded since 1975 at more than double the rate (82% vs. 35%) of such loans to declining areas.

For these programs, at least, federal expenditures seem highly sensitive to population change, particularly for cities experiencing population decline. To the extent that overall federal funds in the Outlays data are reported to the city level, net domestic spending figures reflect these patterns as well. Correlation analysis between various program outlays and count statistics for special population groups (e.g., the number of blacks, poverty families, persons 65 and older, etc.) also produce similar results. If one believes that declining areas "need" disproportionate federal financial assistance, recent federal fund activity clearly appear to have addressed that need.

To be sure, these observations about federal fund flows are not unexpected. The various program patterns examined reflect the manner in which these programs by and large were *intended* to function. Different distribution patterns therefore would be cause for considerable surprise. The bulk of federal spending is directed to people, after all, and most dollars continue to distribute individual benefits by formula. As a recent report by the House Committee on Banking, Finance and Urban Affairs notes:

> By substituting legislatively determined formulas for a method of funding based on specific project review by federal program administrators, the Congress made the distribution pattern an explicit object of deliberation and Congressional decision. By also broadening program scope and content, the Congress made general measures of urban need relevant to the design and evaluation of grant programs.[24]

Based on our analyses, one might add that these congressional determinations have had an impressive record of success. The programs we have examined "work," in the sense of delivering funds to places characterized by various dimensions of need. That optimistic conclusion, however, is subject to at least two obvious criticisms. The first is that the programs examined are so few in number that no "general" assessment of program effectiveness can be derived from them. The second is that the indicators we have used to suggest "need" are too few in number and too limited in scope to accurately assess the multiple dimensions of urban "need." The first criticism seems to us unanswerable within the constraints of existing federal data systems, but the second offers an opportunity to both use and analyze more comprehensive measures of need.

ON THE MEASUREMENT OF URBAN "NEED"

Much of the impetus behind the construction of multiple indicators of "need" originated from efforts undertaken by the Brookings Institution to evaluate General Revenue Sharing, C.D.B.G., and other domestic assistance programs.[25] Nathan and Adams, in particular, have developed two indices of urban social need to "understand central city hardship." [26] Use of these indices permits these authors to document *inter-city hardship*, that is the severity of socio-economic conditions in one city relative to other central cities, and *intra-metropolitan disparity*, that is the severity of conditions in a central city compared to its surrounding suburban areas. According to their analyses, cities in the North East and North Central regions generally exhibit more "hardship" conditions than cities located elsewhere.

The Congressional Budget Office (C.B.O.) has also been active in the development of urban need indicators, having published a summary of its effort under the title "City Need and the Responsiveness of Federal Grant Programs." Identifying three dimensions of urban need—economic, social and fiscal—C.B.O. constructed composite indices for each dimension in order to examine how well current federal programs such as A.R.F.A., L.P.W., G.R.S., C.E.T.A., and C.D.B.G. are targeted to those cities which score highest on need. Since the C.B.O. indices incorporated both the Brookings hardship measures and a comprehensive index of fiscal need developed by the Department of Housing and Urban Development, the C.B.O. measures can be regarded as among the most, if not *the* most comprehensive indices currently in use. Although limited to only five programs in 45 relatively large cities, the C.B.O. study generally found that each program distributed higher per capita amounts to cities with higher levels of need.[27] These results initially seem similar to the results we have reported for seven programs in more than 900 cities, but let us take a closer look.

In order to assess the relationship of these "need" indicators to federal outlays, a data base of 45 cities was constructed from the outlays data, replicating the sample of cities used in the Nathan and Adams and C.B.O. reports. Scores from the various "need" indices were coded for applicable cities and correlated with program outlays, direct payments and net domestic outlay totals for these cities. To make an analytic point, we also correlated program and general outlay totals with selected Census "count" statistics, that is, the actual number of aged, or poor families or overcrowded housing units rather than the percent of the city total such individuals or units comprise.

The results, portrayed in Table 4.8, seem moderately surprising. Apart from the Local Public Works program, relationships between these program outlays and the Brookings "hardship" indices are weak to non-existent. Relationships between outlays and the C.B.O. indices of economic and fiscal need are somewhat stronger, but not markedly so, and are generally quite weak when outlays are related to the C.B.O. social need index— the public works program again excepted. Judging from these figures one would have to conclude that these programs are only moderately responsive to city fiscal and economic need, but hardly responsive at all to "hardship" or social need.

When count statistics rather than multiple-item indices are used, however, a much

Correlations Between Measurements of "Need" and Selected 1978 Programs Outlays

TABLE 4.8

OUTLAY CATEGORY	BROOKINGS INSTITUTION		CONGRESSIONAL BUDGET OFFICE			CENSUS COUNT STATISTICS			
	INTER-CITY	INTRA-CITY	ECONOMIC INDEX	SOCIAL INDEX	FISCAL INDEX	NUMBER OF BLACKS	NUMBER OF 65	NUMBER OF POOR FAMILIES	NUMBER OF CROWDED HOUSES
NET DOMESTIC	-.07	.14	.25	-.02	.53	.93	.99	.98	.84
DIRECT PAYMENTS	-.50	.13	.30	-.01	.37	.89	.98	.97	.97
FOOD STAMPS	.02	.23	.32	.07	.41	.96	.97	.98	.96
LOCAL PUBLIC WORKS	.64	.74	.46	.63	.94	.71	.56	.62	.50
SECTION 8 HOUSES	-.07	.00	.37	.00	.41	.90	.98	.97	.95
C.E.T.A.	-.06	-.03	.17	-.03	.12	.85	.91	.91	.85
C.D.B.G.	-.06	.20	.39	.12	.44	.78	.89	.87	.85
SMALL BUSINESS LOANS	-.29	-.32	-.14	-.32	.09	.58	.59	.63	.63
U.M.T.A.	.03	.16	.37	.16	.72	.94	.92	.92	.67

different picture emerges. Eighteen of the twenty-eight correlations using count statistics report levels of association at .85 or greater and none are below .50. In contrast, only one of the indices correlates with program outlay at .85 or greater while thirty of the thirty-five index-related correlations are below .50. Even net domestic outlays—a suspect number for city-level analysis—shows consistently high relationships to count statistics. Using these figures, one would have to conclude that federal program outlays are not only responsive, but vigorously responsive to, several plausible measures of city need.

We offer these contrasting images less to demonstrate the apparently whimsical relationship between numerical analyses and "truth" than to emphasize the conceptual difficulties inherent in the use of supposedly hard numbers to measure urban need. Quite apart from issues of data quality and availability, there is a *perspective* problem involved in the selection of need indicators that is seldom recognized. Whether such indicators are constructed from a federal, state or local point of view makes a considerable difference in results achieved through analysis. To illustrate, let us ask how these different perspectives might produce different measures of poverty.

An indicator reflecting a local perspective would be the number of residents below the national poverty level in an urban area expressed as a percentage of the total population of that *urban area*. This kind of statistic frequently appears in Census publications. An alternative indicator expressing a state perspective would be the number of poverty residents in an urban area measured as a percentage of the *state-wide* total of residents below the national poverty level. Similarly, an indicator reflecting the federal perspective would be the number of poverty residents in an urban area as a percentage of the *national* total of residents below the national poverty level. Use of an indicator reflecting the local perspective provides one measure of the overall "health" of urban areas. There is a relationship, for example, between the number of poor and the vitality of urban area tax bases or capital stock. Such an indicator, however, is misleading when used to assess the target efficiency of federal (or state) assistance programs, since it bears little relationship to federal (or state) program design.

Many federal programs are distributed by formulas according to the nation-wide percentage of people in certain "need" categories—say, below the national poverty level—*not* according to the percentage of an urban area's population that is below the national poverty level.[28] Urban areas of vastly different sizes in population can have the same proportion of residents below the national poverty level, but clearly manifest different magnitudes of "poverty" from the perspective of federal officials who distribute poverty funds. San Diego, California and Manhattan, Kansas both report 9.3 percent of their families below the poverty level in 1970, but one fraction translates to 72,000 poverty families, the other means 3,000 poverty families. From a federal perspective, these are very different problems. Evaluation of the concentration of federal government aid on these types of assistance programs properly requires indicators that reflect the federal perspective.

Both the Brookings and C.B.O. indices, however, are basically local perspective measures. Many of the variables used to construct these indices are in the form of percentages of some attribute relative to a city unit: percent poverty, percent crowded housing or percent change in per capita income. These variables do not demonstrate a strong relationship to federal aid because they do not reflect federal program design perspectives. Count statistics, which measure magnitudes and thus provide immediate comparability across cities, clearly provide a better reflection of federal perspectives on program design.

Combining count statistics or any other statistics into multiple-indicator indices can be an interesting exercise, but no one should pretend that analyses based on such indices guarantee any improvement in understanding. Analysts who develop these indices certainly offer no such pretensions. C.B.O. analysts, for example, make clear that problems of data availability, data quality and conceptual clarity render any "objective" index impossible. Judgments must be made about what data to use, in what form, under conditions in which most choices must be arbitrary. Census, which collects much of the "data" used in index-construction, goes so far as to suggest that some choices made by index-developers simply cannot be made:

> Trying to define city government fiscal strain and to show the specific degree of this by using the Census data, is virtually impossible. The government data collected and compiled are not designed to reflect surpluses or deficits in the sense of accounting identities. To make the data comparable across a wide variety of cities, we attempt to use actual cash receipts and expenditures. The financial statistics cut across all funds of a city's accounting system, but do not take into consideration such items as accrued liabilities of a government. Certain key items are not collected, such as retirement contribution liabilities, total short-term debt issued and retired during the fiscal year, and long-term debt schedules. Finally, data are not compiled on the source of capital outlays—whether or not they are financed via debt issuance or through current revenues of the city.[29]

If data choices are necessarily arbitrary so, too, are decisions about how data elements are combined. Should indicators for some index be added, multiplied, or divided? Should weights be assigned or not, and if so how? Should trend data be included or not, and if so how should such data be interpreted? These are not "merely" statistical questions. Answers to them reflect some model of how data elements interact in reality and some evaluative judgment about the positive or negative quality of the interaction. Is population loss in a "dense" city good or bad, and what implications do either loss or gain have on government service or fiscal capacity? Is high tax effort a sign of fiscal strain or fiscal health and how does tax effort interact with population change? Index-builders answer such questions on the basis of "hunch" or "feel" as much as anything else, given the poor quality of data available to structure their choices. The resulting measures may seem more or less sensible, but they cannot be regarded as anything more than "best guesses" about exceedingly complicated and poorly understood phenomena.

CONCLUSION: THROUGH A GLASS, DARKLY

We thus conclude more or less where we began. The federal government spends a great deal of money in cities, and recently has expanded its city expenditures very dramatically. Since most federal dollars go to people rather than places, larger cities appear to receive more federal dollars per capita than smaller cities, but growing cities have experienced more rapid rates of increase in over-all federal spending. Recent federal programs designed to assist cities with high concentrations of needy populations or needy conditions appear successful in delivering funds to such cities, although degrees of success vary by program and by the measures of "success" employed. If these conclusions seem overly tentative it is because federal data sources permit nothing more than tentative answers to limited questions. To answer more significant questions, such as the effects of all this federal money on city development or decline, much more information, collected more systematically, would have to be available. Given the billions of federal dollars spent in cities, and the emergence of "urban policy" on the national political agenda, the time seems ripe for a more comprehensive and intensive federal effort to find out what is being spent, how, and with what effects.

NOTES

1. See, for instance, the excellent discussion in Nathan and Dommel, 1977. See also Glickman, 1980; Schultze, Fried, Rivlin, and Teeters, 1971; Bahl, Jump, Schroeder, 1978; Peterson, 1976; and Muller, 1975.

2. This point has been raised by Senator Lugar of Indiana who has noted that

   Public accounting of public administration is woefully inadequate. Especially deficient have been attempts to compare financial data and other sources of fiscal strength and weakness of America's cities or metropolitan areas. National debates have proceeded on the flimsiest of evidence . . . confirming the long held suspicion that public officials are not only poor business managers but unable even to cite accurate figures on payrolls, debts, pension obligations, and intergovernmental transfers, and yet fully prepared to assert need and demand dollars of relief. (Lugar, 1976, p. 289)

3. Nathan, 1978.

4. Bureau of the Census, 1976.

5. This problem is further confounded by the fact that the Census *City Government Finances* series excludes financial data on independent school districts.

6. Bureau of the Census, 1976.

7. Bureau of the Census, 1976.

8. A.C.I.R., 1977b.

9. We refer here, for example, to the basic block grants for vocational education and L.E.A.A.; various associated programs are reported to the city and county level.

10. Based on interviews with H.U.D. officials.

11. For an extended discussion of this point, see Anton, 1980a, 1978.

12. Anton, 1980a.

13. A recent O.M.B. study (Doyle, 1979) has identified at least 185 automated fiscal, budgetary and program related data systems operational in federal departments and agencies. This extensive collection of information on over 770 programs of financial assistance varies in program and geographic detail, type of financial record reported, methods of accounting, comparability, timeliness, manipulability, and public availability. Many of these data bases are quite adequate and often remain untapped information sources for analytical research. Almost all of these systems record a city location for their program reporting. The utility of agency data bases are limited only by their range of coverage which typically does not extend beyond an agency or given program area. To conduct extensive program or spatial analysis at the city level would, thus, require the merger of many separate data bases.

14. For example, see Reid, 1978, 1979.

15. Vernez, 1980; see also Saltzstein, 1977.

16. Dye and Hurley, 1978.

17. Fossett and Nathan, 1980.

18. For an analyses that conceptualizes *cities* as recipients of federal aid, see National Governor's Association, 1979.

19. These are 1975 estimates.

20. Forty-two cities were excluded because of the over-reporting of program outlays in C.S.A. to state capital cities.

21. Examples of such towns include Silver Spring, Maryland (population 220,483), and Babylon, New York (population 212,000).

22. The ideal divisor would not be population, but the special groups for whom the benefits of a program are intended. In the absence of such data, per capita figures are used here. While per capita figures under-report the magnitude of per recipient benefits, the high correlations (.94 and higher) of population with most special population count statistics, suggests that such figures may be a reasonable substitute. Presumably all recipient groups have a linear relationship with population. For a demonstration of these points, see Peter D. Ward, 1979.

23. Since the Section 8 housing assistance program commenced operation in 1975, this judgment is based on data from subsequent years.

24. Cuciti, 1978.

25. Nathan, et al., 1977; and Dommel and Jaffe, 1978.
26. Nathan and Adams, 1976.
27. Cuciti, 1978.
28. Discussions of federal and state formulas may be found in Grasberger, 1978 and Bureau of the Census, 1974. The Grasberger study identifies 146 formula-based categorical grant-in-aid programs for state and local governments in 1975 of which 82% (119) use either a state or national definition of "need."
29. U.S. Bureau of the Census, "Fiscal Environment Indicators of City Government," U.S. Department of Commerce (Washington, D.C.: 1979), p. 24. On a related point, Robert Reischauer has observed that "we do not have crude, let alone good, measures of the impact that concentrations of low-income people have on the service needs or fiscal capacities of big cities," (Reischauer, 1976, p. 302).

Chapter 5

Making Outlays Sense

What theory or theories might be used to account for the patterns of federal spending described in the preceding chapters? The patterns themselves seem sufficiently complex to prohibit early development of a single theoretical explanation, particularly if empirical support is desired for theoretical formulations. We believe the data reported here to be far more accurate and useful than other available data, for example, but we nevertheless remain acutely aware of the distance between these data and "good" data. The problem, of course, is not simply that data may be "inaccurate" for various reasons, or that data for some purposes (i.e., city analyses) may not be available, but more fundamentally that data systems are themselves infused with theoretical assumptions that may be incompatible with alternative theoretical interpretations.

Consider the recent uses of outlays data. These data are collected annually, by program within federal agency, and reported for all states, counties and large cities. Attention is thus focused on federal benefits, as measured by program obligations, and administrative accountability, as measured by the record of state and local jurisdictions into which beneficiary funds are allocated. Extended over time, these data encourage evaluation of the extent to which program administrators are sensitive to political goals. The "theory" implicit in outlays data is very much a theory of federal political and administrative management.

Most published analyses based on outlays data, however, translate the data into outlay "totals," aggregated by state or region, divided by state or regional population, to arrive at an easily manipulated per capita sum. Attention is thus focused on what states or regions receive, rather than on what federal agencies distribute, and on per person allocation rather than *purposive* allocations. Such translations are then used to structure arguments about which regions get more or less from the federal government as a whole or which states show a positive or negative "balance" between federal taxes paid and outlays distributed.

There are two problems inherent in such data transformations. The first, already noted above, is that per capita sums obscure both program differences and the allocation processes that distribute federal dollars. It is therefore difficult to either interpret per capita sums or to use them unambiguously in further analysis. The second, more important, problem is that the theory implicit in such calculations has little if any empirical support. Although all federal expenditure programs have distributional consequences, there is little evidence that funding decisions are designed to increase or decrease total outlays to one region or another, little evidence of any federal interest in taking total per capita distributions into account, and hardly any evidence at all of a federal concern for "balancing" taxes paid and outlays distributed. Individual program may have any or all of these consequences, and it is often useful to understand those distributional results. A vast literature on national budgeting makes clear, however, that programs and agency are the building blocks of federal budgets, that decision-making is fragmented rather than wholistic, and that distributional impact, when it comes into play, is of distinctively less significance than national program purpose.

Of the two analytical themes woven through our analysis, then, we believe that "who gets how much" *in general* is likely to be far less interesting than "what is given" *in particular,* at least in the near future. This is not to say that total state (or county or city) receipts are unimportant, particularly as a political issue. But no state or local government has an uncritical interest in maximizing *all* forms of federal assistance. Larger federal grants for welfare, unemployment compensation or black lung disease, to take some obvious examples, may produce a larger per capita number for a given jurisdiction, yet it is highly unlikely that any jurisdiction would desire continuous expansion of such grants. It seems far more plausible to expect that state and local jurisdictions seek to maximize only the right kinds of assistance, which is to say, assistance that reflects the mix of problems and opportunities peculiar to each jurisdiction. Other forms of assistance may be accepted as necessary, or simply ignored because of a lack of fit between federal purpose and local conditions. For their part, federal program managers also appear to vary the jurisdictions into which they distribute assistance from one year to another, as we have shown. Year-to-year variability in program distributions, coupled with constant change in the number and type of federal assistance activity, give federal assistance patterns a complexity and dynamism that is hidden by the apparent stability of aggregate expenditure totals.

What conceptual scheme might be used to produce theories that explain this system of dynamic but structured complexity? We have already suggested that geographic or ecological frameworks are both unsatisfying in result and unable to capture the inherently political character of expenditure patterns. The more strictly "political" frameworks that have been used, meanwhile, have suffered from conceptual ambiguity, or they have focused on structural properties (such as party allegiance) that have no clear relationship to processes of expenditure determination, or they have simply been too fragmentary, seeking to generate large conclusions through examination of single actions or institutions.[1] A more appropriate "political" framework, we take it, would be (a) substantively clear, (b) linked directly to processes of expenditure determination, (c) capable of illuminating structured relationships, if they exist, (d) capable of summarizing changes in structured relationships through time, (e) linked to plausible and available data, and (f) capable of raising questions for further investigation. Some years ago Phillip Monypenny worked out an analysis of certain federal aid programs that was as useful conceptually as it was empirically interesting.[2] Although our views and purposes are somewhat different from his, we borrow freely from Monypenny's argument in suggesting the following conceptual scheme.

Government activities are organized by *program,* staffed by officials responsible for providing services or goods or both to citizens. Large individual programs or collections of smaller programs taken together can be viewed as policies, generated through *processes of choice.* Depending on the quality of those choice processes, particularly the strength and longevity of *coalitions* that support programs or policies, program activities are maintained or they are changed. Strong coalitions that continue through time can produce programs that also continue through time as institutionalized commitments. Programs supported by weak or brief coalitions can be radically changed or, in some cases, done away with entirely. Because program activity and coalition support can change independently, it can be expected that some programs will continue to operate even as coalition support weakens, or that strong coalitions will exist for some time before a program is enacted.

While simple, these ideas reflect essential political characteristics of outlay programs without imposing artificial summary judgments on the relationships that may exist between those characteristics. A focus on "program" defines activities that can be observed, including funds expended, to which some purpose or purposes have been assigned through official actions. At any given time, a governmental system can be described in terms of an existing mix of programs and, over time, system change can be described in terms of changes in the type and size of programs. Describing governmental systems in terms of programs is plausible, since programs necessarily reflect what governments do, and data for such descriptions are in principle readily available in documents of various kinds, as well as through observation. Built as it is on program-level data, the outlays data series provides an unusually comprehensive and detailed "system" description.

Linking programs to coalitions of actors through choice processes is also plausible. Conceived as purposive activity, programs necessarily represent values, which must be defined and advocated. Value definition and advocacy are pursued by individuals but, to become established as government activities, support for values must be obtained from many individuals, hence the necessity for coalition behavior. Depending on the interaction between types of coalitions and types of values pursued, choice processes associated with government programs will exhibit considerable variety, ranging from "crisis" patterns in which widely shared basic values are re-affirmed or redefined by broad-based coalitions, to the largely hidden processes often associated with incremental adjustments to highly specialized programs designed to serve limited constituencies. Processes associated with program initiation are likely to differ from processes associated with program maintenance or change. As with differences in the size, longevity and resources of coalitions, however, these process differences are in principle observable, thus measurable in one sense or another.[3]

Program, choice and coalition are no more than conceptual boxes that, when elaborated and infused with data, can generate statements that may help to clarify changing federal outlay patterns. Relationships between these concepts are assumed to exist and to be significant, but the quality of those relationships can only be defined by empirical investigation. In that sense the scheme is theoretically open-ended. Answering the questions "how do government programs come into existence, how are they maintained, and how do they change" can produce insights into both the structural and dynamic properties of government action that presumably will vary from time to time as well as from place to place. Indeed, the scheme demands that attention be given to system dynamics, even as it clarifies system structure.

To illustrate, let us suggest that the current "structure" of the federal outlay system is made up of a number of long-lasting programs, supported by stable coalitions, that represent agreed-upon political commitments. *Core program* of this kind are relatively few in number, but they probably represent a large fraction of distributed funds (Figure 5.1).[4] Because they reflect a stable political agreement, core programs are likely to be extremely resistant to anything but incremental change. Fund levels will increase as the national budget increases, but major program changes will occur seldom, usually as a result of some crisis, or perhaps a political realignment that undermines the existing coalition. When such changes occur in core programs, the terms of coalition support are re-negotiated in order to ensure future stability for the revised program. Core programs, in short, represent institutionalized political settlements that are durable as well as purposive. Programs such as highway grants, vocational education grants, A.F.D.C. or mortgage guarantees are good examples.

In addition to core programs, federal outlays support a wide variety of purposes that reflect current political concerns not yet fully institutionalized. These concerns change from one year to another, and coalition-formation is pursued with differing levels of skill. When successful, coalitions organized around new political issues produce new programs to service newly recognized constituencies. At any given time, therefore, the full range of programs can be viewed as a political barometer of sorts, measuring the developing concerns of the political system as well as its lasting political settlements. Success in initiating a new program, however, is no guarantee that the program will become institutionalized; concern over the issue may weaken or coalition members may be unable to sustain cooperative action, or new concerns may arise with stronger claims on national resources. Thus, around the core programs we can observe a fluctuating variety of *barometer programs*, only some of which will achieve stability of support: the Emergency Public Works Program, General Revenue Sharing, or L.E.A.A. appear to be good examples. Seen as a whole, the outlays system is both "structured" around core commitments and coalitions, yet constantly changing to accommodate the interests of new or developing coalitions. Viewed this way, structure and change are equally amenable to observation, measurement and analysis.

PROGRAM: THE FOCUS OF POLITICS

To suggest that the total federal program mix can be grouped into "core" and "barometer" programs is not equivalent to producing such a grouping, however, since what does or does not constitute a "program" is by no means clear. From one point of view, all activities carried out by a departmental sub-unit can be regarded as a program; from another point of view, only similar activities carried out within a unit should be regarded as a program; or from still a third perspective all activities funded from the same source might be characterized as a program. Depending on which among these (or other) perspectives are adopted, a program mix could take on various properties. And depending on how weights are (or are not) assigned to the criteria of longevity, size and coalition strength, distinctions between "core" and "barometer" activities might be drawn very differently.

Outlays data do not resolve these conceptual problems but they can be linked to line

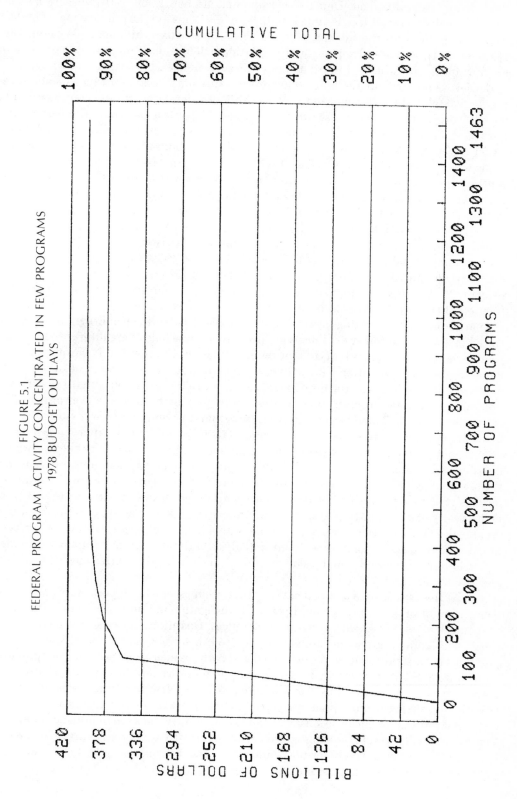

FIGURE 5.1
FEDERAL PROGRAM ACTIVITY CONCENTRATED IN FEW PROGRAMS
1978 BUDGET OUTLAYS

items in the federal budget. Doing so permits operationalization of the "program" concept in a realistic way, if it is assumed that these line items are the primary foci of budget calculations and thus the substance of what federal activity is all about.[5] Without suggesting that this is the only, or the best, operational definition of program, we propose to see how far it can carry us toward a clearer picture of federal activity.

Earlier we pointed out that the recipient structure for federal assistance has been remarkably stable through time, and that the bulk of federal grants were concentrated in only 100 programs, which we also presume to be stable, at least for short-run periods of a few years. Treating each budget line item as a program activity complicates a search for structure by adding many more observations: the 1975 budget contains some 1,312 line items while 1,463 are included in the 1978 budget. Nevertheless a similar pattern of concentration exists, and the pattern is quite stable between 1975 and 1978. Figure 5.2 portrays this stable concentration by showing the number of states into which each of these programs were distributed for the 1975 and 1978 fiscal years as well as their proportion of total domestic outlays for those years. In 1975 there were some 171 programs that benefited every state, but there were also 152 that were distributed to only a single state; these numbers change to 197 and 185, respectively, for 1978. In 1975 the 171 common programs amounted to 83.4 percent of total outlays; in 1978 this fraction declined to 78.9 percent. At the other extreme the single-state programs amounted to no more than a tiny fraction of the outlay totals in both years.

Apart from demonstrating, again, that the bulk of federal expenditures are concentrated in a modest number of "line item" programs, these figures are interesting because they suggest a method for clarifying the distinction between "core" and "barometer" programs. Although observations spread over a larger number of years would be necessary to be wholly persuasive, even the limited time frame of 1975–1978 implies that the common programs distributed to all or most states represent a first approximation of core programs, and that the much larger number of programs distributed to fewer states contain many that approximate barometer programs. These are preliminary approximations, to be sure, but a simple listing of the larger common programs compared to the less widely distributed programs provides considerable support. Among the common programs are the major individual-benefit allocations for the retired, the aged and infirm, veterans, or farmers, together with a few of the larger grants to governments such as C.D.B.G. or highways. Among the latter are special one-time activities such as aid to refugees or geographically limited activities such as geothermal or solar energy grants. It does not seem unreasonable to expect that more detailed analysis of these program groupings, extended over a longer time period, could produce a program classification both conceptually clear and empirically useful.

Among the uses of such a classification, three seem especially important. First, a clear delineation of program types would permit investigation of political process differences that may be associated with program differences. Coalition and choice behavior associated with core programs presumably differ from behavior associated with barometer programs in a fashion that can be described and perhaps measured. Second, the availability of program data across time focuses attention on processes through which programs move into, or out of, the groups of stable core programs. New programs are created every year, as we have seen, and "spreading" benefits to ever-widening constituencies is a time-tested mechanism for ensuring survival that is abundantly reflected in previous chapters. Yet not all programs survive, some survive without growth, others only survive by changing organizations or purposes, or both, and still others not only survive, but expand. Insights into these dynamic processes fill a large case-study literature; intelligent use of

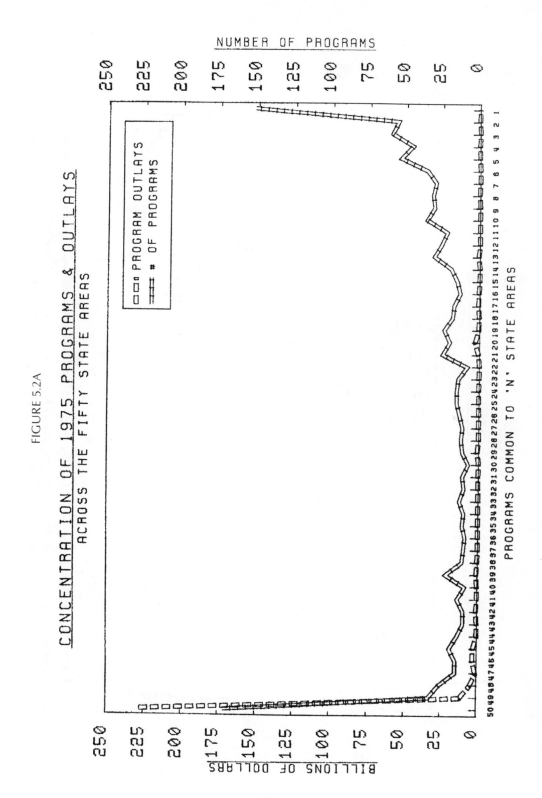

FIGURE 5.2A

CONCENTRATION OF 1975 PROGRAMS & OUTLAYS
ACROSS THE FIFTY STATE AREAS

FIGURE 5.2B

CONCENTRATION OF 1978 PROGRAMS & OUTLAYS
ACROSS THE FIFTY STATE AREAS

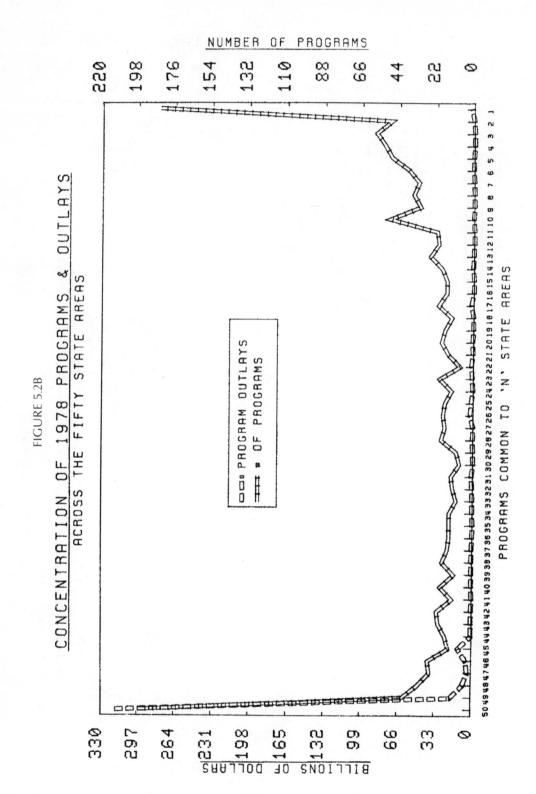

outlays data promises to convert many of these insights into testable propositions of general significance.

The third important use of a better-developed program classification would be to help clarify the extraordinary variety of state patterns of participation in federal assistance programs. Observing core and barometer programs only from a national perspective overlooks the extent to which state officials themselves help to design federal programs, select the activities in which they will or will not participate, and trigger mechanisms for implementation. Although there were 1,312 active programs in 1975 and 1,463 in 1978, for example, the "average" state participated in only 569 and 667 programs respectively, in these two years. As Table 5.1 reveals, populous states such as California and New York participate in twice as many program activities as do the smaller states of Delaware, Vermont and Wyoming. This pattern, clearly evident in both years, reinforces our earlier conclusion that "them that has, gets." Note, furthermore, that the concentration of dollars derived from programs common to all states is essentially identical to the concentration of dollars derived from the multitude of non-common programs. "Them that get" one kind of assistance obviously are "them that gets" all forms of aid.

The evident relationship between state size and number of dollars or number of programs is far from uniform, however. Neither Colorado nor Georgia rank very high in state population, but both are among the top ten states in number of federal programs received. Within that top group, moreover, the least populous state (Colorado) has access to considerably more programs than other states with two to five times more people. If the distribution of these line item programs is thought of as a crude measure of *access* to federal dollars, it is clear that state access varies with size, but that within population or regional groups, similarly situated states exhibit very different access patterns. Using "program" to illuminate access is a valuable supplement to gross dollar or per capita totals because it permits us to reach immediately for political explanations.

Given the data portrayed here "political" explanations are obviously essential. Variation in access within population and regional groupings makes clear that "ecological" explanations cannot explain much, nor is there any pattern of bias in types of program distribution: all states get some of all types of programs, but they get it differently, in different amounts. Why? One plausible political explanation might be that states with larger numbers of governments or government employees generate more interactions with federal program managers, more information about available federal dollars, thus more program awards. The correlations reported in Table 5.2 make clear that this is a promising hunch indeed.[6] Or, characteristics of the governance structure within states, including the professional or other affiliations of public officials, might be related to program access. Still a third plausible idea is that within-state political processes lead some states to greater federal program utilization. Carefully formulated studies of these kinds of hypotheses are essential if we are to explain, as well as describe, patterns of federal spending.

To illustrate, let us consider fund distribution for a single program, the Farmer's Home Administration Emergency Disaster Loan Program, in a single Census division, the East North Central states of Illinois, Indiana, Michigan, Ohio and Wisconsin. These states are annually victimized by tornados, heavy winds and rain, snowstorms and other natural disasters, creating conditions that presumably trigger the allocation of F.M.H.A. emergency loans. Federal responsiveness to these conditions has expanded dramatically since 1949, when F.M.H.A. was established, reaching a level of $3.4 billion in assistance in 1978 (Figure 5.3). Between 1951 and 1978 the East North Central area received some $580 million, of which $490 million (85 percent of the total) was allocated in the period 1975–1978 alone. A full explanation of these funding increases obviously would have to

TABLE 5.1--Profile Of Federal Program Participation By State Areas, FY 1975 And FY 1928, Ordered By FY 1928 Program Participation

State Area	Fiscal Year 1928 Column A Active Programs National Total = 1463			Column B % State Concentration of Program Outlays			Fiscal Year 1925 Column C Active Programs National Total = 1312			Column D % State Concentration of Program Outlays		
	% Of Total Programs (1463)	No.	Total $ in Billions	Total	Common	Other	% Of Total Programs (1312)	No.	Total $ in Billions	Total	Common	Other
CAL....	72.0	1054	43.8	10.9	11.1	10.3	68.5	899	30.4	11.2	11.2	11.2
N.Y....	65.3	955	32.6	8.1	7.9	8.1	60.1	788	22.7	8.3	8.0	10.2
PA.....	60.7	888	18.5	4.6	5.0	3.1	55.5	734	13.5	5.6	5.7	5.8
TEX....	60.7	888	22.8	5.7	5.8	5.2	56.3	739	15.3	5.6	5.7	5.2
COL....	59.3	868	6.7	1.7	1.1	6.0	58.0	761	4.4	1.6	1.5	2.2
ILL....	58.6	858	19.6	4.0	4.5	2.6	57.7	757	13.9	5.1	4.7	2.7
WASH...	58.4	854	8.3	2.5	2.3	2.5	58.4	766	5.7	2.2	2.0	2.2
MASS...	57.4	840	10.1	2.5	2.6	3.2	51.4	674	6.9	2.7	2.6	2.7
MD.....	56.2	822	9.7	2.6	2.5	4.2	51.5	676	7.3	2.7	2.4	1.3
GA.....	56.0	820	11.7	2.6	2.9	2.5	51.5	676	7.3	2.3	2.2	3.8
VA.....	54.1	791	12.1	3.4	3.0	2.5	47.0	617	8.9	3.8	3.5	2.0
MI.....	51.9	760	12.4	3.3	3.7	2.1	47.6	624	10.3	3.3	4.1	3.3
OHIO...	51.9	760	14.9	4.4	4.0	2.5	49.2	645	10.8	4.1	4.7	3.1
MO.....	51.1	747	9.7	2.3	2.3	1.9	47.9	629	6.1	2.3	2.4	2.3
MINN...	50.9	744	7.7	1.7	1.3	2.2	48.6	638	4.8	1.8	1.2	1.3
N.C....	50.0	731	8.9	2.3	2.3	1.0	48.5	636	6.0	2.1	1.4	1.4
FLA....	49.4	722	17.3	4.1	2.4	1.1	49.1	644	11.6	4.3	2.4	2.1
ORE....	48.4	708	4.6	1.1	1.8	1.1	47.6	624	4.3	1.7	1.7	1.5
WIS....	48.3	706	6.6	1.6	1.4	1.4	45.0	590	3.6	1.1	1.6	2.0
N.J....	46.6	682	11.1	3.2	1.1	1.5	44.1	578	7.5	2.9	3.1	2.2
TENN...	45.5	666	5.5	1.4	1.0	1.3	46.0	604	5.3	2.0	1.6	3.4
ARZ....	45.5	665	5.4	1.7	2.4	1.1	44.1	578	2.2	1.3	1.7	1.2
N.M....	44.5	651	3.9	1.9	1.7	1.6	47.4	622	5.0	1.8	2.6	1.8
IND....	44.5		7.9	2.0	1.9	2.3	41.6	546	5.5	1.8	1.8	1.1
ALA....	44.3	648	7.1	1.8	1.9	1.4	41.5	545	5.0	1.8	1.8	1.2

112

TABLE 5.1.--Profile Of Federal Program Participation By State Areas, FY 1925 and FY 1928 Ordered By FY 1928 Program Participation (Continued)

State Area	Fiscal Year 1928						Fiscal Year 1925					
	Columns A			Columns B			Columns C			Columns D		
	Active Programs National Total = 1463			% State Concentration of Program Outlays			Active Programs National Total = 1312			% State Concentration of Program Outlays		
	No. Programs	% Of Total Programs (1463)	$ in Billions	Total	Common	Other	No. Programs	% Of Total Programs (1312)	$ in Billions	Total	Common	Other
OKLA...	641	43.8	5.8	1.5	1.5	1.3	588	44.8	4.0	1.5	1.5	1.2
LA....	637	43.5	6.5	1.6	1.6	1.7	538	41.0	4.4	1.6	1.7	1.5
UTAH..	630	43.1	2.9	1.7	1.7	1.7	571	43.5	1.8	1.7	1.7	1.6
CONN..	624	42.7	4.4	1.1	1.1	1.0	503	38.3	3.3	1.1	1.2	.8
KAN...	616	42.1	4.8	1.2	1.1	1.1	515	39.3	2.9	1.1	1.1	.9
KY....	607	41.5	6.4	1.7	1.7	1.4	510	38.9	4.5	1.7	1.7	1.6
IOWA..	599	40.9	5.2	1.3	1.1	2.1	534	40.7	3.0	1.1	1.7	1.1
NEB...	587	40.1	3.7	1.3	1.3	1.8	512	39.0	2.1	1.1	1.7	1.8
MONT..	580	39.6	2.0	.9	.9	.8	522	39.8	1.0	.4	.4	.6
MISS..	578	39.5	4.8	1.2	1.2	1.3	517	39.4	3.5	1.2	1.2	1.2
S.C...	578	39.5	5.3	1.5	1.3	1.3	530	40.4	2.4	1.3	1.3	1.1
W.VA..	563	38.5	3.1	1.3	1.3	1.3	464	35.4	1.3	.9	.9	1.0
IDA...	554	37.9	4.0	.8	.8	.5	498	38.0	2.7	1.5	1.5	.7
ARK...	546	37.3	4.4	1.0	1.0	1.0	466	35.5	1.5	1.0	1.0	.9
S.D...	533	36.4	1.9	.3	.3	.9	424	32.3	1.1	.6	.6	.7
MAINE.	524	35.8	2.1	.5	.5	.5	444	33.8	1.1	.5	.5	.4
N.D...	506	34.6	1.9	.5	.5	1.2	447	34.1	1.0	.4	.4	.5
NEV...	505	34.5	1.6	.3	.3	.6	436	33.2	.6	.4	.4	.3
WY....	497	34.0	1.4	.4	.4	.4	415	31.6	.7	.6	.6	.3
HA....	496	33.9	2.4	.7	.7	.3	398	30.3	1.7	.7	.7	.5
N.H...	491	33.6	1.5	.4	.4	.2	401	30.6	1.2	.4	.4	.3
R.I...	491	33.6	1.6	.5	.5	.7	433	33.0	.6	.5	.5	.2
ALK...	489	33.4	1.7	.4	.3	.7	389	29.6	.6	.4	.4	.7
VER...	477	32.6	1.8	.2	.2	.2	353	26.9	.7	.2	.2	.2
DEL...	448	30.6	1.0	.3	.3	.2				.3	.3	.2

Source: Calculated from the C.S.A. data.

Table 5.2. Product Moment Correlations, for All Programs

Type of Employees	Oct.–Dec. 1974 Employment Against FY 1975 Programs	Oct.–Dec. 1977 Employment Against FY 1978 Programs
All governments	.79	.84
Federal civilian	.80	.84
State and local total	.78	.83
State total	.82	.86
Local total	.76	.82
State and local FTE	.78	.83
State FTE	.82	.86
Local FTE	.76	.82

Sources: C.S.A. outlays data and Bureau of the Census employment figures.
Note: "FTE" means full time equivalent employees.

take into account federal decisions to liberalize eligibility requirements for disaster loans, among others, since the occurrence of natural disasters can hardly have increased so dramatically. For present purposes, however, the more interesting question is how these five states have participated in this program.

Table 5.3 reveals a clear pattern of varied participation. For the period 1951–1978 Michigan averaged a third of each year's allocation to the area, Illinois received a quarter of annual allocations, on the average and, at the other extreme, Ohio achieved less than 10 percent of annual disbursements. For the more recent period 1975–1978, Wisconsin exceeds Michigan in average annual funding, but Ohio retains its last-place position, behind Indiana. Understanding this pattern requires more than information regarding the occurrence of disasters, since funding is triggered by designation of groups of counties (or the state as a whole) as disaster areas. With some exceptions, such designations are made by the President or the Secretary of Agriculture, *at the request of a state Governor,* which means that state political processes leading to gubernatorial requests must be taken into account. Table 5.3 implies that Michigan and Wisconsin governors have been more active in seeking disaster designations than their East North Central colleagues, although Indiana governors come close, but without the level of funding success achieved by Michigan and Wisconsin.

The political origins of these processes stand out clearly where disaster loan allocations are mapped by county (see Map 5.1). In 1977 Michigan and Wisconsin counties clearly achieved greater allocations than counties in the other states but not, as might have been expected, because of blizzards or frost that might plausibly be associated with colder climate. Indeed both Indiana and Ohio had a higher proportion of disaster designations associated with blizzards than did either Michigan or Wisconsin, whose predominant designation sources were drought (drought and blizzards accounted for 59 and 26 percent of the 744 county disaster designations, respectively, in 1977).[7] Unless drought, blizzard, rain or tornados somehow cease or begin at state boundaries, however, it is difficult to explain the allocation of large amounts to counties in southern Wisconsin and Michigan, and exceedingly small (or no) amounts to immediately adjacent counties in Illinois, Indiana and Ohio. Natural disasters are real enough, but state boundaries obviously have an important impact on how reality is perceived and managed.

Although a full explanation of these patterns is not our purpose here, it is important to

FIGURE 5.3
F.M.H.A. EMERGENCY DISASTER LOAN FUNDING, 1951–1978

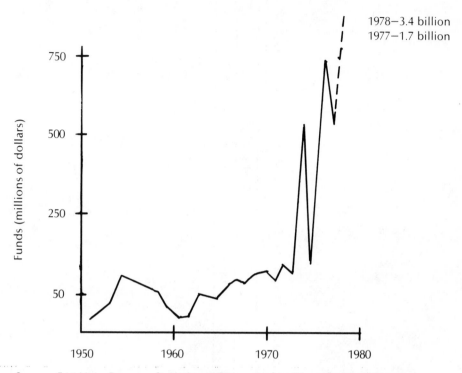

Source: F.M.H.A., Program Statistics, 1978 as cited in Oppenheim, 1980.

emphasize the political nature of state access to federal program dollars—even in a program ostensibly tied to "objective" conditions such as natural disasters. State boundaries structure political processes that are very different, and federal program data offer rich opportunities for posing and answering questions that can illuminate those processes. Identifying the sources of variability in gubernatorial response to disaster, for example, would produce a useful comparison of state political systems, perhaps helping us to understand Ohio's relatively poor level of access in general, no less than its low level of participation in this particular activity. Comparing programs, as well as states, offers further opportunities for understanding. Wisconsin, which does well in the allocation of disaster loans for farmers, does less well in the allocation of food stamps for poor people. Ohio reverses this pattern, with a higher level of participation in food stamps than in disaster loans. Identifying such differences by program emphasizes the need to investigate political processes that determine the dynamics of change within a highly stable structure.

COALITION: THE INSTITUTIONALIZATION
OF PROGRAMS

A political perspective on public spending implies that there is no necessary connection between social condition—whether crisis or opportunity—and governmental pro-

TABLE 5.3--Participation Of East North Central States In FMHA Disaster Loan Program, 1951-1978

Item	State				
	Illinois	Indiana	Michigan	Ohio	Wisconsin
Average % Funding (1951-1978)	25	14	32	9	19
Average % Funding (1975-1978)	17	6	27	4	46
Average % Designation	8	22	29	14	26

Source: FMHA documents, cited in Oppenheim, 1980.

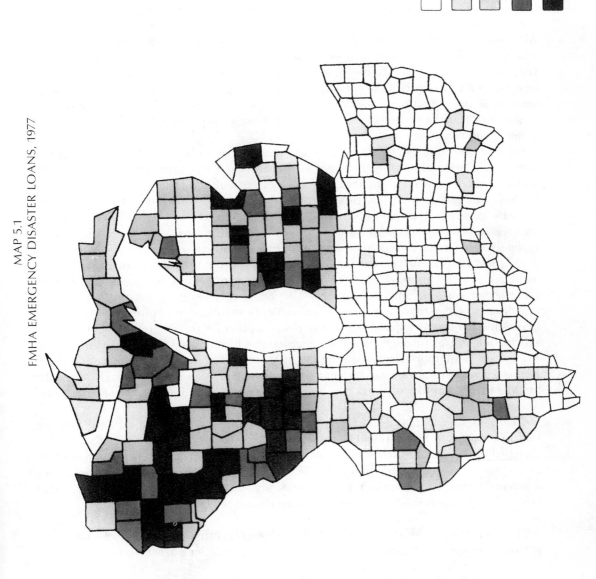

MAP 5.1
FMHA EMERGENCY DISASTER LOANS, 1977

Dollars Loaned

10,000
100,000
500,000
1,000,000

117

gram response. Long-run patterns of national growth, industrialization, urbanization and warfare seem to be associated with patterns of growth in government spending among the more developed nations, most of which can be loosely characterized as "welfare states." But decisions to initiate or suspend public programs are not made "in the long run." Problems or opportunities must be perceived, support for action mobilized, and programs designed in a context of relationships that can change dramatically from one year to another, or one situation to another. Whatever may be said about government expenditures "in general" or "in the long run," understanding the politics of federal spending requires an understanding of the short-run politics of program development.

In the American context one political pattern has been observed with enough regularity and enough consistency to be regarded as the basic model of program development. Often referred to as "the iron triangle," the basic model is based on a coalition of beneficiaries, representatives in Congress, and federal program managers.[8] Programs around which such coalitions develop originate in *advocacy:* some individual or group defines an issue, proposes one course of action to deal with the issue and seeks to mobilize broader support for either the issue-definition or the proposed course of action, or both. Although "objective" social conditions sometimes appear to determine when and whether an "issue" exists, it is more often the case that such conditions exist for some time before they are seen to be "issues" requiring public action. Poverty, air pollution, environmental decay, to take some obvious recent examples, all became "issues" some years after the "coalitions" used to define those issues were well known. It is advocacy rather than fact that defines a "problem" and creates the presumption that government action is necessary.

Advocates need allies, both to create the presumptive public "need" and to translate that need into funds to support a responsive program. Coalitions of actors with a common interest in some program need not be large, particularly if the advocates are already in the federal government (i.e., presidents, congressmen, bureaucrats), but they must include congressional representatives willing to "champion" the cause through the relevant authorization and appropriation committees. Sub-committee and committee support typically is sufficient to secure an appropriation of funds to some agency, for the designated program. Thereafter, the major burden falls on the program manager, who must implement the program in a fashion that produces a reassuring record of "success" for the relevant congressional committees. This commonly involves distribution of funds into districts whose representatives sit on relevant committees *and* into as many districts as possible, in order to expand the base of client support for the program. If congressional satisfaction and/or through clientele expansion can be managed through several successive rounds of appropriations, the program may be said to have become institutionalized. If this clientele-congressional-bureaucrat coalition remains strong enough to ensure funding over a number of years, the resulting program may be thought of as a "core" program.

Coalitions vary a great deal in size, interest, resources and political skill, all of which lead to patterns of institutionalization that vary considerably from the "basic model" sketched above. The basic model seems appropriate for understanding institutionalization of modest new programs, in which there may be little or no visible conflict, producing a process in which program initiation follows advocacy in relatively short order. Other kinds of programs and processes require more elaborate classification:

The Federal Lag Model. Particularly for programs that either require a major departure in precedent or large funding resources, there is often a great deal of public controversy, advocacy proceeds at very high levels for an extended time period (sometimes for decades), and coalition development is difficult. Federal program action occurs only after a winning coalition is in place, thus "lagging" program demand, and sometimes proceeding uncertainly until the winning coalition is solidified. Federal aid for maternal and child care, for example, followed several years of agitation by a feminist-bureaucrat coalition strong enough to pass the program in 1921 but not strong enough to prevent its demise in 1929. A strengthened coalition reinstated the program in 1935 in a different agency, but only after a controversy that included a Supreme Court decision. Federal aid to primary education was advocated for decades before a winning coalition came into existence in 1964. At the present time, coalition-building by environmentalist groups may be a forerunner of a federal "bottle return" program in the future. Advocacy coalitions in this federal lag model include a variety of citizen or corporate organizations but they often include public officials—even federal officials—as well. Thus the Department of Agriculture was an important stimulus for development of the "farm bureau" movement at the turn of the century that ultimately produced federal program assistance for county agricultural organizations.[9]

The Momentum Model. Once established, programs typically possess a momentum of their own, based on the common understanding that budget and personnel commitments for next year will be very similar to current-year commitments. Partly because program objectives are rarely defined with enough precision to exclude different or additional objectives, and partly because program managers recognize the benefits of consistency expansion, however, new program activities often appear to grow from existing programs of very different quality. One consequence of this kind of momentum is that agency program objectives often are highly unstable through time: Section 701 planning assistance changed from a program of assistance to communities of 25,000 or less to a program of assistance for multi-state and even multi-national agencies. Another consequence is that very similar programs are conducted by many agencies: the Defense Department provides aid to local public schools, Commerce provides aid to farmers, Agriculture provides aid to the poor and to local public schools, H.U.D. provides housing assistance, but so do Agriculture, Defense, V.A., and others. Building one program from the momentum of another creates a certain confusion, but it clearly represents a widespread pattern of institutionalization.

The Situational Model. Unusual or unexpected events often produce a pressure to act—to "do something"—that can lead to virtually instant institutionalization. Widespread consensus on the need for action in such situations typically confines advocacy to a search for solutions in the vicinity of existing problem areas, or to quick acceptance of the first proposal that seems reasonable. Situational coalitions tend to be dominated by officials who have the authority to act and are likely to require re-negotiation once the situational source of the original coalition has passed. In some cases, however, program products of these coalitions continue for some time. Thus social security programs developed during the depression crisis have continued and grown, although not without change, as have many of the veterans benefit programs arising from the second world war. In effect, emergency or unusual situations can identify and activate latent coalitions that, in the absence of unexpected events, might have taken longer to develop or might not have developed at all.

These models of program institutionalization are not meant to be exhaustive, nor are they intended to imply that all programs successfully achieve institutionalization. Apparently powerful coalitions often emerge but fail to maintain themselves with enough force to become core commitments. For example, a coalition that included a President, the Attorney General and politically powerful state and local law enforcement officials produced L.E.A.A., but that coalition has failed to sustain itself. Understanding the politics of institutionalization is important, however, not only to account for program longevity but also to perceive the depth of penetration federal program spending has achieved. The drive to broaden the base of coalition support by expanding beneficiaries, repeated thousands of times, has vastly expanded the number of individuals who have a direct stake in federal benefit distributions. In this sense, millions of citizens have become institutionalized beneficiaries of one or more programs, available when necessary to lend support for program continuation or expansion. The federal pot has been enlarged, in part, to accommodate the many new hands that are now in it.

These developments have led a number of observers to suggest that some major change or changes have occurred in the system of federal benefit distribution. Focusing primarily on the expansion of federal grants, one group of observers has argued that the system has become excessively responsive.[10] A better-educated and more demanding population has spawned more groups (or coalitions) whose requests for program benefits have been too easily met, largely because the major mechanism for containing such requests in the past—party discipline—has broken down. Other observers, using a simple "inside-outside" distinction, have argued the "producer hypothesis," i.e., that grant expansion has been caused largely by government officials themselves, seeking budget and program growth.[11] Still others have suggested that federal expansion into virtually all areas of public responsibility through the use of grants has nationalized fiscal politics and "overloaded" the federal government in some way that has not previously been true.[12]

These are interesting ideas, worthy of further investigation, provided they can be appropriately conceptualized. As they have been presented, they suffer from two serious conceptual problems.[13] The first is a difficulty in distinguishing growth from change. That federal spending and government employment have expanded dramatically is clear; whether the political patterns producing that growth are different in any important respect from past patterns is far less clear. Most allegations of change focus on what we have referred to as "the basic model" or the "momentum" model, but those models are derived from historical experiences that date back a half-century or more, as do the "lag" or "situational" models. Unless some new pattern or patterns can be identified and shown to be different from these, or unless some base-line measures from past experience can be shown to differ from currently observable patterns, it is difficult to see how a persuasive case for pattern change, as opposed to mere growth, can be sustained. Increasing the volume of water flowing in a stream may enlarge the stream, but it is still water, not ice or snow.

The second conceptual problem is a matter of perspective: conclusions about change are entirely dependent on *what* is observed and *when* it is observed. To focus so much attention on dramatic increases in grants is to overlook other components of federal spending that arguably are more important or growing more rapidly or both. But even a grants focus requires consideration of time frames more or less appropriate for conclusions derived. Federal grants increased dramatically in the 1970s, but they increased even more dramatically in the 1920s and 1930s, and nearly as dramatically in the 1950s. Choosing one, some or all of these periods as the analytical focus would lead to very different conclusions about change, as would defining periods differently—a point that seems especially relevant in view of the *decline* in grants as a fraction of the budget total that began in the late 1970s. Data we reported earlier, in fact, suggest that growth in grants has not led to any striking changes in the structure of state recipients of federal grant funds. Whether measured in total dollars, concentration of dollars, or dollars-received-for-taxes-paid, the state recipient structure has been remarkably stable, particularly since 1950, when the effects of war-related instabilities had run their course. Viewed in this perspective the "problem" posed by grants is not so much why they increase, but why varying rates of growth and changes in program foci nevertheless result in recipient stability. The question may be more complex, but answers to it are bound to be more interesting.

CHOICE: PROGRAM AS EXPERIMENT

Choice processes associated with the development or change in programs are usually described in terms of a rationality paradigm. In this paradigm, analysis of some record of experience structures a "problem," alternative solutions to this problem are generated and evaluated in terms of some choice criterion (such as cost effectiveness), and a decision is made based on the best fit between the choice criterion and the various available solutions. The rationality paradigm clearly reflects deeply held norms of American politics. It assumes the action should be based on carefully analyzed information, that decision-makers should "know" what they are doing, and that programs should be clearly and carefully linked to the problems they are intended to solve. These norms are explicit in various evaluation studies that test the fit between stated objectives of programs and actual program operations.[14] They are explicit, too, in studies of institutions such as Congress, in which political actors are measured by their success in relating purposes to outcomes.[15] They are also implicit in studies that describe "muddled" or "accidental" decisions, using deviations from rationality to develop such conceptions.[16]

Although examples of rational choice processes can be found, their occurrence has been infrequent enough to stimulate a search for alternative conceptualizations. One promising alternative, the organizational process view,[17] locates the origins of government decisions in the established procedures used to conduct the day-to-day activities of government agencies. Tensions produced by conflict over the results of those procedures or opportunities created by recurrent cycles of activity (i.e., the budget process) create "problems." Solutions are sought in the immediate vicinity of current procedures, rather than searching out all conceivable alternatives, and search ceases when a "satisfactory" rather than optimum solution is found. Goals are thus implicit in decisions rather than derived from an explicit decision criterion. Functionality rather than rationality is the result. This view has considerable utility, particularly for understanding choice processes likely to be associated with what we have referred as the "momentum" model of program development. It seems less likely to illuminate processes associated with major program departures, or with program responses to critical situations. If "rational choice" is rare and "organization process" limited, another choice paradigm seems essential.

Several observations offered earlier suggest what an alternative paradigm might be. We argued above that no necessary relationship exists between "objective" social condition and governmental response. Conditions must be defined as problems by someone, and the problem definition must be accepted by some coalition of actors, before a presumptive need for public action can exist. It follows that advocacy is a more important source of program ideas than analysis, and that coalition strength rather than program purpose is the major source of program initiation and continuation. These twin conclusions both imply and help to account for a third, namely, that program goals are inherently vague and unstable through time. Advocacy designed to mobilize support can hardly be expected to produce carefully thought-out programs, but even if a clear program were proposed, generating enough support to adopt it would normally require either "fudging" the original statement of intent or adding other statements of purpose. Program purposes are typically stated in vague generalities at the outset, therefore, and are typically subject to continuous modification through time to meet the changing requirements of coalition partners. In the beginning the purpose of the coalition may be the program, but, over time, the purpose of the program is the coalition.[18]

The validity of these conclusions is apparent in the design of most programs. Apart from vague statements of purpose most federal program statements are characterized by the absence of any instrumental theory—that is, arguments that federal mechanism X will produce result Y, which is intended; therefore mechanism X rather than mechanisms A, B or C are legislated. Classes of beneficiaries, be they individuals, governments, or groups are often clearly identified as appropriate recipients of federal funds, and functional groupings of eligible recipients are sometimes designated, as in the restriction of certain education grants to school districts, or housing grants to housing authorities. Because of vague goal statements, however, constraints on recipient *uses* of funds are difficult to mandate and even more difficult to monitor.[19] Except in welfare programs, matching requirements are typically loose-to-non-existent, accounting requirements are ambiguous, and few programs are ever subjected to federal audit. Instead, federal programs encourage state and local recipients to follow a strategy of verbal compliance: reports stating what will be, is being, or has been done with federal money are required at stated intervals.[20] Lacking the massive corps of auditors that would be necessary to verify the accuracy of such reports, however, federal program spenders can do no more than selectively check their validity.[21]

If "rational choice" were the only available interpretive paradigm, these qualities of federal program design and implementation might seem bizarre, if not outrageous. They seem politically comprehensible, on the other hand, if program choice is viewed as an experiment, designed as much to test reality as to change it. Federal program histories suggest that decision-makers seldom "know" what they are doing when they enact or continue programs. Although problems may be perfectly evident, solutions seldom are. Is poverty caused by lack of jobs, lack of skills, lack of motivation, family structure, discrimination, or some combination of these and perhaps other equally plausible factors? Are highway fatalities caused by excessive speed, alcohol, automobile design, highway design, or some combination of these and/or other factors? If serious problems have multiple causes, what will be the effect on one if an effort is made to deal with another? Information rarely resolves such issues, either because relevant data are unavailable, inaccessible, or subject to wildly different interpretations. When and if good theories of causation supported by persuasive data are available, furthermore, there remains the problem of instrumental theory: what kind of program, administered by what kinds of governments will produce what effects?

In the absence of either good theories or unambiguous data, the only real choice open to decision-makers is whether to respond to coalition advocacy with the only "program" over which they can exercise some control: dollars. If the coalition seems powerful enough, and the demonstration of "problem" persuasive enough, funds are provided. Mechanisms for distributing dollars to individuals are relatively efficient, and less efficient but serviceable mechanisms for allocating money to governments or groups are also available. Since cause and effect are so unclear, funds distributed to organizations cannot be severely constrained at the outset. Instead, funds are allocated in support of a generally defined cause or problem, with the intention of discovering the uses of those funds at some later point in time. Discovery occurs after a year or two of expenditure experience, usually in the form of a congressional hearing, to which program administrators and selected beneficiaries are invited in order to describe accomplishments achieved with program dollars. Depending on who says what at such hearings, programs can be adjusted by introducing tighter (or less tight) use constraints—again with the purpose of discovering what consequences are produced by such adjustments.

The experimental pattern of program development—"spend some money and see what happens"—offers a useful alternative paradigm for understanding federal expenditure growth, decline or change. Viewing money as the basic federal program permits us to track changing levels of commitment to problems without imposing artificial standards of "rationality" derived from the assumption that instrumental program purposes are clearly defined. Understanding that coalitions of program beneficiaries are the basic sources of program initiation and development avoids the similarly artificial presumption that problems "explain" programs and is consistent with repeated observations of the interest federal program managers and congressional representatives have in being "responsive." Perceiving the experimental nature of much federal program activity allows us to account for both the dynamics of federal program change and the uses of various kinds of information in processes of growth or decline. Finally, this perspective focuses attention on patterns of trust, skill and communication that characterize interpersonal relationships in politics. Spenders and beneficiaries are after all human beings, whose wants and needs drive these intensely political processes.

CONCLUSION

For the moment, the conceptualization we have proposed must be regarded as no more than a preliminary sketch of ideas we believe to be useful in developing explanations of some of the expenditure patterns we have described. Considerably more detailed work on individual programs, agencies, states, and local jurisdictions must be done before the utility of these notions can be truly tested. Both the data system we are developing and our initial interpretations of these data are now in the public domain, however, and we invite all who may be interested to join us in extending these analyses. Although we have tried to be accurate as well as analytically sound, we do not pretend to have been totally successful on either count. To the extent that our conclusions are wrong, we welcome correction. To the extent that our interpretations are wrong-headed, we look forward to stimulation from critics.

However preliminary this exploration may have been, there are two areas of concern that clearly are worth a concluding emphasis. The major premise of our work is that federal expenditures are now, and will continue to be, a major public policy issue. If that premise is granted it is exceedingly difficult to justify the extraordinary carelessness with which the federal government itself keeps track of its own financial activities. Although many federal agencies routinely produce "good" data, the federal government as a whole has yet to develop a comprehensive data system that can unambiguously portray how much money is expended through what programs in which state and local jurisdictions across the country. This is *not,* we suggest, because the problem is too large or too complex, or because appropriate technology is unavailable. Indeed, both the human and mechanical technologies necessary to produce more accurate data are already in place. A few relatively straightforward adjustments in tasks and processes are all that are required to achieve a dramatic improvement (see Epilogue, "Who Knows Where the Money Goes: A Challenge," for an elaboration of this argument). If national policy makers are serious about problems such as city fiscal decline or regional impacts of federal expenditures, a more accurate comprehensive data system is a matter of urgent priority. If state and local policy makers are serious about developing a better appreciation of what they receive and why, they too should develop a sense of urgency in pressing for more accurate information. A coalition of interested data producers and data users is long past due.

Finally, it seems important to emphasize again that the data we have analyzed provide little support for the frequently asserted view that federal government activities are chaotic, incomprehensible or somehow out of control. Proponents of such views seem to us to have based their conclusions on ideological or narrow analytic frameworks that systematically confuse the absence of explicit coordination for the absence of order. When federal expenditures are viewed as a whole, however, and when appropriate conceptual lenses are used to structure analysis, what emerges is a system characterized by remarkable patterns of stability, which are perfectly comprehensible, yet infused with a dynamism derived from political patterns that are also perfectly comprehensible. Recognizing that such patterns exist is the essential first step toward a better understanding of the dynamic complexity of federal government expenditures.

NOTES

1. For a critical review of this literature, see Anton, 1980c.
2. Monypenny, 1960.
3. There are a number of case studies which provide informative legislative and administrative histories of individual federal programs: for instance, Bailey, nd; Reid, 1980; Barton, 1976b; Douglas, 1939; Davidson, 1972; Witte, 1963; McKinley and Frase, 1970; Altmeyer, 1968; Derthick, 1975, 1979b; Dommel, 1974; MacMahon, Millett, Ogden, 1941, as well as A.C.I.R.'s many studies of various programs. In addition, there are large literatures on the subjects of agenda setting and coalition building. But very little attention has been devoted to systematic examination of the origins of programs and the exploration of the diverse ways in which they might evolve over time; important exceptions to this rule are Sundquist's (1968), Walker's (1977), Davidson's (1966), and Polsby's (1971) work on how congressional legislative agendas are set (see also Kingdon, 1973, especially ch. 12), and Anton's (1980c) study of how program efforts evolve over time through congressional and administrative action in response to changing constituent demands.
4. Figure 5.1 shows the concentration of federal expenditures by individual federal programs, as reported in the C.S.A. data. For clarification of how we define "program," see below, note 5.
5. Specifically, we define "program" as each unique O.M.B. line item entry reported in the C.S.A. data. This definition is consistent with the line item definition of program activities used in the budget process, but not identical for two reasons. First, the C.S.A. data does not report on certain types of expenditures either because O.M.B. Circular A-84 does not require information on such expenditures (i.e., congressional expenditures), or because of under-reporting of certain expenditure programs by a few agencies (the agency might either report a single number for a group of O.M.B. line item entries or not report any total at all). Second, in many cases O.M.B. line item entries are reported in even more detailed fashion in the C.S.A. data. For example, Appendix Table 6.3 in the Epilogue presents a comparison of all the line item entries reported in both the O.M.B. *Appendix* volume to the budget and the C.S.A. data for the Elementary and Secondary Act expenditures for FY 1978. Notice that O.M.B. lists ten separate line items in reporting on the different types of "program activities" for ESEA; C.S.A., in contrast, lists 18 separate entries, which correspond to O.M.B.'s listing and, in addition, further distinguish between the very different activities aggregated up by O.M.B. into the "grants to disadvantaged" category through the use of O.M.B.'s *Catalog of Federal Domestic Assistance* classification of all federal assistance activities. Interviews in Washington, D.C. and Lansing, Michigan with federal and state education officials confirmed our hunch that the more detailed breakout of ESEA activities in the C.S.A. data closely corresponds to the "working" definition of "program" they employ in administering ESEA grants.

6. It is worth keeping in mind, however, that aggregate statistics such as these, no matter how they might be further disaggregated, cannot adequately capture the measure of individual talents of state and local officials in obtaining federal assistance. Recall, for instance, the activities of Tom Joe and other state-local officials in obtaining federal assistance, which Derthick (1975) has recounted so well.

7. Calculated from F.M.H.A. data cited in Oppenheim, 1980.

8. A sampling of the large literature exploring some aspect of the "iron triangle" model includes Seidman, 1980; Freeman, 1965; Carter, 1965; Neustadt, 1973; and A.C.I.R., 1978. It should also be noted that Heclo (1979), among other writers, has suggested that more fluid "issue networks," composed of professional advocates of a wide range of (generally "new" politics) causes recently have emerged, overlaying the more traditional "iron triangle" networks. Determination of how "issue networks" may differ from "iron triangles" in their impact on policy processes and outcomes, however, still awaits more detailed empirical research of specific federal program efforts. For, not only do we know very little about "issue networks," but in addition, much of what we think we know about "iron triangles" is based on general descriptions of national policymaking processes, rather than on extensive studies of particular program areas through time.

9. Baker, 1939; Block, 1960; Kile, 1948.

10. See, for example, D. Walker, 1978b, 1979.

11. Beer, 1976.

12. See, for instance, the following A.C.I.R. reports: Anderson, 1980; Beam, 1979a; and Colella, 1979.

13. We do not extensively treat these ideas here because we have done so elsewhere; for extended critiques of these ideas, see Anton 1980c, and Anton, with Cawley, 1980.

14. Useful guides to the evaluation literature, as well as excellent discussions of the limitations of these works because, short of personal preference, it is very difficult to "objectively" determine what "goal" against which to measure program success or failure, are Aaron's (1978) and Levitan and Taggart's (1976, 1976–1977) reviews of the charges that the Great Society programs "failed."

15. Observers of Congress have often criticized "it" for being too parochial and hence unable to formulate and pass comprehensive, goal-oriented legislation. See, for example, Huntington's (1973) statement of this position and contrast Huntington's argument with Orfield's (1975) assessment.

16. See, for example, Lindblom, 1959, 1961, 1966, 1968, 1979; Wildavsky, 1964; Fenno, 1966.

17. Useful discussions of organizational models include Crecine, 1967, 1968, 1969, 1971; Larkey, 1975, 1977a, 1977b, 1979; Cyert and March, 1963; March and Simon, 1958; Cohen, March, Olsen, 1972; Cohen and March, 1974; Mohr, 1976; and Allison, 1971.

18. An earlier statement of this "experimental" model may be found in Anton, 1980c.

19. See Anton, 1979b, 1980c.

20. See Anton, 1980c.

21. See Congressional Budget Office, 1976; and General Accounting Office, 1979, 1980. Recall also the lack of a comprehensive federal data base tracking the flow of federal program dollars into state and local governmental jurisdictions, and the difficulties of tracking federal dollars as they move between and within levels of government because of the maze of state and local account structures, which are often organized on different fiscal year bases than the federal fiscal year and which are generally designed to fulfill other tasks than monitoring the flow of federal dollars. For discussions of the difficulty of tracking federal funds at state and local levels, see Anton, 1979a, 1964, 1966; Larkey, 1979; and Hale and Douglas, 1977.

Chapter 6

Epilogue: Who Knows Where
the Money Goes?

Growth in federal government spending, a recurrent political issue, has become a topic of intensified concern. Apart from the traditional question of whether the federal budget should grow more or less rapidly, the quite extraordinary recent expansion of federal grants to state and local governments has heightened sensitivity to the impact of those decisions on state and local economies. Efforts to discover either who gets what from the federal purse or what difference federal money makes have led to a discovery that seems startling: *no one really knows where federal dollars are spent.* Debates over regional or local inequities produced by federal spending policies occur with increasing frequency but, absent a definitive source of information, there is little hope that these debates can be resolved. Perhaps for that reason, arguments appear to increase in stridency as well as frequency.

Having wandered extensively through the maze of federal reporting systems designed to provide information about spending patterns, we propose now to review the main dimensions of federal data ambiguity, to show that the absence of definitive information is not, after all, so startling, and to offer a series of recommendations that, if implemented, could significantly improve our understanding of the distribution of federal funds.

MONITORING THE MOVEMENT
OF FEDERAL MONIES

By any standard, the massive movement of money in recent years from federal to state and local levels is impressive. Equally impressive is the lack of a single source of information or set of information sources that would enable the federal government (or anybody else) to state with accuracy how much money has been or is being spent by different federal agencies for various programs in different states and localities.

To appreciate how limited our ability to monitor the movement of federal monies is, we need only consider the kinds of data currently available for tracking federal fund flows. Recall that in FY 1978 the federal government spent $461 billion in budget outlays, $124 billion in tax expenditures, and had accumulated $440 billion in outstanding loan assistance. These obligations amounted to more than a trillion dollars ($1,000,000,000,000). Yet, available government-wide federal information systems permit the tracking of less than half of these dollars to state and local geographic areas. No federal information source reports tax expenditures below the national level. Both O.M.B. and Treasury publish national level data on credit activity, but only the Community Services Administration tracks loan assistance to states and localities, and then only for the "face value/obligation" of loans advanced during each fiscal year. No geographic profiles of either total loans outstanding or loan repayment schedules are now available.

Geographic impact of federal budget decisions is available but difficult to interpret. Three government-wide federal information systems report on the geographic distribution of various positions of federal budget outlays; no one report provides complete coverage. Treasury's *Federal Aid to States* report and the bureau of the Census' *Governmental Finances* reports confine their coverage to grants-in-aid: 17% of the total budget in FY 1978. Only the Community Services Administration *Geographic Distribution of Federal Funds* report attempts to comprehensively monitor the movement of federal budget expenditures into states and localities. The C.S.A. data system is thus the only information source that permits a response to the simple question "how much money was distributed by the federal government to states and localities in FY 197?."

Even if the focus is narrowed to grants-in-aid, (recall, only 17% of the budget), the Treasury, Census and C.S.A. information systems yield not one but three "official" answers to the question of where grants flow (see Table 6.1).[1] Whether or not any one of these three data systems is entitled to be judged "harder" than any other seems doubtful, but it is abundantly clear that they are very different systems, supporting very different conclusions regarding "who gets what." The sources of difference are worth noting:

1. Coverage of types of financial assistance programs varies across information systems, as do definitions of what constitutes distinct types of assistance, e.g., grants-in-aid. Census, Treasury and C.S.A. employ similar but not identical definitions of grants-in-aid.
2. Levels of programmatic detail reported by information systems varies considerably. Census reports clusters of distinct federal grants-in-aid programs lumped together into functional classifications. Treasury reports grants-in-aid totals grouped into clusters of related programs (about 90 to 120 separate listings each year). C.S.A. reports data on discrete program activities (over 1,700 in FY 1978).
3. Level of geographic reporting detail varies. Treasury reports state-level data; C.S.A. reports state, county and city data for all cities of 25,000 population or more; Census reports data for states, counties, cities, school and special districts (based on either sampling or census data collection procedures).
4. Information systems report different types of expenditure data. Treasury reports actual outlay data based on checks-issued. C.S.A. reports a mixture of obligations and outlays. Census appears to report mostly outlays for the data derived from O.M.B., Treasury and federal agency sources.

TABLE 6.1.--NATIONAL LEVEL DIFFERENCES IN GRANTS-IN-AID TOTALS REPORTED IN C.S.A., F.A.T.S., AND B.O.C., FISCAL YEARS 1971-78 (THOUSANDS $)

FISCAL YEAR	GRANTS-IN-AID $			$ DIFFERENCES		
	C.S.A.	F.A.T.S.	B.O.C.	C.S.A.-F.A.T.S.	C.S.A.-B.O.C.	F.A.T.S.-B.O.C.
1970-71	31,140,966	29,272,078	26,145,600	1,868,889	4,995,366	3,126,478
1971-72	36,740,792	35,216,970	31,252,900	1,523,822	5,487,892	3,964,070
1972-73	46,734,680	43,056,508	39,255,600	3,678,172	7,479,080	3,800,908
1973-74	45,437,553	45,092,172	41,831,100	345,381	3,606,453	3,261,072
1974-75	63,687,843	48,569,836	46,994,200	15,118,007	16,693,643	1,575,636
1975-76	62,545,702	57,718,501	55,587,100	4,827,201	6,958,602	2,131,401
T.Q.	20,928,318	15,872,201		5,056,117		
1976-77	91,442,548	66,083,740	62,609,800	25,358,808	28,832,748	3,473,940
1977-78	85,953,407	75,293,471	69,592,400	10,659,936	16,361,007	5,701,071

129

5. The timeliness of the data varies. C.S.A. and Treasury data are released within five months after the close of the fiscal year. Census data are released a year or more after the close of the fiscal year; data for the Transition Quarter were never published.

6. Different fiscal years are employed across data bases. Treasury and C.S.A. data correspond to the federal fiscal year. Census employs the federal fiscal year in its collection of data from federal sources, but includes state and local data based on different fiscal years in its reports. If state and local fiscal years end within the fiscal year being reported, Census treats these fiscal years as equivalent to the federal fiscal year.

SOURCES OF VARIETY

Although analysts doubtless regard these varying numbers and the confusion they inevitably produce as perverse, the absence of a single, comprehensive and consistent record of federal spending seems to us quite understandable. No great insight is required to appreciate the enormous diversity of purposes pursued, and the heterogeneity of the agencies created to pursue them, by the entity referred to as "the federal government." It seems perfectly reasonable to suppose, therefore, that information needs will be as diverse as agency purposes require and that absent a strong demonstration of need, there will be no consistent and comprehensive data base. Even the data systems designed to be comprehensive are, as we suggest in Appendix Figures 1.1–1.3, established for different purposes, according to varying mandates, to service somewhat different user communities. Data systems, in short, do not exist in a vacuum; data are "created" because someone wants or needs information.

From this point of view, it is important to understand the fundamental tension involved in seeking to monitor the flow of federal program dollars through data systems oriented to tasks, rather than to programs. All federal spending is organized by programs, administered by bureaus within agencies and, as we have pointed out, program information available within agencies is typically quite accurate and timely. A data system to monitor government expenditures by location and through time would thus have to be built on such program information if it were to reflect the ideals of comprehensiveness and accuracy. Major information systems currently in use, however, are primarily task-oriented in design. The missions served by these information systems—financial control, managerial control, strategic planning—are not organized around individual programs, nor do they require geographic distribution information either at the individual or aggregated-program level.

Financial control information systems are designed to audit the cash flow of receipts and expenditures from accounts/funds, which encompass many and varied program activities. Since detailed program-level data are not required to fulfill this mission, the interest secondary-users may have in program information is far outweighed by the additional investments of time, personnel, and money required to collect it. Accounting systems, data collection procedures, and reporting mechanisms are designed accordingly.

Managerial control information systems are set up to monitor the expenditure of organization resources in the pursuit of program objectives. How much money is being spent on salaries, expenses, equipment replacement, transportation?—these are more pressing concerns than monitoring overall program expenditure patterns by geographic level. Such data are maintained, but usually on a program-by-program basis in separate information bases, not in an integrated information system. Accounting systems in managerial control information systems are thus primarily crafted to provide easily obtainable and intelligible policy evaluation information: assessing cash management policies, productivity, effects of administrative regulations.

Strategic planning information systems are budget oriented. How much money should be spent on what functional needs in the coming year? What revenue sources are available to fund these activities? National budget decisions are facilitated by aggregating clusters of program activities into broader functional and/or organizational categories, e.g., education expenditures or Office of Education expenditures. These categories, in turn, are related to financial control information (i.e., accounts and funds) so that financial disbursements and receipts pursuant to budget decisions can be monitored. Strategic planning information systems thus provide a wealth of information but the organization of this information is not primarily designed to highlight program operations: program-level data is often incomplete, and its presentation in budget tapes and documents often varies in format or detail from year to year, reflecting the changing information needs of the participants in the budget process.

In short, financial control, managerial control and strategic planning information systems offer incomplete program-level data at best. Few of these information systems provide detailed geographic data. Since program-level data reported by geographic levels would be necessary to systematically monitor intergovernmental fiscal flows, and since financial, managerial and strategic planning data bases are generally the only comprehensive information systems available, no single source of information exists that would permit accurate assessment of how much money has been spent, is being spent, or will be spent by department W, on program X, in state Y, for purpose Z, at either the federal, state or local levels.

TOWARD SELF-AWARENESS

It is by no means clear that the information gap we have tried to describe and understand should be regarded as a "problem." The government in Washington may not have a very clear idea of where its resources are being spent, but there is no apparent danger of government collapse as a result. Anyone who wants to, furthermore, can usually find out where individual program dollars are distributed, with a modest investment of time and effort reviewing annual agency reports, or visiting with relevant program managers. Before considering whether anything *can* be done to improve the quality of federal expenditure data, therefore, it is essential to ask whether anything *should* be done.

We believe that a strong case for information reform can be made on both political and practical grounds. Federal funds now constitute the largest single source of revenues available to state and local governments and, as our previous analyses have demonstrated, federal monies are more widely distributed among these jurisdictions than ever before. It is perfectly predictable, therefore, that political pressure to maintain or increase federal disbursements will intensify, and that distributive consequences of federal budget decisions will increasingly be debated. Whether or not federal officials want to know where federal dollars flow, local officials will *demand* to know. As a practical matter, furthermore, these pressures seem certain to create new incentives to generate more adequate program and location-specific information. Large contributions to other governments in a period of fiscal restraint inevitably elevate questions of impact to a higher level of significance. Program evaluation, already a powerful thrust in both Congress and the Executive Branch, can hardly be accomplished unless where, no less than what, is examined. For policy planning and evaluation, in short, better information is essential.

Assuming that information improvement should be a matter of high priority, the question of whether it can be accomplished remains. Washington, we have discovered, is full of skeptics, who deny the possibility even when they grant the utility of achieving a more accurate yet comprehensive data system. The problem is too huge, or too complex, or too costly to resolve, they say. We believe the skeptics are wrong, for two major reasons. First, data systems already exist that, with some additional effort, can become components of a more integrated and consistent data base. These include a large number of program and agency data systems, as well as the O.M.B.-Treasury systems for reporting grants-in-aid, and the C.S.A. system for reporting all federal program activity (see Appendix Figures 1.1–1.3). Second, the technical and personal relationships required to achieve greater accuracy are already in place. O.M.B., Treasury and C.S.A. data are based on accounting systems that are consistent with one another and linked by common inclusion of Treasury/O.M.B. agency-account identification codes. In addition, both O.M.B. and C.S.A. accounting systems employ O.M.B. schedule, type of fund, function and CFDA financial assistance program codes. Officials responsible for compiling and publishing data from these systems, furthermore, have cooperated with one another for years. Together they represent the human base on which a far more useful, technically accurate and comprehensive information system can be built.

What, then, might be done? Strategically, we believe it would be unwise and unproductive to attempt to define some "ideal" system and then seek to meet the requirements of the "ideal" system. Rather, we believe that any approach to reform should:

1. recognize the reality and legitimacy of the multiple purposes for which information systems are designed,
2. recognize the quality of many existing information systems,
3. seek to minimize both the cost and disruption to existing practices likely to follow from proposed changes, and thus
4. aim fundamentally at improving what now exists rather than devising a wholly new or different system.

To these ends, we offer the following recommendations:

A. RECOMMENDATIONS TO STRENGTHEN EXISTING DATA SYSTEMS

1. Automate the Treasury Department's Federal Aid to States report

Justification: *Federal Aid to States,* a major source of information, is now prepared entirely by hand. Changing to electronic data processing would improve the accuracy and versatility of the system by permitting machine verification of information and automated integration with agency and master account codes.

Feasibility: Excellent computer facilities are now available in Treasury. Entering data for all past years can be done in a matter of days, and annual entries into an automated system can easily be organized, at little or no additional cost.

2. Strengthen and enforce existing program-level reporting requirements in the Federal Information Exchange System

Justification: Pursuant to O.M.B. Circular No. A-84, creating the Federal Information Exchange System, C.S.A. (the administering agency) has issued the following instruction:

> The basic level of reporting under each appropriation or fund is the program, for it is through the program that the true impact of the federal effect on community life is best identified. *Every effort should therefore be made to provide information by program.* (Emphasis added.)

Many reporting agencies, however, interpret this O.M.B.-C.S.A. guideline quite broadly, either by reporting obligations only by appropriation or fund, or by failing to report any obligations at all for certain programs. To remedy these deficiencies we recommend that the wording of C.S.A.'s annual "Instructions for Reporting of Federal Outlays By Geographic Location" be changed to read: "Obligations for all government-administered funds *must* be reported by program."

We further recommend that O.M.B. and C.S.A. enforce this requirement, as well as the existing requirement that all financial assistance programs listed in the *Catalog of Federal Domestic Assistance* report separate data for each program.

Feasibility: The Federal Information Exchange System is already in place, thus no additional personnel and only minimal additional effort by existing personnel are required to provide consistent program-level data. A less ambiguous instruction could in fact minimize the occurrence of misunderstandings that sometimes result in underreporting. For example, the Department of Transportation reported one figure for its Urban Mass Transportation Assistance programs in fiscal 1978, while the 1978 *Catalog of Federal Domestic Assistance* listed nine separate programs as active and funded by the same account/appropriation that year. Consultation between D.O.T. and C.S.A. clarified this point and all separate U.M.T.A. programs will be reported as of fiscal 1979.

3. Require agencies reporting to the Federal Information Exchange System to distinguish between grants to state and local governments and grants to non-governmental agencies or to individuals

Justification: Presently used "Type of Assistance" codes in the F.I.X.S. system do not permit a clear identification of formula and project grants to governments as opposed to grants to individuals or other non-governmental recipients. Reporting government grants separately would add clarity, reduce the disparity between F.I.X.S. data and Treasury-O.M.B. data, and bring F.I.X.S. reports into closer conformity with the grants-in-aid definition found in O.M.B. Circular No. A-11.

Feasibility: H.H.S., which accounts for the largest portion of domestic grants, already has the capability of making this distinction in its FARS system. Some additional burden would be placed on C.S.A., which would have to add three "types of assistance" codes to its reports, and on reporting agencies other than H.H.S., which would have to separately report grants to governments. Since this distinction is already required by the A-11 budget circular, the additional reporting burden seems minimal.

4. Identify obligations reported in F.I.X.S. that are allocated to a single unit but largely redistributed to other units

Justification: A number of program obligations reported in the F.I.X.S. system are allocated to a single county or city because the recipient agency is located in that jurisdiction, even though it is known that such obligations are in fact largely re-distributed among other jurisdictions within a given state or area. Many of these obligations are assigned a code (99) that indicates accuracy "at the level reported." While technically correct, this code assignment artificially inflates outlays reported in state capitol or consortium counties and cities. Identifying such reported obligations would alert users to a potential bias in the data and permit more careful secondary analysis.

Feasibility: C.S.A. already has the capacity to identify most of these program obligations and would therefore require little more than a new proration code. Some additional effort would be required from a few reporting agencies.

B. RECOMMENDATIONS TO BRING ABOUT GREATER CONSISTENCY AND INTEGRATION AMONG EXISTING DATA SYSTEMS

5. Develop master geographic crosswalk files and require agency utilization of such files

Justification: Census, F.I.X.S., and G.S.A. all have developed comprehensive codes to identify state and local jurisdictions but their use varies from agency to agency. Individual agencies, moreover, often have their own geographic codes, different from the more comprehensive coding systems. As a result, data from different agencies are often difficult to reconcile geographically or, in some cases, data are not reported at all because such reconciliations cannot be made. H.U.D., for example, does not report data on one of its largest programs, Section 8 Housing Assistance, to the F.I.X.S. system, primarily because H.U.D.'s own place codes have not been reconciled with the G.S.A. codes utilized by F.I.X.S. to identify cities. A simple geographic crosswalk between H.U.D. and G.S.A. codes would entirely resolve this problem.

Feasibility: Geographic code crosswalks are not difficult to develop—indeed, we have included one in this report (see especially the city data file). Only a modest investment of time and resources would be required, although securing agency cooperation in the use of standard codes might impose some additional burden. A central agency such as the Office of Federal Statistical Policy and Standards, or perhaps O.M.B., would presumably have to carry this burden.

6. Reconcile alternative agency classification codes

Justification: O.M.B., Treasury and C.S.A. all use different codes to identify federal spending agencies, primarily because their data systems are designed to serve different purposes. Multiple classification codes, however, confound efforts to discover which agencies are spending how many dollars in any given year. A simple agency identification crosswalk, showing different codes attached by O.M.B., Treasury and C.S.A., would facilitate summaries of federal spending, without disturbing existing classification codes.

Feasibility: Very little time or effort would be required to develop such a crosswalk, either by hand or by machine.

7. Develop agency-account-program crosswalks across time

Justification: New programs, administrative reorganization or simple accounting changes often result in modifications of agency or program identification codes from one year to the next. A single code, that would permit identification of the same agency or program across a number of years, would facilitate construction of historical expenditure records and thus aid both program evaluation and policy planning.

Feasibility: Considerable effort would be required to develop such crosswalks, given the large number of agencies that receive appropriations and expend funds. Technically, however, there are no major obstacles, Appendix Table 6.2 taken from 1978 C.S.A. data, illustrates the feasibility as well as the complexity of such an effort.

8. Perform and publish detailed yearly reconciliations of C.S.A., O.M.B., and Treasury data

Justification: Yearly reconciliations of C.S.A.'s Federal Information Exchange System, O.M.B.'s *Budget Appendix,* "Federal Aid to State and Local Governments," the *Catalog of Federal Domestic Assistance,* and Treasury's *Federal Aid to States* data would provide: (1) a check on the degree of compliance with O.M.B., Treasury and C.S.A. circulars and reporting instructions which require that data submitted for each of the data bases be consistent with data also submitted to one or more of these information systems, (2) a measure of improvement in efforts to establish reporting consistency across information systems, and (3) documentation of how policy recommendations based on one of these data bases might differ with the use of another data base.

Feasibility: O.M.B. and Treasury currently reconcile "Federal Aid to State and Local Governments" with *Federal Aid to States,* and C.S.A. has undertaken reconciliations of the Federal Information Exchange System data with O.M.B.'s *Budget Appendix* and the *Catalog of Federal Domestic Assistance* data. Reconciliations of the Federal Information Exchange System and *Federal Aid to States* data have also been undertaken. (For examples of such reconciliations see Appendix Tables 6.3–6.6.) Technical considerations thus present no major problem, especially if recommendations to develop agency, program and geographic crosswalks are adopted. The major cost of implementing this recommendation would be the time required to perform the reconciliations, a commitment that would progressively decrease after initial start-up costs develop a standard reconciliation procedure.

C. RECOMMENDATIONS TO IMPROVE DATA FOR ANALYTIC OR POLICY-PLANNING PURPOSES

9. Integrate existing program data into comprehensive data systems

Justification: A number of high-quality data systems, not now incorporated into any of the comprehensive data systems, are maintained by program or agency units:

H.E.W.'s (now O.E.'s) Section 437 Education Program Data or the recently-implemented Defense Department Procurement Data System are examples. Integrating such systems into existing comprehensive systems, particularly the F.I.X.S. data base, would greatly enhance the federal government's capacity for management and policy evaluation. If the crosswalks recommended above were developed, furthermore, improved data would in time provide a base for easily accomplished data aggregation by agency or bureau, and thus create a broader base for strategic planning.

Feasibility: Systems for reporting such information are in place, but additional resources would be required for full integration.

10. Integrate available demographic and fiscal information into comprehensive expenditure data systems

Justification: The federal government now maintains a number of useful data bases that measure various social, economic and demographic characteristics of state, county, and local jurisdictions. If existing expenditure data systems were reconciled to provide cross-agency and cross-time consistency, and these data merged into files that included socio-demographic information, a variety of powerful analyses could be easily accomplished (see Appendix Figure 1.1). Formula construction or evaluation, "targeting" issues, impact analyses or agency-program effects by jurisdiction and across time are among the important problems that could be addressed with considerable speed and comprehensiveness.

Feasibility: Technical problems in merging different data bases exist, but are resolvable. Efforts to achieve this objective are already under way, both in the Executive Office of the President (the Domestic Information Display System, or DIDS) and in Congress (organized by the House Information System). Personnel and resources are thus available now. Some increment in resources would be required to add momentum to these efforts.

CONCLUSION

None of the recommendations offered above require major changes in current relationships or resource levels. Most, in fact, can be implemented with existing personnel, existing budgets and existing procedures. In one or two cases resource increments are implied, but we believe those increments would be quite modest. Although these proposals are thus "incremental" rather than "fundamental," implementing them could produce a substantial improvement in our understanding of federal spending patterns. Comprehensive data systems would become more consistent across time, differences between existing data systems would be more easily-identified and understood, analyses of fund distributions would become easier to accomplish and more timely, if more fundamental changes were desired at some later point, they could be more efficiently planned and achieved. We believe these are worthy goals that are achievable in the short rather than the long-run future. What is required most of all, therefore, is a commitment to achieve them.

NOTE

1. Readers interested in state-level difference are directed to Appendix Table 6.1, which reports totals derived from each of these data sources for all states and the District of Columbia from 1971 through 1978.

Appendix Tables

LEVEL OF GEOGRAPHIC AND PROGRAMMATIC DETAIL OF REPORTING IN EIGHT DATA BASES

LEVELS OF ANALYSIS REPORTED IN PUBLISHED HARDCOPY OF DATA BASES

DATA BASE	NATIONAL	REGIONAL	STATE	SMSA	OTHER UNITS*	COUNTY	CITY	NON-CITY	CONG. DIST.	RECIPIENT	AGENCY	FUNCTION	TREASURY/OMB ACCOUNT**	PROGRAM
TCS	YES	NO	NO	NO	NO	NO	NO	NO	NO	NO	YES	NO	YES	A
BOTUSG	YES	NO	NO	NO	NO	NO	NO	NO	NO	NO	YES	YES	YES	A
CFDA	YES	NO	NO	NO	NO	NO	NO	NO	NO	NO	NO	NO	B	YES
FATSLG	YES	NO	YES	NO	NO	NO	NO	NO	NO	NO	YES	YES	YES	A
FATS	YES	C	YES	YES	YES	YES	YES	NO	NO	NO	YES	YES	D	D
CENSUS	YES	F	YES	NO	NO	YES	YES	YES	NO	NO	NO	YES	NO	NO
FIXS	YES	NO	YES	NO	NO	YES	YES	YES	NO	NO	YES	NO	NO	YES
FARS	NO	YES	YES	NO	NO	YES	YES	NO	YES	YES	E	NO	NO	YES

LEVELS OF ANALYSIS OBTAINABLE IN COMPUTER TAPE VERSION OF DATA BASES

DATA BASE	NATIONAL	REGIONAL	STATE	SMSA	OTHER UNITS*	COUNTY	CITY	NON-CITY	CONG. DIST.	RECIPIENT	AGENCY	FUNCTION	TREASURY/OMB ACCOUNT**	PROGRAM
TCS	YES	NO	NO	NO	NO	NO	NO	NO	NO	NO	YES	NO	YES	A
BOTUSG	YES	NO	NO	NO	NO	NO	NO	NO	NO	NO	YES	YES	YES	A
CFDA	YES	NO	NO	NO	NO	NO	NO	NO	NO	NO	YES	YES	YES	YES
FATSLG	YES	NO	YES	NO	NO	NO	NO	NO	NO	NO	YES	YES	YES	A
FATS	***	***	***	***	***	***	***	***	***	***	***	***	***	***
CENSUS	YES	YES	YES	YES	NO	YES	YES	NO	NO	NO	YES	YES	NO	NO
FIXS	YES	YES	YES	NO	YES	YES	YES	YES	YES	YES	YES	YES	YES	YES
FARS	YES	YES	YES	NO	NO	NO	YES	YES	YES	YES	NO	NO	YES	YES

LEVELS OF ANALYSIS OBTAINABLE THROUGH RESTRUCTURING OF COMPUTER TAPE VERSIONS OF DATA BASES

DATA BASE	NATIONAL	REGIONAL	STATE	SMSA	OTHER UNITS*	COUNTY	CITY	NON-CITY	CONG. DIST.	RECIPIENT	AGENCY	FUNCTION	TREASURY/OMB ACCOUNT**	PROGRAM
TCS	YES	NO	NO	NO	NO	NO	NO	NO	NO	NO	YES	YES	YES	A
BOTUSG	YES	NO	NO	NO	NO	NO	NO	NO	NO	NO	YES	YES	YES	A
CFDA	YES	NO	NO	NO	NO	NO	NO	NO	NO	NO	YES	YES	YES	YES
FATSLG	YES	YES	YES	NO	NO	NO	NO	NO	NO	NO	YES	YES	YES	A
FATS	YES	YES	YES	NO	NO	NO	NO	NO	NO	NO	NO	YES	YES	A
CENSUS	YES	YES	YES	YES	YES	YES	YES	YES	YES	YES	YES	YES	NO	NO
FIXS	YES	YES	YES	YES	YES	YES	YES	YES	YES	YES	YES	YES	YES	YES
FARS	YES	YES	YES	YES	YES	YES	YES	YES	YES	YES	YES	YES	YES	YES

* For example, rural areas, special districts, school districts.
** Refers to OMB functional codes, save for Census, which uses its own codes.
*** The Department of Treasury does not maintain a machine readable version of this report.
A Program level detail is available only when individual programs are equivalent to individual accounts. Accounts generally fund multiple programs.
B Reports program data; account data only when program and account level are equivalent.
C The FATS report does not contain regional tables, but the FATS data provides the detailed support documentation for a regional table presented in FATSLG each year.
D Reports expenditure data in columns depicting either individual programs or accounts, or clusters of related programs or accounts for grants-in-aid.
E Provides data on H.E.W.'s POC/Agencies.
F County And City Data Book reports regional figures, as do other Census reports.

Appendix Table 1.2. Eight Major Data Bases: Mandates, Missions, Primary Users

Data Base	Administrative Department	Mandates	Missions	Primary Users
F.A.T.S.	Treasury	Treasury Circular No. 1014 and Part 2, Chapter 7000 of the *Treasury Fiscal Requirements Manual*	Provide state-level detailed support for O.M.B.'s F.A.T.S.L.G. report	Congress, State Officials, O.M.B.
Census	Bureau of the Census	Various legislation and circulars	Compile revenues and expenditure data for federal, state and local governmental units.	State and Local Officials, President, Congress, Federal Agencies, widely used in academic, journalistic and business circles
F.I.X.S.	Community Services Administration	O.M.B. Circular No. A-84	Compilation of data on level of federal obligation and/or expenditures in each state and county and in each city (includes towns, etc.) over 25,000 for all individual appropriations and for related programs.	State and Local Officials, Congress, President, Public, Federal Agencies
F.A.R.S.	Health, Education and Welfare	O.M.B. Circular No. A-84; F.I.X.S. reporting instructions manual by C.S.A.; Additional H.E.W. geographic reporting coverage requirements	To assist H.E.W. managers in providing informed, timely responses to Congress, state and local officials and public inquiries	H.E.W. Officials, Congress, State and Local Officials

Appendix Table 1.2 (continued)

Data Base	Administrative Department	Mandates	Missions	Primary Users
T.C.S.	Treasury	Article 1, Section 9, U.S. Constitution; House of Representatives, Standing Order, December 31, 1791; Section 15, Act of July 31, 1894 (U.S.C. 1020); Section 114, Act of September 12, 1950 (31 U.S.C. 666 (a))	Official documentation on firm accounting basis, of receipts and outlays of U.S. Government, with which all other reports containing similar data must be in agreement.	Congress, O.M.B., G.A.O. Federal Departments and Agencies
B.O.T.U.S.G.	O.M.B.	O.M.B. Circular No. A-11	Presidential Budget Recommendations	President, Congress, Federal Departments and Agencies, Public
C.F.D.A.	O.M.B.	PL 95-220	To assist state, local and other officials to identify federal programs that meet their needs; to improve coordination and communication among federal, state and local governments.	State and Local Officials, Federal Agencies, Congress, Public
F.A.T.S.L.G.	O.M.B.	O.M.B. Circular No. A-11	Relates trends in grants-in aid and credit assistance to state and local governments to budget decisions. Supplemented by F.A.T.S. state-level data.	President, Congress, State and Local Officials, G.A.O.

143

Appendix Table 1.3. Eight Major Data Bases: Coverage, Data, Availability

Data Base	Coverage	Type of Expenditure Record	Source/Timeliness of Data	Availability
F.A.T.S.	Grants-in-aid to State and local governments as defined by O.M.B. Circular No. A-11	Outlays	Data collected from accounting divisions of reporting departments and agencies 30 to 90 days after the close of fiscal year and cash payments (checks-issued) on comparable basis. Report published in January or February following end of the fiscal year.	Hardcopy Only
Census	Revenues and expenditures of federal, state and local governmental units	Outlays/Obligations	Data collected for fiscal year ending June 30. Federal data from O.M.B. budget data, supplemented by Treasury information and detailed agency data in intergovernmental transfers. State data from official state records. (And data from local records by mail survey, depending on size of unit and which Census data collection process data are from; i.e., Census of Governments or Survey of Governments)	Hardcopy and Tape
F.A.R.S.	All H.E.W. Domestic Assistance Programs	Obligations	Data collected from each of H.E.W.'s POCs/Agencies quarterly, cumulated annually. 30 to 90 days after the close of the fiscal year data sent to C.S.A. for F.I.X.S.; published by H.E.W. in February.	Hardcopy and Tape
T.C.S.	Account level statement of all receipts and outlays of U.S. Government on checks-issued and cash payments basis (except for some cases like Interest on Public Debt—accrual basis)	Outlays	Accounting Divisions of Federal Agencies	Hardcopy and Tape

Appendix Table 1.3 (continued)

Data Base	Coverage	Type of Expenditure Record	Source/Timeliness of Data	Availability
B.O.T.U.S.G.	All accounts/programs of federal agencies of the government and privately-owned (government sponsored) enterprises	Outlays/Obligations	Data collected from budget divisions or reporting departments and agencies as part of O.M.B. No. A-11 budget process. Published in January	Hardcopy and Tape
C.F.D.A.	Government-wide compendium of over 1,000 financial and non-financial federal programs, projects, services and activities	Obligations	Data collection from federal agencies	Hardcopy and Tape
F.A.T.S.L.G.	Grants-in-aid and credit assistance (direct and guaranteed) to state and local governments	Actual and Estimated outlays (grants) and obligations (credit assistance)	Data collected from budget divisions of reporting departments and agencies as part of O.M.B. No. A-11 budget process. Published in January.	Hardcopy and Tape
F.I.X.S.	All individual appropriations (accounts) and selected programs of all executive departments and establishments; excludes judicial and Congressional expenditures	Outlays/Obligations	Reporting agencies submit data to C.S.A. 30 to 90 days following the close of the reporting fiscal year. Report published February, data made available to Congress and federal agencies January or February	Hardcopy and Tape

PERCENTAGE CONCENTRATION OF GRANTS-IN-AID TO STATE AND LOCAL GOVERNMENTS, 1924-1978
Ordered BY 1978 CONCENTRATION RANKINGS

AREA	FISCAL YEAR						
	1924	1930	1940	1950	1960	1970	1978
N.Y.	5.1	6.5	8.0	6.9	7.5	10.0	11.1
CAL.	3.2	4.6	8.4	8.7	7.8	12.6	10.6
PA.	2.0	5.2	6.6	4.8	4.5	5.7	5.2
ILL.	6.0	3.5	5.5	4.6	5.3	4.0	4.6
TEX.	6.6	6.5	4.3	5.8	6.0	4.9	4.6
MI.	2.9	2.8	3.8	3.9	3.4	3.2	4.4
OHIO	4.6	3.6	5.3	4.2	4.6	3.7	3.9
MASS.	1.3	3.7	4.1	3.0	4.2	3.6	3.4
N.J.	1.7	2.5	1.4	3.6	1.8	3.6	3.7
FLA.	1.0	1.4	2.2	1.6	2.6	2.3	3.7
GA.	3.1	1.4	4.0	2.6	2.7	2.6	2.2
N.C.	2.3	3.2	2.6	2.0	2.3	2.3	2.1
WIS.	3.0	1.7	1.5	2.2	1.7	1.6	1.9
VA.	3.7	1.3	2.7	1.2	1.8	2.0	1.8
LA.	1.7	2.8	2.8	3.6	3.9	2.7	1.8
MINN.	2.3	2.9	1.2	2.0	1.3	1.7	1.7
TENN.	2.3	1.0	1.8	2.5	2.3	1.7	1.8
MD.	1.8	1.9	1.9	1.0	1.7	1.7	1.7
WASH.	1.0	1.0	2.0	2.0	1.7	1.7	1.7
MO.	4.5	3.6	3.0	3.7	3.0	2.1	1.7
IND.	3.3	2.7	3.0	1.9	3.9	1.5	1.7
ALA.	2.8	1.7	1.3	1.9	2.3	2.2	1.6
KY.	2.6	1.9	1.4	1.8	2.1	1.7	1.5
D.C.	-0.7	0.1	1.5	1.3	1.7	1.3	1.5
ORE.	1.7	2.2	1.4	1.9	1.0	1.3	1.4
CONN.	2.8	1.6	1.2	1.5	1.1	1.2	1.2
OKLA.	2.0	2.2	2.3	3.1	2.1	1.6	1.2
MISS.	1.6	1.3	1.0	1.5	1.3	1.7	1.2
S.C.	1.2	1.6	2.2	1.7	1.4	1.2	1.1
COL.	3.1	2.7	2.0	1.9	1.8	1.0	1.0
IOWA	1.5	1.2	1.2	1.7	1.3	1.6	1.0
ARK.	1.0	1.5	1.2	1.7	1.4	2.0	1.0
ARZ.	3.1	1.1	1.1	1.2	1.4	1.3	0.9
W.VA.	1.0	2.7	1.3	1.7	1.0	0.9	0.9
KAN.	0.9	1.0	1.7	1.8	1.0		0.8
N.M.							0.8

APPENDIX TABLE 1.4

——————— (CONTINUED) PERCENTAGE CONCENTRATION OF GRANTS-IN-AID TO STATE AND LOCAL GOVERNMENTS, 1924-1978 ———————
Ordered BY 1978 CONCENTRATION RANKINGS

FISCAL YEAR

AREA	1924	1930	1940	1950	1960	1970	1978
MAINE.	.9	1.4	.8	.7	.7	.5	.6
NEB...	1.3	1.9	1.3	1.0	.8	.5	.6
UTAH..	1.2	1.0	.9	.6	.8	.7	.5
HA....	-0.	1.3	.3	.4	.7	.5	.5
ALK...		2.1	.1	.8	.7	.6	.5
MONT..	1.1	2.3	1.1	.5	.6	.6	.5
R.I...	1.4	.6	.6	.6	.6	.4	.4
IDA...	1.0	1.0	.8	.7	.5	.3	.4
N.H...	2.3	1.7	.7	.3	.7	.4	.4
S.D...	2.0	1.3	.5	.7	.3	.3	.3
NEV...	2.6	1.9	.5	.3	.7	.4	.3
N.D...	1.6	1.3	.3	.6	.4	.3	
VER...	1.4	1.6	.7	.3	.7	.3	
WY....	1.5	1.8		.6	.7	.4	
DEL...	.5	1.7	.3	.2	.2	.2	.3

147

Yearly State-Area Differences in State-Area Grants-In-Aid Totals Reported by Treasury and Census, FY 1969=1978 (Thousands of Dollars)

Area	Fiscal Year	Reported Grants-In-Aid Treasury	Reported Grants-In-Aid Census	Difference
ALA...	1968-69	419,207	362,900	56,307
ALA...	1969-70	523,508	452,200	71,308
ALA...	1970-71	648,335	537,600	110,735
ALA...	1971-72	677,933	601,100	76,833
ALA...	1972-73	795,952	606,800	189,152
ALA...	1973-74	829,475	713,600	115,875
ALA...	1974-75	820,235	808,000	12,235
ALA...	1975-76	992,934	942,600	50,334
ALA...	1976-77	1,120,519	1,082,700	37,819
ALA...	1977-78	1,240,569	1,155,900	84,669
ALK...	1968-69	106,429	110,800	-4,371
ALK...	1969-70	115,930	108,200	7,730
ALK...	1970-71	159,850	159,400	450
ALK...	1971-72	185,269	174,100	11,169
ALK...	1972-73	209,316	204,000	5,316
ALK...	1973-74	234,207	220,000	14,207
ALK...	1974-75	266,457	258,600	1,857
ALK...	1975-76	318,553	307,800	10,753
ALK...	1976-77	388,004	311,800	70,204
ALK...	1977-78	408,211	346,000	62,211
ARZ...	1968-69	203,645	187,300	16,345
ARZ...	1969-70	237,166	215,200	21,966
ARZ...	1970-71	244,837	233,900	10,937
ARZ...	1971-72	292,172	266,200	25,972
ARZ...	1972-73	381,226	331,900	50,056
ARZ...	1973-74	426,956	358,900	68,056
ARZ...	1974-75	462,604	421,100	41,504
ARZ...	1975-76	530,309	489,100	41,209
ARZ...	1976-77	648,435	523,700	124,735
ARZ...	1977-78	763,318	659,200	104,118
ARK...	1968-69	244,448	205,200	39,248
ARK...	1969-70	274,849	222,100	52,849
ARK...	1970-71	321,235	245,100	76,135
ARK...	1971-72	394,388	314,000	80,388
ARK...	1972-73	468,895	359,200	109,695
ARK...	1973-74	470,181	386,800	83,381
ARK...	1974-75	511,273	466,600	44,673
ARK...	1975-76	613,667	580,800	32,867
ARK...	1976-77	638,790	581,800	56,990
ARK...	1977-78	779,074	708,400	70,674

Yearly State-Area Differences in State-Area Grants-In-Aid Totals
Reported by Treasury and Census, FY 1969-1978 (Thousands of Dollars) (Continued)

Area	Fiscal Year	Reported Grants-In-Aid		Difference
		Treasury	Census	
CAL...	1968-69	2,223,312	2,626,800	-403,488
CAL...	1969-70	2,999,346	3,279,800	-281,454
CAL...	1970-71	3,474,765	3,582,200	-107,435
CAL...	1971-72	4,093,767	4,147,800	-54,033
CAL...	1972-73	4,628,872	5,044,800	-417,928
CAL...	1973-74	4,665,989	4,989,600	-323,611
CAL...	1974-75	4,930,433	5,182,500	-252,067
CAL...	1975-76	5,802,854	6,227,400	-424,546
CAL...	1976-77	6,813,730	7,423,300	-609,570
CAL...	1977-78	8,012,965	8,311,800	-298,835
COL...	1968-69	246,765	241,900	4,865
COL...	1969-70	288,261	276,200	6,061
COL...	1970-71	373,866	333,400	40,466
COL...	1971-72	431,657	413,200	18,457
COL...	1972-73	504,572	488,000	-16,572
COL...	1973-74	503,328	531,300	-27,972
COL...	1974-75	601,832	598,400	3,432
COL...	1975-76	672,597	726,900	-54,303
COL...	1976-77	714,543	767,400	-52,857
COL...	1977-78	825,855	859,600	-33,745
CONN...	1968-69	263,274	237,600	25,674
CONN...	1969-70	295,488	256,600	38,888
CONN...	1970-71	403,358	324,900	78,458
CONN...	1971-72	446,728	370,800	75,928
CONN...	1972-73	550,746	467,800	82,946
CONN...	1973-74	669,431	549,700	119,731
CONN...	1974-75	672,844	589,100	83,744
CONN...	1975-76	723,950	635,500	88,450
CONN...	1976-77	894,981	710,200	184,781
CONN...	1977-78	1,052,697	852,500	200,197
DEL...	1968-69	42,065	40,500	1,565
DEL...	1969-70	51,111	48,400	2,711
DEL...	1970-71	66,184	59,100	7,184
DEL...	1971-72	96,248	98,100	-1,852
DEL...	1972-73	119,891	115,100	4,791
DEL...	1973-74	119,155	121,400	-2,245
DEL...	1974-75	120,216	130,400	-10,184
DEL...	1975-76	160,607	173,900	-12,393
DEL...	1976-77	187,302	199,900	-12,598
DEL...	1977-78	225,033	246,800	-21,767

Yearly State-Area Differences in State-Area Grants-In-Aid Totals
Reported by Treasury and Census, FY 1969-1978 (Thousands of Dollars) (Continued)

Area	Fiscal Year	Reported Grants-In-Aid Treasury	Reported Grants-In-Aid Census	Difference
D.C.	1968-69	251,359	227,200	24,159
D.C.	1969-70	405,135	271,500	133,635
D.C.	1970-71	608,823	361,100	247,723
D.C.	1971-72	563,693	506,000	57,693
D.C.	1972-73	604,574	625,200	-20,626
D.C.	1973-74	610,012	696,600	-86,588
D.C.	1974-75	722,529	716,400	6,129
D.C.	1975-76	749,043	812,400	-63,357
D.C.	1976-77	942,136	1,174,000	-231,864
D.C.	1977-78	1,105,199	1,122,400	-17,201
FLA.	1968-69	427,427	417,400	10,027
FLA.	1969-70	509,409	466,400	43,009
FLA.	1970-71	650,686	577,000	73,686
FLA.	1971-72	830,506	732,500	98,006
FLA.	1972-73	1,114,688	898,800	215,888
FLA.	1973-74	1,160,863	1,069,400	91,463
FLA.	1974-75	1,318,518	1,331,500	-12,982
FLA.	1975-76	1,527,688	1,491,700	35,988
FLA.	1976-77	1,988,414	1,779,700	208,714
FLA.	1977-78	2,364,186	2,130,500	233,686
GA.	1968-69	490,011	422,800	67,211
GA.	1969-70	553,799	456,100	97,699
GA.	1970-71	697,589	591,100	106,489
GA.	1971-72	838,681	729,600	109,081
GA.	1972-73	902,948	882,100	20,848
GA.	1973-74	1,123,869	996,500	127,369
GA.	1974-75	1,179,061	1,141,600	37,461
GA.	1975-76	1,421,097	1,244,300	176,797
GA.	1976-77	1,861,105	1,373,400	487,705
GA.	1977-78	2,036,993	1,676,100	360,893
HA.	1968-69	92,435	126,200	-33,765
HA.	1969-70	123,582	145,100	-21,518
HA.	1970-71	132,839	155,900	-23,061
HA.	1971-72	163,355	190,800	-27,445
HA.	1972-73	210,535	227,300	-16,765
HA.	1973-74	245,308	253,800	-8,492
HA.	1974-75	246,778	291,500	-44,722
HA.	1975-76	309,151	392,600	-83,449
HA.	1976-77	400,144	458,800	-58,656
HA.	1977-78	413,391	478,100	-64,709

Yearly State-Area Differences in State-Area Grants-In-Aid Totals
Reported by Treasury and Census, FY 1969-1978 (Thousands of Dollars) (Continued)

Area	Fiscal Year	Reported Grants-In-Aid		Difference
		Treasury	Census	
IDA...	1968-69	85,784	72,800	12,984
IDA...	1969-70	95,290	82,500	12,790
IDA...	1970-71	108,037	101,100	6,937
IDA...	1971-72	136,036	124,200	11,836
IDA...	1972-73	174,592	152,300	22,292
IDA...	1973-74	187,252	184,100	3,152
IDA...	1974-75	211,639	189,500	22,139
IDA...	1975-76	264,600	236,000	28,600
IDA...	1976-77	287,675	270,400	17,275
IDA...	1977-78	336,315	289,100	47,215
ILL...	1968-69	897,119	982,800	-85,681
ILL...	1969-70	950,809	1,042,100	-91,291
ILL...	1970-71	1,250,042	1,329,900	-79,858
ILL...	1971-72	1,760,275	1,838,400	-78,125
ILL...	1972-73	2,159,129	2,064,400	94,729
ILL...	1973-74	2,265,065	2,396,500	-131,435
ILL...	1974-75	2,226,480	2,180,700	45,780
ILL...	1975-76	2,795,467	2,594,200	201,267
ILL...	1976-77	3,202,188	2,816,100	386,088
ILL...	1977-78	3,467,151	2,904,700	562,451
IND...	1968-69	319,621	351,200	-31,579
IND...	1969-70	352,224	341,300	10,924
IND...	1970-71	431,229	415,600	15,629
IND...	1971-72	544,675	485,300	59,375
IND...	1972-73	676,024	556,000	120,024
IND...	1973-74	710,720	649,100	61,620
IND...	1974-75	805,790	736,600	69,190
IND...	1975-76	996,144	913,400	82,744
IND...	1976-77	1,095,093	1,003,300	91,193
IND...	1977-78	1,259,679	1,136,300	123,379
IOWA..	1968-69	223,364	221,500	-1,864
IOWA..	1969-70	244,345	255,700	-11,355
IOWA..	1970-71	302,292	273,100	29,192
IOWA..	1971-72	325,075	299,900	25,175
IOWA..	1972-73	438,304	376,900	61,404
IOWA..	1973-74	450,754	433,200	17,554
IOWA..	1974-75	555,820	577,400	-21,580
IOWA..	1975-76	659,337	678,100	-18,763
IOWA..	1976-77	714,420	716,900	-2,480
IOWA..	1977-78	796,893	790,000	6,893

Yearly State-Area Differences in State-Area Grants-In-Aid Totals
Reported by Treasury and Census, FY 1969-1978 (Thousands of Dollars) (Continued)

Area	Fiscal Year	Reported Grants-In-Aid		Difference
		Treasury	Census	
KAN...	1968-69	184,630	186,000	-1,371
KAN...	1969-70	231,657	216,800	14,857
KAN...	1970-71	265,885	250,500	15,385
KAN...	1971-72	297,972	281,600	16,372
KAN...	1972-73	391,383	345,300	46,083
KAN...	1973-74	385,468	356,300	29,168
KAN...	1974-75	445,087	426,100	18,987
KAN...	1975-76	517,947	494,100	23,847
KAN...	1976-77	548,524	546,200	2,324
KAN...	1977-78	615,820	562,900	52,920
KY....	1968-69	457,832	405,900	51,932
KY....	1969-70	456,588	372,900	83,688
KY....	1970-71	548,684	530,400	18,284
KY....	1971-72	598,561	489,300	109,261
KY....	1972-73	773,195	635,000	138,195
KY....	1973-74	826,290	694,600	131,690
KY....	1974-75	837,128	778,600	58,528
KY....	1975-76	1,016,474	898,000	118,474
KY....	1976-77	1,018,066	973,300	44,766
KY....	1977-78	1,133,308	1,066,600	66,708
LA....	1968-69	472,281	423,400	48,881
LA....	1969-70	526,972	436,200	90,772
LA....	1970-71	635,145	490,200	144,945
LA....	1971-72	727,315	601,400	125,915
LA....	1972-73	940,332	683,000	257,332
LA....	1973-74	946,504	788,700	157,804
LA....	1974-75	881,429	849,900	31,529
LA....	1975-76	1,135,477	1,052,500	82,977
LA....	1976-77	1,237,128	1,224,600	12,528
LA....	1977-78	1,358,360	1,352,400	5,960
MAINE.	1968-69	94,492	81,600	12,892
MAINE.	1969-70	112,485	98,900	13,585
MAINE.	1970-71	163,990	134,600	29,390
MAINE.	1971-72	191,263	172,400	18,863
MAINE.	1972-73	245,848	193,100	52,748
MAINE.	1973-74	277,862	238,700	39,162
MAINE.	1974-75	292,288	271,300	20,988
MAINE.	1975-76	376,041	300,200	75,841
MAINE.	1976-77	411,510	399,200	12,310
MAINE.	1977-78	470,379	410,400	59,979

Yearly State-Area Differences in State-Area Grants-In-Aid Totals
Reported by Treasury and Census, FY 1969-1978 (Thousands of Dollars) (Continued)

Area	Fiscal Year	Reported Grants-In-Aid		Difference
		Treasury	Census	
MD....	1968-69	280,362	282,400	-2,038
MD....	1969-70	395,031	356,600	38,431
MD....	1970-71	466,515	456,100	10,415
MD....	1971-72	547,387	499,300	48,087
MD....	1972-73	785,722	775,600	10,122
MD....	1973-74	750,187	756,100	-5,913
MD....	1974-75	965,565	896,700	68,865
MD....	1975-76	1,119,935	1,091,900	28,035
MD....	1976-77	1,244,922	1,228,800	-16,122
MD....	1977-78	1,318,423	1,454,000	-135,577
MASS..	1968-69	575,201	520,500	54,701
MASS..	1969-70	715,830	607,600	108,230
MASS..	1970-71	838,685	733,400	105,285
MASS..	1971-72	1,101,058	925,400	175,658
MASS..	1972-73	1,251,609	1,075,800	175,809
MASS..	1973-74	1,311,763	1,199,900	111,863
MASS..	1974-75	1,456,161	1,297,500	158,661
MASS..	1975-76	1,820,676	1,631,300	189,376
MASS..	1976-77	2,079,940	1,897,100	182,840
MASS..	1977-78	2,581,488	2,311,300	270,188
MI....	1968-69	673,613	711,000	-37,387
MI....	1969-70	768,758	818,200	-49,442
MI....	1970-71	1,044,548	1,019,200	25,448
MI....	1971-72	1,339,027	1,296,200	42,827
MI....	1972-73	1,743,481	1,769,700	-26,219
MI....	1973-74	1,816,207	1,845,200	-28,993
MI....	1974-75	2,113,454	2,124,400	-10,946
MI....	1975-76	2,615,605	2,667,300	-51,695
MI....	1976-77	2,915,254	2,841,100	74,154
MI....	1977-78	3,280,231	3,131,300	148,931
MINN..	1968-69	367,217	355,500	11,717
MINN..	1969-70	407,362	403,500	3,862
MINN..	1970-71	531,698	435,600	46,098
MINN..	1971-72	636,871	572,900	63,971
MINN..	1972-73	780,388	722,300	58,088
MINN..	1973-74	871,023	820,900	50,123
MINN..	1974-75	900,213	961,700	-61,487
MINN..	1975-76	1,088,723	1,114,900	-26,177
MINN..	1976-77	1,224,464	1,236,300	-11,836
MINN..	1977-78	1,350,015	1,302,900	47,015

Yearly State-Area Differences in State-Area Grants-In-Aid Totals
Reported by Treasury and Census, FY 1969-1928 (Thousands of Dollars) (Continued)

Area	Fiscal Year	Reported Grants-In-Aid		Difference
		Treasury	Census	
MD....	1968-69	280,362	282,400	-2,038
MD....	1969-70	395,031	356,600	38,431
MD....	1970-71	466,515	456,100	10,415
MD....	1971-72	547,387	499,300	48,087
MD....	1972-73	785,722	775,600	10,122
MD....	1973-74	750,187	756,100	-5,913
MD....	1974-75	965,565	896,700	68,865
MD....	1975-76	1,119,935	1,091,900	28,035
MD....	1976-77	1,244,922	1,228,800	16,122
MD....	1977-78	1,318,423	1,454,000	-135,577
MASS..	1968-69	575,201	520,500	54,701
MASS..	1969-70	715,830	607,600	108,230
MASS..	1970-71	838,685	733,400	105,285
MASS..	1971-72	1,101,058	925,400	175,658
MASS..	1972-73	1,251,609	1,075,800	175,809
MASS..	1973-74	1,311,763	1,199,900	111,863
MASS..	1974-75	1,456,161	1,297,500	158,661
MASS..	1975-76	1,820,676	1,711,300	109,376
MASS..	1976-77	2,079,940	1,897,100	182,840
MASS..	1977-78	2,581,488	2,311,300	270,188
MI....	1968-69	673,613	711,000	-37,387
MI....	1969-70	768,758	818,200	-49,442
MI....	1970-71	1,044,548	1,019,100	25,448
MI....	1971-72	1,339,027	1,296,200	42,827
MI....	1972-73	1,743,481	1,769,700	-26,219
MI....	1973-74	1,816,207	1,845,200	-28,993
MI....	1974-75	2,113,454	2,124,400	-10,946
MI....	1975-76	2,615,605	2,667,300	-51,695
MI....	1976-77	2,915,254	2,841,100	74,154
MI....	1977-78	3,280,231	3,131,300	148,931
MINN..	1968-69	367,217	355,500	11,717
MINN..	1969-70	407,362	403,500	3,862
MINN..	1970-71	531,698	485,600	46,098
MINN..	1971-72	636,871	572,900	63,971
MINN..	1972-73	780,388	722,300	58,088
MINN..	1973-74	871,023	820,900	50,123
MINN..	1974-75	900,213	961,700	-61,487
MINN..	1975-76	1,088,723	1,114,900	-26,177
MINN..	1976-77	1,224,464	1,236,300	-11,836
MINN..	1977-78	1,350,915	1,303,900	47,015

Yearly State Area Differences in State Area Grants-In-Aid Totals
Reported by Treasury and Census, FY 1969-1928 (Thousands of Dollars) (Continued)

Area	Fiscal Year	Reported Grants-In-Aid		Difference
		Treasury	Census	
MISS.	1968-69	321,150	219,800	101,350
MISS.	1969-70	413,042	279,400	133,642
MISS.	1970-71	524,570	349,900	174,670
MISS.	1971-72	578,016	401,700	176,316
MISS.	1972-73	680,402	451,800	228,602
MISS.	1973-74	685,910	523,000	162,910
MISS.	1974-75	637,967	575,800	62,167
MISS.	1975-76	783,174	651,000	132,174
MISS.	1976-77	800,688	700,800	99,888
MISS.	1977-78	915,855	849,300	66,555
MO.	1968-69	443,275	386,700	56,575
MO.	1969-70	507,013	455,800	45,213
MO.	1970-71	607,411	518,200	89,211
MO.	1971-72	717,900	617,100	100,800
MO.	1972-73	847,006	677,700	175,306
MO.	1973-74	852,859	727,800	125,059
MO.	1974-75	908,771	835,400	73,371
MO.	1975-76	1,035,936	1,025,800	13,136
MO.	1976-77	1,142,323	1,166,700	-24,377
MO.	1977-78	1,278,467	1,325,100	-46,633
MONT.	1968-69	114,675	93,200	21,475
MONT.	1969-70	135,491	121,800	13,691
MONT.	1970-71	164,966	148,400	16,566
MONT.	1971-72	181,406	163,700	17,706
MONT.	1972-73	212,198	200,900	24,298
MONT.	1973-74	212,860	178,400	34,460
MONT.	1974-75	230,604	222,500	8,104
MONT.	1975-76	288,475	268,400	20,075
MONT.	1976-77	347,632	310,400	37,232
MONT.	1977-78	397,300	365,900	31,400
NEB.	1968-69	124,864	114,700	10,164
NEB.	1969-70	129,783	127,300	2,483
NEB.	1970-71	161,792	159,200	2,592
NEB.	1971-72	203,728	176,800	26,928
NEB.	1972-73	238,228	220,300	17,928
NEB.	1973-74	271,810	249,600	22,210
NEB.	1974-75	338,244	293,700	44,544
NEB.	1975-76	396,312	369,200	27,112
NEB.	1976-77	367,820	359,900	7,920
NEB.	1977-78	458,783	411,100	47,683

APPENDIX TABLE 15

Yearly State-Area Differences in State-Area Grants-In-Aid Totals
Reported by Treasury and Census, FY 1969-1978 (Thousands of Dollars) (Continued)

Area	Fiscal Year	Reported Grants-In-Aid		Difference
		Treasury	Census	
NEV...	1968-69	61,200	70,600	-9,400
NEV...	1969-70	76,828	76,500	328
NEV...	1970-71	82,372	78,000	4,372
NEV...	1971-72	94,609	90,800	3,809
NEV...	1972-73	123,712	115,000	8,712
NEV...	1973-74	126,951	116,300	10,651
NEV...	1974-75	139,056	136,000	3,056
NEV...	1975-76	194,142	168,800	25,342
NEV...	1976-77	206,027	175,000	31,027
NEV...	1977-78	268,909	247,100	21,809
N.H...	1968-69	60,477	56,700	3,777
N.H...	1969-70	72,188	64,000	8,188
N.H...	1970-71	93,064	76,700	16,364
N.H...	1971-72	94,734	88,000	6,734
N.H...	1972-73	144,536	117,800	26,736
N.H...	1973-74	149,617	129,900	19,717
N.H...	1974-75	171,345	163,300	8,045
N.H...	1975-76	212,591	182,700	29,891
N.H...	1976-77	233,703	202,400	31,303
N.H...	1977-78	289,298	246,800	42,498
N.J...	1968-69	502,286	440,000	62,286
N.J...	1969-70	619,739	536,000	83,739
N.J...	1970-71	823,125	761,300	61,825
N.J...	1971-72	1,040,731	906,800	133,931
N.J...	1972-73	1,233,970	1,037,900	196,070
N.J...	1973-74	1,316,469	1,202,400	114,469
N.J...	1974-75	1,501,252	1,399,400	101,852
N.J...	1975-76	1,861,537	1,567,900	293,637
N.J...	1976-77	2,199,862	1,957,500	242,362
N.J...	1977-78	2,552,215	2,031,600	520,615
N.M...	1968-69	189,182	182,300	6,882
N.M...	1969-70	218,815	199,900	18,915
N.M...	1970-71	258,240	219,600	38,640
N.M...	1971-72	294,341	267,400	26,941
N.M...	1972-73	346,553	320,400	26,153
N.M...	1973-74	337,182	317,900	19,282
N.M...	1974-75	399,300	342,500	56,800
N.M...	1975-76	427,588	373,000	54,588
N.M...	1976-77	449,345	427,300	22,045
N.M...	1977-78	608,411	509,000	99,411

APPENDIX TABLE 15

Yearly State-Area Differences in State-Area Grants-In-Aid Totals
Reported by Treasury and Census, FY 1969-1978 (Thousands of Dollars) (Continued)

Area	Fiscal Year	Reported Grants-In-Aid Treasury	Reported Grants-In-Aid Census	Difference
N.Y.	1968-69	2,047,620	1,967,500	80,120
N.Y.	1969-70	2,365,629	2,214,600	151,029
N.Y.	1970-71	3,286,406	2,443,900	842,506
N.Y.	1971-72	4,402,876	3,349,100	1,053,776
N.Y.	1972-73	4,797,242	4,966,300	-169,058
N.Y.	1973-74	5,221,037	4,450,200	770,837
N.Y.	1974-75	5,682,478	5,006,000	676,478
N.Y.	1975-76	6,417,280	6,064,300	352,980
N.Y.	1976-77	6,446,787	6,515,100	931,687
N.Y.	1977-78	8,372,465	7,085,500	1,286,965
N.C.	1968-69	440,913	352,000	88,913
N.C.	1969-70	507,068	414,100	92,968
N.C.	1970-71	643,043	567,100	75,943
N.C.	1971-72	736,262	625,000	111,262
N.C.	1972-73	937,331	835,700	101,631
N.C.	1973-74	975,396	873,200	102,196
N.C.	1974-75	1,049,787	1,216,100	-166,313
N.C.	1975-76	1,275,040	1,179,700	95,340
N.C.	1976-77	1,511,942	1,555,000	-43,058
N.C.	1977-78	1,655,955	1,603,000	52,955
N.D.	1968-69	75,675	72,400	3,275
N.D.	1969-70	87,725	78,000	9,725
N.D.	1970-71	113,514	116,200	-2,686
N.D.	1971-72	127,008	109,600	17,408
N.D.	1972-73	163,515	142,700	20,815
N.D.	1973-74	152,208	147,400	4,808
N.D.	1974-75	170,856	161,100	9,756
N.D.	1975-76	204,909	179,000	25,909
N.D.	1976-77	224,401	238,900	-14,499
N.D.	1977-78	259,138	246,200	12,933
OHIO	1968-69	785,045	748,400	36,645
OHIO	1969-70	888,453	772,300	116,153
OHIO	1970-71	1,015,912	867,400	148,512
OHIO	1971-72	1,208,151	1,020,100	188,051
OHIO	1972-73	1,592,115	1,246,200	345,915
OHIO	1973-74	1,760,225	1,569,300	190,925
OHIO	1974-75	1,788,060	1,763,800	24,260
OHIO	1975-76	2,134,818	1,988,800	146,618
OHIO	1976-77	2,510,305	2,260,900	249,405
OHIO	1977-78	2,904,685	2,594,500	310,185

Yearly State-Area Differences in State-Area Grants-In-Aid Totals
Reported by Treasury and Census, FY 1969-1978 (Thousands of Dollars) (Continued)

Area	Fiscal Year	Reported Grants-In-Aid		Difference
		Treasury	Census	
OKLA..	1968-69	376,400	342,500	33,900
OKLA..	1969-70	403,759	366,100	37,659
OKLA..	1970-71	458,380	383,800	74,580
OKLA..	1971-72	500,668	443,900	56,768
OKLA..	1972-73	589,233	514,300	74,933
OKLA..	1973-74	597,776	559,100	38,676
OKLA..	1974-75	713,914	625,600	88,314
OKLA..	1975-76	688,866	681,300	7,566
OKLA..	1976-77	782,019	803,900	-21,881
OKLA..	1977-78	937,180	864,200	72,980
ORE...	1968-69	236,303	244,100	-7,797
ORE...	1969-70	297,956	284,100	13,856
ORE...	1970-71	384,901	388,600	-3,699
ORE...	1971-72	439,259	412,600	26,659
ORE...	1972-73	577,789	543,300	34,489
ORE...	1973-74	557,718	547,900	9,818
ORE...	1974-75	600,487	722,800	-122,313
ORE...	1975-76	795,997	789,100	6,897
ORE...	1976-77	836,132	891,100	-54,968
ORE...	1977-78	1,075,400	1,053,900	21,500
PA....	1968-69	989,562	904,200	85,362
PA....	1969-70	1,343,171	1,005,100	338,071
PA....	1970-71	1,391,169	1,301,600	89,569
PA....	1971-72	1,621,145	1,439,300	181,845
PA....	1972-73	2,357,661	1,801,000	556,461
PA....	1973-74	2,390,490	2,178,000	212,490
PA....	1974-75	2,697,909	2,376,200	321,709
PA....	1975-76	3,121,571	2,975,300	146,271
PA....	1976-77	3,628,059	3,145,600	482,459
PA....	1977-78	3,912,086	3,438,600	473,486
R.I...	1968-69	104,671	92,200	12,471
R.I...	1969-70	132,690	117,100	15,590
R.I...	1970-71	138,180	127,100	11,080
R.I...	1971-72	178,307	153,300	25,007
R.I...	1972-73	238,667	225,800	12,867
R.I...	1973-74	248,846	209,400	39,446
R.I...	1974-75	248,917	230,900	18,017
R.I...	1975-76	311,639	310,800	839
R.I...	1976-77	357,546	345,400	12,146
R.I...	1977-78	388,000	358,700	29,300

Yearly State-Area Differences in State-Area Grants-In-Aid Totals
Reported by Treasury and Census, FY 1969-1978 (Thousands of Dollars) (Continued)

Area	Fiscal Year	Reported Grants-In-Aid		Difference
		Treasury	Census	
S.C...	1968-69	228,532	181,300	47,232
S.C...	1969-70	278,078	217,700	60,378
S.C...	1970-71	365,873	274,500	91,373
S.C...	1971-72	407,913	319,700	88,213
S.C...	1972-73	556,630	456,200	100,430
S.C...	1973-74	559,268	486,600	72,668
S.C...	1974-75	574,740	558,300	16,440
S.C...	1975-76	697,106	671,200	25,906
S.C...	1976-77	802,540	750,700	51,840
S.C...	1977-78	903,414	851,000	52,414
S.D...	1968-69	92,794	88,800	3,994
S.D...	1969-70	103,686	92,600	11,086
S.D...	1970-71	116,778	103,300	13,478
S.D...	1971-72	132,169	115,400	16,769
S.D...	1972-73	198,675	156,600	42,075
S.D...	1973-74	210,032	178,700	31,332
S.D...	1974-75	213,232	191,200	22,032
S.D...	1975-76	228,249	215,000	13,249
S.D...	1976-77	240,454	218,900	21,554
S.D...	1977-78	288,446	250,700	37,746
TENN...	1968-69	393,452	343,800	49,652
TENN...	1969-70	487,031	416,500	70,531
TENN...	1970-71	616,720	529,600	87,120
TENN...	1971-72	703,618	549,600	154,018
TENN...	1972-73	816,365	709,700	106,665
TENN...	1973-74	851,141	730,600	120,541
TENN...	1974-75	910,734	837,400	73,334
TENN...	1975-76	1,083,348	1,015,800	67,548
TENN...	1976-77	1,188,617	1,098,400	90,217
TENN...	1977-78	1,330,860	1,254,700	76,160
TEX...	1968-69	944,867	874,800	70,067
TEX...	1969-70	1,153,405	1,022,200	131,205
TEX...	1970-71	1,388,135	1,240,300	147,835
TEX...	1971-72	1,647,956	1,441,400	206,556
TEX...	1972-73	2,055,628	1,691,700	363,928
TEX...	1973-74	2,128,082	1,900,000	228,082
TEX...	1974-75	2,200,105	2,196,500	3,605
TEX...	1975-76	2,604,263	2,558,700	45,563
TEX...	1976-77	2,885,381	2,726,300	159,081
TEX...	1977-78	3,295,287	3,038,300	256,987

APPENDIX TABLE 1.5

Yearly State-Area Differences in State-Area Grants-In-Aid Totals
Reported by Treasury and Census, FY 1969-1928 (Thousands of Dollars) (Continued)

Area	Fiscal Year	Reported Grants-In-Aid		Difference
		Treasury	Census	
UTAH...	1968-69	134,472	149,600	-15,128
UTAH...	1969-70	173,847	174,800	-953
UTAH...	1970-71	185,022	198,800	-13,778
UTAH...	1971-72	220,179	225,200	-5,021
UTAH...	1972-73	260,802	270,400	-9,598
UTAH...	1973-74	275,247	268,000	-7,247
UTAH...	1974-75	294,104	307,100	-13,296
UTAH...	1975-76	359,361	381,100	-21,739
UTAH...	1976-77	387,837	415,800	-27,963
UTAH...	1977-78	434,261	466,600	-32,339
VER...	1968-69	75,451	73,200	2,251
VER...	1969-70	77,105	72,600	4,505
VER...	1970-71	96,438	93,800	2,638
VER...	1971-72	108,505	102,500	6,005
VER...	1972-73	138,112	123,000	15,112
VER...	1973-74	150,773	141,900	8,873
VER...	1974-75	154,252	158,100	-3,848
VER...	1975-76	176,963	190,400	-13,437
VER...	1976-77	222,501	202,900	19,601
VER...	1977-78	240,659	239,300	1,359
VA...	1968-69	370,223	358,900	11,323
VA...	1969-70	465,682	408,700	56,982
VA...	1970-71	571,854	520,600	51,254
VA...	1971-72	622,860	582,600	40,260
VA...	1972-73	828,077	752,300	75,777
VA...	1973-74	890,559	807,800	82,759
VA...	1974-75	1,004,305	995,200	9,105
VA...	1975-76	1,185,831	1,116,300	69,531
VA...	1976-77	1,311,454	1,298,300	13,154
VA...	1977-78	1,468,126	1,500,000	-31,874
WASH...	1968-69	324,093	352,100	-28,007
WASH...	1969-70	400,451	399,200	1,251
WASH...	1970-71	501,772	472,100	29,672
WASH...	1971-72	633,633	557,100	76,533
WASH...	1972-73	829,474	800,200	29,274
WASH...	1973-74	792,930	702,400	90,530
WASH...	1974-75	798,108	886,400	-88,292
WASH...	1975-76	979,689	959,200	20,489
WASH...	1976-77	1,118,893	1,273,900	-155,007
WASH...	1977-78	1,311,062	1,185,700	125,362

Yearly State-Area Differences in State-Area Grants-in-Aid Totals
Reported by Treasury and Census, FY 1969-1978 (Thousands of Dollars) (Continued)

Area	Fiscal Year	Reported Grants-In-Aid		Difference
		Treasury	Census	
W.VA..	1968-69	264,849	232,200	32,649
W.VA..	1969-70	303,698	264,300	39,398
W.VA..	1970-71	405,148	341,800	63,348
W.VA..	1971-72	448,176	350,300	97,876
W.VA..	1972-73	536,022	450,000	86,022
W.VA..	1973-74	581,623	483,900	97,723
W.VA..	1974-75	551,472	505,300	46,172
W.VA..	1975-76	689,874	552,700	137,174
W.VA..	1976-77	631,233	580,000	51,233
W.VA..	1977-78	707,622	656,700	50,922
WIS...	1968-69	314,187	325,700	-11,513
WIS...	1969-70	368,704	361,400	7,304
WIS...	1970-71	422,299	397,500	24,799
WIS...	1971-72	524,980	516,500	8,480
WIS...	1972-73	778,284	725,100	53,184
WIS...	1973-74	817,868	791,000	26,868
WIS...	1974-75	919,714	919,100	614
WIS...	1975-76	1,165,409	1,188,800	-23,391
WIS...	1976-77	1,493,308	1,250,300	243,008
WIS...	1977-78	1,607,427	1,433,300	174,127
WY....	1968-69	84,086	83,500	586
WY....	1969-70	83,493	84,300	-807
WY....	1970-71	85,876	86,100	-224
WY....	1971-72	127,428	96,400	31,028
WY....	1972-73	115,059	109,400	5,659
WY....	1973-74	119,426	109,900	9,526
WY....	1974-75	132,289	142,100	-9,811
WY....	1975-76	166,657	188,100	-21,443
WY....	1976-77	185,644	197,800	-12,156
WY....	1977-78	235,707	225,500	10,207
NATION*	1968-69	19,742,197	19,152,400	589,797
NATION*	1969-70	23,717,466	21,857,400	1,860,066
NATION*	1970-71	29,272,078	26,145,600	3,126,478
NATION*	1971-72	35,216,970	31,252,900	3,964,070
NATION*	1972-73	43,056,508	39,255,600	3,800,908
NATION*	1973-74	45,092,172	41,831,100	3,261,072
NATION*	1974-75	48,569,836	46,994,200	1,575,636
NATION*	1975-76	57,718,501	55,587,100	2,131,401
NATION*	1976-77	66,083,740	62,609,800	3,473,940
NATION*	1977-78	75,293,471	69,592,400	5,701,071

AREA	NET DOMESTIC	AG	COM	DOD	EPA	GSA	HEW	HUD	INT	JUST	LABOR	NASA	SBA	DOT	TREA	VA	OTHER AGENCIES
ALA....	1.72	1.71	1.27	2.31	1.61	1.07	.66	1.68	.36	.88	1.17	5.03	2.76	1.18	1.16	2.01	1.59
ALK....	.41	.38	1.04	.86	.11	.30	.12	1.08	6.77	.28	.44		.02	1.60	.27	.91	.18
ARZ....	.33	.94	1.27	1.71	.70	.50	1.02	3.39	8.64	1.49	1.78	.33	.64	.93	.88	1.93	.84
ARK....	.96	1.85	.34	1.80	.51	.57	1.04	.69	.53	1.56	1.46	.00	.70	.79	.68	1.11	.58
CAL....	10.61	4.92	8.29	14.48	9.52	8.04	10.39	14.21	12.63	11.01	12.41	39.97	8.28	6.87	9.87	13.01	8.85
COL....	.66	.66	2.51	2.26	.91	1.99	1.41	2.19	8.19	1.47	1.15		1.43	6.14	.91	3.14	.43
CONN...	1.07	.79	2.73	4.06	.33	.51	1.43	.91	.18	1.17	.80	1.39	.89	1.36	.99	.27	.87
DEL....	.25	.16		.30	.14	.51	.24	.17	.08	.28	.26	1.64	.33	.95	.51		
D.C....	3.03	1.00	11.13	1.50	7.54	21.43	4.87	1.57	8.23	17.43	5.69	.01	1.08	.01	5.73	1.94	5.00
FLA....	4.17	2.31	1.37	5.24	2.81	.90	4.45	1.45	.07	3.29	5.54	1.63	3.33	3.05	2.66	5.18	3.20
GA.....	2.82	2.89	.77	3.21	2.67	.79	3.01	3.11	1.01	2.40	1.93	8.09	5.68	1.46	12.77	.98	.08
HA.....	.58	.36	.35	2.14	.84	.10	.34	.26	1.95	.40	.62	.05	.24	.80	.26	.67	.38
IDA....	.52	1.17	.39	.43	.82	.13	.32	.47	2.47	.22	.90	.34	.72	.55	.44	.57	.74
ILL....	1.90	3.36	1.51	2.34	2.98	5.84	5.00	2.66	.71	4.30	4.52	.19	1.07	6.68	3.93	3.64	9.27
IND....	1.26	1.16	.95	1.16	.99	1.16	1.24	1.58	.65	1.42	2.18	.09	1.46	1.91	1.40	1.59	1.32
IOWA...	.17	1.55	.11	.23	.48	.29	.99	.73	.46	1.05	.67	.05	1.80	.88	.76	1.05	.81
KAN....	1.55	3.16	.31	.38	.92	.86	1.54	1.45	.40	1.46	1.64	.34	.80	1.18	.59	.91	.24
KY.....	1.57	1.55	.61	2.24	.75	.42	1.52	1.29	.43	1.10	1.68	.01	.93	.30	1.42	1.62	2.12
LA.....	2.05	2.05	9.58	1.53	.30	2.68	2.18	2.24	.18	1.44	1.61	2.46	.78	1.38	1.73	1.19	1.07
MAINE..	.48	.56	.43	1.48	.20	.83	3.18	.36	.85	.89	.68	.02	.06	1.00	.50	.54	.35
MD.....	2.38	.96	11.58	3.24	1.41	1.14	4.74	3.00	1.15	2.62	3.33	.90	.79	1.38	2.90	2.08	3.21
MASS...	2.47	.86	1.03	1.45	4.20	.18	1.08	.36	.84	1.27	1.16	.14	3.06	.17	.56	2.10	.18
MI.....	3.01	2.95	.93	1.23	1.78	.42	1.74	.87	1.23	2.31	1.95	.39	.83	1.70	.43	2.08	1.86
MINN...	.88	2.63	.89	.46	.21	.68	1.08	2.00	.02	.29	.22	.36	.06	.51	.23	1.77	.24
MISS...	1.16	2.65	.67	1.71	.47	.25	.32	.50	1.62	.30	.40	.15	.79	.49	.82	.42	.56
MO.....	2.17	1.38	2.67	2.04	.90	4.75	.65	1.49	2.62	.27	.52	.03	.13	.36	.82	.80	2.48
MONT...	.48	1.37	.16	.29	.81	.16	.24	1.84	.35	.23	.40	.03	.56	.87	.43	.63	.72
NEB....	.90	.15	.15	.71	.47	.03	.36	.88	1.10	.52	.39	.05	1.24	.76	.23	.66	.63
NEV....	.36	.35	.07	.62	.51	.48	.19	.49	1.35	.23	.47	.03	.15	.87	.52	.53	.27
N.H....	.82	.79	3.07	2.04	.44	5.13	.43	.56	.54	.52	.55	.04	.25	.35	2.82	2.16	2.51
N.J....	7.91	6.26	1.35	2.12	.72	7.76	3.46	.80	.43	.23	4.67	1.25	1.37	1.45	.52	.80	1.81
N.Y....	2.15	2.18	17.38	3.54	.19	1.37	10.13	8.50	1.00	8.11	11.18	1.34	.89	.76	10.87	5.04	.96
N.C....	1.52	2.12	1.08	3.46	.78	.19	2.18	1.59	.14	.24	1.54	1.08	5.63	.35	1.62	2.39	1.17
N.D....	.62	2.03	.08	.65	1.45	.31	.28	.61	.67	.23	.23	.79	.41	.03	.18	.30	.21
OHIO...	3.62	1.86	.80	2.46	2.19	.20	4.46	3.61	4.67	2.23	4.00	3.01	1.68	3.03	.07	4.19	3.84
OKLA...	1.40	2.03	.69	2.35	.51	.68	1.27	1.50	1.00	.88	1.11	.04	.71	.52	.80	1.51	.21
ORE....	1.12	2.12	.08	.50	.72	.19	1.13	3.57	4.67	.03	.99	.02	2.88	1.69	.87	.83	.95
PA.....	4.49	2.01	2.08	3.03	2.51	2.71	6.09	.36	.04	2.59	4.64	.25	2.86	.26	4.88	3.71	1.17
R.I....	.29	.11	1.40	.50	.35	.13	.09	1.38	1.73	.61	.87	.01	.21	4.12	.37	.30	.31
S.C....	1.45	1.40	.57	2.30	.34	.09	.29	2.55	.44	.21	.20	.11	1.84	.67	.91	.67	1.31
S.D....	.20	.83	.22	.15	.66	.66	.84	.94	.52	.92	.45	.59	.32	.25	.56	.01	.20
TENN...	.51	7.25	2.17	18.11	4.35	.48	4.72	1.13	2.52	.38	.18	9.59	1.84	1.43	1.01	.53	5.74
TEX....	.69	.26	.26	8.41	.19	.50	4.40	4.06	2.46	.35	1.31	1.49	7.15	1.54	.76	7.52	.59
UTAH...	.20	.14	.43	1.16	1.56	3.91	.83	.87	3.18	2.28	.66	1.01	.32	.21	.24	.15	.16
VER....	.92	.81	2.43	7.88	.71	3.07	1.83	2.22	.63	2.08	.26	.86	1.26	2.89	1.25	4.85	4.02
VA.....	2.92	1.81	2.28	6.41	.76	.36	.95	1.67	3.18	.85	.79	.09	2.28	1.08	.85	1.98	2.82
WASH...	.20	1.53	.83	2.88	2.93	.28	2.18	.43	.62	1.32	1.72	5.15	.74	1.29	1.49	1.72	.61
W.VA...	.74	1.74		.21	.11	.36	.13	.08		.11	.14	.00	.98	.35	.85	1.45	1.05
WIS....	1.60	2.17	.07	.38		.08		.13	2.62			.01	.62		.12	.35	.29
WY.....	.25	.47		.20													

APPENDIX TABLE 6.1--STATE LEVEL DOLLAR DIFFERENCES (THOUSANDS $), IN GRANTS-IN-AID REPORTED IN C.S.A., F.A.T.S., AND B.O.C.

AREA	FY YEAR	DOLLAR DIFFERENCES		
		CSA-FATS	CSA-BOC	FATS-BOC
ALA...	1970-71	-79,602	31,132	110,735
ALA...	1971-72	-13,182	63,651	76,833
ALA...	1972-73	-28,832	160,320	189,152
ALA...	1973-74	-83,501	32,374	115,875
ALA...	1974-75	200,478	212,713	12,235
ALA...	1975-76	35,244	85,578	50,334
ALA...	T.Q.	22,281		
ALA...	1976-77	263,528	301,347	37,819
ALA...	1977-78	136,670	221,339	84,669
ALK...	1970-71	-18,342	-17,892	450
ALK...	1971-72	71,326	82,495	11,169
ALK...	1972-73	12,809	18,125	5,316
ALK...	1973-74	21,993	36,200	14,207
ALK...	1974-75	110,199	112,056	1,857
ALK...	1975-76	-64,063	-53,310	10,753
ALK...	T.Q.	75,018		
ALK...	1976-77	-9,914	145,222	70,204
ALK...	1977-78		52,297	62,211
ARZ...	1970-71	36,729	47,666	10,937
ARZ...	1971-72	63,542	89,514	25,972
ARZ...	1972-73	-28,853	78,879	50,026
ARZ...	1973-74	-18,363	49,693	68,056
ARZ...	1974-75	155,738	197,242	41,504
ARZ...	1975-76	27,567	68,776	41,209
ARZ...	T.Q.	69,534		
ARZ...	1976-77	252,741	377,476	124,735
ARZ...	1977-78	84,524	188,642	104,118
ARK...	1970-71	-3,370	72,765	76,135
ARK...	1971-72	-41,346	39,042	80,388
ARK...	1972-73	-44,973	64,722	109,695
ARK...	1973-74	-56,480	26,901	83,381
ARK...	1974-75	123,735	168,408	44,673
ARK...	1975-76	99,829	132,696	32,867
ARK...	T.Q.	46,740		
ARK...	1976-77	250,449	307,439	56,990
ARK...	1977-78	31,302	101,976	70,674

APPENDIX TABLE 6.1—STATE LEVEL DOLLAR DIFFERENCES, (THOUSANDS $), IN GRANTS-IN-AID REPORTED IN C.S.A., F.A.T.S., AND B.O.C. (CONTINUED)

AREA	FY YEAR	DOLLAR DIFFERENCES		
		CSA-FATS	CSA-BOC	FATS-BOC
CAL...	1970-71	76,862	-30,573	-107,435
CAL...	1971-72	36,270	-17,763	-54,033
CAL...	1972-73	20,194	-397,734	-417,928
CAL...	1973-74	217,019	-106,592	-323,611
CAL...	1974-75	1,417,655	1,165,588	-252,067
CAL...	1975-76	799,042	374,496	-424,546
CAL...	T.Q.	374,021		
CAL...	1976-77	2,979,300	2,369,730	-609,570
CAL...	1977-78	879,729	580,894	-298,835
COL...	1970-71	57,544	98,009	40,466
COL...	1971-72	59,446	77,903	18,457
COL...	1972-73	74,138	90,710	16,572
COL...	1973-74	72,516	44,544	-27,972
COL...	1974-75	233,071	236,503	3,432
COL...	1975-76	53,284	-1,019	-54,303
COL...	T.Q.	10,657		
COL...	1976-77	341,142	288,285	-52,857
COL...	1977-78	202,326	168,581	-33,745
CONN.	1970-71	6,729	85,187	78,458
CONN.	1971-72	70,853	146,781	75,928
CONN.	1972-73	83,472	166,418	82,946
CONN.	1973-74	63	119,794	119,731
CONN.	1974-75	106,567	190,311	83,744
CONN.	1975-76	154,959	243,409	88,450
CONN.	T.Q.	46,296		
CONN.	1976-77	340,883	525,664	184,781
CONN.	1977-78	23,839	224,036	200,197
DEL...	1970-71	10,431	17,615	7,184
DEL...	1971-72	14,985	13,133	-1,852
DEL...	1972-73	6,625	11,416	4,791
DEL...	1973-74	26,080	23,835	-2,245
DEL...	1974-75	56,601	46,417	-10,184
DEL...	1975-76	15,363	2,970	-12,393
DEL...	T.Q.	-1,737		
DEL...	1976-77	102,191	89,593	-12,598
DEL...	1977-78	-14,651	-36,418	-21,767

AREA	FY YEAR	DOLLAR DIFFERENCES		
		CSA-FATS	CSA-BOC	FATS-BOC
D.C...	1970-71	228,538	476,261	247,723
D.C...	1971-72	190,334	248,027	57,693
D.C...	1972-73	706,259	685,633	-20,626
D.C...	1973-74	542,168	455,580	-86,588
D.C...	1974-75	672,815	678,944	6,129
D.C...	1975-76	863,716	800,359	-63,357
D.C...	T.Q.	1,278,175		
D.C...	1976-77	1,276,925	1,045,061	-231,864
D.C...	1977-78	1,664,450	1,647,249	-17,201
FLA...	1970-71	47,944	121,631	73,686
FLA...	1971-72	176,475	274,481	98,006
FLA...	1972-73	-42,644	173,244	215,888
FLA...	1973-74	-23,590	67,873	-91,463
FLA...	1974-75	557,833	544,851	-12,982
FLA...	1975-76	348,108	384,796	36,688
FLA...	T.Q.	152,140		
FLA...	1976-77	980,307	1,189,021	208,714
FLA...	1977-78	95,856	329,542	233,686
GA...	1970-71	35,913	142,402	106,489
GA...	1971-72	40,076	149,157	109,081
GA...	1972-73	216,345	237,193	20,848
GA...	1973-74	-158,309	-30,940	127,369
GA...	1974-75	469,489	506,950	37,461
GA...	1975-76	-42,093	134,704	176,797
GA...	T.Q.	122,102		
GA...	1976-77	602,239	1,089,944	487,705
GA...	1977-78	-71,260	289,633	360,893
HA...	1970-71	22,168	-893	-23,061
HA...	1971-72	-292	-27,737	-27,445
HA...	1972-73	20,312	-3,547	-16,765
HA...	1973-74	-7,807	-16,299	-8,492
HA...	1974-75	180,946	-136,224	-44,722
HA...	1975-76	5,586	-77,863	-83,449
HA...	T.Q.	59,783		
HA...	1976-77	30,415	-28,241	-58,656
HA...	1977-78	75,630	10,921	-64,709

APPENDIX TABLE 6.1—STATE LEVEL DOLLAR DIFFERENCES (THOUSANDS $) IN GRANTS-IN-AID REPORTED IN C.S.A., F.A.T.S., AND B.O.C. (CONTINUED)

| AREA | FY YEAR | DOLLAR DIFFERENCES | | |
		CSA–FATS	CSA–BOC	FATS–BOC
IDA...	1970-71	10,864	17,801	6,937
IDA...	1971-72	8,905	20,741	11,836
IDA...	1972-73	538	22,830	22,292
IDA...	1973-74	-15,073	-11,921	3,152
IDA...	1974-75	59,889	82,028	22,139
IDA...	1975-76	-47,728	-19,128	28,600
IDA...	T.Q.	36,484		
IDA...	1976-77	91,855	109,130	17,275
IDA...	1977-78	1,937	49,152	47,215
ILL...	1970-71	112,177	32,319	-79,858
ILL...	1971-72	36,351	-41,774	-78,125
ILL...	1972-73	174,937	-269,666	-94,729
ILL...	1973-74	-119,368	-250,803	-131,435
ILL...	1974-75	993,097	1,038,877	45,780
ILL...	1975-76	80,345	281,612	201,267
ILL...	T.Q.	481,919		
ILL...	1976-77	908,572	1,294,660	386,088
ILL...	1977-78	1,119,468	1,681,919	562,451
IND...	1970-71	40,444	56,072	15,629
IND...	1971-72	32,169	91,544	59,375
IND...	1972-73	39,506	159,530	120,024
IND...	1973-74	13,011	74,631	61,620
IND...	1974-75	360,115	429,305	69,190
IND...	1975-76	23,948	106,692	82,744
IND...	T.Q.	131,501		
IND...	1976-77	456,807	548,000	91,193
IND...	1977-78	165,470	288,849	123,379
IOWA...	1970-71	-6,482	22,710	29,192
IOWA...	1971-72	9,950	35,125	25,175
IOWA...	1972-73	20,495	81,899	61,404
IOWA...	1973-74	39,222	56,776	17,554
IOWA...	1974-75	78,019	56,439	-21,580
IOWA...	1975-76	77,240	58,477	-18,763
IOWA...	T.Q.	6,443		
IOWA...	1976-77	127,938	125,458	-2,480
IOWA...	1977-78	65,685	72,578	6,893

APPENDIX TABLE 6.1--STATE LEVEL DOLLAR DIFFERENCES (THOUSANDS $) IN
GRANTS-IN-AID REPORTED IN C.S.A., F.A.T.S., AND B.O.C. (CONTINUED)

AREA	FY YEAR	DOLLAR DIFFERENCES		
		CSA-FATS	CSA-BOC	FATS-BOC
KAN....	1970-71	41,714	57,099	15,385
KAN....	1971-72	20,022	36,394	16,372
KAN....	1972-73	-3,806	42,277	46,083
KAN....	1973-74	-26	29,142	29,168
KAN....	1974-75	82,638	101,625	18,987
KAN....	1975-76	-3,826	20,021	23,847
KAN....	T.Q.	47,660		
KAN....	1976-77	219,979	222,303	2,324
KAN....	1977-78	64,686	117,606	52,920
KY.....	1970-71	-17,218	1,066	18,284
KY.....	1971-72	37,033	146,294	109,261
KY.....	1972-73	-51,764	86,431	138,195
KY.....	1973-74	-139,444	-7,754	131,690
KY.....	1974-75	243,438	301,966	58,528
KY.....	1975-76	29,804	148,278	118,474
KY.....	T.Q.	45,226		
KY.....	1976-77	380,122	424,888	44,766
KY.....	1977-78	250,118	316,826	66,708
LA.....	1970-71	-24,428	120,516	144,945
LA.....	1971-72	-93,900	32,015	125,915
LA.....	1972-73	-48,075	209,257	257,332
LA.....	1973-74	-166,650	-8,846	157,804
LA.....	1974-75	299,601	331,130	31,529
LA.....	1975-76	129,298	212,275	82,977
LA.....	T.Q.	74,817		
LA.....	1976-77	340,662	353,190	12,528
LA.....	1977-78	120,855	126,815	5,960
MAINE.	1970-71	9,603	38,993	29,390
MAINE.	1971-72	-3,613	15,250	18,863
MAINE.	1972-73	32,739	85,487	52,748
MAINE.	1973-74	-24,043	15,119	39,162
MAINE.	1974-75	78,706	99,694	20,988
MAINE.	1975-76	53,794	129,635	75,841
MAINE.	T.Q.	13,418		
MAINE.	1976-77	63,604	75,914	12,310
MAINE.	1977-78	12,842	72,821	59,979

APPENDIX TABLE 6.1--STATE-LEVEL DOLLAR DIFFERENCES (THOUSANDS $) IN GRANTS-IN-AID REPORTED IN C.S.A., F.A.T.S., AND B.O.C. (CONTINUED)

AREA	FY YEAR	DOLLAR DIFFERENCES		
		CSA-FATS	CSA-BOC	FATS-BOC
MD.....	1970-71	324,423	334,838	10,415
MD.....	1971-72	140,253	188,340	48,087
MD.....	1972-73	379,959	390,081	10,122
MD.....	1973-74	229,179	223,266	-5,913
MD.....	1974-75	518,626	587,491	68,865
MD.....	1975-76	204,712	232,747	28,035
MD.....	T.Q.	18,346		
MD.....	1976-77	753,066	769,188	16,122
MD.....	1977-78	564,383	428,806	-135,577
MASS...	1970-71	165,117	270,402	105,285
MASS...	1971-72	41,556	217,214	175,658
MASS...	1972-73	413,902	589,711	175,809
MASS...	1973-74	260,143	372,006	111,863
MASS...	1974-75	590,426	749,087	158,661
MASS...	1975-76	261,820	371,196	109,376
MASS...	T.Q.	212,418		
MASS...	1976-77	1,048,032	1,230,872	182,840
MASS...	1977-78	600,668	870,856	270,188
MI.....	1970-71	107,773	133,222	25,448
MI.....	1971-72	126,153	168,980	42,827
MI.....	1972-73	195,841	169,622	-26,219
MI.....	1973-74	-49,195	-78,188	-28,993
MI.....	1974-75	714,561	703,615	-10,946
MI.....	1975-76	-123,888	-175,583	-51,695
MI.....	T.Q.	350,012		
MI.....	1976-77	1,059,657	1,133,811	74,154
MI.....	1977-78	393,870	542,801	148,931
MINN...	1970-71	-19,897	65,995	46,098
MINN...	1971-72	-36,881	27,090	63,971
MINN...	1972-73	103,410	161,498	58,088
MINN...	1973-74	-40,393	9,730	50,123
MINN...	1974-75	275,560	214,073	-61,487
MINN...	1975-76	92,195	66,018	-26,177
MINN...	T.Q.	40,494		
MINN...	1976-77	299,281	287,445	-11,836
MINN...	1977-78	92,415	139,430	47,015

AREA	FY YEAR	DOLLAR DIFFERENCES		
		CSA-FATS	CSA-BOC	FATS-BOC
MISS...	1970-71	-88,499	86,171	174,670
MISS...	1971-72	-96,919	79,397	176,316
MISS...	1972-73	-80,336	148,266	228,602
MISS...	1973-74	-151,123	11,787	162,910
MISS...	1974-75	197,865	260,032	62,167
MISS...	1975-76	-15,935	116,239	132,174
MISS...	T.Q.	78,255		
MISS...	1976-77	281,282	381,170	99,888
MISS...	1977-78	184,418	250,973	66,555
MO...	1970-71	-2,914	86,297	89,211
MO...	1971-72	-10,177	90,623	100,800
MO...	1972-73	-3,253	178,559	175,306
MO...	1973-74	-258,342	102,928	125,059
MO...	1974-75	213,924	331,713	73,371
MO...	1975-76	111,975	227,060	13,136
MO...	T.Q.	324,700		
MO...	1976-77	300,687	300,323	-24,377
MO...	1977-78		254,054	-46,633
MONT...	1970-71	11,125	27,690	16,566
MONT...	1971-72	6,164	23,870	17,706
MONT...	1972-73	-13,882	10,416	24,298
MONT...	1973-74	-6,964	27,496	34,460
MONT...	1974-75	100,742	108,846	8,104
MONT...	1975-76	11,857	31,932	20,075
MONT...	T.Q.	-3,139		
MONT...	1976-77	66,759	103,991	37,232
MONT...	1977-78	-25,893	5,507	31,400
NEB...	1970-71	18,718	21,310	2,592
NEB...	1971-72	5,216	32,144	26,928
NEB...	1972-73	40,709	58,637	17,928
NEB...	1973-74	-7,671	14,539	22,210
NEB...	1974-75	68,117	112,661	44,544
NEB...	1975-76	-54,434	-27,322	27,112
NEB...	T.Q.	-15,840		
NEB...	1976-77	97,725	105,645	7,920
NEB...	1977-78	11,071	58,754	47,683

AREA	FY YEAR	DOLLAR DIFFERENCES CSA-FATS	DOLLAR DIFFERENCES CSA-BOC	DOLLAR DIFFERENCES FATS-BOC
NEV.	1970-71	-150	4,222	4,372
NEV.	1971-72	19,570	23,379	3,809
NEV.	1972-73	-1,838	6,874	8,712
NEV.	1973-74	2,699	13,350	10,651
NEV.	1974-75	49,859	52,915	3,056
NEV.	1975-76	8,534	33,876	25,342
NEV.	T.Q.	21,451		
NEV.	1976-77	48,711	79,738	31,027
NEV.	1977-78	14,806	36,615	21,809
N.H.	1970-71	10,586	26,950	16,364
N.H.	1971-72	22,562	29,296	6,734
N.H.	1972-73	2,943	47,679	26,736
N.H.	1973-74	2,654	22,371	19,717
N.H.	1974-75	59,833	67,878	8,045
N.H.	1975-76	11,413	41,304	29,891
N.H.	T.Q.	15,860		
N.H.	1976-77	103,988	135,291	31,303
N.H.	1977-78	3,242	45,740	42,498
N.J.	1970-71	66,147	127,972	61,825
N.J.	1971-72	-31,166	102,765	133,931
N.J.	1972-73	273,138	469,208	196,070
N.J.	1973-74	-27,439	87,030	114,469
N.J.	1974-75	470,379	572,231	101,852
N.J.	1975-76	342,941	636,578	293,637
N.J.	T.Q.	125,143		
N.J.	1976-77	681,819	924,181	242,362
N.J.	1977-78	1,182	521,797	520,615
N.MEX.	1970-71	-7,562	31,078	38,640
N.MEX.	1971-72	-9,941	36,882	26,941
N.MEX.	1972-73	-31,303	-5,150	26,153
N.MEX.	1973-74	-692	18,590	19,282
N.MEX.	1974-75	68,348	125,148	56,800
N.MEX.	1975-76	4,507	59,095	54,588
N.MEX.	T.Q.	27,127		
N.MEX.	1976-77	210,492	232,537	22,045
N.MEX.	1977-78	38,319	137,730	99,411

APPENDIX TABLE 6.1--STATE LEVEL DOLLAR DIFFERENCES (THOUSANDS $) IN
GRANTS IN AID REPORTED IN C.S.A., F.A.I.S., AND B.O.C. (CONTINUED)

AREA	FY YEAR	DOLLAR DIFFERENCES		
		CSA-FATS	CSA-BOC	FATS-BOC
N.Y....	1970-71	112,818	955,325	842,506
N.Y....	1971-72	11,578	1,065,354	1,053,776
N.Y....	1972-73	996,989	827,931	-169,058
N.Y....	1973-74	559,262	1,330,099	770,837
N.Y....	1974-75	-901,000	1,577,478	676,478
N.Y....	1975-76	-174,893	178,087	352,980
N.Y....	T.Q.	-767,670		
N.Y....	1976-77	3,118,844	4,050,531	931,687
N.Y....	1977-78	1,221,912	2,568,877	1,286,965
N.C....	1970-71	41,676	117,619	75,943
N.C....	1971-72	39,723	150,985	111,262
N.C....	1972-73	-14,035	115,666	101,631
N.C....	1973-74	-58,043	44,153	102,196
N.C....	1974-75	423,085	256,772	-166,313
N.C....	1975-76	207,957	303,297	95,340
N.C....	T.Q.	174,504		
N.C....	1976-77	475,267	432,209	-43,058
N.C....	1977-78	200,174	253,129	52,955
N.D....	1970-71	7,046	4,360	-2,686
N.D....	1971-72	22,367	39,775	17,408
N.D....	1972-73	22,727	23,542	20,815
N.D....	1973-74	7,887	12,695	4,808
N.D....	1974-75	61,034	70,790	9,756
N.D....	1975-76	-7,571	18,338	25,909
N.D....	T.Q.	5,374		
N.D....	1976-77	62,792	48,293	-14,499
N.D....	1977-78	244	13,182	12,938
OHIO...	1970-71	93,951	242,464	148,512
OHIO...	1971-72	-44,626	143,425	188,051
OHIO...	1972-73	78,907	424,822	345,915
OHIO...	1973-74	-222,694	-531,769	190,925
OHIO...	1974-75	518,578	542,838	24,260
OHIO...	1975-76	431,438	578,056	146,618
OHIO...	T.Q.	150,232		
OHIO...	1976-77	1,208,309	1,457,714	249,405
OHIO...	1977-78	336,290	646,475	310,185

APPENDIX TABLE 6.1--STATE LEVEL DOLLAR DIFFERENCES (THOUSANDS $) IN
GRANTS-IN-AID REPORTED IN C.S.A., F.&I.S., AND B.O.C. (CONTINUED)

AREA	FY YEAR	DOLLAR DIFFERENCES		
		CSA-FATS	CSA-BOC	FATS-BOC
OKLA...	1970-71	22,600	97,179	74,580
OKLA...	1971-72	17,579	74,347	56,768
OKLA...	1972-73	-1,207	73,726	74,933
OKLA...	1973-74	-58,475	-19,799	38,676
OKLA...	1974-75	24,140	112,454	88,314
OKLA...	1975-76	23,155	30,721	7,566
OKLA...	T.Q.	-9,898		
OKLA...	1976-77	287,996	266,115	-21,881
OKLA...	1977-78	39,539	112,519	72,980
ORE...	1970-71	2,022	-1,677	-3,699
ORE...	1971-72	26,174	52,833	26,659
ORE...	1972-73	-37,155	-2,666	34,489
ORE...	1973-74	-26,739	36,557	9,818
ORE...	1974-75	181,876	59,563	-122,313
ORE...	1975-76	-74,535	-67,638	6,897
ORE...	T.Q.	-3,287		
ORE...	1976-77	262,520	207,552	-54,968
ORE...	1977-78	91,876	113,376	21,500
PA...	1970-71	124,247	213,816	89,569
PA...	1971-72	47,768	229,613	181,845
PA...	1972-73	60,822	617,283	556,461
PA...	1973-74	-8,507	203,983	212,490
PA...	1974-75	731,864	1,053,573	321,709
PA...	1975-76	117,575	263,846	146,271
PA...	T.Q.	156,261		
PA...	1976-77	1,205,627	1,688,086	482,459
PA...	1977-78	280,307	753,793	473,486
R.I...	1970-71	23,880	34,959	11,080
R.I...	1971-72	-6,200	18,807	25,007
R.I...	1972-73	-10,063	22,930	12,867
R.I...	1973-74	-17,066	22,383	39,446
R.I...	1974-75	70,066	88,083	18,017
R.I...	1975-76	21,759	22,598	839
R.I...	T.Q.	12,032		
R.I...	1976-77	94,805	106,951	12,146
R.I...	1977-78	27,777	57,077	29,300

APPENDIX TABLE 6.1--STATE LEVEL DOLLAR DIFFERENCES (THOUSANDS $) IN GRANTS-IN-AID REPORTED IN C.S.A., F.A.T.S., AND B.O.C. (CONTINUED)

AREA	FY YEAR	DOLLAR DIFFERENCES		
		CSA-FATS	CSA-BOC	FATS-BOC
S.C...	1970-71	-41,045	50,329	91,373
S.C...	1971-72	-38,604	49,609	88,213
S.C...	1972-73	-49,935	50,495	100,430
S.C...	1973-74	-70,474	2,194	72,668
S.C...	1974-75	192,752	209,192	16,440
S.C...	1975-76	148,522	174,428	25,906
S.C...	T.Q.	61,268		
S.C...	1976-77	299,860	351,700	51,840
S.C...	1977-78	86,977	139,391	52,414
S.D...	1970-71	618	14,096	13,478
S.D...	1971-72	26,968	43,737	16,769
S.D...	1972-73	34,675	76,750	42,075
S.D...	1973-74	-25,832	5,500	31,332
S.D...	1974-75	-29,493	51,525	22,032
S.D...	1975-76	-6,963	6,286	13,249
S.D...	T.Q.	-9,792		
S.D...	1976-77	111,241	132,795	21,554
S.D...	1977-78	-4,583	33,163	37,746
TENN...	1970-71	-14,797	72,323	87,120
TENN...	1971-72	-51,643	102,375	154,018
TENN...	1972-73	-108,738	-2,073	106,665
TENN...	1973-74	-108,809	11,732	120,541
TENN...	1974-75	193,782	267,116	73,334
TENN...	1975-76	108,685	176,233	67,543
TENN...	T.Q.	-8,460		
TENN...	1976-77	443,491	533,708	90,217
TENN...	1977-78	189,224	265,384	76,160
TEX...	1970-71	108,278	256,112	147,835
TEX...	1971-72	203,618	410,174	206,556
TEX...	1972-73	-21,010	342,918	363,928
TEX...	1973-74	-150,174	77,908	228,082
TEX...	1974-75	760,909	764,514	3,605
TEX...	1975-76	272,911	318,474	45,563
TEX...	T.Q.	417,516		
TEX...	1976-77	1,009,931	1,169,012	159,081
TEX...	1977-78	664,502	921,489	256,987

173

APPENDIX TABLE 6.1—STATE LEVEL DOLLAR DIFFERENCES (THOUSANDS $) IN GRANTS-IN-AID REPORTED IN C.S.A., F.A.T.S., AND B.O.C. (CONTINUED)

AREA	FY YEAR	DOLLAR DIFFERENCES CSA-FATS	CSA-BOC	FATS-BOC
UTAH	1970-71	30,861	17,083	-13,778
UTAH	1971-72	38,725	33,704	-5,021
UTAH	1972-73	41,160	31,562	-9,598
UTAH	1973-74	12,387	19,634	-7,247
UTAH	1974-75	114,680	101,384	-13,296
UTAH	1975-76	-3,507	-25,246	-21,739
UTAH	T.Q.	29,347		
UTAH	1976-77	156,158	128,195	-27,963
UTAH	1977-78	55,279	22,940	-32,339
VER	1970-71	-4,493	-1,855	2,638
VER	1971-72	29,292	35,297	6,005
VER	1972-73	2,829	17,941	15,112
VER	1973-74	4,243	13,116	8,873
VER	1974-75	26,128	22,280	-3,848
VER	1975-76	21,065	7,628	-13,437
VER	T.Q.	-4,768		
VER	1976-77	98,974	118,575	19,601
VER	1977-78	1,517	2,876	1,359
VA	1970-71	-26,153	25,101	51,254
VA	1971-72	98,366	138,626	43,260
VA	1972-73	42,802	118,579	75,777
VA	1973-74	52,609	135,368	82,759
VA	1974-75	202,315	211,420	9,105
VA	1975-76	218,065	287,596	69,531
VA	T.Q.	120,627		
VA	1976-77	422,752	435,906	13,154
VA	1977-78	100,591	68,717	-31,874
WASH	1970-71	76,537	106,210	29,672
WASH	1971-72	113,851	190,384	76,533
WASH	1972-73	113,772	43,046	29,274
WASH	1973-74	87,222	90,530	90,530
WASH	1974-75	253,624	165,332	-88,298
WASH	1975-76	74,705	95,194	20,489
WASH	T.Q.	37,050		
WASH	1976-77	518,676	363,669	-155,007
WASH	1977-78	152,862	278,224	-125,362

174

APPENDIX TABLE 6.1--STATE LEVEL DOLLAR DIFFERENCES (THOUSANDS $) IN
GRANTS-IN-AID REPORTED IN C.S.A., F.A.T.S., AND B.O.C. (CONTINUED)

AREA	FY YEAR	DOLLAR DIFFERENCES		
		CSA-FATS	CSA-BOC	FATS-BOC
W.VA..	1970-71	12,963	76,311	63,348
W.VA..	1971-72	26,381	124,257	97,876
W.VA..	1972-73	2,303	88,325	86,022
W.VA..	1973-74	-94,636	3,087	97,723
W.VA..	1974-75	-181,826	227,998	46,172
W.VA..	1975-76	-130,995	6,179	137,174
W.VA..	T.Q.	53,103		
W.VA..	1976-77	261,810	313,043	51,233
W.VA..	1977-78	85,644	136,566	50,922
WIS...	1970-71	83,047	107,846	24,799
WIS...	1971-72	68,388	76,868	8,480
WIS...	1972-73	75,049	128,233	53,184
WIS...	1973-74	107,174	134,042	26,868
WIS...	1974-75	333,291	333,905	614
WIS...	1975-76	37,730	14,339	-23,391
WIS...	T.Q.	107,744		
WIS...	1976-77	251,355	494,363	243,008
WIS...	1977-78	45,743	219,870	174,127
WY....	1970-71	-1,956	1,733	-224
WY....	1971-72	-17,559	13,469	31,028
WY....	1972-73	-839	4,820	5,659
WY....	1973-74	-5,921	3,605	9,526
WY....	1974-75	-64,276	54,465	-9,811
WY....	1975-76	-54,967	-76,410	-21,443
WY....	T.Q.	-19,869		
WY....	1976-77	8,207	-3,949	-12,156
WY....	1977-78	5,332	15,539	10,207
NATION*	1970-71	1,868,889	4,995,366	3,126,478
NATION*	1971-72	1,523,822	5,487,892	3,964,070
NATION*	1972-73	3,678,172	7,479,080	3,800,908
NATION*	1973-74	3,345,381	3,606,453	3,261,072
NATION*	1974-75	15,118,007	16,693,643	1,575,636
NATION*	1975-76	4,827,201	6,958,602	2,131,401
NATION*	T.Q.	5,056,117		
NATION*	1976-77	25,358,808	28,832,748	3,473,940
NATION*	1977-78	10,659,936	16,361,007	5,701,071

Note: "*" National figures were calculated from state-level data.

APPENDIX TABLE 6.2--Listing Of Agencies Reporting In I.F.X.S., FY 1970-78, Ordered By I.F.A.P. Agency Code

I.F.A.P. AGENCY CODE	NAME	REPORTING AGENCY CODE IN F.I.X.S., FY									
		1970	1971	1972	1973	1974	1975	1976	T.Q.	1977	1978
1	DEPARTMENT OF AGRICULTURE	10	10	10	10	10	10	10	10	10	10
2	DEPARTMENT OF COMMERCE	20	20	20	20	20	20	20	20	20	20
3	DEPARTMENT OF DEFENSE	30	30	30	30	30	30	30	30	30	30
4	DEPARTMENT OF HEALTH, EDUCATION AND WELFARE	40	40	40	40	40	40	40	40	40	40
5	DEPARTMENT OF HOUSING AND URBAN DEVELOPMENT	50	50	50	50	50	50	50	50	50	50
6	DEPARTMENT OF THE INTERIOR	60	60	60	60	60	60	60	60	60	60
7	DEPARTMENT OF JUSTICE	70	70	70	70	70	70	70	70	70	70
8	DEPARTMENT OF LABOR	80	80	80	80	80	80	80	80	80	80
9	DEPARTMENT OF STATE	100	100	100	100	100	100	100	100	100	100
10	DEPARTMENT OF TRANSPORTATION	110	110	110	110	110	110	110	110	110	110
11	TREASURY DEPARTMENT	110	110	110	110	110	110	110	110	110	110
12	ACTION	125	125	125	125	125	125	125	125	125	125
13	ADMINISTRATIVE CONFERENCE OF THE U.S.							128	128	128	128
14	ADVISORY COMM ON INTERGOVERNMENTAL RELATIONS	130	130	130	130	130	130	130	130	130	130
15	ADVISORY COMMITTEE ON FEDERAL PAY							135	135	135	135
16	AGENCY FOR INTERNATIONAL DEVELOPMENT	140	140	140	140	140	140	140	140	140	140
17	ALASKA DEVELOPMENT COMMITTEES	150	150	150	150	150	150	150	154		
18	AMERICAN BATTLE MONUMENTS COMMISSION	160	160	160	160	160	160	160	160	160	160
19	APPALACHIAN REGIONAL COMMISSION	170	170	170	170	170	170	170	170	170	170
20	BOARD FOR INTERNATIONAL BROADCASTING	180	180	180	180	180	180	180	180	180	180
21	CIVIL AERONAUTICS BOARD	200	200	200	200	200	200	200	200	200	200
22	CIVIL SERVICE COMMISSION	210	210	210	210	210	210	210	210	210	210
23	COMMISSION ON AMERICAN SHIPBUILDING							214	214	214	214
24	COMMISSION ON EXECUTIVE, LEGISLATIVE, JUDICIAL SAL							216	216	216	216
25	COMMISSION ON FEDERAL PAPERWORK							218	218	218	218
26	COMMISSION ON ORG FOR GOV FOR CONDCT FORGN PLC	220	220	220	220	220	220				
27	COMMISSION ON CIVIL RIGHTS							219	219	219	219
28	COMMITTEE ON REVIEW OF NATL POLICY-GAMBLING							221	221	221	221
29	COMMITTEE FOR PURCHASE FROM BLIND & OTHER HDC							222	222	222	222
30	COMMODITY FUTURES TRADING COMMISSION							223	223	223	223
31	COMMUNITY SERVICES ADMINISTRATION						225	225	225	225	225
32	COUNCIL OF ECONOMIC ADVISERS						230	230	230	230	230
33	COUNCIL ON & OFFICE OF ENVIRONMENTAL QUALITY							231	231	231	231
34	COUNCIL ON INTERNATIONAL ECONOMIC POLICY	230	230	230	230	230					
35	COUNCIL ON WAGE AND PRICE STABILITY					233	233	233	233	233	233
36	DEFENSE MANPOWER COMMISSION					234	234	234			
37	DOMESTIC COUNCIL	235	235	235	235	235	235	235	235	235	235
38	ENERGY RESEARCH & DEVELOPMENT ADMINISTRATION						236	236	236	236	236
39	ENVIRONMENTAL PROTECTION AGENCY	237	237	237	237	237	237	237	237	237	237
40	EQUAL EMPLOYMENT OPPORTUNITY COMMISSION	240	240	240	240	240	240	240	240	240	240
41	EXPORT-IMPORT BANK OF WASHINGTON	250	250	250	250	250	250	250	250	250	250
42	FARM CREDIT ADMINISTRATION	260	260	260	260	260	260	260	260	260	260
43	FEDERAL COAL MINE SAFETY BOARD OF REVIEW	270	270	270	270	270	270	270	270	270	260

APPENDIX TABLE 6.2: (CONTINUED)=Listing Of Agencies Reporting In F.I.X.S., FY 1970-78, Ordered By I.F.A.P. Agency Code

I.F.A.P. AGENCY CODE	NAME	REPORTING AGENCY CODE IN F.I.X.S., FY									
		1970	1971	1972	1973	1974	1975	1976	T.Q.	1977	1978
44	FEDERAL COMMUNICATIONS COMMISSION	280	280	280	280	280	280	280	280	280	280
45	FEDERAL ELECTION COMMISSION							283	283	283	283
46	FEDERAL ENERGY ADMINISTRATION						285	285	285	285	285
47	FEDERAL HOME LOAN BANK BOARD	290	290	290	290	290	290	290	290	290	290
48	FEDERAL MARITIME COMMISSION	300	300	300	300	300	300	300	300	300	300
49	FEDERAL MEDIATION AND CONCILIATION SERVICE	310	310	310	310	310	310	310	310	310	310
50	FEDERAL POWER COMMISSION	320	320	320	320	320	320	320	320	320	320
51	FEDERAL RADIATION COUNCIL	330	330	330	330	330	330	330	330	330	330
52	FEDERAL TRADE COMMISSION	340	340	340	340	340	340	340	340	340	340
53	FOREIGN CLAIMS SETTLEMENT COMMISSION	350	350	350	350	350	350	350	350	350	350
54	GENERAL SERVICES ADMINISTRATION	360	360	360	360	360	360	360	360	360	360
55	GOVERNMENT PRINTING OFFICE							365	365	365	365
56	HARRY S TRUMAN SCHOLARSHIP FOUNDATION							368	368	368	368
57	INDIAN CLAIMS COMMISSION	370	370	370	370	370	370	370	370	370	370
58	INTER-AMERICAN FOUNDATION							373	373	373	373
59	INTERNATIONAL TRADE COMMISSION						375	375	375	375	375
60	INTERSTATE COMMERCE COMMISSION	380	380	380	380	380	380	380	380	380	380
61	JAPAN-UNITED STATES FRIENDSHIP COMMISSION							383	383	383	383
62	LEGAL SERVICES CORPORATION							385	385		
63	LOWELL HISTORIC CANAL DISTRICT COMMISSION							387	387	387	
64	MARINE MAMMAL COMMISSION							388	388	388	
65	NATIONAL AERONAUTICS AND SPACE ADMINISTRATION	390	390	390	390	390	390	390	390	390	390
66	NATIONAL AERONAUTICS AND SPACE COUNCIL	400	400	400	400						
67	NATIONAL CAPITAL HOUSING AUTHORITY	410	410	410	410	410	410	410	410	410	410
68	NATIONAL CAPITAL PLANNING COMMISSION	420	420	420	420	420	420	420	420	420	420
69	NATIONAL CAPITAL TRANSPORTATION AGENCY	430	430	430	430						
70	NATL CENTER FOR PROD & QUALITY OF WORKNG LIFE							433	433	433	433
71	NATL COMM REV FEDERAL & STATE LAWS W/T & E/S							435	435	435	435
72	NATL COMMISSION ON ELECTRONIC FUND TRANSFERS							437	437	437	437
73	NATIONAL COMMISSION ON SUPPLIES AND SHORTAGES							438	438	438	438
74	NATIONAL COMMISSION ON WATER QUALITY							439	439	439	439
75	NATL COUNCIL/COMM ON MARINE RES & ENGR DEV	440	440								
76	NATIONAL FOUNDATION ON ARTS AND HUMANITIES	450	450	450	450	450	450	450	450	450	450
77	NATIONAL LABOR RELATIONS BOARD	460	460	460	460	460	460	460	460	460	460
78	NATIONAL MEDIATION BOARD	470	470	470	470	470	470	470	470	470	470
79	NATIONAL SCIENCE FOUNDATION	480	480	480	480	480	480	480	480	480	480
80	NATIONAL SECURITY COUNCIL	490	490	490	490	490	490	490	490	490	490
81	NAT STUDY COMM REC & DOC OF FEDERAL OFFICIALS							500	500	500	500
82	NATIONAL TRANSPORTATION SAFETY BOARD							503	503	503	503
83	OCCUPATIONAL SAFETY AND HEALTH REVIEW COMM							505	505	505	505
84	OFFICE OF DRUG ABUSE POLICY							510	510	510	510
85	OFFICE OF MANAGEMENT AND BUDGET	190	190	515	515	515	515	515	515	515	515
86	OFFICE OF SCIENCE AND TECHNOLOGY	520	520	520	520	520	520	520	520	520	520

APPENDIX TABLE 6.2 (CONTINUED): Listing Of Agencies Reporting In F.I.X.S., FY 1970-78, Ordered By I.F.A.P. Agency Code

I.F.A.P. AGENCY CODE	NAME	REPORTING AGENCY CODE IN F.I.X.S., FY									
		1970	1971	1972	1973	1974	1975	1976	T.Q.	1977	1978
87	OFFICE OF TELECOMMUNICATIONS POLICY	530	530	530	530	530	530				
88	PANAMA CANAL							525	525	525	525
89	PENNSYLVANIA AVENUE DEVELOPMENT CORPORATION							530	530	530	530
90	POSTAL SERVICE	90	90	540	540	540	540	535	535	535	535
91	PRESIDENT'S COMMISSION ON MENTAL HEALTH							540	540	543	543
92	PRIVACY PROTECTION STUDY COMMISSION							545	545	545	545
93	PUBLIC LAND LAW REVIEW COMMISSION	550	550	550	550	550	550	550	550	550	550
94	RAILROAD RETIREMENT BOARD	560	560	560	560	560	560	560	560	560	560
95	RENEGOTIATION BOARD	570	570	570	570	570	570	570	570	570	570
96	SECURITIES AN DEXCHANGE COMMISSION	580	580	580	580	580	580	580	580	580	580
97	SELECT COMM ON WESTERN HEMISPHERE IMMIGRATION	590	590	590	590	590	590	590	590	590	590
98	SELECTIVE SERVICE SYSTEM	600	600	600	600	600	600	600	600	600	600
99	SMALL BUSINESS ADMINISTRATION	610	610	610	610	610	610	610	610	610	610
100	SMITHSONIAN INSTITUTION	620	620	620	620	620	620	620	620	620	620
101	SPECIAL REPRESENTATIVE FOR TRADE NEGOTIATIONS	630	630	630	630	630	630	630	630	630	630
102	SUBVERSIVE ACTIVITIES CONTROL BOARD	640	640	640	640	640	640	640	640	640	640
103	UNITED STATES TAX COURT	660	660	660	660	660	660	660	660	660	660
104	TENNESSEE VALLEY AUTHORITY	670	670	670	670	670	670	670	670	670	670
105	THE WHITE HOUSE	680	680	680	680	680	680	680	680	680	680
106	ARMS CONTROL AND DISARMAMENT AGENCY	690	690	690	690	690	690	690	690	690	690
107	U.S. INFORMATION AGENCY	700	700	700	700	700	700	700	700	700	175
108	U.S. SINAI SUPPORT MISSION	710	710	710	710	710		705	705	705	705
109	U.S. SOLDIERS' AND AIRMEN'S HOME	720	720	720	720	720		710	710	710	710
110	VETERANS ADMINISTRATION	730	730	730	730	730		720	720	720	720
111	WATER RESOURCES COUNCIL	510	510	510	510	510	510	730	730	730	730
112	OFFICE OF EMERGENCY PREPAREDNESS	650	650	650	650	650	650				
113	TARIFF COMMISSION	180	180	180	180	180					
114	ATOMIC ENERGY COMMISSION	500	500	500	500	500					
115	OFFICE OF ECONOMIC OPPORTUNITY	500	500								
116	PEACE CORPS	540	540								
117	DEPARTMENT OF ENERGY										35
118	INTERNATIONAL COMMUNICATION AGENCY										374
119	NATIONAL COMM-INTERNATIONAL YEAR OF THE CHILD										434
120	NATIONAL COMMISSION ON NEIGHBORHOODS										436
121	NATIONAL ENDOWMENT FOR THE ARTS										444
122	NATIONAL ENDOWMENT FOR THE HUMANITIES										445
123	NATIONAL TRANSPORTATION POLICY STUDY COMM										502
124	OFFICE OF ADMINISTRATION										508
125	OFFICE OF THE VICE PRESIDENT										527
126	PRESIDENTIAL COMMISSION ON WORLD HUNGER										542
127	PRESIDENT'S COMMISSION ON PENSION POLICY										544
128	UNITED STATES METRIC BOARD										650
129	U.S. NUCLEAR REGULATORY COMMISSION										702

APPENDIX TABLE 6.3

DETAILED NATIONAL LEVEL RECONCILIATION OF ESEA EXPENDITURES REPORTED IN F.I.X.S. AND O.M.B. "APPENDIX" VOLUME
(IN THOUSANDS $) (BASE=OMB FIGURES)

LINE ITEM ENTRIES	O.M.B. APPENDIX VOLUME OBLIGATIONS $	DIFFERENCE: FIXS FROM OMB $	DIFFERENCE: FIXS FROM OMB %	F.I.X.S. $	APPROPRIATION NAME IN F.I.X.S.	OMB CFDA CODE
GRANTS FOR DISADVANTAGED	2,759,311	-32,689	-1.2	12,074	EDUC DEPRIVED CHILDREN--HANDICAPPED,OE	13427
				2,329,031	EDUC DEPRIVED CHILDREN--LEA'S,OE	13428
				307,889	EDUC DEPRIVED CHILDREN--MIGRANTS,OE	13429
				27,933	EDUC DEPRIVED CHILDREN--STATE ADMIN,OE	13430
				31,807	EDUC DEPRIVED CHILDREN--IN STATE INST,OE	13431
				7,127	EDUC DEPRIVED CHILDREN--SPEC.INCENT.GTS,OE	13512
				11,361	ELEMENTARY & SECONDARY EDUC--EVALUATION,OE	
				2,726,622		
SUPPORT AND INNOVATION GRANTS	214,270	+19,826	+9.3	234,096	EDUCATIONAL INNOVATION AND SUPPORT,OE	13571
BILINGUAL EDUCATION	134,781	-2,140	-1.6	132,641	BILINGUAL EDUCATION,OE	13403
BASIC SKILLS IMPROVEMENT	26,807	-6,164	-23.0	20,643	RIGHT TO READ--ELIMINAT OF ILLITERACY,OE	13533
FOLLOW THROUGH	59,000	-455	-.8	58,545	FOLLOW THROUGH,OE	13433
ALCOHOL AND DRUG ABUSE EDUCATION	2,000	-530	-26.5	1,470	ALCOHOL AND DRUG ABUSE PREVENTION,OE	13420
ENVIRONMENTAL EDUCATION	3,500	0	0	3,500	ENVIRONMENTAL EDUCATION,OE	13522
EDUC. BROADCAST. FACILITIES	14,923	+1,077	+7.2	16,000	EDUCATIONAL BROADCASTING FACILITIES,OE	13413
ELLENDER FELLOWSHIP	750	0	0	750	ELLENDER FELLOWSHIP	
ETHNIC HERITAGE STUDIES	2,300	-46	-2.0	2,254	ETHNIC HERITAGE STUDIES PROGRAM,OE	13549
ITEMS NOT EXPLICITLY LISTED		+239	+100.0	72	ELEMENTARY AND SECONDARY EDUCATION,OE	13570
				167	SCHOOL LIBRARY RES.,TEXTBOOKS,ETC,OE	
				239	NOT EXPLICITLY RELATED TO OMB ENTRIES	
TOTAL	3,217,642	-20,882	-.6	3,196,760	TOTAL	

SOURCES: BOTUSG,APPENDIX VOLUME, FY 1980; and FIXS computer tapes for FY 1978.

APPENDIX TABLE 6.4
HUMAN DEVELOPMENT PROGRAM BY STATE & SELECTED STATISTICS, FY 1922

STATE	DOLLAR AMOUNT ($ 1,000S)			PERCENTAGE		RANKING		RANK DIFFERENCE
	FIXS	FATS	DIFF	FIXS	FATS	FIXS	FATS	FATS-FIXS
ALABAMA	40,952	30,353	10,599	2.3	2.5	15	13	-2
ALASKA	7,832	22,908		2.4		44	51	7
ARIZONA	29,001	20,705	8,296	1.4	1.7	27	24	-3
ARKANSAS	24,705	19,006	5,699	1.4	1.6	29	25	-4
CALIFORNIA	144,876	112,912	31,964	8.0	9.4	1	1	0
COLORADO	24,401	11,013	7,388	1.4	1.0	30	28	-2
CONNECTICUT	16,885	12,026	4,859	0.9	1.0	35	33	-2
DELAWARE	5,866	4,165	1,701	0.3	0.3	50	49	-1
DISTRICT OF COLUMBIA	47,461	27,805	19,656	2.6	2.3	17	14	3
FLORIDA	67,327	48,625	19,202	3.8	4.4	11	7	-1
GEORGIA	45,003	21,600	23,403	2.5	1.8	14	21	7
HAWAII	8,516	7,582	934	0.5		43	41	-2
IDAHO	8,717	6,774	1,943	0.5	0.6	42	43	1
ILLINOIS	74,339	36,137	38,202	4.1	3.0	5	10	5
INDIANA	31,131	17,936	16,209	1.7	1.5	23	30	-5
IOWA	21,660			1.2		32	27	1
KANSAS	18,594	16,027	2,567	1.0	1.3	34	29	0
KENTUCKY	36,350	23,756	12,594	1.4	2.0	20	19	2
LOUISIANA	37,677	24,092	13,585	2.1	2.0	18	18	0
MAINE	9,224	8,488	736	0.5		41	39	-2
MARYLAND	29,930	24,757	5,173	1.7	2.1	24	17	-7
MASSACHUSETTS	45,132	34,123	11,009	2.5	2.8	13	11	-6
MICHIGAN	56,319	57,640	-1,321	3.1	4.8	9	6	3
MINNESOTA	33,729	33,394	30,335	1.9	2.8	22	8	28
MISSISSIPPI	60,718	55,650	5,068	3.4	4.6	8	5	3
MISSOURI	40,238	30,672	9,566	2.2	2.5	16	12	-4
MONTANA	10,009	9,245	764	0.6	0.8	39	37	-2
NEBRASKA	12,950	10,203	2,747	0.7	0.8	37	35	-2
NEVADA	12,349	16,418	-69	0.7	0.5	47	44	-4
NEW HAMPSHIRE	6,651	8,008	-1,357	0.4	0.7	48	46	-7
NEW JERSEY	45,218	26,609	18,609	2.5	2.2	12	15	3
NEW MEXICO	15,897	10,150	5,747	0.4		36	36	0
NEW YORK	134,746	49,211	85,535	7.5	4.1	2	9	5
NORTH CAROLINA	50,517	42,870	7,647	2.8	3.6	10	7	-3
NORTH DAKOTA	71,472	47,000	472			45	42	0
OHIO	71,772	49,321	22,451	4.1	4.1	6	4	-10
OKLAHOMA	29,796	25,440	4,356	1.7	2.1	26	16	0
OREGON	20,664	14,841	5,823	1.1	1.4	33	31	0
PENNSYLVANIA	86,751	57,334	29,417	4.8	4.8	4	4	-6
RHODE ISLAND	7,112	5,720	1,392	1.6		46	40	-6
SOUTH CAROLINA	28,266	21,101	7,165	1.6	1.8	28	22	-5
SOUTH DAKOTA	39,313	10,306	3,007	1.5	1.9	40	45	17
TENNESSEE	39,255	10,616	28,639	2.2		17	34	17
TEXAS	103,495	73,488	30,007	5.7	6.1	3	3	-1
UTAH	11,384	8,947	2,437	0.6	0.7	38	38	0
VERMONT	5,954	4,372	1,582	0.3		49	47	-2
VIRGINIA	36,194	20,929	15,265	2.0	1.7	21	23	2
WASHINGTON	29,871	22,580	7,291	1.7	1.9	25	20	-5
WEST VIRGINIA	24,151	18,772	5,379	1.3	1.6	31	26	-5
WISCONSIN	37,366	12,220	25,146	2.1	1.0	19	32	13
WYOMING	5,451	4,371	1,080	0.3	0.4	51	48	-3

BREAKOUT OF PROGRAMS IN E.A.I.S. UNDER "HUMAN DEVELOPMENT" (Col. 32)

AS CULLED FROM ACCOUNT #1636 IN EIXS, FY 1922

FIXS AGENCY CODE	FIXS PROG CODE	OMB ACCOUNT NUMBER AGENCY	POC	ACCOUNT	SCH TYPE	FUND TYPE	FUNC	FIXS T.A.	OMB CFDA	NATIONAL DOLLAR AMOUNT	ACCOUNT NAME
40	649	9	80	1636	0	1	500	2		16,629,058	REHAB SVCS & FACILITIES-INNOV & EXPAN, OS
543	0	9	80	1636	0	1	500	8		52,186,196	HUMAN DEVELOPMENT, OS
		9	80	1636	0	1	500		13600	35,000	HUMAN DEVELOPMENT, OS
40	600	9	80	1636	0	1	500	2	13608	441,559,045	CHILD DEVELOPMENT-HEAD START, OS
40	608	9	80	1636	0	1	500	2	13612	13,620,685	CHILD DEV-CHILD WELFARE R & D GRANTS, OS
40	612	9	80	1636	0	1	500	2	13623	32,542,671	NATIVE AMERICAN PROGRAMS, OS
40	623	9	80	1636	0	1	500	2	13624	8,728,917	RUNAWAY YOUTH ACT, OS
40	624	9	80	1636	0	1	500	1	13626	722,137,163	REHAB SVCS & FACILITIES-BASIC SUPPORT, OS
40	626	9	80	1636	0	1	500	2	13627	29,971,594	REHAB SVCS & FACILITIES-SPECIAL PROJS, OS
40	627	9	80	1636	0	1	500	2	13628	28,904,446	REHABILITATION RESEARCH & DEMOS, OS
40	628	9	80	1636	0	1	500	2	13629	17,044,806	CHILD DEV-CHILD ABUSE PREV & TREATMENT, OS
40	629	9	80	1636	0	1	500	1	13630	30,016,565	REHABILITATION TRAINING, OS
40	630	9	80	1636	0	1	500	2	13631	32,186,592	DEVELOPMENTAL DISABILITIES-BASIC SUPP, OS
40	631	9	80	1636	0	1	500	2	13632	19,067,854	DEVELOPMENTAL DISABILITIES-SPEC PROJ, OS
40	632	9	80	1636	0	1	500	1	13633	5,206,811	DEVELOPMENTAL DISABILITIES-DEMO & TRNG, OS
40	633	9	80	1636	0	1	500	2	13634	137,148,160	PROG FOR AGING-STATE AGENCY ACTIVITIES, OS
40	634	9	80	1636	0	1	500	1	13635	25,379,008	PROG FOR AGING-TITLE III-MODEL PROJ, OS
40	635	9	80	1636	0	1	500	2	13636	198,884,768	PROG FOR AGING-NUTRITION PROGRAM, OS
40	636	9	80	1636	0	1	500	1	13637	6,849,778	PROG FOR AGING-RESEARCH AND DEMO, OS
40	637	9	80	1636	0	1	500	2	13638	14,432,312	PROG FOR AGING-AGING TRAINING, OS
40	638	9	80	1636	0	1	500	2	13639	3,489,037	PROG FOR AGING-MULTIDISCIPLINARY CTRS, OS
40	639	9	80	1636	0	1	500	2		19,784,415	PROG FOR AGING-TITLE V SENIOR CENTERS, OS

APPENDIX TABLE 6.6: STATE BY STATE BREAKOUT OF PROGRAMS LISTED IN TABLE 5 ($ in 1,000s)

CATALOG OF FEDERAL DOMESTIC ASSISTANCE CODE

STATE	13600	13608	13612	13623	13624	13626	13627	13628	13629	13630	13631	13632
ALABAMA	12793	82	48	146	18516	345	611	82	607	704	394	228
ALASKA	1855		48	38	2000	15		175		170	48	
ARIZONA	7524	420	1513	93	8231	379	42	270	374	311	617	0
ARKANSAS	6578		6739	69	10882	497	892	157	724	395	21	0
CALIFORNIA	32042	1222	1985	1387	55996	1563	2736	1461	2412	2541	1088	353
COLORADO	6840	690	1257	152	8388	374	724	737	552	335	483	134
CONNECTICUT	2893	353	0	36	6838	241		345	187	382		
DELAWARE	1282		0	0	2037	257		234		171	31	0
DISTRICT OF COLUMBIA	9503	2160	0	622	5505	2483	1878	2435	822	170	1543	119
FLORIDA	14401		84	469	28458	1419	168	136	409	1138	293	138
GEORGIA	10389	12		69	21175	2623	856	443	637	784	176	312
HAWAII	2053		642	4	3633	148		339	227	172	248	0
IDAHO	18375	394	58	168	27011	107	1388	310	159	170	201	0
ILLINOIS	4047		169	460	12294	939	0	723	2000	1431	765	214
INDIANA	3900	25	67	168	10130	122	0	274	341	809	435	117
IOWA	12204	183	239	75	7593	241	265	68	310	464	381	313
KANSAS	11251	46	183	68	16363	111	416	102	163	329	82	90
KENTUCKY	2180		134	269	18836	40		89	247	663	346	
LOUISIANA	7289	722	114	84	4000	538	81	41	76	669	149	274
MAINE	9230	1024	75	248	11323	256	1687	257	659	519	776	277
MARYLAND	10510	286	456	139	17317	281	1512	1213	1326	793	588	149
MASSACHUSETTS	6478		856	198	24976	715	1547	231	907	1285	574	
MICHIGAN	41493	187	160	45	13810	150	150	366	270	593	654	78
MINNESOTA	11015	193	103	138	13401	141		262	821	483	258	158
MISSISSIPPI	2958		149	91	16700	24		118		743	224	
MISSOURI	2631		296	48	2956	108	175	176		171		131
MONTANA	1228			81	5152	285	0	60		245	507	
NEBRASKA	11990	463	57	133	2032	293	0	37	260	172	60	
NEVADA	1161		1517	736	3064	140	0	886	71	910	458	85
NEW HAMPSHIRE	5276	2245	444	68	16688	4029	0	327	187	139	85	
NEW JERSEY	30455	135	796		5741	277	3617	1194	4580	179	344	
NEW MEXICO	1689	304	889	418	43611	106		383	320	2329	966	82
NEW YORK	14892	889	65	66	24301	318	0	35	93	957	887	261
NORTH CAROLINA	8100		357	99	2472	63	329	222	812	170	451	
NORTH DAKOTA	3436	9983	92	139	3058	338	67	65	635	1557	126	186
OHIO	13991	25	22	68	18178	1422	548	407	383	452	611	85
OKLAHOMA	1308			33	49392	390	1743	38	1306	330	1124	
OREGON	7846	100	1531	107	5566	156		95	56	1837	27	344
PENNSYLVANIA	2255	68	132	555	2219	997	325	29	267	170	613	122
RHODE ISLAND	10904	441	150	37	17850	218	3515	334	897	170	73	85
SOUTH CAROLINA	23442			76	14341	1183		1298	1135	747	852	172
SOUTH DAKOTA	2435		22	210	2955	1059		46	227	1843	55	162
TENNESSEE	1251	301	1519	119	18871	3982	873	32	129	198	27	
TEXAS	6147	98		230	17063	498	1373	178	841	752	354	232
UTAH	6075		978	49	2000	35	776	288	283	468	295	185
VERMONT	5569	133	114				1212	52	685	732	560	143
WYOMING	1002							13	21	171	46	0

APPENDIX TABLE 6.61 STATE-BY-STATE BREAKOUT OF PROGRAMS LISTED IN TABLE 5 (Continued)

STATE	CATALOG OF FEDERAL DOMESTIC ASSISTANCE CODE										OVERALL TOTAL ($1,000s)
	13633	13634	13635	13636	13637	13638	13639	T.A.2	T.A.8	AG.543	
ALABAMA	2168	20	3267	0	203	126	321	291	0	0	40952
ALASKA	804	9	1007	0	30	0	100	50	0	0	7832
ARIZONA	1353	138	1942	0	135	0	266	168	0	0	29001
ARKANSAS	1556	205	2262	46	267	67	225	168	0	0	24705
CALIFORNIA	11878	4095	17225	1437	1247	249	1760	1699	3328	0	144876
COLORADO	1295	3	1845	0	188	0	181	203	2360	0	24401
CONNECTICUT	1876	225	2824	0	83	52	278	241	0	0	16885
DELAWARE	2079	229	1007	0	80	0	100	56	0	0	5866
DISTRICT OF COLUMBIA	9638	129	1007	0	1635	0	100	56	26260	35	47461
FLORIDA	7222	122	10776	1319	489	134	1070	632	0	0	67827
GEORGIA	2506	118	3739	268	276	0	371	388	5527	0	45003
HAWAII	804	30	1018	128	188	77	100	66	0	0	8516
IDAHO	6659	4	1018	0	30	60	100	65	0	0	8717
ILLINOIS	3027	1244	4937	241	639	0	986	917	2470	0	74339
INDIANA	2001	224	3015	0	135	0	448	390	0	0	31131
IOWA	1598	111	2356	84	189	77	296	64	0	0	21660
KANSAS	2089	236	3117	0	185	122	232	121	0	0	18594
KENTUCKY	1994	26	2976	0	237	125	309	273	0	0	36350
LOUISIANA	1827	24	3057	0	339	0	295	306	0	0	37677
MAINE	2846	40	3057	274	376	0	104	81	0	0	9224
MARYLAND	3798	148	5668	237	339	1	300	333	0	0	29930
MASSACHUSETTS	4751	572	7161	464	734	260	563	471	2171	0	45132
MICHIGAN	2431	10	3664	290	238	66	704	564	0	0	56319
MINNESOTA	1469	95	2138	0	63	0	210	318	0	0	33729
MISSISSIPPI	3312	110	4943	128	344	132	491	189	2243	0	60718
MISSOURI	804	18	1018	0	30	0	100	371	0	0	40238
MONTANA	1149	118	1582	0	176	57	157	57	0	0	10009
NEBRASKA	804	24	1018	0	55	0	175	125	0	0	12950
NEVADA	804	26	1018	0	370	0	100	150	0	0	6349
NEW HAMPSHIRE	4503	196	6786	2	370	0	667	66	0	0	6651
NEW JERSEY	804	240	1088	0	30	0	1000	596	0	0	45218
NEW MEXICO	11729	5374	17679	373	1377	440	1750	1472	0	0	15897
NEW YORK	2903	186	4331	270	325	180	1430	436	0	0	134746
NORTH CAROLINA	804	13	1007	0	30	0	100	52	0	0	50517
NORTH DAKOTA	6131	184	9241	0	605	155	908	858	0	0	7472
OHIO	1864	113	2802	0	88	186	275	216	0	0	71772
OKLAHOMA	1529	113	2216	118	371	0	307	180	0	0	29796
OREGON	7938	96	12003	594	564	447	1183	962	2924	0	20664
PENNSYLVANIA	1421	384	1018	0	61	0	100	273	0	0	86751
RHODE ISLAND	804	92	2057	0	54	0	202	222	0	0	7112
SOUTH CAROLINA	2527	100	1018	0	229	54	374	53	0	0	28266
SOUTH DAKOTA	6645	511	3809	0	248	222	984	336	3371	0	9313
TENNESSEE	804	13	10018	13	648	136	100	979	0	0	39255
TEXAS	804	33	1007	0	30	0	372	93	0	0	103495
UTAH	2513	13	3788	342	192	52	391	51	0	0	11384
VERMONT	2074	82	3115	189	117	149	220	271	1533	0	5954
VIRGINIA	1293	176	1841	0	136	53	181	140	0	0	36194
WASHINGTON	2891	13	4357	33	313	131	428	371	0	0	29871
WEST VIRGINIA	804	13	1018	0	53	0	99	12	0	0	24151
WISCONSIN	2891	176	4357	33	313	131	428	371	0	0	37356
WYOMING	804	13	1018	0	53	0	99	12	0	0	5451

References and
Selected Bibliography

References and
Selected Bibliography

The following citations provide the full references for works referred to in the text, as well as a selected introduction to the large body of research, past and present, bearing on the study of federal spending patterns. We have provided these supplementary references for the convenience of readers who may wish to further explore the themes that have concerned us in this work. While no adequate bibliography of research on federal expenditure patterns currently exists, readers interested in additional bibliographic leads are directed to Anton, with Cawley, 1980.

Aaron, 1972—Henry J. Aaron, *Shelter and Subsidies: Who Benefits from Federal Housing Policies?* (Washington, D.C.: The Brookings Institution, 1972)

Aaron, 1973—Henry J. Aaron, *Why Is Welfare So Hard to Reform?* (Washington, D.C.: The Brookings Institution, 1973)

Aaron, 1978—Henry J. Aaron, *Politics and the Professors: The Great Society in Perspective* (Washington, D.C.: The Brookings Institution, 1978)

Academy for Contemporary Problems, 1978—The Academy for Contemporary Problems, *Revitalizing the Northeastern Economy—An Action Survey, General Report and Recommendations* (Columbus, Ohio: The Academy for Contemporary Problems, 1978, Second Printing)

A.C.I.R., 1962—Advisory Commission on Intergovernmental Relations, *Measures Of State And Local Fiscal Capacity And Tax Effort* (Washington, D.C.: U.S. Government Printing Office, M-16, October 1962)

A.C.I.R., 1971—Advisory Commission on Intergovernmental Relations, *Measuring The Fiscal Capacity And Effort Of State And Local Areas* (Washington, D.C.: U.S. Government Printing Office, M-58, March 1971)

A.C.I.R., 1972—Advisory Commission on Intergovernmental Relations, *Measuring The Fiscal Effort Of State And Local Areas* (Washington, D.C.: U.S. Government Printing Office, M-58R, January 1972)

A.C.I.R., 1977a—Advisory Commission on Intergovernmental Relations, *Improving Federal Grants Management* (Washington, D.C.: U.S. Government Printing Office, February 1977, A-53)

A.C.I.R., 1977b—Advisory Commission on Intergovernmental Relations, *The States and Intergovernmental Aids* (Washington, D.C.: U.S. Government Printing Office, A-55, 1977)

A.C.I.R., 1977c—Advisory Commission on Intergovernmental Relations, *Federal Grants: Their Effects on State-Local Expenditure, Employment Levels, Wage Rates* (Washington, D.C.: U.S. Government Printing Office, A-61, 1977)

A.C.I.R., 1977d—Advisory Commission on Intergovernmental Relations, *Safe Streets Reconsidered: The Block Grant Experience 1968–1975* (Washington, D.C.: U.S. Government Printing Office, A-55, 1977)

A.C.I.R., 1977e—Advisory Commission on Intergovernmental Relations, *Safe Streets Reconsidered: The Block Grant Experience 1968–1975—Part B, Case Studies* (Washington, D.C.: U.S. Government Printing Office, A-55a, 1977)

A.C.I.R., 1977f—Advisory Commission on Intergovernmental Relations, *A Catalog of Federal Grant-In-Aid Programs to State and Local Governments: Grants Funded FY 1975* (Washington, D.C.: U.S. Government Printing Office, A-52a, 1977)

A.C.I.R., 1977g—Advisory Commission on Intergovernmental Relations, *The Partnership For Health Act: Lessons From A Pioneering Block Grant* (Washington, D.C.: U.S. Government Printing Office, 1977, A-56)

A.C.I.R., 1977h—Advisory Commission on Intergovernmental Relations, *The Comprehensive Employment and Training Act: Early Readings from a Hybrid Block Grant* (Washington, D.C.: U.S. Government Printing Office, A-58, 1977)

A.C.I.R., 1977i—Advisory Commission on Intergovernmental Relations, *Community Development: The Workings of a Federal-Local Block Grant* (Washington, D.C.: U.S. Government Printing Office, A-57, 1977)

A.C.I.R., 1977j—Advisory Commission on Intergovernmental Relations, *The Intergovernmental Grant System as Seen by Local, State, and Federal Officials* (Washington, D.C.: U.S. Government Printing Office, 1977, A-54)

A.C.I.R., 1978—Advisory Commission on Intergovernmental Relations, *Categorical Grants: Their Role and Design* (Washington, D.C.: U.S. Government Printing Office, A-52, 1978)

A.C.I.R., 1979—Advisory Commission on Intergovernmental Relations, *A Catalog of Federal Grant-In-Aid Programs to State and Local Governments: Grants Funded FY 1978* (Washington, D.C.: U.S. Government Printing Office, A-72, 1979)

Alford, 1977—Robert R. Alford, *Health Care Politics* (Chicago: The University Of Chicago Press, 1977)

Allison, 1969—Graham T. Allison, "Conceptual Models and the Cuban Missile Crisis," *American Political Science Review* 63,3 (September 1969), 689–718

Allison, 1971—Graham T. Allison, *Essence of Decision: Explaining the Cuban Missile Crisis* (Boston: Little, Brown and Company, 1971)

Allison and Halperin, 1972—Graham T. Allison and Morton H. Halperin, "Bureaucratic Politics: A Paradigm and Some Policy Implications," in Raymond Tanter and Richard H. Ullman, eds., *Theory and Policy in International Relations* (Princeton, New Jersey: Princeton University Press, 1972), pp. 40–79

Allman, 1978—T. D. Allman, "The Urban Crisis Leaves Town and Moves to the Suburbs," *Harpers* 257,1543 (December 1978), 41–56

Almond and Verba, 1963—Gabriel A. Almond and Sidney Verba, *The Civic Culture: Political Attitudes and Democracy in Five Nations* (Princeton, New Jersey: Princeton University Press, 1963)

Altman and Sapolsky, 1976—Drew Altman and Harvey M. Sapolsky, "Writing the Regulations for Health," *Policy Sciences* 7,4 (December 1976), 417–437

Altmeyer, 1968—Arthur J. Altmeyer, *The Formative Years of Social Security* (Madison, Milwaukee, and London: University of Wisconsin Press, 1968)

Altshuler, 1969—Alan A. Altshuler, *The City Planning Process: A Political Analysis* (Ithaca: Cornell University Press, 1969)

American Political Science Association, 1950—A Report of the Committee on Political Parties, American Political Science Association, *Toward a More Responsible Two-Party System* (New York: Rinehart & Company, Inc., 1950)

Anderson, 1980—Wayne F. Anderson, "Intergovernmental Aid: Relief or Intrusion?" *National Civic Review* 69,3 (March 1980), 127–132

Anderson, 1955a—William Anderson, *The Nation and the States, Rivals or Partners?* (Minneapolis: University of Minnesota Press, 1955)

Anderson, 1955b—William Anderson, "The Intention of the Farmers: A Note on Constitutional Interpretation," *American Political Science Review* 49,2 (June 1955) 340–352

Anderson, 1956a—William Anderson, "The Commission On Intergovernmental Relations And The United States Federal System," *Journal of Politics* 18,2 (May 1956), 211–231

Anderson, 1956b—William Anderson, *Intergovernmental Fiscal Relations* (Minneapolis: The University Of Minnesota Press, 1956)

Anderson, 1960—William Anderson, *Intergovernmental Relations In Review* (Minneapolis: The University Of Minnesota Press, 1960)

Anton, 1963a—Thomas J. Anton, "Power, Pluralism, and Local Politics," *Administrative Science Quarterly* 7,4 (March 1963), 425–457

Anton, 1963b—Thomas J. Anton, "State Planning, Gubernatorial Leadership, and Federal Funds: Three Cases," in Gilbert Y. Steiner, ed., *The Office Of Governor* (Urbana, Illinois: University of Illinois, Institute of Governmental and Public Affairs, May 1963), pp. 63–79

Anton, 1964—Thomas J. Anton, *Budgeting in Three Illinois Cities* (Urbana, Illinois: Institute of Government and Public Affairs, University of Illinois, 1964)

Anton, 1966—Thomas J. Anton, *The Politics of State Expenditures in Illinois* (Urbana and London: University of Illinois Press, 1966)

Anton, 1967—Thomas J. Anton, "Roles and Symbols in the Determination of State Expenditures," *Midwest Journal of Political Science* 11,1 (February 1967), 27–43

Anton, 1969a—Thomas J. Anton, "Policy-Making and Political Culture in Sweden," in Olaf Ruin, ed., *Scandinavian Political Studies* Volume 4 (1969) (New York: Columbia University Press, 1969), pp. 88–102

Anton, 1969b—Thomas J. Anton, "Administration 'Blowin' In The Wind," *Public Administration Review* 29,3 (May–June, 1969), 309–316

Anton, 1975a—Thomas J. Anton, "The Imagery Of Policy Analysis: Stability, Determinism, And Reaction," *Policy Studies Journal* 3,3 (Spring 1975), 225–233

Anton, 1975b—Thomas J. Anton, *Governing Greater Stockholm: A Study Of Policy Development And System Change* (Berkeley: University of California Press, 1975)

Anton, 1976—Thomas J. Anton, "Toward A Performance-Based Conception Of Local Responsibility," in Stephanie Cole, ed., *Partnerships Within States: Local Self-Government In The Federal System* (Urbana, Illinois: Institute of Governmental and Public Affairs, 1976), pp. 59–75

Anton, 1977a—Thomas J. Anton, "General Revenue Sharing and State-Local Governmental Structure," in F. Thomas Juster, ed., *The Economic And Political Impact Of General Revenue Sharing* (Ann Arbor, Michigan: Survey Research Center, Institute for Social Research, The University of Michigan, 1977), pp. 131–142

Anton, 1977b—Thomas J. Anton, "On Implementing The Vocational Education Amendments of 1976," in The National Institute Of Education, *The Planning Papers For The Vocational Education Study* (Washington, D.C.: U.S. Government Printing Office, 1979), pp. 3–21

Anton, 1977c—Thomas J. Anton, "Notes on Swedish National Government Grants to Local Governments," Unpublished paper, The University of Michigan, 1977

Anton, 1978—Thomas J. Anton, *Creating a Data Base for Intergovernmental Fiscal Analysis,* (Ann Arbor, Michigan: Ph.D. Program in Urban and Regional Planning, The University of Michigan, The Intergovernmental Fiscal Analysis Project, Analysis Series Paper #1, 1978)

Anton, 1979a—Thomas J. Anton, "Data Systems For Urban Fiscal Policy: Toward Reconstruction," Paper prepared for the N.S.F. Conference on Comparative Urban Research, Chicago, Illinois, April 26–27, 1979

Anton, 1979b—Thomas J. Anton, "Notes On Fungibility," Paper prepared for presentation at the 40th National Conference on Public Administration, Baltimore, Maryland, April 1–4, 1979

Anton, 1980a—Thomas J. Anton, "Outlays Data and the Analysis of Federal Policy Impact," in Norman Glickman, ed., *The Urban Impacts of Federal Policies* (Baltimore, Maryland: The Johns Hopkins University Press, 1980), pp. 121–150

Anton, 1980b—Thomas J. Anton, *Administered Politics: Elite Political Culture in Sweden* (Boston: Martinus Nijhoff Publishing, 1980)

Anton, 1980c—Thomas J. Anton, "Federal Assistance Programs: The Politics Of System Transformation," in Douglas E. Ashford, ed., *National Resources And Urban Policy* (New York: Methuen, 1980), pp. 15–44

Anton, with Cawley, 1980—Thomas J. Anton, with the assistance of Jerry P. Cawley, "Intergovernmental Change in the United States: Myth and Reality or Where did you go? To Washington. What did you see? Nothin'," Paper prepared for the National Science Foundation, 1980

Anton and Hofferbert, 1975—Thomas J. Anton and Richard Hofferbert, *Assessing The Political Impact Of General Revenue Sharing: Local Perspectives* (Ann Arbor, Michigan: Institute for Social Research, The University of Michigan, 1975)

Anton, Cawley, Kramer, forthcoming—Thomas J. Anton, Jerry P. Cawley, Kevin L. Kramer, "Federal Spending in States and Regions: Patterns of Stability and Change," to appear in a volume published by Rutgers University Press.

Anton, Cawley, Kramer, Jones, 1980—Thomas J. Anton (Principal Investigator), Jerry P. Cawley, Kevin L. Kramer, Kathryn A. Jones, *Project Report on Federal Spending Patterns to the U.S. Department Of Housing And Urban Development* (Ann Arbor, Michigan: The University of Michigan, Ph.D. Program in Urban and Regional Planning, Intergovernmental Fiscal Analysis Project, 1980)

Anton, Cawley, Kramer, Ward, 1978—Thomas J. Anton, Jerry P. Cawley, Kevin L. Kramer, and Peter D. Ward, *The Impact of the Tisch Amendment on Federal Aid to Michigan* (Ann Arbor, Michigan: Ph.D. Program in Urban and Regional Planning, The University of Michigan, The Intergovernmental Fiscal Analysis Project, Analysis Series Paper #2, October 1978)

Anton, Larkey, Linton, *et al.*, 1975—Thomas J. Anton, Patrick D. Larkey, Toni R. Linton, *et al.*, *Understanding The Fiscal Impact Of General Revenue-Sharing* (Ann Arbor, Michigan: Institute of Public Policy Studies, The University of Michigan, 1975)

Ascher, 1979—William Ascher, *Forecasting: An Appraisal for Policy-makers and Planning* (Baltimore: The Johns Hopkins University Press, 1979)

Axelrod, 1972—Robert Axelrod, "Where the Votes Come From: An Analysis of Electoral Coalitions, 1952–1968," *American Political Science Review* 66,1 (March 1972), 11–20

Axelrod, 1974—Robert Axelrod, "Communication," *American Political Science Review* 68,2 (June 1974), 717–720

Axelrod, 1978—Robert Axelrod, "1976 Update," *American Political Science Review* 72,2 (June 1978), 622–624

Bahl and Saunders, 1965—Roy W. Bahl, Jr. and Robert J. Saunders, "Determinants Of Changes In State And Local Government Expenditures," *National Tax Journal* 18,1 (March 1965), 50–57

Bahl and Warford, 1971—Roy W. Bahl and J. J. Warford, "Interstate Distributions Of Benefits From The Federal Budgetary Process," *National Tax Journal* 24,2 (June 1971), 169–176

Bahl, Jump, and Schroeder, 1978—Roy Bahl, Bernard Jump, Jr., and Larry Schroeder, "The Outlook for City Fiscal Performance in Declining Regions," in Roy Bahl, ed., *The Fiscal Outlook For Cities: Implications of a National Urban Policy* (Syracuse: Syracuse University Press, 1978), pp. 1–47

Bailey and O'Connor, 1975—John J. Bailey and Robert J. O'Connor, "Operationalizing Incrementalisms: Measuring the Muddles," *Public Administration Review* 35,1 (January–February 1975), 60–66

Bailey, 1966—Stephen K. Bailey, "Co-ordinating The Great Society," *The Reporter* 34,6 (March 24, 1966), 39–41

Bailey, 1968—Stephen K. Bailey, "Managing The Federal Government," in Kermit Gordon, ed., *Agenda for the Nation* (Washington, D.C.: The Brookings Institution, 1968), pp. 301–332

Bailey, 1975—Stephen K. Bailey, *Educational Interest Groups in the Nation's Capital* (Washington, D.C.: American Council on Education, 1975)

Bailey, nd—Stephen Kemp Bailey, *Congress Makes a Law: The Story Behind the Employment Act of 1946* (New York: Vintage Books, nd; originally published by Columbia University Press, 1950)

Bailey and Mosher, 1968—Stephen K. Bailey and Edith K. Mosher, *ESEA: The Office of Education Administers a Law* (Syracuse, New York: Syracuse University Press, 1968)

Bailey, Frost, Marsh, Wood, 1962—Stephen K. Bailey, Richard T. Frost, Paul E. Marsh, and Robert C. Wood, *Schoolmen and Politics: A Study of State Aid to Education in the Northeast* (Syracuse, New York: Syracuse University Press, 1962)

Baker, 1939—Gladys Baker, *The County Agent* (Chicago, Illinois: The University Of Chicago Press, 1939)

Baldwin, 1968—Sidney Baldwin, *Poverty and Politics: The Rise and Decline of the Farm Security Administration* (Chapel Hill: The University of North Carolina Press, 1968)

Banfield, 1964—Edward C. Banfield, "In Defense of the American Party System," in Robert A. Goldwin, ed., *Political Parties, U.S.A.* (Chicago: Rand McNally and Company, 1964), pp. 21–39

Banfield, 1965—Edward C. Banfield, *Political Influence* (New York: The Free Press, 1965)

Banfield, 1973—Edward C. Banfield, "Making a New Federal Program: Model Cities, 1964–68," in Allan P. Sindler, ed., *Policy and Politics in America: Six Case Studies* (Boston: Little, Brown and Company, 1973), pp. 125–158

Bardach, 1979—Eugene Bardach, *The Implementation Game: What Happens After A Bill Becomes A Law* (Cambridge, Massachusetts: The M.I.T. Press, 1979)

Barnard, 1968—Chester I. Barnard, *The Functions of the Executive* (Cambridge, Massachusetts: Harvard University Press, 1968)

Barone, Ujifusa, and Matthews, 1972—Michael Barone, Grant Ujifusa, and Douglas Matthews, eds., *The Almanac of American Politics, 1972* (Boston: Gambit, 1972)

Barone, Ujifusa, and Matthews, 1974—Michael Barone, Grant Ujifusa, and Douglas Matthews, eds., *The Almanac of American Politics, 1974* (Boston: Gambit, 1973)

Barone, Ujifusa, and Matthews, 1975—Michael Barone, Grant Ujifusa, and Douglas Matthews, eds., *The Almanac of American Politics, 1976* (New York: E. P. Dutton and Company, Inc., 1975)

Barone, Ujifusa, and Matthews, 1977—Michael Barone, Grant Ujifusa, and Douglas Matthews, eds., *The Almanac of American Politics, 1978* (New York: E. P. Dutton and Company, Inc., 1977)

Barone, Ujifusa, and Matthews, 1979—Michael Barone, Grant Ujifusa, and Douglas Matthews, eds., *The Almanac of American Politics, 1980* (New York: E. P. Dutton and Company, Inc., 1979)

Barton, 1976a—Weldon V. Barton, "Food, Agriculture, and Administrative Adaptation to Political Change," *Public Administration Review* 36,2 (March–April 1976), 148–154

Barton, 1976b—Weldon V. Barton, "Coalition-Building in the United States House of Representatives: Agricultural Legislation in 1973," in James E. Anderson, ed., *Cases in Public Policy-Making* (New York: Praeger Publishers, 1976), pp. 1411–1461

Bauer, Pool, and Dexter, 1972—Raymond A. Bauer, Ithiel De Sola Pool, and Lewis Anthony Dexter, *American Business & Public Policy: The Politics Of Foreign Trade* (Chicago: Aldine Publishing Company, 1972, Second Edition)

Beam, 1979a—David R. Beam, "The Accidental Leviathan: Was the Growth of Government A Mistake," *Intergovernmental Perspective* 5,4 (Fall 1979), 12–19

Beam, 1979b—David Beam, "Theoretical Perspectives On Government Growth: Interpretation In The Social Sciences," Draft chapter to be included in a forthcoming A.C.I.R. report, 1979

Beam and Colella, 1979—David R. Beam and Cynthia C. Colella, "One Thing Leads To Another: An Evolutionary Perspective on Governmental Growth," Paper prepared for presentation at the 40th National Conference on Public Administration, Baltimore, Maryland, April 1–4, 1979

Beer, 1972—Samuel H. Beer, "The Disorders of Modernity: The American Case," *Political Quarterly* 43,1 (January–March 1972), 19–28

Beer, 1973—Samuel H. Beer, "The Modernization Of American Federalism," *Publius* 3,2 (Fall 1973), 49–95

Beer, 1974—Samuel H. Beer, "Government and Politics: An Imbalance," *The Center Magazine* 7,2 (March–April 1974), 10–22

Beer, 1976—Samuel H. Beer, "The Adoption Of General Revenue Sharing: A Case Study in Public Sector Politics," *Public Policy* 24,2 (Spring 1976), 127–195

Beer, 1977a—Samuel H. Beer, "Political Overload & Freedom," *Polity* 10,1 (Fall 1977), 5–17

Beer, 1977b—Samuel H. Beer, "A Political Scientist's View of Fiscal Federalism," in Wallace E. Oates, ed., *The Political Economy of Fiscal Federalism* (Lexington, Massachusetts: D. C. Heath and Company, 1977), pp. 21–46

Beer, 1978—Samuel H. Beer, "Federalism, Nationalism, and Democracy in America," *American Political Science Review* 72,1 (March 1978), 9–21

Beer, 1979—Samuel H. Beer, "In Search of a New Public Philosophy," in Anthony King, ed., *The New American Political System* (Washington, D.C.: American Enterprise Institute for Public Policy Research, 1979), pp. 5–44

Beer, 1980—Samuel H. Beer, "The Future of the States in the Federal System," (unpublished paper, January 1980)

Bell, 1975—Daniel Bell, "The Revolution of Rising Entitlements," *Fortune* 91,44 (April 1975), 98–103, 182, 185

Bell, 1976—Daniel Bell, *The Coming of Post-Industrial Society: A Venture in Social Forecasting* (New York: Basic Books, Inc., Publishers, 1976)

Bell, 1978—Daniel Bell, *The Cultural Contradictions of Capitalism* (New York: Basic Books, Inc., Publishers, 1978)

Bell and Gabler, 1976—Michael Bell and L. Richard Gabler, "Government Growth: An Intergovernmental Concern," *Intergovernmental Perspective* 2,4 (Fall 1976), 8–14

Bendiner, 1964—Robert Bendiner, *Obstacle Course on Capitol Hill* (New York: McGraw-Hill Book Company, 1964)

Berke and Kirst, 1972—Joel S. Berke and Michael W. Kirst, eds., *Federal Aid To Education: Who Benefits? Who Governs?* (Lexington, Massachusetts: D. C. Heath and Company, 1972)

Berry, 1977—Jeffrey M. Berry, *Lobbying for the People: The Political Behavior of Public Interest Groups* (Princeton, New Jersey: Princeton University Press, 1977)

Bish, 1971—Robert L. Bish, *The Public Economy of Metropolitan Areas* (Chicago: Markham Publishing Company, 1971)

Bish and Ostrom, 1973—Robert L. Bish and Vincent Ostrom, *Understanding Urban Government: Metropolitan Reform Reconsidered* (Washington, D.C.: American Enterprise Institute for Public Policy Research, 1973)

Bitterman, 1938—Henry J. Bitterman, *State and Federal Grants-In-Aid* (New York: Mentzer, Bush & Company, 1938)

Blechman, Gramlich and Hartman, 1974—Barry M. Blechman, Edward M. Gramlich, and Robert W. Hartman, *Setting National Priorities: The 1975 Budget* (Washington, D.C.: The Brookings Institution, 1974)

Blechman, Gramlich and Hartman, 1975—Barry M. Blechman, Edward M. Gramlich, and Robert W. Hartman, *Setting National Priorities: The 1976 Budget* (Washington, D.C.: The Brookings Institution, 1975)

Block, 1960—William J. Block, *The Separation of the Farm Bureau and the Extension Service: Political Issue in a Federal System* (Urbana: The University of Illinois Press, 1960)

Blough, 1952—Roy M. Blough, *The Federal Taxing Process* (New York: Prentice-Hall, 1952)

Bolton, 1966—Roger E. Bolton, *Defense Purchases and Regional Growth* (Washington, D.C.: The Brookings Institution, 1966)

Boorstin, 1953—Daniel J. Boorstin, *The Genius of American Politics* (Chicago: University of Chicago Press, 1953)

Borcherding, 1977—Thomas E. Borcherding, "One Hundred Years of Public Spending, 1870–1970," in Thomas E. Borcherding, ed., *Budgets and Bureaucrats: The Sources of Government Growth* (Durham, North Carolina: Duke University Press, 1977), pp. 19–44

Brady, Cooper, Hurley, 1979—David W. Brady, Joseph Cooper, Patricia A. Hurley, "The Decline of Party in the U.S. House of Representatives, 1887–1968," *Legislative Studies Quarterly* 4,3 (August 1979), 381–407

Branch, 1972—Taylor Branch, "Government Subsidies: Who Gets The $63 Billion?" *Washington Monthly* 4,1 (March 1972), 9–27

Break, 1967—George F. Break, *Intergovernmental Fiscal Relations in the United States* (Washington, D.C.: The Brookings Institution, 1967)

Break, 1980—George F. Break, "Intergovernmental Fiscal Relations," in Joseph A. Pechman, ed., *Setting National Priorities: Agenda for the 1980s* (Washington, D.C.: The Brookings Institution, 1980), pp. 247–281

Brittan, 1975—Samuel Brittan, "The Economic Contradictions of Democracy," *British Journal of Political Science* 5,2 (April 1975), 129–159

Broder, 1972—David S. Broder, *The Party's Over: The Failure of Politics in America* (New York: Harper & Row, Publishers, 1972)

Brown, 1978—Lawrence D. Brown, "Mayors and Models: Notes on the Study of Urban Politics," in Walter Dean Burnham and Martha Wagner Weinberg, eds., *American Politics and Public Policy* (Cambridge, Massachusetts: The M.I.T. Press, 1978), pp. 251–279

Brown and Frieden, 1976—Lawrence D. Brown and Bernard J. Frieden, "Rulemaking by Improvisation: Guidelines and Goals in the Model Cities Program," *Policy Sciences* 7,4 (December 1976), 455–488

Browning, 1973—Clyde E. Browning, *The Geography Of Federal Outlays: An Introduction and Comparative Inquiry* (Chapel Hill, North Carolina: University of North Carolina at Chapel Hill, Department of Geography, Studies in Geography, No. 4, 1973)

Bryce, 1895—James Bryce, *The American Commonwealth* (New York: MacMillan And Company, 1895, Third Edition, Two Volumes)

Buchanan, 1950—James M. Buchanan, "Federalism And Fiscal Equity," *American Economic Review* 40,4 (September 1950), 583–599

Buchanan, 1952a—James M. Buchanan, "Federal Grants And Resource Allocation," *Journal of Political Economy* 40,3 (June 1952), 208–217

Buchanan, 1952b—James M. Buchanan, "A Reply (to A. D. Scott)," *Journal of Political Economy* 40,6 (December 1952), 536–538

Burch, 1962—Philip H. Burch, Jr., *Highway Revenue And Expenditure Policy In The United States* (New Brunswick, New Jersey: Rutgers University Press, 1962)

Burdick, 1923—Charles K. Burdick, "Federal Aid Legislation," *Cornell Law Quarterly* 8,4 (June 1923), 324–337

Bureau of the Census, 1974—Bureau of the Census, *1972 Census of Governments, Topical Studies, Volume 6, Number 3: State Payments to Local Governments* (Washington, D.C.: U.S. Government Printing Office, 1974)

Bureau of the Census, 1976—Bureau of the Census, *Classification Manual Government Finances* (Washington, D.C.: U.S. Department of Commerce, Bureau of the Census, 1976)

Burnham, 1965—Walter Dean Burnham, "The Changing Shape of the American Political Universe," *American Political Science Review* 59,1 (March 1965), 7–28

Burnham, 1969—Walter Dean Burnham, "The End of American Party Politics," *Trans-action* 7,2 (December 1969), 12–22

Burnham, 1970—Walter Dean Burnham, *Critical Elections and the Mainsprings of American Politics* (New York: W. W. Norton & Company, Inc., 1970)

Burnham, 1974a—Walter Dean Burnham, "Theory and Voting Research: Some Reflections on Converse's 'Change in the American Electorate,' " *American Political Science Review* 68,3 (September 1974), 1002–1023

Burnham, 1974b—Walter Dean Burnham, "Rejoinder to 'Comments' by Philip Converse and Jerrold Rusk," *American Political Science Review* 68,3 (September 1974), 1050–1057

Burns, 1973—James MacGregor Burns, *Presidential Government: The Crucible of Leadership* (Boston: Houghton Mifflin Company, 1973)

Business Week, 1976–"The Second War Between The States," Business Week (May 17, 1976), pp. 92–95

Caddell, 1979a–Patrick H. Caddell, "Trapped in a Downward Spiral," Public Opinion 2,5 (October–November 1979), 2–7, 52–55, 58–60

Caddell, 1979b–Patrick H. Caddell, "Caddell Rebuts Miller," Public Opinion 2,5 (October–November 1979), 59

Campbell, Gurin, Miller, 1971–Angus Campbell, Gerald Gurin, and Warren E. Miller, The Voter Decides (Westport, Connecticut: Greenwood Press, Publishers, 1971–originally published by Row, Peterson and Company, 1954)

Campbell, Converse, Miller, Stokes, 1960–Angus Campbell, Philip E. Converse, Warren E. Miller, and Donald E. Stokes, The American Voter (New York: John Wiley and Sons, Inc., 1960)

Campbell, Converse, Miller, Stokes, 1966–Angus Campbell, Philip E. Converse, Warren E. Miller, and Donald E. Stokes, Elections and the Political Order (New York: John Wiley and Sons, Inc., 1966)

Cameron, 1978–David R. Cameron, "The Expansion of the Public Economy: A Comparative Analysis," American Political Science Review 72,4 (December 1978), 1243–1261

Caraley, 1976–Demetrios Caraley, "Congressional Politics and Urban Aid," Political Science Quarterly 91,1 (Spring 1976), 19–45

Caraley, 1978a–Demetrios Caraley, "Congressional Politics and Urban Aid: A 1978 Postscript," Political Science Quarterly 93,3 (Fall 1978), 411–419

Caraley, 1978b–Demetrios Caraley, "The Carter Congress and Urban Programs: First Soundings," in Walter Dean Burnham and Martha Wagner Weinberg, eds., American Politics and Public Policy (Cambridge, Massachusetts: The M.I.T. Press, 1978), pp. 188–221

Caro, 1975–Robert A. Caro, The Power Broker: Robert Moses and the Fall of New York (New York: Vintage Books, 1975)

Carson, nd–Rachel Carson, Silent Spring (Greenwich, Connecticut: Fawcett Publications, Inc., nd; originally published by Houghton Mifflin Company, 1962)

Cater, 1965–Douglass Cater, Power In Washington (New York: Random House, Vintage Books, 1965)

Catsambas, 1978–Thanos Catsambas, Regional Impacts of Federal Fiscal Policy: Theory and Estimation of Economic Incidence (Lexington, Massachusetts: D. C. Heath and Company, 1978)

Cavala and Wildavsky, 1970–Bill Cavala and Aaron Wildavsky, "The Political Feasibility Of Income By Right," Public Policy 18,3 (Spring 1970), 321–354

Cawley and Kramer, 1979–Jerry P. Cawley and Kevin L. Kramer, Reconciling Treasury's "Federal Aid to States" Report with Community Services Administration's "Geographic Distribution Of Federal Funds" Report (Ann Arbor, Michigan: Ph.D. Program in Urban and Regional Planning, The University of Michigan, The Intergovernmental Fiscal Analysis Project, Analysis Series Paper #10, April, 1979)

Cawley, Fossett, Kramer, 1980–Jerry P. Cawley, James W. Fossett, and Kevin L. Kramer, Estimates of the Geographic Impact of Alternative 1981 Budget Proposals (Ann Arbor, Michigan: Ph.D. Program in Urban and Regional Planning, The University of Michigan, The Intergovernmental Fiscal Analysis Project, Information Report #5, May, 1980)

Cawley, Kramer, Ward, Anton, 1979–Jerry P. Cawley, Kevin L. Kramer, Peter D. Ward, Thomas J. Anton, Indirect Federal Support Activities: Patterns in the FIXS Data (Ann Arbor, Michigan: Ph.D. Program in Urban and Regional Planning, The University of Michigan, The Intergovernmental Fiscal Analysis Project, Working Paper Series, Analysis #4, February, 1979)

Chamberlain, 1946–Lawrence H. Chamberlain, The President, Congress, and Legislation (New York: Columbia University Press, 1946)

Citrin, 1974–Jack Citrin, "Comment: The Political Relevance of Trust in Government," American Political Science Review 68,3 (September 1974), 973–988

Citrin, 1979–Jack Citrin, "Do People Want Something for Nothing: Public Opinion on Taxes and Government Spending," National Tax Journal 32,2 (June 1979, Supplement), 113–129

Clark, 1938–Jane Perry Clark, The Rise of a New Federalism: Federal-State Cooperation in the United States (New York: Columbia University Press, 1938)

Clark, 1945—Colin Clark, "Public Finance and Changes in the Value of Money," *Economic Journal* 55 (December 1945), 371–389

Clark, 1980—Timothy B. Clark, "The Public and the Private Sectors—The Old Distinctions Grow Fuzzy," *National Journal* 12,3 (January 19, 1980), 99–104

Cleaveland, 1969—Frederic N. Cleaveland, ed., *Congress "and" Urban Problems: A Casebook on the Legislative Process* (Washington, D.C.: The Brookings Institution, 1969)

Clotfelter, 1970—James Clotfelter, "Senate Voting And Constituency Stake In Defense Spending," *Journal of Politics* 32,4 (November 1970), 979–983

Cnudde and McCrone, 1969—Charles Cnudde and Donald J. McCrone, "Party Competition and Welfare Policies in the American States," *American Political Science Review* 58,3 (September 1969), 858–866

Cobb and Elder, 1971—Roger W. Cobb and Charles D. Elder, "The Politics of Agenda-Building: An Alternative Perspective for Modern Democratic Theory," *Journal of Politics* 33,4 (November 1971), 892–915

Cobb and Elder, 1972—Roger W. Cobb and Charles D. Elder, *Participation in American Politics: The Dynamics of Agenda-Building* (Baltimore: The Johns Hopkins University Press, 1972)

Cobb, Ross, Ross, 1976—Roger Cobb, Jennie-Keith Ross, Marc Howard Ross, "Agenda Building as a Comparative Political Process," *American Political Science Review* 70,1 (March 1976), 126–138

Cohen and Grodzins, 1963—Jacob Cohen and Morton Grodzins, "How Much Economic Sharing in American Federalism?" *American Political Science Review* 57,1 (March 1963), 5–23

Cohen and March, 1974—Michael D. Cohen and James G. March, *Leadership and Ambiguity: The American College President* (New York: McGraw-Hill Book Company, 1974)

Cohen, March and Olsen, 1972—Michael D. Cohen, James G. March and Johan P. Olsen, "A Garbage Can Model of Organizational Choice," *Administrative Science Quarterly* 17,1 (March 1972), 1–25

Colella, 1979—Cynthia Cates Colella, "The Creation, Care and Feeding of Leviathan: Who and What Makes Government Grow," *Intergovernmental Perspective* 5,4 (Fall 1979), 6–11

Commentary, 1973—"Nixon, the Great Society, and the Future of Social Policy: A Symposium," *Commentary* 55,5 (May 1973), 31–61

Commission on Intergovernmental Relations, 1955—Commission on Intergovernmental Relations (Kestnbaum Commission), *A Report To The President* (Washington, D.C.: U.S. Government Printing Office, 1955)

Congressional Budget Office, 1976—Congressional Budget Office, Comptroller General's Office, *The Number of Federal Employees Engaged in Regulatory Activities,* Staff paper prepared for the Subcommittee on Oversight and Investigations of the Committee on Interstate and Foreign Commerce, House of Representatives (Washington, D.C.: U.S. Government Printing Office, 1976)

Congressional Budget Office, 1977—The Congressional Budget Office, The Congress Of The United States (Peggy L. Cuciti main author) *Troubled Local Economies And The Distribution Of Federal Dollars* (Washington, D.C.: United States Government Printing Office, 1977)

Congressional Budget Office, 1980—Congressional Budget Office (Mark Stertz main author), *Tax Expenditures: Current Issues and Five-Year Budget Projections for Fiscal Years 1981–1985—A Report to the Senate and House Committees on the Budget—Part III* (Washington, D.C.: U.S. Government Printing Office, 1980)

Converse, 1972—Philip E. Converse, "Change in the American Electorate," in Angus Campbell and Philip E. Converse, eds., *The Human Meaning of Social Change* (New York: Russell Sage Foundation, 1972), pp. 263–337

Converse, 1974—Philip E. Converse, "Comment on Burnham's 'Theory and Voting Research,'" *American Political Science Review* 68,3 (September 1974), 1024–1027

Converse, 1975—Philip E. Converse, "Public Opinion and Voting Behavior," in Fred I. Greenstein and Nelson W. Polsby, eds., *Handbook Of Political Science, Volume 4: Nongovernmental Politics* (Reading, Massachusetts: Addison-Wesley Publishing Company, 1975), pp. 75–169

Converse, 1976—Philip E. Converse, *The Dynamics of Party Support: Cohort-Analyzing Party Identification* (Beverly Hills: Sage Publications, 1976)

Converse and Markus, 1979—Philip E. Converse and Gregory B. Markus, "Plus ça change . . . : The New CPS Election Study Panel," *American Political Science Review* 73,1 (March 1979), 32–49

Cook, 1979—Robert F. Cook, "Fiscal Implications of CETA Public Service Employment," in L. Kenneth Hubbell, ed., *Fiscal Crisis in American Cities: The Federal Response* (Cambridge, Massachusetts: Ballinger Publishing Company, 1979), pp. 193–228

Corwin, 1923—Edward S. Corwin, "The Spending Power Of Congress—Apropos The Maternity Act," *Harvard Law Review* 36,5 (March 1923), 548–582

Corwin, 1950—Edward S. Corwin, "The Passing of Dual Federalism," *Virginia Law Review* 36,1 (February 1950), 1–24

Coser and Howe, 1976—Lewis A. Coser and Irving Howe, eds., *The New Conservatives: A Critique from the Left* (New York: New American Library, A Meridian Book, 1976, Revised Edition)

Council of State Governments, 1949—The Council of State Governments, *Federal Grants-In-Aid: Report Of The Committee On Federal Grants-In-Aid* (np.: The Council of State Governments, 1949)

Courant, Gramlich and Rubinfeld, 1979a—Paul N. Courant, Edward M. Gramlich, and Daniel L. Rubinfeld, *The Tax Limitation Movement: Conservative Drift or the Search for a Free Lunch?* (Ann Arbor, Michigan: University of Michigan, Institute of Public Policy Studies, Discussion Paper No. 141, 1979)

Cover and Mayhew, 1977—Albert D. Cover and David R. Mayhew, "Congressional Dynamics and the Decline of Competitive Congressional Elections," in Lawrence C. Dodd and Bruce I. Oppenheimer, eds., *Congress Reconsidered* (New York: Praeger Publishers, 1977), pp. 54–72

Crecine, 1967—John P. Crecine, "A Computer Simulation Model Of Municipal Budgeting," *Management Science* 13,11 (July 1967), 786–815

Crecine, 1968—John P. Crecine, "A Simulation of Municipal Budgeting: The Impact of Problem Environment," in William D. Coplin, ed., *Simulation in the Study of Politics* (Chicago: Markham Publishing Company, 1968), pp. 115–146

Crecine, 1969—John P. Crecine, *Governmental Problem-Solving: A Computer Simulation of Municipal Budgeting* (Chicago: Rand McNally and Company, 1969)

Crecine, 1971—John P. Crecine, "Defense Budgeting: Organizational Adaptation to Environmental Constraints," in R. F. Byrne, A. Charnes, W. W. Cooper, O. A. Davis, and Dorothy Gilford, eds., *Studies in Budgeting* (Amsterdam: North-Holland Publishing Company, 1971), pp. 210–261

Crenson, 1972—Matthew A. Crenson, *The Un-Politics of Air Pollution: A Study of Non-Decision-making in the Cities* (Baltimore: The Johns Hopkins University Press, 1972)

Crenson, 1975—Matthew A. Crenson, *The Federal Machine: Beginnings of Bureaucracy in Jacksonian America* (Baltimore: The Johns Hopkins University Press, 1975)

Cronin, 1970—Thomas E. Cronin, "The Textbook Presidency And Political Science," Paper prepared for delivery at the Annual Meeting of the American Political Science Association, 1970

Crozier, 1975—Michel Crozier, "Western Europe," in Michel Crozier, Samuel P. Huntington, Joji Watanuki, eds., *The Crisis of Democracy* (New York: New York University Press, 1975), pp. 11–57

Crozier and Thoenig, 1976—Michel Crozier and Jean-Claude Thoenig, "The Regulation of Complex Organized Systems," *Administrative Science Quarterly* 21,4 (December 1976), 547–570

Cuciti, 1978—Peggy L. Cuciti, main author, Subcommittee on the City of the Committee on Banking, Finance and Urban Affairs, House of Representatives, *City Need and the Responsiveness of Federal Grant Programs,* 95th Congress, Second Session (Washington, D.C.: U.S. Government Printing Office, August 1978)

C.S.A., 1976—Community Services Administration, "Instructions for Reporting of Federal Outlays by Geographic Location," Interagency memo to heads of executive departments and agencies dated March 4, 1976

Cyert and March, 1963—Richard M. Cyert and James G. March, *A Behaviorial Theory of the Firm* (Englewood Cliffs, New Jersey: Prentice-Hall, Inc., 1963)

Dahl and Lindblom, 1963—Robert A. Dahl and Charles E. Lindblom, *Politics, Economics, and Welfare: Planning and Politico-Economic Systems Resolved into Basic Social Processes* (New York: Harper and Row, Publishers, 1963)

Davidson, 1966—Roger H. Davidson, *Coalition-Building for Depressed Areas Bills: 1955–1965* (Indianapolis: The Bobbs-Merrill Company, Inc., Inter-University Case Program, No. 103, 1966)

Davidson, 1972—Roger H. Davidson, *The Politics of Comprehensive Manpower Legislation* (Baltimore: The Johns Hopkins University Press, 1972)

Davidson, 1974a—Roger H. Davidson, "Representation and Congressional Committees," *Annals of the American Academy of Political and Social Science,* vol. 411 (January 1974), 48–62

Davidson, 1974b—Roger H. Davidson, "Policy Making in the Manpower Subgovernment," in Michael P. Smith, ed., *Politics in America: Studies in Policy Analysis* (New York: Random House, 1974), pp. 82–106

Davidson, 1977—Roger H. Davidson, "Breaking Up Those 'Cozy Triangles': An Impossible Dream?" in Susan Welch and John G. Peters, eds., *Legislative Reform and Public Policy* (New York: Praeger, 1977), pp. 30–53

Davis, Dempster, Wildavsky, 1966—Otto A. Davis, M. A. H. Dempster, Aaron Wildavsky, "A Theory of the Budgetary Process," *American Political Science Review* 60,3 (September 1966), 529–547

Davis, Dempster, Wildavsky, 1971—Otto A. Davis, M. A. H. Dempster, Aaron Wildavsky, "On the Process of Budgeting II: An Empirical Study of Congressional Appropriations," in R. F. Byrne, A. Charnes, W. W. Cooper, O. A. Davis, and Dorothy Gilford, eds., *Studies in Budgeting* (Amsterdam: North-Holland Publishing Company, 1971), pp. 292–375

Davis, Dempster, Wildavsky, 1974—Otto A. Davis, M. A. H. Dempster, Aaron Wildavsky, "Towards a Predictive Theory of Government Expenditure: U.S. Domestic Appropriations," *British Journal of Political Science* 4,4 (October 1974), 419–452

Dawson and Gray, 1971—Richard E. Dawson and Virginia Gray, "State Welfare Policies," in Herbert Jacob and Kenneth N. Vines, eds., *Politics In The American States: A Comparative Analysis* (Boston: Little, Brown and Company, 1971, Second Edition), pp. 433–476

Dawson and Robinson, 1963—Richard E. Dawson and James A. Robinson, "Inter-Party Competition, Economic Variables, and Welfare Policies in the American States," *Journal of Politics* 25,2 (May 1963), 265–289

Dearing, 1942—Charles L. Dearing, *American Highway Policy* (Washington, D.C.: The Brookings Institution, 1942)

Derthick, 1968—Martha Derthick, "Intercity Differences in Administration of the Public Assistance Program: The Case of Massachusetts," in James Q. Wilson, ed., *City Politics and Public Policy* (New York: John Wiley and Sons, Inc., 1968), pp. 243–266

Derthick, 1970—Martha Derthick, *The Influence of Federal Grants: Public Assistance in Massachusetts* (Cambridge, Massachusetts: Harvard University Press, 1970)

Derthick, 1972—Martha Derthick, *New Towns In-Town: Why a Federal Program Failed* (Washington, D.C.: The Urban Institute, 1972)

Derthick, 1974—Martha Derthick, *Between State and Nation: Regional Organizations of the United States* (Washington, D.C.: The Brookings Institution, 1974)

Derthick, 1975—Martha Derthick, *Uncontrollable Spending For Social Services Grants* (Washington, D.C.: The Brookings Institution, 1975)

Derthick, 1976a—Martha Derthick, "Guidelines for Social Services Grants," *Policy Sciences* 7,4 (December 1976), 489–504

Derthick, 1976b—Martha Derthick, "Professional Fiefdoms Appraised: The Case of Social Services," *Publius* 6,2 (Spring 1976), 121–134

Derthick, 1979a—Martha Derthick, "How Easy Votes On Social Security Came To An End," *The Public Interest* No. 54 (Winter 1979), 94–105

Derthick, 1979b—Martha Derthick, *Policymaking for Social Security* (Washington, D.C.: The Brookings Institution, 1979)

Deutsch, 1966—Karl W. Deutsch, *The Nerves of Government: Models of Political Communication and Control* (New York: The Free Press, 1966)

Dluhy, 1979—Milan J. Dluhy, "Design and Delivery of Social Welfare Services: Politics and Issues at the Local Level," in Gary Tobin, ed., *The Changing Structure of the City: What Happened to the Urban Crisis* (Beverly Hills: Sage Publications, 1979), pp. 141–156

Dodd, 1977—Lawrence C. Dodd, "Congress and the Quest for Power," in Lawrence C. Dodd and Bruce I. Oppenheimer, eds., *Congress Reconsidered* (New York: Praeger Publishers, 1977), pp. 269–307

Dommel, 1974—Paul R. Dommel, *The Politics of Revenue Sharing* (Bloomington and London: Indiana University Press, 1974)

Dommel, 1979—Paul R. Dommel, "Block Grants for Community Development: Decentralized Decisionmaking," in L. Kenneth Hubbell, ed., *Fiscal Crisis in American Cities: The Federal Response* (Cambridge, Massachusetts: Ballinger Publishing Company, 1979), pp. 229–255

Dommel and Jaffe, 1978—Paul R. Dommel and Jacob M. Jaffe, *Report On The Allocation Of Community Development Funds To Small Cities* (Washington, D.C.: The Brookings Institution, 1978, processed)

Dommel, *et al.,* 1978—Paul R. Dommel, Richard P. Nathan, Sara Liebschutz and Margaret T. Wrightson, and associates, *Decentralizing Community Development* (Washington, D.C.: U.S. Government Printing Office, 1978)

Douglas, 1976—James Douglas, "Review Article: The Overloaded Crown," *British Journal of Political Science* 6,4 (October 1976), 483–505

Douglas, 1920a—Paul H. Douglas, "The Development of a System of Federal Grants-In-Aid I," *Political Science Quarterly* 35,2 (June 1920), 255–271

Douglas, 1920b—Paul H. Douglas, "The Development of a System of Federal Grants-In-Aid II," *Political Science Quarterly* 35,4 (December 1920), 522–544

. Douglas, 1939—Paul H. Douglas, *Social Security in the United States: An Analysis and Appraisal of the Federal Social Security Act* (New York: McGraw-Hill Book Company, Inc., Whittlese House, 1939, Second Edition)

Downs, 1960—Anthony Downs, "Why the Government Budget Is Too Small in a Democracy," *World Politics* 12,4 (July 1960), 541–563

Downs, 1967—Anthony Downs, *Inside Bureaucracy* (Boston: Little, Brown and Company, 1967)

Downs, 1972—Anthony Downs, "Up and Down with Ecology—The 'Issue-Attention Cycle'," *The Public Interest* No. 28 (Summer 1972), 38–50

Downs and Larkey, 1979—George Downs and Patrick Larkey, "Theorizing about Public Expenditure Decision-Making: (as) if Wishes Were Horses . . . ," *Policy Sciences* 11,2 (November 1979), 143–156

Downs and Mohr, 1976—George W. Downs, Jr., and Lawrence B. Mohr, "Conceptual Issues in the Study of Innovation," *Administrative Science Quarterly* 21,3 (December 1976), 700–714

Doyle, 1979—James Doyle, "Review of Federal Agency System" Office of Management and Budget internal report, 1979.

Drucker, 1966—Peter F. Drucker, "Notes on the New Politics," *The Public Interest,* No. 4 (Summer 1966), 13–30

Drucker, 1969—Peter F. Drucker, "The Sickness Of Government," *The Public Interest,* No. 14 (Winter 1969), 3–23

Drummond, 1949—Roscoe Drummond, "Are We Maintaining Our Federal System?" *State Government* 22,2 (February 1949 Supplement), 1–4

Duncan and Shelton, 1978a—Joseph W. Duncan and William C. Shelton, *Revolution in United States Government Statistics, 1926–1976* (Washington, D.C.: U.S. Government Printing Office, 1978)

Duncan and Shelton, 1978b—Joseph W. Duncan and William C. Shelton, *A Framework for Planning U.S. Federal Statistics for the 1980s* (Washington, D.C.: U.S. Government Printing Office, 1978)

Dye, 1966—Thomas R. Dye, *Politics, Economics, and the Public: Policy Outcomes in the American States* (Chicago: Rand McNally and Company, 1966)

Dye and Hurley, 1978—Thomas R. Dye and Thomas L. Hurley, "The Responsiveness of Federal and State Governments to Urban Problems, *Journal of Politics* 40,1 (February 1978), 196–207

Edelman, 1964—Murray Edelman, *The Symbolic Uses Of Politics* (Urbana, Chicago, and London: University of Illinois Press, 1964)

Edelman, 1971—Murray Edelman, *Politics as Symbolic Action: Mass Arousal and Quiescence* (Chicago: Markham Publishing Company, 1971)

Edelman, 1977—Murray Edelman, *Political Language: Words That Succeed and Policies That Fail* (New York: Academic Press, 1977)

Eidenberg and Morey, 1969—Eugene Eidenberg and Roy D. Morey, *An Act of Congress: The Legislative Process and the Making of Educational Policy* (New York: W. W. Norton and Company, 1969)

Elazar, 1962—Daniel J. Elazar, *The American Partnership: Intergovernmental Co-operation in the Nineteenth-Century United States* (Chicago: University of Chicago Press, 1962)

Elazar, 1965—Daniel J. Elazar, "The Shaping of Intergovernmental Relations in the Twentieth Century," *Annals of the American Academy of Political and Social Science* Volume 359 (May 1965), 10–22

Elazar, 1967—Daniel J. Elazar, "Urban Problems and the Federal Government: A Historical Inquiry," *Political Science Quarterly* 84,4 (December 1967), 505–525

Elazar, 1972—Daniel J. Elazar, *American Federalism: A View from the States* (New York: Thomas Y. Crowell Company, 1972, Second Edition)

Elazar, 1973—Daniel J. Elazar, "Cursed By Bigness Or Toward A Post-Technocratic Federalism," *Publius* 3,2 (Fall 1973), 239–298

Elazar, 1976—Daniel J. Elazar, "Federalism vs. Decentralization: The Drift From Authenticity," *Publius* 6,4 (Fall 1976), 9–20

Elazar, 1978—Daniel J. Elazar, "Is Federalism Compatible with Prefectorial Administration?" Paper prepared for delivery at the 1978 Annual Meeting of The American Political Science Association, The New York Hilton Hotel, New York, New York, August 31–September 3, 1978

Etzioni, 1967—Amitai Etzioni, "Mixed-Scanning: A 'Third' Approach to Decision-Making," *Public Administration Review* 27,5 (December 1967), 385–392

Etzioni, 1977–1978—Amitai Etzioni, "Societal Overload: Sources, Components, and Corrections," *Political Science Quarterly* 92,4 (Winter 1977–1978), 607–631

Eulau, 1973—Heinz Eulau, "Polarity In Representational Federalism: A Neglected Theme of Political Theory," *Publius* 3,2 (Fall 1973), 153–171

Eyestone, 1977—Robert Eyestone, "Confusion, Diffusion, and Innovation," *American Political Science Review* 71,2 (June 1977), 441–447

Fabricant, 1952—Solomon Fabricant, *The Trend of Government Activity in the United States since 1900* (New York: National Bureau of Economic Research, Inc., 1952)

Farkas, 1971—Suzanne Farkus, *Urban Lobbying: Mayors in the Federal Arena* (New York: New York University Press, 1971)

Fenno, 1966—Richard F. Fenno, Jr., *The Power of the Purse: Appropriation Politics in Congress* (Boston: Little, Brown and Company, 1966)

Fenno, 1973—Richard F. Fenno, Jr., *Congressmen In Committees* (Boston: Little, Brown and Company, 1973)

Fenno, 1977—Richard F. Fenno, Jr., "U.S. House Members in Their Constituencies: An Exploration," *American Political Science Review* 71,3 (September 1977), 883–917

Fenno, 1978—Richard F. Fenno, Jr., *Home Style: House Members in Their Districts* (Boston: Little, Brown And Company, 1978)

Fenton, 1957—John H. Fenton, *Politics In The Border States* (New Orleans, La.: Hauser Press, 1957)

Fenton, 1966—John H. Fenton, *Midwest Politics* (New York: Holt, Rinehart and Winston, 1966)

Fenton and Chamberlayne, 1969—John H. Fenton and Donald W. Chamberlayne, "The Literature Dealing With The Relationships Between Political Processes, Socioeconomic Conditions & Public Policies in the American States: A Bibliography Essay," *Polity* 1,3 (Spring 1969), 388–404

Ferejohn, 1974—John A. Ferejohn, *Pork Barrel Politics: Rivers and Harbors Legislation, 1947–1968* (Stanford, California: Stanford University Press, 1974)

Fesler, 1940—James W. Fesler, "The Independence of State Utility Commissions, I," *Journal of Politics* 2,4 (November 1940), 367–390

Fesler, 1941—James W. Fesler, "The Independence of State Utility Commissions, II," *Journal of Politics* 3,1 (February 1941), 42–66

Fesler, 1949—James W. Fesler, *Area And Administration* (Alabama: University of Alabama Press, 1949)

Fesler, 1957—James W. Fesler, "Administrative Literature and the Second Hoover Commission Reports," *American Political Science Review* 51,1 (March 1957), 135–157

Fesler, 1965—James W. Fesler, "Approaches To The Understanding Of Decentralization," *Journal of Politics* 27,3 (August 1965), 536–566

Fine, 1964—Sidney Fine, *Laissez Faire and the General-Welfare State: A Study of Conflict in American Thought, 1865–1901* (Ann Arbor, Michigan: University of Michigan Press, 1964)

Fiorina, 1977a—Morris P. Fiorina, "Big Government: A Congressman's Best Friend," *Washington Monthly* 9,1 (March 1977), 55–61

Fiorina, 1977b—Morris P. Fiorina, "The Case of the Vanishing Marginals: The Bureaucracy Did It," *American Political Science Review* 71,1 (March 1977), 177–181

Fiorina, 1977c—Morris P. Fiorina, *Congress: Keystone of the Washington Establishment* (New Haven and London: Yale University Press, 1977)

Fiorina, 1979—Morris P. Fiorina, "Legislative Facilitation of Government Growth: Universalism and Reciprocity Practices in Majority Rule Institutions" (St. Louis, Missouri: Washington University, Center for the Study of American Business, Working Paper Number 48, October 1979)

First National Bank of Boston, 1979—The First National Bank of Boston/Toucher Ross & Co., *Urban Fiscal Stress: A Comparative Analysis of 66 U.S. Cities* (Boston, Massachusetts: Economics Department, First National Bank of Boston, 1979)

Fisher, 1961—Glenn W. Fisher, "Determinants Of State And Local Government Expenditures: A Preliminary Analysis," *National Tax Journal* 14,4 (December 1961), 349–355

Fisher, 1964—Glenn W. Fisher, "Interstate Variation In State And Local Governmental Expenditures," *National Tax Journal* 17,1 (March 1964), 57–74

Fisher, 1969—Glenn W. Fisher, *Taxes And Politics: A Study Of Illinois Public Finance* (Urbana: University of Illinois Press, 1969)

Ford, 1909—Henry Jones Ford, "The Influence Of State Politics In Expanding Federal Power," *Proceedings Of The American Political Science Association At Its 5th Annual Meeting, Washington, D.C. And Richmond, Virginia, December 28–31, 1908* (Baltimore, Maryland: The Waverly Press, 1909), pp. 53–63

Fossett, 1979—James W. Fossett, "Federal Grants and Big City Politics—Some Preliminary Findings," Paper prepared for delivery at the Midwest Political Science Association Annual Convention, April 20, 1979

Fossett and Nathan, 1980—James W. Fossett and Richard P. Nathan, *The Prospects for Urban Revival* (forthcoming, 1980)

Fox and Hammond, 1977—Harrison W. Fox, Jr. and Susan Webb Hammond, *Congressional Staffs: The Invisible Force in American Lawmaking* (New York: The Free Press, 1977)

Freeman, 1965—J. Leiper Freeman, *The Political Process: Executive Bureau-Legislative Committee Relations* (New York: Random House, 1965, Revised Edition)

Freeman, 1975—Roger A. Freeman, *The Growth of American Government: A Morphology of the Welfare State* (Stanford, California: Stanford University, The Hoover Institution Press, 1975)

Fried, 1975—Robert C. Fried, "Comparative Urban Policy and Performance," in Fred I. Greenstein and Nelson W. Polsby, eds., *Handbook of Political Science, Volume 6: Policies and Policymaking* (Reading, Massachusetts: Addison-Wesley Publishing Company, 1975), pp. 305–379

Fried, Rivlin, Schultze, and Teeters, 1973—Edward R. Fried, Alice M. Rivlin, Charles L. Schultze, and Nancy E. Teeters, *Setting National Priorities: The 1974 Budget* (Washington, D.C.: The Brookings Institution, 1973)

Frieden and Kaplan, 1977—Bernard J. Frieden and Marshall Kaplan, *The Politics of Neglect: Urban Aid from Model Cities to Revenue Sharing* (Cambridge, Massachusetts: The M.I.T. Press, 1977)

Friedman, 1953—Milton Friedman, "The Methodology of Positive Economics," in Milton Friedman, *Essays in Positive Economics* (Chicago: University of Chicago Press, 1953), pp. 3–43

Friedman, 1962—Milton Friedman, *Capitalism & Freedom* (Chicago: The University of Chicago Press, 1962)

Friedman, 1976—Milton Friedman, "The Line We Dare Not Cross: The Fragility of Freedom at 60%," *Encounter* 47,5 (November 1976), 8–14

Friedman, 1978—Milton Friedman, "From Galbraith To Economic Freedom," in Milton Friedman, *Tax Limitation, Inflation And The Role Of Government* (Dallas: The Fisher Institute, 1978), pp. 52–81

Friedman, 1971—Robert S. Friedman, "State Politics and Highways," in Herbert Jacob and Kenneth N. Vines, eds., *Politics In The American States: A Comparative Analysis* (Boston: Little, Brown and Company, 1971, Second Edition), pp. 477–519

Friedrich, 1968—Carl J. Friedrich, *Trends of Federalism in Theory and Practice* (New York: Praeger, 1968)

Furniss and Tilton, 1977—Norman Furniss and Timothy Tilton, *The Case for the Welfare State: From Social Security to Social Equality* (Bloomington: Indiana University Press, 1977)

Gardner, 1973—John W. Gardner, *In Common Cause* (New York: W. W. Norton & Company, Inc., 1973, Revised Edition)

Gates, 1934—Paul Wallace Gates, *The Illinois Central Railroad and Its Colonization Work* (Cambridge, Massachusetts: Harvard University Press, 1934)

Gates, 1954—Paul Wallace Gates, *Fifty Million Acres: Conflicts over Kansas Land Policy, 1854–1890* (Ithaca, New York: Cornell University Press, 1954)

General Accounting Office, 1977a—General Accounting Office, *Changing Patterns of Federal Aid to State and Local Governments, 1969–1975* (Washington, D.C.: U.S. Government Printing Office, 1977)

General Accounting Office, 1977b—General Accounting Office, *Federal Information Sources and Systems* (Washington, D.C.: U.S. Government Printing Office, 1977)

General Accounting Office, 1979—General Accounting Office, *Grant Auditing: A Maze of Inconsistency, Gaps, and Duplication That Needs Overhauling* (Washington, D.C.: U.S. Government Printing Office, 1979)

General Accounting Office, 1980—General Accounting Office, *GAO Findings on Federal Internal Audit—A Summary* (Washington, D.C.: U.S. Government Printing Office, 1980)

Gifford, 1978—Bernard R. Gifford, "New York City and Cosmopolitan Liberalism," *Political Science Quarterly* 93,4 (Winter 1978), 559–584

Ginzberg and Solow, 1974—Eli Ginzberg and Robert M. Solow, eds., *The Great Society: Lessons for the Future* (New York: Basic Books, Inc., Publishers, 1974)

Glazer and Kristol, 1976—Nathan Glazer and Irving Kristol, eds., *The American Commonwealth—1976* (New York: Basic Books, Inc., Publishers, 1976)

Glickman, 1980—Norman J. Glickman, ed., *The Urban Impacts Of Federal Policies* (Baltimore: Johns Hopkins University Press, 1980)

Goldenberg, Fossett, and Anton, 1976—Edie N. Goldenberg, James W. Fossett, and Thomas J. Anton, "Program Evaluation and the Policy Process: The Case of General Revenue Sharing," in David A. Caputo and Richard L. Cole, eds., *Revenue Sharing: Methodological Approaches and Problems* (Lexington, Massachusetts: D. C. Heath and Company, 1976), pp. 85–107

Goldwin, 1978—Robert A. Goldwin, "That May Be All Right in Practice, but It Doesn't Work in Theory: Comments on Daniel Elazar's 'Is Federalism Compatible with Prefectorial Administration?' " Paper prepared for delivery at the 1978 Annual Meeting of The American Political Science Association, The New York Hilton Hotel, New York, New York, August 31–September 3, 1978

Golembiewski, 1977a—Robert T. Golembiewski, "A Critique of 'Democratic Administration' and Its Supporting Ideation," *American Political Science Review* 71,4 (December 1977), 1488–1507

Golembiewski, 1977b—Robert T. Golembiewski, "Observations on 'Doing Political Theory': A Rejoinder," *American Political Science Review* 71,4 (December 1977), 1526–1531

Goodrich, 1948—Carter Goodrich, "National Planning of Internal Improvements," *Political Science Quarterly* 63,1 (March 1948), 16–44

Goodrich, 1956—Carter Goodrich, "American Development Policy: The Case of Internal Improvements," *Journal of Economic History* 16,4 (December 1956), 449–460

Goodrich, 1960—Carter Goodrich, *Government Promotion of American Canals and Railroads 1800–1890* (New York: Columbia University Press, 1960)

Goodrich, 1961—Carter Goodrich, ed., *Canals and American Economic Development* (New York: Columbia University Press, 1961)

Goss, 1972—Carol F. Goss, "Military Committee Membership And Defense-Related Benefits In The House Of Representatives," *Western Political Quarterly* 25,2 (June 1972), 215–233

Gramlich, 1970—Edward M. Gramlich, "The Effect Of Federal Grants On State-Local Expenditures: A Review Of The Econometric Literature," in Stanley J. Bowers, ed., *Proceedings Of The 62nd Annual Conference On Taxation, National Tax Association* (Columbus, Ohio: National Tax Association, 1970), pp. 569–593

Gramlich, 1977—Edward M. Gramlich, "Intergovernmental Grants: A Review of the Empirical Literature," in Wallace E. Oates, ed., *The Political Economy of Fiscal Federalism* (Lexington, Massachusetts: D. C. Heath and Company, 1977), pp. 219–239

Gramlich, 1978a—Edward M. Gramlich, "State and Local Budgets the Day after It Rained: Why Is the Surplus so High?" in Arthur M. Okun and George L. Perry, eds., *Brookings Papers on Economic Activity* 1(1978), 191–216

Gramlich, 1978b—Edward M. Gramlich, "The Role of Economics in the Study of Intergovernmental Relations," Preliminary Draft, American Political Science Association, September 1978

Gramlich and Galper, 1973—Edward M. Gramlich and Harvey Galper, "State and Local Fiscal Behavior and Federal Grant Policy," in Arthur M. Okun and George L. Perry, eds., *Brookings Papers On Economic Activity* 1(1973), 15–58

Grasberger, *et al.*, 1978—Frederick J. Grasberger, *et al.*, *A Typology and Review of Federal Categorical Grant-In-Aid Formulas for Fiscal Year 1975* (Rochester: Center for Governmental Research, Inc., 1978)

Graves, 1934—W. Brooke Graves, "Stroke Oar," *State Government* 7,12 (December 1934), 259–262

Graves, 1936a—W. Brooke Graves, "The Future Of The American States," *American Political Science Review* 30,1 (February 1936), 24–50

Graves, 1936b—W. Brooke Graves, "Federal Leadership in State Legislation," *Temple Law Quarterly* 10,4 (July 1936), 385–405

Graves, 1938—W. Brooke Graves, "Influence of Congressional Legislation on Legislation in the States," *Iowa Law Review* 23,4 (May 1938), 519–538

Graves, 1964—W. Brooke Graves, *American Intergovernmental Relations: Their Origins, Historical Development, And Current Status* (New York: Charles Scribner's Sons, 1964)

Gray, 1973a—Virginia Gray, "Innovation in the States: A Diffusion Study," *American Political Science Review* 67,4 (December 1973), 1174–1185

Gray, 1973b—Virginia Gray, "Rejoinder to 'Comment' by Jack I. Walker," *American Political Science Review* 67,4 (December 1973), 1192–1193

Gray, 1974—Virginia Gray, "Expenditures and Innovation as Dimensions of 'Progressivism': A Note on the American States," *American Journal of Political Science* 18,4 (November 1974), 693–699

Greenberg, 1979—George D. Greenberg, with Robert C. Luskin, *Federal Program Implementation In Selected States: A Study Of The Implementation Of The Partnership For Health Act And Of The Early And Periodic Screening, Diagnosis, And Treatment Program In Michigan, Pennsylvania, And Alabama* Project Report To The National Center for Health Services Research, U.S. Public Health Service, U.S. Department of Health, Education, And Welfare, Washington, D.C., June 1979.

Greenberg, forthcoming—George Greenberg, "Block Grants and State Discretion: A Study of the Implementation of the Partnership for Health Act in Three States," *Policy Sciences* (forthcoming)

Greenberg, Miller, Mohr, and Vladeck, 1977—George D. Greenberg, Jeffrey A. Miller, Lawrence B. Mohr and Bruce C. Vladeck, "Developing Public Policy Theory: Perspectives from Empirical Research," *American Political Science Review* 71,4 (December 1977), 1532–1543

Greenstone, 1975—J. David Greenstone, "Group Theories," in Fred I. Greenstein and Nelson W. Polsby, eds., *Handbook of Political Science, Volume 2: Micropolitical Theory* (Reading, Massachusetts: Addison-Wesley Publishing Company, 1975), 243–318

Greer, 1965—Scott Greer, *Urban Renewal and American Cities: The Dilemma of Democratic Intervention* (Indianapolis: The Bobbs-Merrill Company, 1965)

Gregg, 1974—Phillip M. Gregg, "Units and Levels of Analysis: A Problem Policy Analysis in Federal Systems," *Publius* 4,4 (Fall 1974), 59–86

Grodzins, 1960a—Morton Grodzins, "The Federal System," in The Report of the President's Commission on National Goals, *Goals for Americans* (Englewood Cliffs, New Jersey: Prentice-Hall, Inc., 1960), pp. 265–282

Grodzins, 1960b—Morton Grodzins, "American Political Parties And The American System," *Western Political Quarterly* 13,4 (December 1960), 978–998

Grodzins, 1963a—Morton Grodzins, "Centralization and Decentralization In The American Federal System," in Robert A. Goldwin, ed., *A Nation of States: Essays on the American Federal System* (Chicago: Rand McNally and Company, 1963), pp. 1–23

Grodzins, 1963b—Morton Grodzins, "Local Strength In the American Federal System: The Mobilization Of Public-Private Influence," in Marian D. Irish, ed., *Continuing Crises in American Politics* (Englewood Cliffs, New Jersey: Prentice-Hall, Inc., 1963), pp. 132–152

Grodzins, 1966—Morton Grodzins, *The American System: A New View of Government in the United States,* edited by Daniel J. Elazar (Chicago: Rand McNally and Company, 1966)

Hadwiger, 1976—Don F. Hadwiger, "The Old, the New, and the Emerging United States Department of Agriculture," *Public Administration Review* 36,2 (March–April 1976), 155–165

Hadwiger, 1978—Don F. Hadwiger, "Agriculture Policy," in Theodore J. Lowi and Alan Stone, eds., *Nationalizing Government: Public Policies in America* (Beverley Hills: Sage Publications, 1978), pp. 85–100

Haider, 1974—Donald H. Haider, *When Governments Come To Washington: Governors, Mayors, and Intergovernmental Lobbying* (New York: The Free Press, 1974)

Hale, 1977—George E. Hale, "Executive Leadership Versus Budgetary Behavior," *Administration and Society* 9,2 (August 1977), 169–190

Hale, 1979—George E. Hale, "Federal Courts and the State Budgetary Process," *Administration and Society* 11,3 (November 1979), 357–368

Hale and Douglass, 1977—George E. Hale and Scott R. Douglass, "The Politics of Budget Execution: Financial Manipulation in State and Local Government," *Administration and Society* 9,3 (November 1977), 367–379

Hale and Palley, 1978—George E. Hale and Marian Lief Palley, "The Impact of Federal Funds on the State Budgetary Process," *National Civic Review* 67,10 (November 1978), 461–464, 473

Hale and Palley, 1979—George E. Hale and Marian Lief Palley, "Federal Grants to the States: Who Governs?," *Administration and Society* 11,1 (May 1979), 3–26

Halperin, 1974—Morton H. Halperin, with the assistance of Priscilla Clapp and Arnold Kanter, *Bureaucratic Politics and Foreign Policy* (Washington, D.C.: The Brookings Institution, 1974)

Halperin and Kanter, 1973—Morton H. Halperin and Arnold Kanter, "The Bureaucratic Perspective: A Preliminary Framework," in Morton H. Halperin and Arnold Kanter, eds., *Readings in American Foreign Policy: A Bureaucratic Perspective* (Boston: Little, Brown and Company, 1973), pp. 1–42

Halstead, 1978—D. Kent Halstead, *Tax Wealth in Fifty States* (Washington, D.C.: U.S. Government Printing Office, 1978)

Hamilton, 1978—Edward K. Hamilton, "On Nonconstitutional Management of a Constitutional Problem," *Daedalus* 107 (Winter 1978), 111–128

Handlin, 1943—Oscar Handlin, "Laissez-Faire Thought in Massachusetts, 1790–1880," *Journal of Economic History* 3, Supplement (December 1943), 55–65

Handlin and Handlin, 1969 (revision of 1947 edition)—Oscar Handlin and Mary Flug Handlin, *Commonwealth—A Study of the Role of Government in the American Economy: Massachusetts, 1774–1861* (Cambridge, Massachusetts: The Belknap Press of Harvard University Press, 1969, Revised Edition)

Hardin, 1946—Charles M. Hardin, "The Bureau of Agricultural Economics under Fire: A Study in Valuation Conflicts," *Journal of Farm Economics* 28,3 (August 1946), 635–668

Hardin, 1947—Charles M. Hardin, "Programmatic Research and Agricultural Policy," *Journal of Farm Economics* 29,2 (May 1947), 359–382

Hardin, 1948—Charles M. Hardin, "Reflections on Agricultural Policy Formation in the United States," *American Political Science Review* 42,5 (October 1948), 881–905

Hardin, 1952—Charles M. Hardin, *The Politics of Agriculture: Soil Conservation and the Struggle for Power in Rural America* (Glencoe, Illinois: The Free Press, 1952)

Hardin, 1955—Charles M. Hardin, *Freedom in Agricultural Education* (Chicago: The University of Chicago Press, 1955)

Hardin, 1965—Charles M. Hardin, "Present and Prospective Policy Problems of U.S. Agriculture: As Viewed by a Political Scientist," *Journal of Farm Economics* 47,5 (December 1965), 1091–1115

Hardin, 1974—Charles M. Hardin, *Presidential Power and Accountability: Toward a New Constitution* (Chicago: University of Chicago Press, 1974)

Hardin, 1978—Charles M. Hardin, "Agricultural Price Policy: The Political Role of Bureaucracy," *Policy Studies Journal* 6,4 (Summer 1978), 467–472

Hargrove, 1975—Erwin C. Hargrove, *The Missing Link: The Study of the Implementation of Social Policy* (Washington, D.C.: The Urban Institute, 1975)

Harrington, 1971—Michael Harrington, *The Other America: Poverty in the United States* (Baltimore, Maryland: Penguin Books, Inc., 1971, Revised Edition; originally published by Macmillan Company, 1962)

Harris, 1940—Joseph P. Harris, "The Future Of Federal Grants-In-Aid," *Annals of the American Academy of Political and Social Science,* vol. 207 (January 1940), 14–26

Harris 1956—Seymour E. Harris, "Taxes and Treasury Disbursements, Regional and State Differences, 1934–1954, 1939, 1952, 1953, 1954," in Carl J. Friedrich and Seymour E. Harris, eds., *Public Policy, 1956: Volume 7* (Cambridge, Massachusetts: Harvard University Press, 1956), pp. 177–231

Hartman and Pechman, 1977—Robert W. Hartman and Joseph A. Pechman, "Issues in Budget Accounting," in Joseph A. Pechman, ed., *Setting National Priorities: The 1978 Budget* (Washington, D.C.: The Brookings Institution, 1977), pp. 425–435

Hartz, 1943—Louis Hartz, "Laissez-Faire Thought in Pennsylvania, 1776–1860," *Journal of Economic History* 3, Supplement (December 1943), 66–77

Hartz, 1955—Louis Hartz, *The Liberal Tradition in America: An Interpretation of American Political Thought Since the Revolution* (New York: Harcourt, Brace & World, Inc., 1955)

Hartz, 1968—Louis Hartz, *Economic Policy and Democratic Thought: Pennsylvania, 1776–1860* (Chicago: Quadrangle Books, 1968)

Havemann and Stanfield, 1977—Joel Havemann and Rochelle L. Stanfield, "A Year Later, The Frostbelt Strikes Back," *National Journal* 9,27 (July 2, 1977), 1028–1037

Havemann, Stanfield, Peirce, *et al.,* 1976—Joel Havemann, Rochelle L. Stanfield, Neal R. Peirce, *et al.,* "Federal Spending: The North's Loss Is The Sunbelt's Gain," *National Journal* 8,26 (June 26, 1976), 878–891

Hawkins and Stein, 1977—Brett W. Hawkins and Robert M. Stein, "Regional Planning Assistance: Its Distribution to Local Governments and Relationship to Local Grant Getting," *Journal of the American Institute of Planners* 43,3 (July 1977), 279–288

Heath, 1943—Milton S. Heath, "Laissez-Faire in Georgia, 1732–1860," *Journal of Economic History* 3, Supplement (December 1943), 78–100

Heath, 1954—Milton Sydney Heath, *Constructive Liberalism: The Role of the State in Economic Development in Georgia to 1860* (Cambridge, Massachusetts: Harvard University Press, 1954)

Heclo, 1974—Hugh Heclo, *Modern Social Politics in Britain and Sweden: From Relief to Income Maintenance* (New Haven and London: Yale University Press, 1974)

Heclo, 1977—Hugh Heclo, "A Question of Priorities," *The Humanist* 37,2 (March–April 1977), 21–24

Heclo, 1979—Hugh Heclo, "Issue Networks And The Executive Establishment," in Anthony King, ed., *The New American Political System* (Washington, D.C.: American Enterprise Institute for Public Policy Research, 1979), pp. 87–124

Heidenheimer, Heclo, and Adams, 1975—Arnold J. Heidenheimer, Hugh Heclo, and Carolyn Terch Adams, *Comparative Public Policy: The Politics of Social Choice in Europe and America* (New York: St. Martin's Press, 1975)

Heinz, 1962—John P. Heinz, "The Political Impasse in Farm Support Legislation," *Yale Law Journal* 71,5 (April 1962), 952–978

Herring, 1929—E. Pendleton Herring, *Group Representation Before Congress* (Baltimore, Maryland: The Johns Hopkins University Press, 1929)

Herring, 1965—Pendleton Herring, *The Politics of Democracy: American Parties in Action* (New York: W. W. Norton & Company, Inc., 1965; originally published in 1940)

Hibbard, 1965—Benjamin Horace Hibbard, *A History Of The Public Land Policies* (Madison and Milwaukee: University of Wisconsin Press, 1965)

Hibbs, 1977—Douglas A. Hibbs, Jr., "Political Parties and Macroeconomic Policy," *American Political Science Review* 71,4 (December 1977), 1467–1487

Hines and Reid, 1977a—Fred K. Hines and J. Norman Reid, *Using Federal Outlays Data To Measure Program Equity—Opportunities And Limitations* (Washington, D.C.: Department of Agriculture, Working Paper No. 7711, 1977). This working paper is a longer version of a like titled paper published in *American Journal of Agricultural Economics* 59,5 (December 1977), 1013–1019

Hines and Reid, 1977b—Fred K. Hines and J. Norman Reid, "Using Federal Outlays Data To Measure Program Equity: Opportunities and Limitations," *American Journal of Agricultural Economics* 59,5 (December 1977), 1013–1019

Hirschman, 1973—Albert O. Hirschman, *Journeys Toward Progress: Studies of Economic Policy-Making in Latin America* (New York: W. W. Norton & Company, Inc., 1973)

Hirschman, 1975—Albert O. Hirschman, "Policymaking and Policy Analysis in Latin America—A Return Journey," *Policy Sciences* 6,4 (December 1975), 385–402

Hofferbert, 1972—Richard I. Hofferbert, "State and Community Policy Studies: A Review of Comparative Input-Output Analyses," in James A. Robinson, ed., *Political Science Annual: An International Review, Volume Three, 1972* (Indianapolis, Indiana: The Bobbs-Merrill Company, Inc., 1972), pp. 3–72

Holden, 1964—Matthew Holden, Jr., "The Governance Of The Metropolis As A Problem In Diplomacy," *Journal of Politics* 26,3 (August 1964), 627–647

Homans, 1964—George C. Homans, "Bringing Men Back In," *American Sociological Review,* Volume 29, No. 5, December, 1964

Hoogenboom and Hoogenboom, 1976—Ari Hoogenboom and Olive Hoogenboom, *A History of the ICC: From Panacea to Palliative* (New York: W. W. Norton and Company, Inc., 1976)

Horowitz, 1977—Donald L. Horowitz, *The Courts and Social Policy* (Washington, D.C.: The Brookings Institution, 1977)

Howards and Brehm, 1978—Irving Howards and Henry Brehm, "The Impossible Dream: The Nationalization Of Welfare? A Look At Disability Insurance And State Influence Over The Federal Government," *Polity* 11,1 (Fall 1978), 7–26

Huitt, 1963—Ralph K. Huitt, "Congressional Organization and Operations in the Field of Money and Credit," in Commission on Money and Credit, *Fiscal and Debt Management Policies* (Englewood Cliffs, New Jersey: Prentice-Hall, Inc., 1963), pp. 399–495

Huntington, 1952—Samuel P. Huntington, "The Marasmus of the ICC: The Commission, the Railroads, and the Public Interest," *Yale Law Journal* 61,4 (April 1952), 467–509

Huntington, 1973—Samuel P. Huntington, "Congressional Responses to the Twentieth Century," in David B. Truman, ed., *The Congress and America's Future* (Englewood Cliffs, N.J.: Prentice-Hall, Inc., 1973, Second Edition), pp. 6–38

Huntington, 1974a—Samuel P. Huntington, "Postindustrial Politics: How Benign Will It Be?" *Comparative Politics* 6,2 (January 1974), 163–191

Huntington, 1974b—Samuel P. Huntington, "Paradigms of American Politics: Beyond the One, the Two, and the Many," *Political Science Quarterly* 89,1 (March 1974), 1–26

Huntington, 1975a—Samuel P. Huntington, "The United States," in Michael Crozier, Samuel P. Huntington and Joji Watanuki, *The Crisis Of Democracy* (New York: New York University Press, 1975), pp. 59–118

Huntington, 1975b—Samuel P. Huntington, "The Democratic Distemper," *The Public Interest,* No. 41 (Fall 1975), 9–38

Huntington, 1976—Samuel P. Huntington, "The Democratic Distemper," in Nathan Glazer and Irving Kristol, eds., *The American Commonwealth—1976* (New York: Basic Books, Inc., Publishers, 1976), pp. 9–38, originally published in *The Public Interest* No. 41 (April 1975)

Hurley, 1979—Patricia A. Hurley, "Assessing the Potential for Significant Legislative Output in the House of Representatives," *Western Political Quarterly* 32,1 (March 1979), 45–58

Hurley, Brady, Cooper, 1977—Patricia Hurley, David Brady, Joseph Cooper, "Measuring Legislative Potential for Policy Change," *Legislative Studies Quarterly* 2,4 (November 1977), 385–398

Hurst, 1964—James Willard Hurst, *Law and Economic Growth: The Legal History of the Lumber Industry in Wisconsin 1836–1915* (Cambridge, Massachusetts: The Belknap Press of Harvard University Press, 1964)

Ingram, 1977—Helen Ingram, "Policy Implementation Through Bargaining: The Case Of Federal Grants-In-Aid," *Public Policy* 25,4 (Fall 1977), 499–520

Interagency Task Team Report, 1974—A-84 Task Team, *Interagency Task Team Report On Improvements To The Federal Outlays Report By Geographic Region, OMB Circular A-84 Policy and Associated Processes* (Washington, D.C.: July, 1974)

Intergovernmental Task Force, 1968—*The Dynamics of Information Flow: Recommendations to Improve the Flow of Information Within and Among Federal, State and Local Governments* (Washington, D.C.: Intergovernmental Task Force on Information Systems, 1968)

Jackson, 1970—Charles O. Jackson, *Food And Drug Legislation In The New Deal* (Princeton, New Jersey: Princeton University Press, 1970)

Jacob and Lipsky, 1968—Herbert Jacob and Michael Lipsky, "Outputs, Structure, And Power: An Assessment Of Changes In The Study Of State And Local Politics," *Journal of Politics* 30,2 (May 1968), 510–538

Jensen, 1965—Merrill Jensen, ed., *Regionalism In America* (Madison: The University of Wisconsin Press, 1965)

Johnson, 1962—E. A. J. Johnson, "Federalism, Pluralism, and Public Policy," *Journal of Economic History* 22,4 (December 1962), 427–444

Joint Federal-State Action Committee, 1957—Joint Federal-State Action Committee, *Report Of The Joint Federal-State Action Committee To The President Of The United States And To The Chairman Of The Governor's Conference, Progress Report No. 1* (Washington, D.C.: U.S. Government Printing Office, December 1957)

Joint Federal-State Action Committee, 1958—Joint Federal-State Action Committee, *Second Report Of The Joint Federal-State Action Committee To The President Of The United States And To The Chairman Of The Governor's Conference, Progress Report No. 2* (Washington, D.C.: U.S. Government Printing Office, December 1958)

Joint Federal-State Action Committee, 1960—Joint Federal-State Action Committee, *Final Report Of The Joint Federal-State Action Committee To The President Of The United States And To The Chairman Of The Governor's Conference* (Washington, D.C.: U.S. Government Printing Office, February 1960)

Jones, 1961—Charles O. Jones, "Representation in Congress: The Case of the House Agricultural Committee," *American Political Science Review* 55,2 (June 1961), 358–367

Jones, 1962—Charles O. Jones, "The Role of the Congressional Subcommittee," *Midwest Journal of Political Science* 6,4 (November 1962), 327–344

Jones, 1973—Charles O. Jones, "State and Local Public Policy Analysis: A Review of Progress," in Evron M. Kirkpatrick, *et al., Political Science and State and Local Government* (Washington, D.C.: American Political Science Association, 1973), pp. 27–54

Jones, 1974—Charles O. Jones, "Federal-State-Local Sharing in Air Pollution Control," *Publius* 4,1 (Winter 1974), 69–85

Jones, 1976—Charles O. Jones, "Regulating The Environment," in Herbert Jacob and Kenneth N. Vines, eds., *Politics In The American States: A Comparative Analysis* (Boston: Little, Brown and Company, 1976, Third Edition), pp. 354–387, pp. 388–427

Jones, 1977—Charles O. Jones, *An Introduction to the Study of Public Policy* (North Scituate, Massachusetts: Duxbury Press, 1977, Second Edition)

Jones, 1978—Charles O. Jones, *Clean Air: The Policies and Politics of Pollution Control* (Pittsburgh: University of Pittsburgh Press, 1978)

Jusenius and Ledebur, 1976—C. L. Jusenius and L. C. Ledebur, *A Myth In The Making: The Southern Economic Challenge And Northern Economic Decline* (Springfield, Virginia: U.S. Department of Commerce, Economic Development Administration, Economic Development Research Paper PB 263 631, National Technical Information Service, 1976)

Juster and Anton, 1977—F. Thomas Juster and Thomas J. Anton, "Introduction and Summary," in F. Thomas Juster, ed., *The Economic And Political Impact Of General Revenue Sharing* (Ann Arbor, Michigan: Survey Research Center, Institute for Social Research, The University of Michigan, 1977), pp. 1–12

Kaufman, 1956—Herbert Kaufman, "Emerging Conflicts In The Doctrines Of Public Administration," *American Political Science Review* 50,4 (December 1956), 1057–1073

Kaufman, 1963—Herbert Kaufman, *Politics and Policies in State and Local Governments* (Englewood Cliffs, New Jersey: Prentice-Hall, Inc., 1963)

Kaufman, 1967—Herbert Kaufman, *The Forest Ranger: A Study In Administrative Behavior* (Baltimore: The Johns Hopkins University Press, 1967)

Kaufman, 1969—Herbert Kaufman, "Administrative Decentralization And Political Power," *Public Administration Review* 29,1 (January–February, 1969), 3–15

Kaufman, 1976—Herbert Kaufman, *Are Government Organizations Immortal?* (Washington, D.C.: The Brookings Institution, 1976)

Kaufman, 1977a—Herbert Kaufman, "Reflections on Administrative Reorganization," in Joseph A. Pechman, ed., *Setting National Priorities: The 1978 Budget* (Washington, D.C.: The Brookings Institution, 1977), pp. 391–418

Kaufman, 1977b—Herbert Kaufman, *Red Tape: Its Origins, Uses, and Abuses* (Washington, D.C.: The Brookings Institution, 1977)

Kaufman, with Couzens, 1973—Herbert Kaufman with the collaboration of Michael Couzens, *Administrative Feedback: Monitoring Subordinates' Behavior* (Washington, D.C.: The Brookings Institution, 1973)

Kee, 1965—Woo Sik Kee, "Central City Expenditures And Metropolitan Areas," *National Tax Journal* 18,4 (December 1965), 337–353

Kendrick, 1955—M. Slade Kendrick, *A Century and a Half of Federal Expenditures* (New York: National Bureau of Economic Research, Inc., 1955, Revised)

Key, 1937—V. O. Key, Jr., *The Administration Of Federal Grants To States* (Chicago: Public Administration Service, 1937)

Key, 1940—V. O. Key, Jr., "State Legislation Facilitative of Federal Action," *Annals of the American Academy of Political and Social Science,* vol. 207 (January 1940), 7–13

Key, 1942—V. O. Key, Jr., *The Matching Requirement In Federal Grant Legislation In Relation To Variations In State Fiscal Capacity* (Washington, D.C.: Federal Security Agency, Social Security Board, Bureau of Research and Statistics, 1942)

Key, 1956—V. O. Key, Jr., *American State Politics: An Introduction* (New York: Alfred A. Knopf, 1956)

Key, 1964—V. O. Key, Jr., *Politics, Parties, & Pressure Groups* (New York: Thomas Y. Crowell Company, 1964, Fifth Edition)

Key, with Heard, 1949—V. O. Key, Jr., with the Assistance of Alexander Heard, *Southern Politics* (New York: Vintage Books, n.d., originally published by Alfred A. Knopf, 1949)

Kile, 1948—Orville Merton Kile, *The Farm Bureau Through Three Decades* (Baltimore, Maryland: The Waverly Press, 1948)

King, 1973a—Anthony King, "Ideas, Institutions and the Policies of Governments: A Comparative Analysis: Parts I and II," *British Journal of Political Science* 3,3 (July 1973), 291–313

King, 1973b—Anthony King, "Ideas, Institutions and the Policies of Governments: A Comparative Analysis: Part III," *British Journal of Political Science* 3,4 (October 1973), 409–423

King, 1975—Anthony King, "Overload: Problems Of Governing In The 1970s," *Political Studies* 23,2–3 (July–September, 1975), 284–296

Kingdon, 1966—John W. Kingdon, "A House Appropriations Subcommittee: Influences on Budgetary Decisions," *Southwestern Social Science Quarterly* 47,1 (June 1966), 68–78

Kingdon, 1973—John W. Kingdon, *Congressmen's Voting Decisions* (New York: Harper and Row, Publishers, 1973)

Kingdon, 1977—John W. Kingdon, "Models of Legislative Voting," *Journal of Politics* 39,3 (August 1977), 563–595

Kirkpatrick, 1971—Evron M. Kirkpatrick, " 'Toward a More Responsible Two-Party System': Political Science, Policy Science, or Pseudo-Science?" *American Political Science Review* 65,4 (December 1971), 965–990

Kirkpatrick, 1978—Jeane Jordan Kirkpatrick, *Dismantling the Parties: Reflections on Party Reform and Party Decomposition* (Washington, D.C.: American Enterprise Institute for Public Policy Research, 1978)

Kirlin, 1979—John J. Kirlin, "Adapting The Intergovernmental Fiscal System to the Demands of an Advanced Economy," in Gary Tobin, ed., *The Changing Structure Of The City: What Happened to the Urban Crisis* (Beverly Hills: Sage Publications, 1979), pp. 77–103

Kneese and Schultze, 1975—Allen V. Kneese and Charles L. Schultze, *Pollution, Prices, and Public Policy* (Washington, D.C.: The Brookings Institution, 1975)

Kraemer, 1978—Kenneth L. Kraemer, "An Assessment of Federal Research and Development for State and Local Government Information Processing," in American Association for the Advancement of Science, Intergovernmental Research and Development Project, *Report from the Workshop on Management, Finance and Personnel* (Washington, D.C.: A.A.A.S., 1978), pp. 84–130

Labovitz, 1978—I. M. Labovitz, "Federal Expenditures and Revenues in Regions and States," *Intergovernmental Perspective* 4,4 (Fall 1978), 16–23

Ladd, 1970—Everett Carll Ladd, Jr., *American Political Parties: Social Change and Political Response* (New York: W. W. Norton & Company, Inc., 1970)

Ladd, 1978—Everett Carll Ladd, Jr., *Where Have All the Voters Gone? The Fracturing of America's Political Parties* (New York: W. W. Norton & Company, Inc., 1978)

Ladd, 1979—Everett Carll Ladd, Jr., "Note to Readers," *Public Opinion* 2,5 (October–November 1979), 27

Ladd and Hadley, 1975—Everett Carll Ladd, Jr. and Charles D. Hadley, *Transformations of the American Party System: Political Coalitions from the New Deal to the 1970s* (New York: W. W. Norton & Company, Inc., 1975)

Lapp, 1916a—John A. Lapp, "Highway Administration and State Aid," *American Political Science Review* 10,4 (November 1916), 735–738

Lapp, 1916b—John A. Lapp, "Federal Grants in Aid," *American Political Science Review* 10,4 (November 1916), 738–743

Larkey, 1975—Patrick Daniel Larkey, "Process Models and Program Evaluation: The Impact of General Revenue Sharing on Municipal Fiscal Behavior" (Unpublished Ph.D. Dissertation, University of Michigan, 1975)

Larkey, 1977a—Patrick D. Larkey, "Process Models and Program Evaluation: The Impact of General Revenue Sharing on Municipal Fiscal Behavior—A Summary," in Stanley J. Bowers, ed., *1976 Proceedings of the Sixty-Ninth Annual Conference On Taxation, National Tax*

Association—Tax Institute of America, at Phoenix, Arizona, November 14–18, 1976 (Columbus, Ohio: National Tax Association, 1977), pp. 167–178

Larkey, 1977b—Patrick D. Larkey, "Process Models of Governmental Resource Allocation and Program Evaluation," *Policy Sciences* 8,3 (September 1977), 269–301

Larkey, 1979—Patrick D. Larkey, *Evaluating Public Programs: The Impact of General Revenue Sharing on Municipal Government* (Princeton, New Jersey: Princeton University Press, 1979)

Larkins, 1972—Dan Larkins, *$300 Billion in Loans: An Introduction to Federal Credit Programs* (Washington, D.C.: American Enterprise Institute for Public Policy Research, 1972)

Laski, 1939—Harold J. Laski, "The Obsolescence of Federalism," *The New Republic* 98,1274 (May 3, 1939), 367–369

Laski, 1940—Harold J. Laski, *The American Presidency: An Interpretation* (New York: Harper and Brothers Publishers, 1940)

Leacock, 1909—Stephen Leacock, "The Limitations Of Federal Government," *Proceedings Of The American Political Science Association At Its 5th Annual Meeting, Washington, D.C. And Richmond, Virginia, December 28–31, 1908* (Baltimore, Maryland: The Waverly Press, 1909), pp. 37–52

LeLoup, 1978—Lance T. LeLoup, "The Myths of Incrementalism: Analytical Choices in Budgetary Theory," *Polity* 10,4 (Summer 1978), 488–509

Levitan and Taggart, 1976—Sar A. Levitan and Robert Taggart, *The Promise of Greatness* (Cambridge, Massachusetts: Harvard University Press, 1976)

Levitan and Taggart, 1976–1977—Sar A. Levitan and Robert Taggart, "The Great Society Did Succeed," *Political Science Quarterly* 91,4 (Winter 1976–1977), 601–608

Levitin and Miller, 1979—Teresa E. Levitin and Warren E. Miller, "Ideological Interpretations of Presidential Elections," *American Political Science Review* 73,3 (September 1979), 751–771

Lilla, 1978—Mark T. Lilla, "Where Has All The Money Gone? The Distribution Of Federal Grants-In-Aid" Unpublished B.A.—Seniors Honors Thesis, Department of Political Science, The University of Michigan, 1978

Lindbeck, 1976—Assar Lindbeck, "Stabilization Policy in Open Economies with Endogenous Politicians," *American Economic Review* 66,2 (May 1976), 1–19

Lindblom, 1959—Charles E. Lindblom, "The Science of 'Muddling Through'," *Public Administration Review* 19,2 (Spring 1959), 79–88

Lindblom, 1961—Charles E. Lindblom, "Decision-Making in Taxation and Expenditures," in *Public Finances: Needs, Sources, and Utilization* (Princeton, New Jersey: Princeton University Press, 1961), pp. 295–329

Lindblom, 1966—Charles E. Lindblom, *The Intelligence Of Democracy* (New York: The Free Press, 1966)

Lindblom, 1968—Charles E. Lindblom, *The Policy-Making Process* (Englewood Cliffs, New Jersey: Prentice-Hall, Inc., 1968)

Lindblom, 1977—Charles E. Lindblom, *Politics and Markets: The World's Political-Economic Systems* (New York: Basic Books, Inc., Publishers, 1977)

Lindblom, 1979—Charles E. Lindblom, "Still Muddling, Not Yet Through," *Public Administration Review* 39,6 (November–December 1979), 517–526

Lineberry and Fowler, 1967—Robert L. Lineberry and Edmund P. Fowler, "Reformism and Public Policies In American Cities," *American Political Science Review* 61,3 (September 1967), 701–716

Lipset, 1967—Seymour Martin Lipset, *The First New Nation: The United States in Historical and Comparative Perspective* (Garden City, New York: Doubleday & Company, Inc., Anchor Books, 1967)

Lockard, 1968a—Duane Lockard, *New England State Politics* (Chicago: Henry Regnery Company, 1968—originally published by Princeton University Press, 1959)

Lockard, 1968b—Duane Lockard, "State Party Systems and Policy Outputs," in Oliver Garceau, ed., *Political Research and Political Theory* (Cambridge, Massachusetts: Harvard University Press, 1968), pp. 190–220

Long, 1958—Norton E. Long, "The Local Community As An Ecology Of Games," *American Journal of Sociology* 64,3 (November 1958), 251–261

Lowi, 1964a—Theodore J. Lowi, "How the Farmers Get What They Want," *The Reporter* 30,11 (May 21, 1964), 34–37

Lowi, 1964b—Theodore J. Lowi, "American Business, Public Policy, Case Studies and Political Theory," *World Politics* 16,4 (July 1964), 677–715

Lowi, 1969—Theodore J. Lowi, *The End of Liberalism: Ideology, Policy, and The Crisis of Public Authority* (New York: W. W. Norton and Company, Inc., 1969)

Lowi, 1972—Theodore J. Lowi, "Four Systems of Policy, Politics and Choice," *Public Administration Review* 27,4 (July/August 1972), 298–310

Lowi, 1974—Theodore J. Lowi, "Permanent Receivership: The New Governmental Pattern," *The Center Magazine* 7,2 (March–April, 1974), 33–42

Lowi, 1978—Theodore J. Lowi, "Europeanization Of America? From United States To United State," in Theodore J. Lowi and Alan Stone, eds., *Nationalizing Government: Public Policies In America* (Beverly Hills: Sage Publications, 1978), pp. 15–29

Lowi, 1979—Theodore J. Lowi, *The End Of Liberalism: The Second Republic Of The United States* (New York: W. W. Norton and Company, 1979, Second Edition)

Lowrie, 1922—S. Gale Lowrie, "Centralization Versus Decentralization," *American Political Science Review* 16,3 (August 1922), 379–386

Lugar, 1976—Richard G. Lugar, "The Federal Government's Role in Relieving Cities of the Fiscal Burden of Low Income Concentration," *National Tax Journal* 29,3 (September 1976), pp. 286–292

Maass, 1950—Arthur A. Maass, "Congress and Water Resources," *American Political Science Review* 44,3 (September 1950), 576–593

Maass, 1951—Arthur Maass, *Muddy Waters* (Cambridge, Massachusetts: Harvard University Press, 1951)

Maass, 1959—Arthur Maass, "Division of Powers: An Areal Analysis," in Arthur Maass, ed., *Area and Power: A Theory of Local Government* (Glencoe, Illinois: Free Press, 1959), pp. 9–26

MacDonald, 1923—Austin F. MacDonald, *Federal Subsidies To The States: A Study In American Administration* (Philadelphia: University of Pennsylvania, 1923)

MacDonald, 1928a—Austin F. MacDonald, *Federal Aid: A Study of the American Subsidy System* (New York: Thomas Y. Crowell Company, 1928)

MacDonald, 1928b—Austin F. MacDonald, "Federal Aid to the States: Report of the Committee on Federal Aid to the States of the National Municipal League," *National Municipal Review* 17,10 (October 1928), 619–659

MacDonald, 1931—Austin F. MacDonald, "Recent Trends in Federal Aid to the States," *American Political Science Review* 25,3 (August 1931), 628–634

MacDonald, 1940—Austin F. MacDonald, "Federal Aid to the States: 1940 Model," *American Political Science Review* 34,3 (June 1940), 489–499

Macmahon, Millett, Ogden, 1941—Arthur W. Macmahon, John D. Millett, Gladys Ogden, *The Administration of Federal Work Relief* (Chicago: Public Administration Service, 1941)

Manley, 1968—John F. Manley, "Congressional Staff and Public Policy-Making: The Joint Committee on Internal Revenue Taxation," *Journal of Politics* 30,4 (November 1968), 1046–1067

Manley, 1970a—John F. Manley, *The Politics of Finance: The House Committee on Ways and Means* (Boston: Little, Brown and Company, 1970)

Manley, 1970b—John F. Manley, "The Family Assistance Plan: An Essay On Incremental And Nonincremental Policy-Making," Paper prepared for delivery at the Annual Meeting of the American Political Science Association, September 7–12, 1970, Biltmore Hotel, Los Angeles, California

Manvel, 1971—Allen D. Manvel, "Differences in Fiscal Capacity and Effort: Their Significance for a Federal Revenue-Sharing System," *National Tax Journal* 14,2 (June 1971), 193–204

March and Simon, 1958—James G. March and Herbert A. Simon, *Organizations* (New York: John Wiley and Sons, Inc., 1958)

Marcus, 1979—Robert S. Marcus, "House Voting on Rivers and Harbors Legislation: The Impact of Party, Ideology, and Federal Spending," Paper prepared for delivery at the 1979 Annual Meeting of the Southwest Social Science Association, Fort Worth, Texas, March 28–31, 1979

Margolis, H., 1977—Howard Margolis, "The Politics of Auto Emissions," *The Public Interest,* No. 49 (Fall 1977), 3–21

Margolis, M., 1977—Michael Margolis, "From Confusion to Confusion: Issues and the American Voter (1956–1972)," *American Political Science Review* 71,1 (March 1977), 31–43

Markusen, 1980—Ann R. Markusen, "Urban Impact Analysis: A Critical Forecast," in Norman J. Glickman, ed., *The Urban Impacts Of Federal Policies* (Baltimore: The Johns Hopkins University Press, 1980), pp. 103–118

Markusen and Fastrup, 1978—Ann R. Markusen and Jerry Fastrup, "The Regional War for Federal Aid," *The Public Interest* No. 53 (Fall 1978), 87–89

Markusen, Saxenian, and Weiss, 1979—Ann R. Markusen, Annalee Saxenian and Marc A. Weiss, "Who Benefits From Intergovernmental Transfers?" Paper presented at the Conference on Municipal Fiscal Squeeze in Miami, Florida, March 8 and 9, 1979

Marmor, 1973—Theodore R. Marmor, *The Politics Of Medicare* (Chicago: Aldine Publishing Company, 1973)

Martin, 1965—Roscoe C. Martin, *The Cities and the Federal System* (New York: Atherton Press, 1965)

Marvick, 1952—L. Dwaine Marvick, "Congressional Appropriation Politics: A Study of Institutional Conditions for Expressing Supply Intent," Unpublished Ph.D. dissertation, Columbia University, 1952

Maxwell, 1946—James A. Maxwell, *The Fiscal Impact Of Federalism In The United States* (Cambridge, Massachusetts: Harvard University Press, 1946)

Maxwell and Aronson, 1977—James A. Maxwell and J. Richard Aronson, *Financing State and Local Governments* (Washington, D.C.: The Brookings Institution, 1977, Third Edition)

Mayhew, 1966—David R. Mayhew, *Party Loyalty Among Congressmen: The Difference Between Democrats And Republicans, 1947–1962* (Cambridge, Massachusetts: Harvard University Press, 1966)

Mayhew, 1974—David R. Mayhew, *Congress: The Electoral Connection* (New Haven: Yale University Press, 1974)

Mazmanian and Nienaber, 1979—Daniel A. Mazmanian and Jeanne Nienaber, *Can Organizations Change: Environmental Protection, Citizen Participation, and the Corps of Engineers* (Washington, D.C.: The Brookings Institution, 1979)

McConnell, 1966—Grant McConnell, *Private Power and American Democracy* (New York: Alfred A. Knopf, 1966)

McConnell, 1977—Grant McConnell, *The Decline of Agrarian Democracy* (New York: Atheneum, 1977)

McCune, 1956—Wesley McCune, *Who's Behind Our Farm Policy?* (New York: Frederick A. Praeger, 1956)

McFarland, 1976—Andrew S. McFarland, *Public Interest Lobbies: Decision Making on Energy* (Washington, D.C.: American Enterprise Institute for Public Policy Research, 1976)

McKay, 1979—David H. McKay, "The United States in Crisis: A Review of the American Political Literature," *Government and Opposition* 14,3 (Summer 1979), 373–385

McKinley and Frase, 1970—Charles McKinley and Robert W. Frase, *Launching Social Security: A Capture-And-Record Account 1935–1937* (Madison: University of Wisconsin Press, 1970)

Meltsner, 1970—Arnold J. Meltsner, "Local Revenue: A Political Problem," in John P. Crecine, ed., *Financing the Metropolis: Public Policy in Urban Economics* (Beverly Hills, California: Sage Publications, 1970), pp. 103–135

Meltsner, 1974—Arnold J. Meltsner, *The Politics of City Revenue* (Berkeley: University of California Press, 1974)

Meltsner and Wildavsky, 1970—Arnold J. Meltsner and Aaron Wildavsky, "Leave City Budgeting Alone: A Survey, Case Study, and Recommendations for Reform," in John R. Crecine, ed., *Financing The Metropolis: Public Policy in Urban Economics* (Beverly Hills, California: Sage Publications, 1970), pp. 311–358

Meltzer and Richard, 1978—Allan H. Meltzer and Scott F. Richard, "Why Government Grows (and Grows) in a Democracy," *The Public Interest* No. 52 (Summer 1978), 111–118

Meranto, 1967—Philip Meranto, *The Politics of Federal Aid to Education in 1965: A Study in Political Innovation* (Syracuse, New York: Syracuse University Press, 1967)

Meyerson and Banfield, 1964—Martin Meyerson and Edward C. Banfield, *Politics, Planning, And The Public Interest: The Case of Public Housing in Chicago* (New York: The Free Press, 1964)

Miller, 1974a—Arthur H. Miller, "Political Issues and Trust in Government," *American Political Science Review* 68,3 (September 1974), 951–972

Miller, 1974b—Arthur H. Miller, "Rejoinder to 'Comment' by Jack Citrin: Political Discontent or Ritualism?" *American Political Science Review* 68,3 (September 1974), 989–1001

Miller, 1977—Arthur H. Miller, "The Majority Party Revisited?: A Summary Comparison of the 1972 and 1976 Elections" (Ann Arbor, Michigan: The University of Michigan, The Center For Political Studies, 1977)

Miller, 1979—Warren E. Miller, "Misreading the Public Pulse," *Public Opinion* 2,5 (October–November 1979), 9–15, 60

Miller and Levitan, 1976—Warren E. Miller and Teresa E. Levitan, *Leadership & Change: Presidential Elections From 1952 To 1976* (Cambridge, Massachusetts: Winthrop Publishers, Inc., 1976)

Moe and Teel, 1970—Ronald C. Moe and Steven C. Teel, "Congress as Policy-Maker: A Necessary Reappraisal," *Political Science Quarterly* 85,3 (September 1970), 443–470

Mohr, 1969—Lawrence B. Mohr, "Determinants of Innovation in Organizations," *American Political Science Review* 63,1 (March 1969), 111–126

Mohr, 1973—Lawrence B. Mohr, "The Concept of Organizational Goal," *American Political Science Review* 67,2 (June 1973), 470–481

Mohr, 1976—Lawrence B. Mohr, "Organizations, Decisions, And Courts," *Law & Society Review* 10,4 (Summer 1976), 621–642

Monypenny, 1958—Phillip Monypenny, *The Impact Of Federal Grants In Illinois* (Urbana, Illinois: University of Illinois, Institute of Governmental and Public Affairs, January 1958)

Monypenny, 1960—Phillip Monypenny, "Federal Grants-In-Aid To State Governments: A Political Analysis," *National Tax Journal* 13,1 (March 1960), 1–16

Mosher and Poland, 1964—Frederick C. Mosher and Orville F. Poland, *The Costs Of American Governments: Facts, Trends, Myths* (New York: Dodd, Mead and Company, 1964)

Moynihan, 1970—Daniel P. Moynihan, *Maximum Feasible Misunderstanding: Community, Action in the War on Poverty* (New York: The Free Press, 1970)

Moynihan, 1973—Daniel P. Moynihan, *The Politics of a Guaranteed Income: The Nixon Administration and the Family Assistance Plan* (New York: Vintage Books, 1973)

Moynihan, 1978—Daniel P. Moynihan, "The Politics And Economics Of Regional Growth," *The Public Interest* No. 51 (Spring 1978), 3–21

Moynihan, 1979—Daniel Patrick Moynihan, "New York State and the Federal Fisc: III Fiscal Year 1978" (Washington, D.C.: U.S. Senate Office of Senator Moynihan, New York, June 10, 1979)

Moynihan, 1980—Daniel Patrick Moynihan, "What Will They Do For New York?" *New York Times Magazine* (January 27, 1980), 30, 32–33, 38, 39

Muller, 1975—Thomas Muller, *Growing and Declining Urban Areas: A Fiscal Comparison* (Washington, D.C.: The Urban Institute, 1975)

Munger and Fenno, 1962—Frank J. Munger and Richard F. Fenno, Jr., *National Politics and Federal Aid to Education* (Syracuse, New York: Syracuse University Press, 1962)

Murphy, 1973a—Jerome T. Murphy, "Title V of ESEA: The Impact of Discretionary Funds on State Education Bureaucracies," *Harvard Educational Review* 43,3 (August 1973), 362–385

Murphy, 1973b—Jerome T. Murphy, "The Education Bureaucracies Implement Novel Policy: The Politics of Title I of ESEA, 1965–1972," in Allan P. Sindler, ed., *Policy And Politics In America: Six Case Studies* (Boston: Little, Brown and Company, 1973), pp. 161–198

Murphy, Jerome, 1974—Jerome T. Murphy, *State Education Agencies and Discretionary Funds: Grease the Squeaky Wheel* (Lexington, Massachusetts: D. C. Heath and Company, 1974)

Murphy and Cohen, 1974—Jerome T. Murphy and David K. Cohen, "Accountability in Education—The Michigan Experience," *The Public Interest*, No. 36 (Spring 1974), 53–81

Murphy, James T., 1974—James T. Murphy, "Political Parties and the Porkbarrel: Party Conflict and Cooperation in House Public Works Committee Decision Making," *American Political Science Review* 68,1 (March 1974), 169–185

Mushkin, 1956—Selma J. Mushkin, "Distribution of Federal Taxes Among the States," *National Tax Journal* 9,2 (June 1956), 148–165

Mushkin, 1957—Selma Mushkin, "Federal Grants And Federal Expenditures," *National Tax Journal* 10,3 (September 1957), 193–213

Myers and Shannon, 1979—Will Myers and John Shannon, "Revenue Sharing for States: An Endangered Species," *Intergovernmental Perspective* 5,3 (Summer 1979), 10–18

Nash, 1964—Gerald D. Nash, *State Government and Economic Development: A History of Administrative Policies in California, 1849–1933* (Berkeley, California: University of California, Institute of Governmental Studies, 1964)

Nathan, 1975a—Richard P. Nathan, *The Plot That Failed: Nixon and the Administrative Presidency* (New York: John Wiley and Sons, Inc., 1975)

Nathan, 1975b—Richard P. Nathan, "The New Federalism Versus The Emerging New Structuralism," *Publius* 5,3 (Summer 1975), 111–129

Nathan, 1978—Richard P. Nathan, "The Outlook for Federal Grants to Cities," in Roy Bahl, ed., *The Fiscal Outlook for Cities: Implications of a National Urban Policy* (Syracuse: Syracuse University Press, 1978), pp. 75–92

Nathan, 1979—Richard P. Nathan, "The Brookings Monitoring Research Methodology for Studying the Effects of Federal Grant-In-Aid Programs," Paper prepared for presentation at the annual meeting of the American Political Science Association, Washington, D.C., September 1979

Nathan and Adams, 1976—Richard P. Nathan and Charles Adams, "Understanding Central City Hardship," *Political Science Quarterly* 91,1 (Spring 1976), 47–62

Nathan and Dommel, 1977—Richard P. Nathan and Paul R. Dommel, "The Cities," in Joseph A. Pechman, ed., *Setting National Priorities: The 1978 Budget* (Washington, D.C.: The Brookings Institution, 1977), pp. 283–316

Nathan and Fossett, 1979—Richard P. Nathan and James W. Fossett, "Urban Conditions—The Future Of The Federal Role," in Stanley J. Bowers, ed., *1978 Proceedings Of The Seventy-First Annual Conference On Taxation, National Tax Association—Tax Institute Of America At Philadelphia, Pennsylvania, November 12–16, 1978* (Columbus, Ohio: National Tax Association, 1979), pp. 30–41

Nathan, Adams, *et al.*, 1977—Richard P. Nathan, Charles F. Adams, Jr., *et al.*, *Revenue Sharing: The Second Round* (Washington, D.C.: The Brookings Institution, 1977)

Nathan, Manvel, Calkins, *et al.*, 1975—Richard P. Nathan, Allen D. Manvel, Susannah E. Calkins, *et al.*, *Monitoring Revenue Sharing* (Washington, D.C.: The Brookings Institution, 1975)

Nathan, *et al.*, 1977—Richard P. Nathan, *et al.*, *Block Grants for Community Development* (Washington, D.C.: The Brookings Institution, contracted by the U.S. Department of Housing and Urban Development, 1977)

Nathan, Jaffe, Dommel, Fossett, 1977—Richard P. Nathan, Jacob M. Jaffe, Paul R. Dommel, and James W. Fossett, *Feasibility of Measuring the Geographic Impact of Federal Economic and Community Development Programs* (Washington, D.C.: The Brookings Institution, Report to the Office of Management and Budget, August 8, 1977)

National Governors' Association, 1979—National Governors' Association, *Bypassing the States: Wrong Turn for Urban Aid* (Washington, D.C.: National Governors' Association, 1979)

Nelson, 1969—Daniel Nelson, *Unemployment Insurance: The American Experience 1915–1935* (Madison: University of Wisconsin Press, 1969)

Neustadt, 1969—Richard E. Neustadt, *Presidential Power: The Politics of Leadership* (New York: John Wiley and Sons, Inc., 1969)

Neustadt, 1970—Richard E. Neustadt, *Alliance Politics* (New York: Columbia University Press, 1970)

Neustadt, 1973—Richard E. Neustadt, "Politicians and Bureaucrats," in David B. Truman, ed., *The Congress and America's Future* (Englewood Cliffs, N.J.: Prentice-Hall, Inc., Second Edition, 1973), pp. 118–140

Neustadt and Fineberg, 1978—Richard E. Neustadt and Harvey V. Fineberg, *The Swine Flu Affair: Decision-making on a Slippery Disease* (Washington, D.C.: U.S. Government Printing Office, Department of Health, Education and Welfare, 1978)

Newcomer, 1928—Mabel Newcomer, "Tendencies in State and Local Finance and Their Relation to State and Local Functions," *Political Science Quarterly* 43,1 (March 1928), 1–31

Nutter, 1978—G. Warren Nutter, *Growth of Government in the West* (Washington, D.C.: American Enterprise Institute for Public Policy Research, 1978)

Oates, 1972—Wallace E. Oates, *Fiscal Federalism* (New York: Harcourt, Brace, Jovanovich, Inc., 1972)

Oates, 1977—Wallace E. Oates, "An Economist's Perspective on Fiscal Federalism," in Wallace E. Oates, ed., *The Political Economy of Fiscal Federalism* (Lexington, Massachusetts: D. C. Heath and Company, 1977), pp. 3–20

O'Connor, 1973—James O'Connor, *The Fiscal Crisis Of The State* (New York: St. Martin's Press, 1973)

Office of Policy Development and Research, 1979—Office of Policy Development and Research, Department of Housing and Urban Development, "The Urban Fiscal Crisis: Fact or Fantasy? A Reply to the Touche Ross/First National Bank Study, Urban Fiscal Stress" (Washington, D.C.: Department of Housing and Urban Development, 1979)

Olson, 1967—Kenneth G. Olson, "The Service Function Of The United States Congress," in Alfred de Grazia, ed., *Congress: The First Branch Of Government* (New York: Anchor Books, 1967), pp. 323–364

Oppenheim, 1980—John Oppenheim, "An Assessment of Farmers Home Administration Emergency Disaster Loans in the East North Central Region," unpublished manuscript, 1980

Orfield, 1975—Gary Orfield, *Congressional Power: Congress And Social Change* (New York: Harcourt Brace Jovanovich, Inc., 1975)

Orfield, 1978—Gary Orfield, *Must We Bus? Segregated Schools and National Policy* (Washington, D.C.: The Brookings Institution, 1978)

Osman, 1966—Jack W. Osman, "The Dual Impact Of Federal Aid On State And Local Government Expenditures," *National Tax Journal* 19,4 (December 1966), 362–372

Ostrom, V., 1976—Vincent Ostrom, "The Contemporary Debate Over Centralization and Decentralization," *Publius* 6,4 (Fall 1976), 21–32

Ostrom, 1977—Vincent Ostrom, "Some Problems In Doing Political Theory: A Response to Golembiewski's 'Critique'," *American Political Science Review* 71,4 (December 1977), 1508–1525

Owen and Schultze, 1976—Henry Owen and Charles L. Schultze, eds., *Setting National Priorities: The Next Ten Years* (Washington, D.C.: The Brookings Institution, 1976)

Pack with Foldman, 1978—Janet Rothenberg Pack, with the assistance of Gordon Folkman, "Frostbelt and Sunbelt: Convergence Over Time," *Intergovernmental Perspective* 4,4 (Fall 1978), 8–15

Patterson, 1967—James T. Patterson, *Congressional Conservatism and the New Deal: The Growth of the Conservative Coalition in Congress, 1933–1939* (Lexington: University of Kentucky Press, 1967)

Patterson, 1969—James T. Patterson, *The New Deal and the States: Federalism in Transition* (Princeton, New Jersey: Princeton University Press, 1969)

Pechman, 1977a—Joseph A. Pechman, *Federal Tax Policy* (Washington, D.C.: The Brookings Institution, Third Edition, 1977)

Pechman, 1977b—Joseph A. Pechman, ed., *Setting National Priorities: The 1978 Budget* (Washington, D.C.: The Brookings Institution, 1977)

Pechman, 1978a—Joseph A. Pechman, "Tax Expenditures," in Joseph A. Pechman, ed., *Setting National Priorities: The 1979 Budget* (Washington, D.C.: The Brookings Institution, 1978), pp. 315–319

Pechman, 1978b—Joseph A. Pechman, ed., *Setting National Priorities: The 1979 Budget* (Washington, D.C.: The Brookings Institution, 1978)

Pechman, 1979a—Joseph A. Pechman, "Tax Expenditures," in Joseph A. Pechman, ed., *Setting*

National Priorities: The 1980 Budget (Washington, D.C.: The Brookings Institution, 1979), pp. 225–229

Pechman, 1979b—Joseph A. Pechman, ed., *Setting National Priorities: The 1980 Budget* (Washington, D.C.: The Brookings Institution, 1979)

Pechman, 1980—Joseph A. Pechman, ed., *Setting National Priorities: Agenda for the 1980s* (Washington, D.C.: The Brookings Institution, 1980)

Perry and Kraemer, 1978—James L. Perry and Kenneth L. Kraemer, "Innovation Attributes, Policy Intervention, and the Diffusion of Computer Applications Among Local Governments," *Policy Sciences* 9,2 (April 1978), 179–205

Peters and Rose, 1980—B. Guy Peters and Richard Rose, "The Growth of Government and the Political Consequences of Economic Overload," in Charles H. Levine, ed., *Managing Financial Stress: The Crisis In The Public Sector* (Chatham, New Jersey: Chatham House Publishers, Inc., 1980), pp. 33–51

Peterson, 1976—George E. Peterson, "Finance," in William Gorham and Nathan Glazer, eds., *The Urban Predicament* (Washington, D.C.: The Urban Institute, 1976), pp. 35–118

Pierce, 1971—Lawrence C. Pierce, *The Politics of Fiscal Policy Formation* (Pacific Palisades, California: Goodyear Publishing Company, Inc., 1971)

Piven and Cloward, 1972—Frances Fox Piven and Richard A. Cloward, *Regulating the Poor: The Functions of Public Welfare* (New York: Vintage Books, 1972)

Plott, 1968—Charles R. Plott, "Some Organizational Influences On Urban Renewal Decisions," *American Economic Review* 58,2 (May 1968), 306–321

Polsby, 1968—Nelson W. Polsby, "The Institutionalization of the U.S. House of Representatives," *American Political Science Review* 62,1 (March 1968), 144–168

Polsby, 1971—Nelson W. Polsby, "Policy Initiation in the American Political System," in Irving Louis Horowitz, ed., *The Use and Abuse of Social Science* (New Brunswick, New Jersey: E. P. Dutton and Company, Transaction Books, 1971), pp. 296–308

Polsby, 1976—Nelson W. Polsby, *Congress and the Presidency* (Englewood Cliffs, New Jersey: Prentice-Hall, Inc., 1976, Third Edition)

Polsby, Gallagher, Rundquist, 1969—Nelson W. Polsby, Miriam Gallagher, and Barry Spencer Rundquist, "The Growth of the Seniority System in the U.S. House of Representatives," *American Political Science Review* 63,3 (September 1969), 787–807

Porter, Warner and Porter, 1973—David O. Porter, with David C. Warner and Teddie W. Porter. *The Politics of Budgeting Federal Aid: Resource Mobilization By Local School Districts* (Beverly Hills: Sage Publications, 1973)

Potter, 1954—David M. Potter, *People of Plenty: Economic Abundance and the American Character* (Chicago: University of Chicago Press, 1954)

Pressman, 1974—Jeffrey L. Pressman, "Federal Programs and Political Development in Cities," in Willis D. Hawley and David Rogers, eds., *Improving The Quality Of Urban Management* (Beverly Hills, California: Sage Publications, 1974), pp. 583–605

Pressman, 1975a—Jeffrey L. Pressman, *Federal Programs and City Politics: The Dynamics of the Aid Process in Oakland* (Berkeley: University of California Press, 1975)

Pressman, 1975b—Jeffrey L. Pressman, "Political Implications of the New Federalism," in Wallace E. Cates, ed., *Financing the New Federalism: Revenue Sharing, Conditional Grants, and Taxation* (Baltimore and London: The Johns Hopkins University Press, 1975), pp. 13–39

Pressman and Wildavsky, 1974—Jeffrey L. Pressman and Aaron Wildavsky, *Implementation: How Great Expectations In Washington Are Dashed In Oakland: Or, Why It's Amazing That Federal Programs Work At All This Being A Saga of the Economic Development Administration As Told By Two Sympathetic Observers Who Seek To Build Morals on a Foundation of Ruined Hopes* (Berkeley: University of California Press, 1974)

Pressman and Wildavsky, 1979—Jeffrey L. Pressman and Aaron Wildavsky, *Implementation: How Great Expectations in Washington Are Dashed in Oakland: Or, Why It's Amazing That Federal Programs Work at All* (Berkeley: University of California Press, 1979, Second Edition)

Preston, 1979—Michael E. Preston, *The Politics Of Bureaucratic Reform: Improving The Adminis-*

tration Of Minority Employment Programs (Unpublished manuscript, University of Illinois, Urbana, 1979)

Price, D. E., 1972–David E. Price, *Who Makes The Laws? Creativity and Power in Senate Committees* (Cambridge, Massachusetts: Schenkman Publishing Company, 1972)

Price, D. E., 1975–David E. Price, Director, *The Commerce Committees: A Study of the House and Senate Commerce Committees* The Ralph Nader Congress Project (New York: Grossman Publishers, 1975)

Price, D. E., 1978–David E. Price, "Policy Making in Congressional Committees: The Impact of 'Environmental' Factors," *American Political Science Review* 72,2 (June 1978), 548–574

Price, H. D., 1962–H. Douglas Price, "Race, Religion, and the Rules Committee: The Kennedy Aid-to-Education Bills," in Alan F. Westin, ed., *The Uses of Power: 7 Cases in American Politics* (New York: Harcourt, Brace & World, Inc., 1962), pp. 1–71

Price, H. D., 1970–H. Douglas Price, "Computer Simulation and Legislative 'Professionalism': Some Quantitative Approaches to Legislative Evolution," Paper prepared for delivery at the 1970 Annual Meeting of the American Political Science Association, Biltmore Hotel, Los Angeles, California, September 7–12, 1970

Price, H. D., 1971–H. Douglas Price, "The Congressional Career Then and Now," in Nelson W. Polsby, ed., *Congressional Behavior* (New York: Random House, 1971), pp. 14–27

Price, H. D., 1973–H. Douglas Price, "The Electoral Arena," in David B. Truman, ed., *The Congress and America's Future* (Englewood Cliffs, New Jersey: Prentice-Hall, Inc., Second Edition, 1973), pp. 39–62

Price, H. D., 1975–H. Douglas Price, "Congress and the Evolution of Legislative 'Professionalism'," in Norman Ornstein, ed., *Congress in Change: Evolution and Reform* (New York: Praeger Publishers, 1975), pp. 2–23

Price, H. D., 1977–H. Douglas Price, "Careers and Committees in the American Congress: The Problem of Structural Change," in William O. Aydelotte, ed., *The History of Parliamentary Behavior* (Princeton, New Jersey: Princeton University Press, 1977), pp. 28–62

Rabinovitz, Pressman and Rein, 1976–Francine Rabinovitz, Jeffrey Pressman and Martin Rein, "Guidelines: A Plethora of Forms, Authors, and Functions," *Policy Sciences* 7,4 (December 1976), 399–400

Rafuse, 1977–Robert W. Rafuse, Jr., *The New Regional Debate: A National Overview* (Washington, D.C.: National Governors' Conference, Center for Policy Research and Analysis, Agenda Setting Series, April 1977)

Ratner, 1967–Sidney Ratner, *Taxation And Democracy In America* (New York: John Wiley and Sons, 1967)

Ray, 1976a–Bruce A. Ray, "Congressional Committees and the Geographical Distribution of Federal Spending," Paper prepared for delivery at the 1976 Annual Meeting of the Midwest Political Science Association, Chicago, Illinois, 1976

Ray, 1976b–Bruce A. Ray, "Investigating the Myth of Congressional Influence: The Geographic Distribution of Federal Spending," Paper prepared for delivery at the 1976 Annual Meeting of the American Political Science Association, Chicago, Illinois, September 2–5, 1976

Ray, 1977–Bruce A. Ray, "Congressional Influence and the Geographic Distribution of Federal Spending," Unpublished Ph.D., Washington University, St. Louis, 1977

Reagan, 1972–Michael D. Reagan, *The New Federalism* (New York: Oxford University Press, 1972)

Reagan, 1975–Michael D. Reagan, "Accountability and Independence in Federal Grants-in-aid," in Bruce L. R. Smith, eds., *The New Political Economy: The Public Use of the Private Sector* (New York: John Wiley and Sons, 1975), pp. 181–213

Redman, 1973–Eric Redman, *The Dance Of Legislation* (New York: Simon and Schuster, 1973)

Reich, 1964–Charles A. Reich, "The New Property," *Yale Law Journal* 73,5 (April 1964), 733–787

Reich, 1965–Charles A. Reich, "Individual Rights and Social Welfare: The Emerging Legal Issues," *Yale Law Journal* 74,7 (June 1965), 1245–1257

Reich, 1966a–Charles A. Reich, "The New Property," *The Public Interest* No. 3 (Spring 1966), 57–89

Reich, 1966b—Charles A. Reich, "The Law of the Planned Society," *Yale Law Journal* 75,8 (July 1966), 1227–1270

Reid, 1975—John Norman Reid, "The Interstate Distribution of Federal Health Grants: An Analysis of Causal Factors," Unpublished Ph.D. Dissertation, University of Illinois at Urbana-Champaign, 1975

Reid, 1978—J. Norman Reid, *On Interpreting Federal Spending Data: Some Considerations* (Washington, D.C.: Department of Agriculture, Working Paper No. 7813, 1978)

Reid, 1979—J. Norman Reid, "Understanding Federal Programs: The Need for a Coordinated Data System," *State and Local Government Review,* Vol. 11, No. 2 (May 1979), 42–47

Reid, Godsey, Hines, 1978—J. Norman Reid, W. Maureen Godsey, Fred K. Hines, *Federal Outlays in Fiscal 1976* (Washington, D.C.: U.S. Department of Agriculture, Economics, Statistics, and Cooperatives Service, Rural Development Research Report No. 1, 1978)

Reid, 1980—T. R. Reid, *Congressional Odyssey: The Saga of a Senate Bill* (San Francisco: W. H. Freeman and Company, 1980)

Rein and Heclo, 1973—Martin Rein and Hugh Heclo, "What Welfare Crisis?—A Comparison Among the United States, Britain, and Sweden," *The Public Interest* No. 33 (Fall 1973), 61–83

Rein and Rabinovitz, 1978—Martin Rein and Francine F. Rabinovitz, "Implementation: A Theoretical Perspective," in Walter Dean Burnham and Martha Wagner Weinber, eds., *American Politics and Public Policy* (Cambridge, Massachusetts: The M.I.T. Press, 1978), pp. 307–335

Reischauer, 1974—Robert D. Reischauer, *Rich Governments—Poor Governments: Determining the Fiscal Capacity and Revenue Requirements of State and Local Government* (Washington, D.C.: The Brookings Institution, unpublished draft, December 1979)

Reischauer, 1975—Robert D. Reischauer, "General Revenue Sharing—The Program's Incentives," in Wallace A. Oates, ed., *Financing the New Federalism: Revenue Sharing, Conditional Grants, and Taxation* (Baltimore: The Johns Hopkins University Press, 1975), pp. 40–87

Reischauer, 1976—Robert D. Reischauer, "The Federal Government's Role In Relieving Cities Of The Fiscal Burdens Of Concentrations Of Low-Income Persons," *National Tax Journal* 29,3 (September 1976), 293–311

Reischauer, 1977—Robert D. Reischauer, "Government Diversity: Bane of the Grants Strategy in the United States," in Wallace E. Cates, ed., *The Political Economy of Fiscal Federalism* (Lexington, Massachusetts: D. C. Heath and Company, 1977), pp. 115–127

Reischauer, 1978—Robert D. Reischauer, "The Economy, the Federal Budget, and the Prospects for Urban Aid," in Roy Bahl, ed., *The Fiscal Outlook for Cities: Implications of a National Urban Policy* (Syracuse, New York: Syracuse University Press, 1978), pp. 93–110

Reischauer, 1979—Robert D. Reischauer, "Federal Countercyclical Policy—The State And Local Role," in Stanley J. Bowers, ed., *1978 Proceedings of the Seventy-First Annual Conference on Taxation, National Tax Association—Tax Institute of America at Philadelphia, Pennsylvania, November 12–16, 1978* (Columbus, Ohio: National Tax Association, 1979), pp. 53–64

Reuss, 1977—Henry S. Reuss, *To Save Our Cities: What Needs to Be Done* (Washington, D.C.: Public Affairs Press, 1977)

Rifkin and Barber, 1978—Jeremy Rifkin and Randy Barber, *The North Will Rise Again: Pensions, Politics and Power in the 1980s* (Boston: Beacon Press, 1978)

Ripley, 1969—Randall B. Ripley, "Legislative Bargaining and the Food Stamp Act, 1964," in Frederic N. Cleaveland, et al., *Congress "and" Urban Problems* (Washington, D.C.: The Brookings Institution, 1969), pp. 279–310

Ripley and Franklin, 1975—Randall B. Ripley and Grace A. Franklin, eds., *Policy-Making in the Federal Executive Branch* (New York: The Free Press, 1975)

Ripley and Franklin, 1976—Randall B. Ripley and Grace A. Franklin, *Congress, The Bureaucracy, and Public Policy* (Homewood, Illinois: The Dorsey Press, 1976)

Ritt, 1976—Leonard G. Ritt, "Committee Position, Seniority, And The Distribution Of Governmental Expenditures," *Public Policy* 24,4 (Fall 1976), 463–489

Rivlin, 1971—Alice M. Rivlin, *Systematic Thinking for Social Action* (Washington, D.C.: The Brookings Institution, 1971)

Rivlin, 1973—Alice M. Rivlin, *Social Policy: Alternative Strategies For The Federal Government* (Ann Arbor, Michigan: The University of Michigan, The Department of Economics and The Institute Of Public Policy Studies, W. S. Woytinsky Lecture No. 3, 1973)

Roach, 1925—Hannah Grace Roach, "Sectionalism in Congress (1870 To 1890)," *American Political Science Review* 19,3 (August 1925), 500–526

Rockefeller, 1962—Nelson A. Rockefeller, *The Future Of Federalism* (Cambridge: Harvard University Press, 1962)

Rose and Peters, 1978—Richard Rose and Guy Peters, *Can Government Go Bankrupt?* (New York: Basic Books, 1978)

Ross, 1979—John P. Ross, "Countercyclical Revenue Sharing," in L. Kenneth Hubbell, ed., *Fiscal Crisis in American Cities: The Federal Response* (Cambridge, Massachusetts: Ballinger Publishing Company, 1979), pp. 257–288

Rudder, 1977—Catherine E. Rudder, "Committee Reform and the Revenue Process," in Lawrence C. Dodd and Bruce I. Oppenheimer, eds., *Congress Reconsidered* (New York: Praeger Publishers, 1977), pp. 117–139

Rundquist, 1973—Barry Spencer Rundquist, "Congressional Influences on the Distribution of Prime Military Contracts," A dissertation submitted to the Department of Political Science and the Committee on graduate studies at Stanford University in partial fulfillment of the requirements for the degree of doctor of philosophy (Ann Arbor, Michigan: University Microfilms)

Russett, 1970—Bruce M. Russett, *What Price Vigilance? The Burdens Of National Defense* (New Haven and London: University of California Press, 1970)

Sacks and Harris, 1964—Seymour Sacks and Robert Harris, "The Determinants Of State And Local Government Expenditures And Intergovernmental Flows Of Funds," *National Tax Journal* 17,1 (March 1964), 75–85

Salamon, 1975—Lester M. Salamon, Director, *The Money Committees: A Study of the House Banking and Currency Committee and the Senate Banking, Housing, and Urban Affairs Committees* (New York: Grossman Publishers, 1975)

Salamon, 1976—Lester M. Salamon, "Follow-up, Letdowns, and Sleepers: The Time Dimension in Policy Evaluation," in Charles O. Jones and Robert D. Thomas, eds., *Public Policy Making In A Federal System* (Beverly Hills: Sage, 1976), pp. 257–284

Salisbury, 1975—Robert H. Salisbury, "Interest Groups," in Fred I. Greenstein and Nelson W. Polsby, eds., *Handbook of Political Science, Volume 2: Micropolitical Theory* (Reading, Massachusetts: Addison-Wesley Publishing Company, 1975), pp. 243–318

Salisbury, 1977—Robert H. Salisbury, "Peak Associations and the Tensions of Interest Intermediation, or Why No Corporatism in America," Paper prepared for delivery at the Annual Meeting of the American Political Science Association, Washington-Hilton Hotel, Washington, D.C., September 1–4, 1977

Saltzstein, 1977—Alan L. Saltzstein, "Federal Categorical Aid to Cities: Who Needs It Versus Who Wants It," *Western Political Quarterly* 30,3 (September 1977), 377–383

Samuelson, 1963—Paul A. Samuelson, "Discussion," *American Economic Review* 53,2 (May 1963), 231–236

Sanders, 1979—Heywood T. Sanders, "Urban Renewal And The Revitalized City: A Reconsideration Of Recent History" (Unpublished paper, Institute of Governmental and Public Affairs, University of Illinois, Urbana, 1979)

Sanford, 1967—Terry Sanford, *Storm Over The States* (New York: McGraw-Hill Book Company, 1967)

Sayre and Kaufman, 1965—Wallace S. Sayre and Herbert Kaufman, *Governing New York City: Politics In The Metropolis* (New York: W. W. Norton and Company, 1965)

Schattschneider, 1935—E. E. Schattschneider, *Politics, Pressures and the Tariff: A Study of Free Enterprise in Pressure Politics, as Shown in the 1929–1930 Revision of the Tariff* (New York: Prentice-Hall, Inc., 1935)

Schattschneider, 1960—E. E. Schattschneider, *The Semisovereign People: A Realist's View of Democracy in America* (New York: Holt, Rinehart and Winston, 1960)

Scheiber, 1966—Harry N. Scheiber, *The Condition Of American Federalism: An Historian's View* (Washington, D.C.: U.S. Government Printing Office, 89th Congress, 2nd Session, Senate Committee On Governmental Operations, Subcommittee On Intergovernmental Relations, Committee Print, October 15, 1966)

Scheiber, 1969—Harry N. Scheiber, *Ohio Canal Era: A Case Study of Government and the Economy, 1820–1861* (Athens, Ohio: Ohio University Press, 1969)

Scheiber, 1972—Harry N. Scheiber, "Government and the Economy: Studies of the 'Commonwealth' Policy in Nineteenth-Century America," *Journal of Interdisciplinary History* 3,1 (Summer 1972), 135–151

Scheiber, 1973—Harry Scheiber, "Property Law, Expropriation, and Resource Allocation by Government: The United States, 1789–1910," *Journal of Economic History* 33,1 (March 1973), 232–251

Scheiber, 1975—Harry N. Scheiber, "Federalism And The American Economic Order, 1789–1910," *Law And Society Review* 10,1 (Fall 1975), 57–118

Schlesinger, 1965—Joseph A. Schlesinger, "Political Party Organization," in James G. March, ed., *Handbook Of Organizations* (Chicago: Rand McNally and Company, 1965), pp. 764–801

Schmitter, 1974—Philippe C. Schmitter, "Still the Century of Corporatism?" *Review of Politics* 36,1 (January 1974), 85–131

Schmitter, 1977a—Philippe C. Schmitter, "Modes of Interest Intermediation and Modes of Societal Change in Western Europe," *Comparative Politics* 10,1 (April 1977), 7–38

Schmitter, 1977b—Philippe C. Schmitter, "Interest Intermediation and Regime Governability in Contemporary Western Europe," Paper prepared for delivery at the 1977 Annual Meeting of the American Political Science Association, Washington, D.C., September 1–4, 1977

Schultze, 1968—Charles L. Schultze, *The Politics and Economics of Public Spending* (Washington, D.C.: The Brookings Institution, 1968)

Schultze, 1970—Charles L. Schultze, "The Role of Incentives, Penalties, and Rewards in Attaining Effective Policy," in Robert H. Haveman and Julius Margolis, eds., *Public Expenditures And Policy Analysis* (Chicago: Markham Publishing Company, 1970), pp. 145–172

Schultze, 1971—Charles L. Schultze, *The Distribution Of Farm Subsidies: Who Gets The Benefits? A Staff Paper* (Washington, D.C.: The Brookings Institution, 1971)

Schultze, 1974—Charles L. Schultze, "Sorting Out The Social Grant Programs: An Economist's Criteria," *American Economic Review* 64,2 (May 1974), 181–189

Schultze, 1976—Charles L. Schultze, "Federal Spending: Past, Present, and Future," in Henry Owen and Charles L. Schultze, eds., *Setting National Priorities: The Next Ten Years* (Washington, D.C.: The Brookings Institution, 1976), pp. 323–369

Schultze, 1977—Charles L. Schultze, *The Public Use of Private Interest* (Washington, D.C.: The Brookings Institution, 1977)

Schultze, Fried, Rivlin and Teeters, 1971—Charles L. Schultze, Edward R. Fried, Alice M. Rivlin and Nancy H. Teeters, *Setting National Priorities: The 1972 Budget* (Washington, D.C.: The Brookings Institution, 1971)

Schultze, Fried, Rivlin, and Teeters, 1972—Charles L. Schultze, Edward R. Fried, Alice M. Rivlin, and Nancy E. Teeters, *Setting National Priorities: The 1973 Budget* (Washington, D.C.: The Brookings Institution, 1972)

Schultze, Hamilton and Schick, 1970—Charles L. Schultze, Edward K. Hamilton and Allen Schick, *Setting National Priorities: The 1971 Budget* (Washington, D.C.: The Brookings Institution, 1970)

Seidman, 1972—Harold Seidman, "Crisis of Confidence in Government," *Political Quarterly* 43,1 (January–March, 1972), 79–88

Seidman, 1980—Harold Seidman, *Politics, Position, and Power: The Dynamics of Federal Organization* (New York: Oxford University Press, 1980, Third Edition)

Selznick, 1966—Philip Selznick, *TVA and the Grass Roots: A Study in the Sociology of Formal Organization* (New York: Harper & Row, Publishers, 1966)

Sharkansky, 1968—Ira Sharkansky, *Spending In The American States* (Chicago: Rand McNally and Company, 1968)

Sharkansky, 1969—Ira Sharkansky, *The Politics of Taxing and Spending* (Indianapolis and New York: The Bobbs-Merrill Company, Inc., 1969)

Sharkansky, 1970a—Ira Sharkansky, *Regionalism In American Politics* (Indianapolis and New York: The Bobbs-Merrill Company, Inc., 1970)

Sharkansky, 1970b—Ira Sharkansky, *The Routines Of Politics* (New York: Van Nostrand Reinhold Company, 1970)

Sharkansky, 1978—Ira Sharkansky, *The Maligned States: Policy Accomplishments, Problems, and Opportunities* (New York: McGraw-Hill Book Company, 1978)

Sharkansky, 1979—Ira Sharkansky, *Wither the State?* (Chatham, New Jersey: Chatham House Publishers, Inc., 1979)

Sharkansky and Hofferbert, 1971—Ira Sharkansky and Richard I. Hofferbert, "Dimensions of State Policy," in Herbert Jacob and Kenneth N. Vines, eds., *Politics In The American States: A Comparative Analysis* (Boston: Little, Brown and Company, 1971, Second Edition), pp. 315–353

Shover, 1965—John L. Shover, "Populism in the Nineteen-Thirties: The Battle for the AAA," *Agricultural History* 39,1 (January 1965), 17–24

Simon, 1963—Herbert A. Simon, "Discussion," *American Economic Review* 53,2 (May 1963), 229–231

Simon, 1970—Herbert A. Simon, *The Sciences of the Artificial* (Cambridge, Massachusetts: The M.I.T. Press, 1970)

Simon, 1979—Herbert A. Simon, "Rational Decision Making in Business Organizations," *American Economic Review* 69,4 (September 1979), 493–513

Sinclair, 1977a—Barbara Deckard Sinclair, "Determinants of Aggregate Party Cohesion in the U.S. House of Representatives, 1901–1956," *Legislative Studies Quarterly* 2,2 (May 1977), 155–175

Sinclair, 1977b—Barbara Deckard Sinclair, "Party Realignment and the Transformation of the Political Agenda: The House of Representatives, 1925–1938," *American Political Science Review* 71,3 (September 1977), 940–953

Sinclair, 1978—Barbara Deckard Sinclair, "The Policy Consequences of Party Realignment—Social Welfare Legislation in the House of Representatives, 1933–1954," *American Journal of Political Science* 22,1 (February 1978), 83–105

Smithies, 1955—Arthur Smithies, *The Budgetary Process in the United States* (New York: McGraw-Hill Book Company, Inc., 1955)

Snowiss, 1971—Sylvia Snowiss, "Presidential Leadership of Congress: An Analysis of Roosevelt's First Hundred Days," *Publius* 1,1 (Spring 1971), 59–87

Snyder, 1958—Richard C. Snyder, "A Decision-Making Approach to the Study of Political Phenomena," in Roland A. Young, ed., *Approaches to the Study of Politics* (Evanston, Illinois: Northwestern University Press, 1958), pp. 3–38

Sonenblum, Kirlin and Ries, 1977—Sidney Sonenblum, John J. Kirlin, and John C. Ries, *How Cities Provide Services: An Evaluation of Alternative Delivery Structures* (Cambridge, Massachusetts: Ballinger Publishing Company, 1977)

Sorokin, 1956—Pitirim Aleksandrovich Sorokin, *Fads and Foibles in Modern Sociology and Related Sciences* (Chicago: H. Regnery Company, 1956)

Spohn and McCollum, 1975—Richard Spohn and Charles McCollum, directors, *The Revenue Committees: A Study of the House Ways and Means Senate Finance Committees and the House and Senate Appropriations Committees* The Ralph Nader Congress Project (New York: Grossman Publishers, 1975)

Stanfield, 1976—Rochelle L. Stanfield, "The PIGS: Out of the Sty, Into Lobbying with Style," *National Journal* 8,33 (August 14, 1976), 1134–1139

Stanfield, 1978—Rochelle L. Stanfield, "The Development of Carter's Urban Policy: One Small Step for Federalism," *Publius* 8,1 (Winter 1978), 39–62

Stanfield, 1979a—Rochelle L. Stanfield, "Fighting Among Themselves," *National Journal* 11,16 (April 21, 1979), 652

Stanfield, 1979b—Rochelle L. Stanfield, "A New Breed of Mayors with a New View of Washington," *National Journal* 11,21 (May 26, 1979), 866–870

Stanfield, 1979c—Rochelle L. Stanfield, "Federal Aid Comes Out of the Closet in the Mountain and Desert West," *National Journal* 11,50 (December 15, 1979), 2096–2099

Stanfield, 1979d—Rochelle L. Stanfield, "Revenue Sharing Survived This Year, but 1980 May Be a Different Story," *National Journal* 11,32 (August 11, 1979), 1331–1335

Stanfield, 1979e—Rochelle L. Stanfield, "Toward an Urban Policy with a Small-Town Accent," *Publius* 9,1 (Winter 1979), 31–43

Stanfield, 1980—Rochelle L. Stanfield, "If You Want The Federal Dollars, You Have To Accept Federal Controls," *National Journal* 12,3 (January 19, 1980), 105–109

Statistical Policy Division, 1975—Statistical Policy Division, Executive Office of the President, Office of Management and Budget, *Statistical Services of the United States Government* (Washington, D.C.: U.S. Government Printing Office, 1975, Revised Edition)

Statistical Policy Division, 1976—Statistical Policy Division, Executive Office of the President, Office of Management and Budget, *Federal Statistical Directory* (Washington, D.C.: U.S. Government Printing Office, 1976, 25th Edition)

Stein, 1979—Robert M. Stein, "Federal Categorical Aid: Equalization and the Application Process," *Western Political Quarterly* 32,4 (December 1979), 396–408

Steiner, 1966—Gilbert Y. Steiner, *Social Insecurity: The Politics of Welfare* (Chicago, Illinois: Rand McNally and Company, 1966)

Steiner, 1971—Gilbert Y. Steiner, *The State of Welfare* (Washington, D.C.: The Brookings Institution, 1971)

Steiner, with Milius, 1976—Gilbert Y. Steiner, with the assistance of Pauline H. Milius, *The Children's Cause* (Washington, D.C.: The Brookings Institution, 1976)

Steinfels, 1979—Peter Steinfels, *The Neoconservatives: The Men Who Are Changing America's Politics* (New York: Simon and Schuster, 1979)

Stellwagen, 1967—Marvin Allan Stellwagen, "An Analysis of the Spatial Impact of Federal Revenues and Expenditures: 1950 and 1960," unpublished Ph.D. dissertation, the University of Washington, 1967

Stenberg, 1980—Carl W. Stenberg, "Federalism in Transition: 1959–79," *Intergovernmental Perspective* 6,1 (Winter 1980), 4–13

Stephens, 1974—G. Ross Stephens, "State Centralization and the Erosion of Local Autonomy," *Journal of Politics* 36,1 (February 1974), 44–76

Stephens, 1979—G. Ross Stephens, "The Great Reform in Federal Grant Policy or What Ever Happened to General Revenue Sharing?" in L. Kenneth Hubbell, ed., *Fiscal Crisis in American Cities: The Federal Response* (Cambridge, Massachusetts: Ballinger Publishing Company, 1979), pp. 85–119

Stephens and Olson, 1979—G. Ross Stephens and Gerald W. Olson, *Pass-Through Federal Aid and Interlevel Finance in the American Federal System, 1957 to 1977, Volumes 1 and 2* (Kansas City, Missouri: The University of Missouri, Kansas City and The National Science Foundation, 1979)

Stern, 1964—Philip M. Stern, *The Great Treasury Raid* (New York: Random House, 1964)

Stern, 1973—Philip M. Stern, *The Rape of the Taxpayer* (New York: Random House, 1973)

Stockman, 1975—David A. Stockman, "The Social Pork Barrel," *The Public Interest* No. 39 (Spring 1975), 3–30

Stonecash, 1977—Jeff Stonecash, "Urban Policy Analysis; Systems, Assumptions, and Multiple Planes of Influence," *Publius* 7,1 (Winter 1977), 59–89

Stonecash, 1979—Jeff Stonecash, "Interjurisdictional Transfers and Local Response Patterns: A Refocusing of Aid Impact Studies," *Publius* 9,3 (Summer 1979), 101–117

Strom, 1975—Gerald S. Strom, "Congressional Policy Making: A Test of a Theory," *Journal of Politics* 37,3 (August 1975), 711–735

Studenski and Baikie, 1949—Paul Studenski and E. J. Baikie, "Federal Grants-In-Aid," *National Tax Journal* 2,3 (September 1949), 193–214.

Sullivan, 1972—Gerald E. Sullivan, "Incremental Budget-Making in the American States: A Test of the Anton Model," *Journal of Politics* 34,2 (May 1972), 639–647

Sundelson and Mushkin, 1944—J. Wilner Sundelson and S. J. Mushkin, *The Measurement of State and Local Tax Effort* (Washington, D.C.: Bureau of Research and Statistics, 1944)

Sundquist, 1968—James L. Sundquist, *Politics and Policy: The Eisenhower, Kennedy and Johnson Years* (Washington, D.C.: The Brookings Institution, 1968)

Sundquist, 1973—James L. Sundquist, *Dynamics of the Party System: Alignment and Realignment of Political Parties in the United States* (Washington, D.C.: The Brookings Institution, 1973)

Sundquist, 1976—James L. Sundquist, "Congress and the President: Enemies or Partners?" in Henry Owen and Charles L. Schultze, eds., *Setting National Priorities: The Next Ten Years* (Washington, D.C.: The Brookings Institution, 1976), pp. 583–618

Sundquist, 1978a—James L. Sundquist, "In Defense of Pragmatism—A Response to Daniel J. Elazar's 'Is Federalism Compatible with Prefectorial Administration?' " Paper prepared for delivery at the 1978 Annual Meeting of The American Political Science Association, The New York Hilton Hotel, New York, New York, August 31–September 3, 1978

Sundquist, 1978b—James L. Sundquist, "Research Brokerage: The Weak Link," in Laurence E. Lynn, Jr., ed., *Knowledge and Policy: The Uncertain Connection* (Washington, D.C.: National Academy of Sciences, 1978), pp. 126–144

Sundquist, 1979—James L. Sundquist, "Jimmy Carter as Public Administrator: An Appraisal at Mid-Term," *Public Administration Process* 39,1 (January–February 1979), 3–11

Sundquist, 1980—James L. Sundquist, "The Crisis of Competence in Government," in Joseph A. Pechman, ed., *Setting National Priorities: Agenda for the 1980s* (Washington, D.C.: The Brookings Institution, 1980), pp. 531–563

Sundquist, with Davis, 1969—James L. Sundquist with the collaboration of David W. Davis, *Making Federalism Work: A Study of Program Coordination at the Community Level* (Washington, D.C.: The Brookings Institution, 1969)

Surrey, 1957—Stanley S. Surrey, "The Congress and the Tax Lobbyist—How Special Tax Provisions Get Enacted," *Harvard Law Review* 70,7 (May 1957), 1145–1182

Surrey, 1970—Stanley S. Surrey, "Tax Incentives as a Device for Implementing Government Policy: A Comparison with Direct Government Expenditures," *Harvard Law Review* 83,4 (February 1970), 705–738

Surrey, 1973—Stanley S. Surrey, *Pathways to Tax Reform: The Concept of Tax Expenditures* (Cambridge, Massachusetts: Harvard University Press, 1973)

Surrey, 1976—Stanley S. Surrey, "Treasury Department Regulatory Material Under the Tax Code," *Policy Sciences* 7,4 (December 1976), 505–518

Tarschys, 1975—Daniel Tarschys, "The Growth In Public Expenditures: Nine Modes Of Explanation," *Scandinavian Political Studies* 10 (1975), 9–31

Tarschys and Eduards, 1975—Daniel Tarschys and Maud Eduards, *Petita: Hur svenska myndigheter argumenterar for hogre anslag* (Stockholm: LiberForlag, 1975)

Temporary Commission on City Finances, 1978—Members of the Temporary Commission on City Finances, *The City in Transition: Prospects and Policies for New York* (New York: Arno Press, 1978)

Thomas, 1975—Norman C. Thomas, *Education in National Politics* (New York: David McKay Company, Inc., 1975)

Thomas and Wolman, 1969—Norman C. Thomas and Harold L. Wolman, "Policy Formulation in the Institutionalized Presidency: The Johnson Task Forces," in Thomas E. Cronin and Sanford D. Greenberg, eds., *The Presidential Advisory System* (New York: Harper and Row Publishers, 1969), pp. 124–143

Thomas, 1980—John Clayton Thomas, "Governmental Overload in the United States: A Problem of Distributive Policies?" *Administration & Society* 11,4 (February 1980), 371–391

Thurow, 1976—Lester Thurow, "The Theory of Grants-In-Aid," *National Tax Journal* 10,4 (December 1976), 373–377

Tiedt, 1966—Sidney W. Tiedt, *The Role Of The Federal Government In Education* (New York: Oxford University Press, 1966)

Tilly, 1978—Charles Tilly, *From Mobilization to Revolution* (Reading, Massachusetts: Addison-Wesley Publishing Company, 1978)

Trescott, 1955—Paul B. Trescott, "Federal-State Financial Relations, 1790–1960," *Journal of Economic History* 15,3 (September 1955), 227–245

Trescott, 1960—Paul B. Trescott, "The United States Government and National Income, 1790–1860," in National Bureau of Economic Research, *Trends in the American Economy in the Nineteenth Century* (Princeton, New Jersey: Princeton University Press, 1960), pp. 337–361

Truman, 1962—David B. Truman, "Federalism and the Party System," in Arthur W. Macmahon, ed., *Federalism: Mature and Emergent* (New York: Russell and Russell, Inc., 1962, originally published in 1955 by Columbia University Press), pp. 115–136

Truman, 1971—David B. Truman, *The Governmental Process: Political Interests and Public Opinion* (New York: Alfred A. Knopf, 1971, Second Edition)

Turner, 1951a—Julius Turner, "Responsible Parties: A Dissent from the Floor," *American Political Science Review* 45,1 (March 1951), 143–152

Turner, 1951b—Julius Turner, *Party and Constituency: Pressures on Congress* (Baltimore: The Johns Hopkins Press, 1951)

Turner, revised by Schneier, 1970—Julius Turner, revised edition by Edward V. Schneier, Jr., *Party and Constituency: Pressures on Congress* (Baltimore: The Johns Hopkins Press, Revised Edition, 1970)

United States Senate, Committee on the Budget, 1976—Committee on the Budget, United States Senate, *Tax Expenditures: Compendium of Background Material on Individual Provisions*, Committee Print, 94th Congress, Second Session (Washington, D.C.: U.S. Government Printing Office, 1976)

Van Horn and Van Meter, 1976—Carl E. Van Horn and Donald S. Van Meter, "The Implementation of Intergovernmental Policy," in Charles O. Jones and Robert D. Thomas, eds., *Public Policy Making in a Federal System* (Beverly Hills: Sage Publications, 1976), pp. 39–62

Van Meter and Van Horn, 1975—Donald S. Van Meter and Carl E. Van Horn, "The Policy Implementation Process: A Conceptual Framework," *Administration and Society* 6,4 (February 1975), 445–488

Vehorn, 1977—Charles L. Vehorn, *The Regional Distribution of Federal Grants-In-Aid* (Columbus, Ohio: Academy for Contemporary Problems, 1977)

Vernez, 1980—Georges Vernez, "Overview of the Spatial Dimensions of the Federal Budget," in Norman J. Glickman, ed., *The Urban Impact Of Federal Policies* (Baltimore: The Johns Hopkins University Press, 1980), pp. 67–102

Vose, 1958—Clement E. Vose, "Litigation as a Form of Pressure Group Activity," *Annals of the American Academy of Political and Social Science,* vol. 319 (September 1958), 20–31

Walker, D., 1972—David B. Walker, "Curbing the 'New Feudalists,' " *The Bureaucrat* 1,1 (Spring, 1972), 42–45

Walker, D., 1975—David B. Walker, "The New System of Intergovernmental Assistance: Some Initial Notes," *Publius* 5,3 (Summer 1975), 131–145

Walker, D., 1977—David B. Walker, "Categorical Grants: Some Clarifications and Continuing Concerns," *Intergovernmental Perspective* 3,2 (Spring 1977), 14–19

Walker, D., 1978a—David B. Walker, "A New Intergovernmental System in 1977," *Publius* 8,1 (Winter 1978), 101–116

Walker, D., 1978b—David B. Walker, "Recent Trends in Intergovernmental Relations," in Ellis Katz and Benjamin R. Schuster, eds., *The Practice of American Federalism* (Philadelphia: Center for the Study of Federalism, Temple University, 1978)

Walker, D., 1979—David B. Walker, "Localities under the New Intergovernmental System," in L. Kenneth Hubbell, ed., *Fiscal Crisis in American Cities: The Federal Response* (Cambridge, Massachusetts: Ballinger Publishing Company, 1979), pp. 27–57

Walker and Richter, 1977—David B. Walker and Albert J. Richter, "States and the Impact of Federal Grants," *State Government* 50,2 (Spring 1977), 83–88

Walker, J., 1969—Jack L. Walker, "The Diffusion Of Innovations Among The American States," *American Political Science Review* 63,3 (September 1969), 880–899

Walker, J., 1971—Jack L. Walker, "Innovation in State Politics," in Herbert Jacob and Kenneth N. Vines, eds., *Politics In The American States: A Comparative Analysis* (Boston: Little, Brown and Company, 1971, Second Edition), pp. 354–387

Walker, J., 1973—Jack L. Walker, "Comment: Problems in Research on the Diffusion of Policy Innovation," *American Political Science Review* 67,4 (December 1973), 1186–1191

Walker, J., 1974—Jack L. Walker, "The Diffusion of Knowledge and Policy Change: Toward a Theory of Agenda Setting," Paper prepared for delivery at the 1974 Annual Meeting of the American Political Science association, Palmer House, Chicago, Illinois, August 29–September 2, 1974.

Walker, J., 1976—Jack L. Walker, "Setting the Agenda in the U.S. Senate: A Theory of Problem Selection," Paper prepared for delivery at the 1976 Annual Meeting of the American Political Science Association, The Palmer House, Chicago, Illinois, September 2–5, 1976

Walker, J., 1977—Jack L. Walker, "Setting the Agenda in the U.S. Senate: A Theory of Problem Selection," *British Journal of Political Science* 7,4 (October 1977), 423–445

Ward, 1979—Peter D. Ward, *The Measurement Of Federal And State Responsiveness To Urban Problems* (Ann Arbor, Michigan: The University of Michigan, The Ph.D. Program in Urban and Regional Planning, The Intergovernmental Fiscal Analysis Project, 1979). Revised version to be published in the *Journal of Politics*.

Warren, Rose, Bergunder, 1974—Roland L. Warren, Stephen M. Rose and Ann F. Bergunder, *The Structure Of Urban Reform* (Lexington, Massachusetts: D. C. Heath and Company, 1974)

Weaver, 1977—Paul H. Weaver, "Do the American People Know What They Want?" *Commentary* 64,6 (December 1977), 62–67

Weaver, 1978—Paul H. Weaver, "Regulation, Social Policy, and Class Conflict," *The Public Interest*, No. 50 (Winter 1978), 45–63

Webb, 1920—Sidney Webb, *Grants in Aid: A Criticism and a Proposal* (London: Longmans, Green And Company, 1920, Revised and Enlarged Edition—originally published in 1911)

Weidenbaum, 1972—Murray L. Weidenbaum, "Subsidies in Federal Credit Programs," in Joint Economic Committee of Congress, U.S. Congress, *The Economics of Federal Credit Programs: Part I—General Study Paper, May 1972* (Washington, D.C.: U.S. Government Printing Office, 1972), pp. 106–119

White, 1953—Leonard D. White, *The States and The Nation* (Baton Rouge: Louisiana State University Press, 1953)

White, 1956—Leonard D. White, *The Federalists: A Study in Administrative History* (New York: Macmillan Company, 1956)

White, 1965a—Leonard D. White, *The Jacksonians: A Study in Administrative History 1829–1861* (New York: The Free Press, 1965)

White, 1965b—Leonard D. White, *The Republican Era: A Study in Administrative History 1869–1901* (New York: The Free Press, 1965)

White, 1965c—Leonard C. White, *The Jeffersonians: A Study in Administrative History 1801–1829* (New York: The Free Press, 1965)

Wildavsky, 1964—Aaron Wildavsky, *The Politics Of The Budgetary Process* (Boston: Little, Brown and Company, 1964)

Wildavsky, 1973—Aaron Wildavsky, "Government and the People," *Commentary* 56,2 (August 1973), 25–32

Wildavsky, 1976—Aaron Wildavsky, "A Bias Toward Federalism: Confronting the Conventional Wisdom on the Delivery of Governmental Services," *Publius* 6,2 (Spring 1976), 95–120

Wildavsky, 1977—Aaron Wildavsky, *Budgeting: A Comparative Theory Of Budgetary Processes* (Boston: Little, Brown and Company, 1977)

Wilensky, 1970—Gail Wilensky, "Determinants of Local Government Expenditures," in John P. Crecine, ed., *Financing the Metropolis: Public Policy in Urban Economics* (Beverly Hills, California: Sage Publications, 1970), pp. 197–218

Williams, E., 1939—Edward Ainsworth Williams, *Federal Aid for Relief* (New York: Columbia University Press, 1939)

Williams, J., 1936—J. Kerwin Williams, "The Status of Cities under Recent Federal Legislation," *American Political Science Review* 30,6 (December 1936), 1107–1114

Williams, J., 1939—J. Kerwin Williams, *Grants-In-Aid Under the Public Works Administration: A Study in Federal-State-Local Relations* (New York: Columbia University Press, 1939)

Williams and Williams, 1940—J. Kerwin Williams and Edward A. Williams, "New Techniques in Federal Aid," *American Political Science Review* 34,5 (October 1940), 947–954

Willoughby, 1927—W. F. Willoughby, *The National Budget System, With Suggestions For Its Improvement* (Baltimore, Maryland: The Johns Hopkins University Press, 1927)

Wilson, 1967—James Q. Wilson, "The Bureaucracy Problem," *The Public Interest* No. 6 (Winter 1967), 3–9

Wilson, 1969—James Q. Wilson, "The Mayors vs. The Cities," *The Public Interest* No. 16 (Summer 1969), 25–37

Wilson, 1976—James Q. Wilson, "The Rise Of The Bureaucratic State," in Nathan Glazer and Irving Kristol, eds., *The American Commonwealth 1976* (New York: Basic Books, Inc., 1976), pp. 77–103

Wilson, 1979—James Q. Wilson, "American Politics, Then and Now," *Commentary* 67,2 (February 1979), 39–46

Wilson and Rachal, 1977—James Q. Wilson and Patricia Rachal, "Can the Government Regulate Itself?," *The Public Interest,* No. 46 (Winter 1977), 3–14

Wirt, 1974—Frederick M. Wirt, *Power in the City: Decision Making in San Francisco* (Berkeley: University of California Press, 1974)

Wirt, 1976—Frederick M. Wirt, "Education Politics and Policies," in Herbert Jacob and Kenneth N. Vines, eds., *Politics In The American States: A Comparative Analysis* (Boston: Little, Brown and Company, 1976, Third Edition), pp. 284–348

Wirt, 1978a—Frederick Wirt, "Does Control Follow the Dollar? Value Analysis, School Policy, and State-Local Linkages," Paper prepared for delivery at the 1978 Annual Meeting of The American Political Science Association, The New York Hilton Hotel, New York, New York, August 31–September 3, 1978

Wirt, 1978b—Frederick M. Wirt, "Territorial Constraints on System Maintenance: Local Control of American School Policy" (Unpublished paper, The University of Illinois, 1978)

Wirt, 1979—Frederick M. Wirt, "Neo-Conservatism and National School Policy," Paper prepared for delivery at the American Research Association Convention, April 1979

Wirt and Kirst, 1972—Frederick M. Wirt and Michael W. Kirst, *The Political Web of American Schools* (Boston: Little, Brown and Company, 1972)

Witte, 1963—Edwin E. Witte, *The Development of the Social Security Act* (Madison: University of Wisconsin Press, 1963)

Wolanin, 1976—Thomas R. Wolanin, " 'Don't Trouble Me with the Facts': Congress, Information, and Policy Making for Postsecondary Education," in Samuel K. Gove and Frederick M. Wirt, eds., *Political Science and School Politics: The Princes and Pundits* (Lexington, Massachusetts: D. C. Heath and Company, Lexington Books, 1976), pp. 91–119

Wolf, 1976—Eleanor P. Wolf, "Social Science and the Courts: The Detroit Schools Case," *The Public Interest* No. 42 (Winter 1976), 102–120

Wolman, 1971—Harold Wolman, *Politics of Federal Housing* (New York: Dodd, Mead & Company, 1971)

Wooddy, 1934—Carroll H. Wooddy, *The Growth of the Federal Government 1915–1932* (New York: McGraw-Hill Book Company, Inc., 1934)

Wright, 1968—Deil S. Wright, *Federal Grants-In-Aid: Perspectives And Alternatives* (Washington, D.C.: American Enterprise Institute, 1968)

Wright, 1974—Deil S. Wright, "Intergovernmental Relations: An Analytical Overview," *Annals Of The American Academy Of Political and Social Science* Volume 416 (November 1974), 1–16

Wright, 1978—Deil S. Wright, *Understanding Intergovernmental Relations: Public Policy and Participants' Perspectives in Local, State, and National Governments* (North Scituate, Massachusetts: Duxbury Press, 1978)

Yin, 1977—Robert K. Yin, "Production Efficiency Versus Bureaucratic Self-Interest: Two Innovative Processes?" *Policy Sciences* 8,4 (December 1977), 381–399

Yin, 1980—Robert K. Yin, "Creeping Federalism: The Federal Impact on the Structure and Function of Local Government," in Norman J. Glickman, ed., *The Urban Impact Of Federal Policies* (Baltimore: The Johns Hopkins University Press, 1980), pp. 595–618

Yin, *et al.*, 1979—Robert K. Yin, *et al.*, *Federal Aid And Urban Economic Development: A Local Perspective* (Santa Monica, California: The Rand Corporation, 1979)

Young, 1966—James Sterling Young, *The Washington Community 1800–1828* (New York: Harcourt, Brace & World, Inc., 1966)

Zeigler and Olexa, 1976—Harmon Zeigler and Joseph S. Olexa, "The Energy Issue: Oil and the Emergency Energy Act of 1973–1974," in Robert L. Peabody, ed., *Cases in American Politics* (New York: Praeger Publishers, 1976), pp. 159–205

Zeigler and Peak, 1972—L. Harmon Zeigler and G. Wayne Peak, *Interest Groups in American Society* (Englewood Cliffs, New Jersey: Prentice-Hall, Inc., 1972)

National Summary
Data

NAME	GEOGRAPHIC CODES				POPULATION CHARACTERISTICS							ECONOMY
	FIPS REGION CODE	FIPS DIV. REGION CODE	FEDERAL REGION CODE	FIPS STATE CODE	LAND AREA IN SQ.MI. (1977)	POPULATION (1975)	DENSITY IN SQ.MI. (1975)	POP. CHANGE 70-75 %	% TOTAL POP. 65 YRS. (1975)	% TOTAL URBAN POP. (1970)	% TOTAL POP. BLACK (1970)	PER CAPITA INCOME (1974)
STATES...												
ALA....	3.	6.	4.	1.	50708.	3615907.	71.	4.9	10.4	58.4	26.2	3624.
ALK....	4.	9.	10.	2.	569600.	364487.	1.	16.2	2.3	48.8	3.0	6315.
ARZ....	4.	8.	9.	4.	113417.	2225077.	20.	25.2	10.0	79.5	3.0	4530.
ARK....	3.	7.	6.	5.	51945.	2106793.	41.	10.0	12.7	50.0	18.3	3378.
CAL....	4.	9.	9.	6.	156361.	21022559.	136.	6.7	8.7	90.7	7.0	5114.
COL....	4.	8.	8.	8.	103766.	2541311.	24.	14.7	8.3	78.7	3.0	4884.
CONN...	1.	1.	1.	9.	4862.	3100188.	638.	1.3	10.0	77.3	6.0	5348.
DEL....	3.	5.	3.	10.	1982.	579405.	292.	8.6	8.0	72.1	14.3	4809.
D.C....	3.	5.	3.	11.	61.	711518.	11664.	-5.4	10.0	100.0	71.1	5659.
FLA....	3.	5.	4.	12.	54090.	8283074.	153.	22.4	16.3	80.5	15.3	4815.
GA.....	3.	5.	4.	13.	58073.	4931083.	85.	27.4	8.7	60.3	25.8	4091.
HA.....	4.	9.	9.	15.	6425.	863396.	135.	12.3	6.6	83.0	1.0	4963.
IDA....	4.	8.	10.	16.	82677.	813765.	10.	15.0	10.3	54.3	.3	4119.
ILL....	2.	3.	5.	17.	55748.	11206393.	201.	2.0	10.0	83.0	12.8	5107.
IND....	2.	3.	5.	18.	36097.	5309197.	147.	1.8	10.2	64.9	6.9	4458.
IOWA...	2.	4.	7.	19.	55941.	2860686.	51.	1.8	12.5	57.2	1.2	4628.
KAN....	2.	4.	7.	20.	81787.	2279890.	28.	5.4	12.0	66.1	4.8	4669.
KY.....	3.	6.	4.	21.	39650.	3387860.	85.	4.6	10.9	52.4	7.2	3712.
LA.....	3.	7.	6.	22.	44930.	3803937.	85.	4.2	9.1	66.1	29.8	3545.
MAINE.	1.	1.	1.	23.	30920.	1057955.	34.	3.1	11.8	50.9	.3	3694.
MD....	3.	5.	3.	24.	9891.	4121603.	417.	5.8	8.2	76.6	17.8	5299.
MASS..	1.	1.	1.	25.	7826.	5812489.	743.	-1.7	11.6	84.6	3.1	4755.
MI....	2.	3.	5.	26.	56817.	9116699.	160.	3.0	8.9	73.9	11.2	4751.
MINN..	2.	4.	5.	27.	79289.	3916455.	49.	8.8	10.8	66.4	.9	4675.
MISS..	3.	6.	4.	28.	47296.	2342592.	50.	3.8	10.8	44.5	36.8	3098.
MO....	2.	4.	7.	29.	68995.	4769816.	69.	1.8	12.6	70.1	10.3	4254.
MONT..	4.	8.	8.	30.	76483.	746244.	5.	3.0	10.0	53.6	.3	4347.
NEB...	2.	4.	7.	31.	76483.	1543678.	20.	3.8	12.4	61.6	2.7	4508.
NEV...	4.	8.	9.	32.	109889.	590268.	5.	21.8	7.5	80.9	5.7	5149.
N.H...	1.	1.	1.	33.	9027.	811804.	90.	10.8	10.8	56.5	.4	4281.
N.J...	1.	2.	2.	34.	7521.	7332965.	975.	2.8	10.5	88.9	10.7	5237.
N.M...	4.	8.	6.	35.	121412.	1143287.	9.	-.7	7.2	70.0	1.9	3601.
N.Y...	1.	2.	2.	36.	47831.	18075487.	378.	-.7	11.2	85.6	11.9	4903.
N.C...	3.	5.	4.	37.	48798.	5441366.	112.	7.2	9.1	45.0	22.2	3875.
N.D...	2.	4.	8.	38.	69273.	642888.	9.	2.9	11.4	44.3	.4	5087.
OHIO..	2.	3.	5.	39.	40975.	10735280.	262.	1.0	9.9	75.3	9.1	4561.
OKLA..	3.	7.	6.	40.	68782.	2711263.	39.	5.9	12.3	68.0	6.7	3983.
ORE...	4.	9.	10.	41.	96184.	2284335.	24.	9.4	11.3	67.1	1.3	4660.
PA....	1.	2.	3.	42.	44966.	11863710.	264.	.2	11.6	71.5	8.6	4449.

(cont.)

NATIONAL SUMMARY DATA -- TABLE ONE

	GEOGRAPHIC CODES					POPULATION CHARACTERISTICS						ECONOMY
NAME	FIPS REGION CODE	FIPS DIV. CODE	FEDERAL REGION CODE	FIPS STATE CODE	LAND AREA IN SQ. MI. (1977)	POPULATION (1975)	DENSITY IN SQ. MI. (1975)	POP. CHANGE 70-75 %	% TOTAL POP. 65 YRS. (1975)	% TOTAL POP. URBAN (1970)	% TOTAL POP. BLACK (1970)	PER CAPITA INCOME (1974)
STATES (CONT)												
R.I....	1.	1.	1.	44.	1049.	931208.	888.	-2.4	12.1	87.0	2.7	4558.
S.C....	3.	5.	4.	45.	30225.	2815762.	93.	8.8	8.1	47.6	30.4	3635.
S.D....	2.	4.	8.	46.	75955.	682744.	9.	2.6	12.5	44.6	.3	4167.
TENN...	3.	6.	4.	47.	41328.	4174100.	101.	6.7	10.6	58.8	15.8	3821.
TEX....	3.	7.	6.	48.	262134.	12244678.	47.	9.3	9.6	79.8	12.5	4188.
UTAH...	4.	8.	8.	49.	82096.	1202672.	15.	13.9	7.6	80.6	.6	4022.
VER....	1.	1.	1.	50.	9267.	472073.	51.	6.1	11.0	32.2	.2	3907.
VA.....	3.	5.	3.	51.	39780.	4980570.	125.	6.8	8.5	63.1	18.5	4701.
WASH...	4.	9.	10.	53.	66570.	3553231.	53.	3.9	10.4	72.6	2.1	4864.
W.VA...	3.	5.	3.	54.	24070.	1799349.	75.	3.4	11.7	39.0	3.8	3617.
WIS....	2.	3.	5.	55.	54464.	4577343.	84.	4.2	11.2	65.9	2.9	4468.
WY.....	4.	8.	8.	56.	97203.	376309.	4.	12.6	8.9	60.4	.7	4566.
DIVISIONS												
N.ENG.	1.	1.	0.	0.	62951.	12185717.	194.	2.9	11.2	76.4	3.3	4734.
M.A...	1.	2.	0.	0.	100318.	37272162.	372.	.1	11.2	81.7	10.6	4824.
E.N.C.	2.	3.	0.	0.	244101.	40944912.	168.	1.8	10.0	74.7	9.6	4729.
W.N.C.	2.	4.	0.	0.	507730.	16695816.	33.	2.9	12.0	63.6	3.9	4526.
S.A...	3.	5.	0.	0.	266970.	33663730.	126.	9.9	10.7	63.6	20.8	4454.
E.S.C.	3.	6.	0.	0.	178982.	13520459.	76.	5.7	10.7	54.6	20.1	3616.
W.S.C.	3.	7.	0.	0.	427791.	20866671.	49.	7.9	10.1	72.7	15.6	3962.
MOUNT.	4.	8.	0.	0.	856047.	9639473.	11.	16.4	8.7	73.2	1.7	4440.
PAC...	4.	9.	0.	0.	895140.	28273008.	32.	6.2	9.7	86.0	5.7	5057.
REGIONS												
N.E...	1.	0.	0.	0.	163269.	49457879.	303.	.8	11.2	80.4	8.8	4802.
N.CT..	2.	0.	0.	0.	751831.	57640728.	77.	1.9	10.6	71.5	8.1	4670.
SOUTH.	3.	0.	0.	0.	873743.	68050860.	78.	8.4	10.5	64.6	19.0	4137.
WEST..	4.	0.	0.	0.	1751187.	37912481.	22.	8.6	9.5	82.9	4.9	4900.
NATION	0.	0.	0.	0.	3540023.	213030000.	60.	4.8	10.5	73.5	11.1	4572.

NATIONAL SUMMARY DATA -- TABLE TWO

NAME	ECONOMY (CONT) MEDIAN FAMILY INCOME (1969)	% FAMILY BELOW POVERTY LEVEL (1969)	% OF TOTAL EMP. MANUF. (1970)	% OF TOTAL EMP. WHOLE-SALE & RETAIL (1970)	HOUSING (1970) % ONE UNIT STUCTURES	% OF OCCUP. UNITS OWNER OCCUP.	% OF OCCUP. UNITS LACK SOME PLUMB.	% OF OCCUP. UNITS 1.01 PERSONS PER ROOM	GOVERNMENT FINANCE (1971-72) TOTAL GENERAL REV. (MIL.)	TOTAL TAXES (MIL.)	GEN. EXPD. PER CAP	DEBT OUT-STAND. PER CAP
STATES												
ALA...	7263.	20.7	28.6	19.0	82.9	66.7	15.4	10.9	1034.0	297.7	25.	41.
ALK...	12441.	9.3	7.1	18.8	51.3	50.3	13.2	19.0	215.5	53.8	61.	107.
ARZ...	9185.	11.5	15.6	21.8	73.0	65.3	4.3	12.3	913.2	406.9	43.	40.
ARK...	6271.	22.9	26.1	19.4	85.3	66.7	16.0	10.5	533.0	162.3	23.	40.
CAL...	10729.	8.4	14.6	21.1	67.8	55.0	3.0	7.7	15108.1	7365.3	64.	38.
COL...	9552.	9.1	34.8	22.2	71.4	63.6	3.2	6.6	1187.3	589.7	45.	37.
CONN..	11808.	5.3	29.7	18.5	59.1	62.5	2.2	5.8	1473.8	981.5	40.	55.
DEL...	10209.	8.7	9.9	19.2	75.5	68.2	4.1	5.8	231.2	457.8	35.	52.
D.C...	9576.	12.7	8.7	14.4	36.4	28.2	4.6	12.8	1068.7	457.1	118.	105.
FLA...	8261.	12.7	14.1	23.5	69.4	68.6	11.9	8.6	3110.6	1203.0	40.	36.
GA....	8165.	16.8	27.2	19.5	74.8	61.1	5.2	10.7	1790.5	629.3	33.	32.
HA....	11552.	7.9	10.7	21.9	64.4	46.9	3.7	9.1	629.0	125.9	19.	34.
IDA...	8380.	10.9	14.7	22.7	80.4	70.1	5.1	9.6	263.5	112.2	31.	21.
ILL...	10957.	7.7	30.3	20.2	59.2	59.4	3.7	7.8	5626.1	3130.4	41.	48.
IND...	9966.	7.4	35.9	19.1	78.0	71.7	18.4	5.8	2313.7	1247.6	37.	33.
IOWA..	9016.	8.7	20.4	21.8	81.6	71.7	10.1	5.7	1381.1	676.6	41.	31.
KAN...	8690.	9.7	17.4	21.5	79.8	69.1	10.8	10.3	1036.1	522.1	38.	39.
KY....	7439.	19.3	25.6	18.7	78.0	66.9	3.7	14.2	853.3	305.2	22.	35.
LA....	7527.	21.6	15.9	21.2	68.8	63.0	2.9	7.1	1342.5	500.1	32.	55.
MAINE.	8205.	10.7	31.6	19.5	50.4	70.8	2.5	6.3	346.4	224.7	31.	57.
MD....	11057.	7.7	19.5	19.2	75.3	58.8	22.1	5.7	2227.9	996.8	47.	45.
MASS..	10833.	6.2	29.2	20.1	73.6	57.5	7.6	7.2	2832.9	1929.5	41.	53.
MI....	11029.	7.3	35.9	19.4	85.6	74.4	5.3	14.9	4853.8	2184.7	46.	75.
MINN..	9928.	8.3	21.1	22.0	73.7	71.5	3.2	8.0	2443.6	824.3	55.	30.
MISS..	6068.	29.0	25.4	17.9	79.4	66.3	22.1	6.1	723.4	189.8	28.	46.
MO....	8908.	11.6	24.4	21.5	60.1	67.2	7.6	5.9	1852.1	958.1	34.	24.
MONT..	8509.	10.4	9.7	22.3	63.5	65.6	5.3	3.2	320.8	191.1	36.	42.
NEB...	8562.	10.1	13.7	19.1	57.9	66.5	5.4	4.3	700.6	384.9	37.	81.
NEV...	10687.	7.0	35.5	18.5	81.4	58.2	2.4	8.3	326.5	136.3	57.	35.
N.H...	9682.	6.7	32.0	19.2	40.3	68.2	4.3	15.3	291.3	210.4	33.	54.
N.J...	11403.	6.1	6.8	21.6	82.3	60.5	8.3	7.3	4080.8	2475.6	51.	22.
N.M...	7845.	18.6	24.2	19.6	73.8	47.4	13.9	10.0	425.1	85.3	35.	97.
N.Y...	10609.	8.6	35.5	17.5	84.6	65.4	4.1	9.3	16686.9	7453.4	84.	23.
N.C...	7770.	16.5	4.7	23.1	76.9	68.4	4.1	6.4	1784.9	526.3	31.	29.
N.D...	7836.	12.4	35.6	19.2	72.6	67.7	2.6	7.1	241.8	110.6	32.	44.
OHIO..	10309.	7.6	15.8	21.6		69.2	4.4	5.3	4428.2	2372.9	36.	29.
OKLA..	7720.	15.1	21.4	22.1		69.1		5.3	857.6	334.2	29.	37.
ORE...	9487.	8.6	34.1	18.8		68.8			1060.3	540.5	43.	34.
PA....	9554.	7.9							4908.5	2362.9	35.	50.

(cont.)

NATIONAL SUMMARY DATA -- TABLE TWO

NAME	ECONOMY (CONT)				HOUSING (1970)				GOVERNMENT FINANCE (1971-72)			
			% OF TOTAL EMP.			% OF OCCUP. UNITS						
	MEDIAN FAMILY INCOME (1969)	% FAMILY BELOW POVERTY LEVEL (1969)	MANUF. (1970)	WHOLE-SALE &RETAIL (1970)	% ONE UNIT STUCTURES	OWNER OCCUP.	LACK SOME PLUMB.	1.01 PERSONS PER ROOM	TOTAL GENERAL REV. (MIL.)	TOTAL TAXES (MIL.)	GEN. EXPD. PER CAP	DEBT OUT-STAND. PER CAP
STATES (CONT)												
R.I.	9733.	8.5	35.1	19.0	51.6	57.9	2.7	5.9	330.6	200.3	31.	42.
S.C.	7620.	19.1	36.2	16.7	82.8	66.1	16.8	12.0	733.0	230.4	25.	24.
S.D.	7490.	14.8	7.4	21.6	80.9	69.6	8.6	8.7	264.4	174.1	31.	12.
TENN.	7446.	18.3	30.6	18.7	79.9	66.7	13.0	9.5	1371.8	546.9	29.	49.
TEX.	8486.	14.7	18.5	22.2	80.3	64.7	6.0	11.1	4230.9	1971.8	33.	53.
UTAH.	9320.	9.1	14.5	21.5	75.1	69.4	1.8	10.5	391.2	167.6	30.	30.
VER.	8928.	12.4	23.9	18.1	65.7	69.1	4.9	6.5	182.1	122.5	32.	34.
VA.	9044.	7.6	22.4	21.5	74.7	62.8	11.6	7.7	1789.4	819.5	33.	47.
WASH.	10404.	18.1	21.6	21.6	75.6	66.8	2.3	5.2	1686.1	653.4	41.	51.
W.VA.	7414.	7.4	23.2	18.9	82.6	68.9	15.4	8.9	477.4	167.7	24.	16.
WIS.	10065.	9.3	31.0	19.9	70.5	69.1	4.8	7.0	2482.5	1181.7	49.	43.
WY.	8944.		6.4	20.3	74.3	66.4	3.3	8.5	170.4	70.4	46.	39.
DIVISIONS												
N.ENG.	10613.	6.7	34.7	25.4	55.7	61.0	3.5	6.0	5456.7	3668.9	38.	44.
M.A.	10395.	7.9	31.5	24.9	53.7	56.6	2.9	6.4	25675.7	12291.4	62.	74.
E.N.C.	10560.	7.5	37.6	26.2	69.8	67.5	4.0	7.2	19704.3	10116.5	41.	46.
W.N.C.	8982.	10.1	26.9	31.2	76.8	69.5	5.8	7.0	7919.7	3751.0	41.	47.
S.A.	8539.	14.0	28.4	27.8	74.0	63.5	9.5	9.0	13263.3	5098.5	37.	37.
E.S.C.	7166.	21.0	36.1	26.3	81.6	66.7	16.5	11.0	3982.5	1339.6	26.	40.
W.S.C.	7964.	16.8	23.4	29.4	81.0	65.3	7.7	11.0	6964.0	2968.8	31.	50.
MOUNT.	9070.	10.9	16.9	31.6	73.2	65.5	4.0	9.8	3998.0	1759.5	40.	35.
PAC.	10600.	8.3	26.4	28.9	68.7	57.1	1.8	7.6	18273.2	8738.9	58.	40.
REGIONS												
N.E.	10449.	7.6	32.3	25.0	54.2	57.6	3.0	6.3	31132.4	15960.8	56.	67.
N.CT.	10112.	8.3	34.7	27.6	71.6	68.0	4.5	7.1	27624.0	13867.5	41.	46.
SOUTH.	8075.	16.3	28.2	28.0	77.7	64.7	10.4	10.0	24209.8	9406.9	33.	42.
WEST.	10225.	8.9	24.1	29.5	69.9	59.0	2.3	8.1	22271.2	10498.4	54.	39.
NATION	9586.	10.7	30.3	27.4	69.1	62.9	5.5	8.0	105243.0	49739.0	39.	49.

NAME	GOVT. EMPLOY. IN FTE (1972)	CRIME RATE PER 100,000 (1975)	TOTAL REPORTED OUTLAYS			DEFENSE PROCUREMENTS			INTEREST ON PUBLIC DEBT		
			1975	1977	1978	1975	1977	1978	1975	1977	1978
STATES											
ALA.	101030	3471	5725616	7044535	7969711	602512	560079	580409	106607	104111	204319
ALK.	10065	5984	1444637	1859046	1954176	186950	180480	238082	11771	17630	20403
ARZ.	66690	8337	4259524	5566164	6405855	723779	581101	700282	65301	101098	114085
ARK.	50373	3556	2884224	4200983	4357641	134022	134868	158717	83742	116197	125981
CAL.	750583	7199	40380608	54935632	57627959	8379425	10650083	11163714	774794	160453	1342991
COL.	78286	6656	5008313	7373823	7490044	406830	479102	554017	120111	178346	194310
CONN.	84716	4949	5974945	6746373	8655284	2360522	1991420	3506280	557055	491375	528750
DEL.	14925	6664	800477	1094804	1185194	52067	65645	87061	22636	39369	42682
D.C.	50268	7752	10059494	12386460	14583652	1221770	1309245	1259112	18562	28003	33394
FLA.	254164	7790	12940744	17524216	19419372	1144381	1267850	1595274	210141	343596	402748
GA.	163372	4621	8262177	10912191	13022902	820283	647644	345381	142042	44801	272232
HA.	10080	6003	2164024	2331642	2839668	353200	277873	204413	29912	41457	51848
IDA.	23623	4173	1331176	1632204	2406640	41413	39657	45483	27680	44801	47978
ILL.	352071	5353	15632241	20040232	22060650	663449	663470	8565563	661058	970048	1029503
IND.	157230	4913	6247163	7888021	9433423	871341	901972	978620	306970	450017	477772
IOWA	90581	3921	3384660	4687894	5999025	191229	307010	483345	174530	257545	272758
KAN.	75345	4720	3643308	4927448	5692223	256439	418158	270569	122371	181701	197966
KY.	80021	3272	4968395	7250263	6974528	646622	341111	690531	141917	204090	222962
LA.	117364	4109	5243517	6438395	7510336	57363	557287	350243	112857	187015	213118
MAINE	29145	3963	1568653	2244622	2436971	947752	333147	1419954	41918	76730	89248
MD.	129589	5874	8587285	10889641	11834237	1419954	1419954	1654040	96154	145057	172985
MASS.	188550	6094	9170353	12760870	13894330	1829414	2453760	2849438	239921	439173	510819
MI.	284007	6830	10611228	14665207	15406814	817144	1315239	1484789	544200	802738	849103
MINN.	130332	4310	5550874	7807645	8930796	448766	687275	750136	182217	265015	267592
MISS.	73756	2414	4269340	4916940	5625733	1450434	600278	1542071	80327	121327	137278
MO.	140749	5390	7856074	11406469	12564333	58654	2521715	3136962	216677	306995	333359
MONT.	22963	4199	1290069	2028427	2094428	80081	195713	48802	33234	48335	48805
NEB.	54791	3619	2190104	3064840	4014844	62306	124646	113610	80709	119840	130567
NEU.	21276	8177	1088255	1658221	1995508	199264	48728	64347	18983	28432	32904
N.H.	20034	3372	1258526	1635161	1815010	1071760	185503	252902	31120	56965	66258
N.J.	232293	5132	12321417	14429836	15425304	141765	1320409	1590293	3162159	2258833	2331385
N.M.	34880	5856	2443979	3413750	3764546	476517	220904	260058	44679	71405	76732
N.Y.	764384	5650	38467745	52915308	46720813	3852046	4430414	4691975	10613511	16055133	7518081
N.C.	143791	3823	6830785	9019555	9742609	200237	449714	497673	124611	187988	224181
N.D.	18484	2308	1284536	1902403	2280455	1339193	71540	85839	29596	43044	43462
OHIO	325353	4925	12363039	16790873	17792366	347132	1566031	1696038	477237	718933	792801
OKLA.	78019	4579	4493761	4311706	6555054	103902	429438	464534	136677	203784	221725
ORE.	70761	6763	3232852	5021920	5021920	120135	120135	151321	81168	121571	140693
PA.	317230	3339	15975810	21482174	22293070	1601424	2360269	2350619	500194	831074	905685

(cont.)

NATIONAL SUMMARY DATA -- TABLE THREE

NAME	GOVT. EMPLOY. IN FTE (1972)	CRIME RATE PER 100,000 (1975)	TOTAL REPORTED OUTLAYS			DEFENSE PROCUREMENTS			INTEREST ON PUBLIC DEBT		
			1975	1977	1978	1975	1977	1978	1975	1977	1978
STATES (CONT)											
R.I...	23446	5618	1335547	1784995	1945016	83631	138016	173457	40067	73342	85307
S.C...	77144	4645	3874183	5164309	5798506	276293	266123	300865	63540	95856	114311
S.D...	20952	2740	1175407	2182318	1963269	33465	27869	39042	31892	46383	46834
TENN..	129554	4285	6013144	9439774	9998113	389445	740222	552637	136487	210286	240137
TEX...	380041	5404	18056528	23845334	29079115	2354100	3269200	5442682	347794	601298	624836
UTAH..	33040	5127	2097640	2947811	3248271	203749	293198	295386	41122	61591	71279
VER...	12232	3473	718511	999674	975461	123613	120137	110813	18765	34350	39953
VA....	137933	4534	9878965	13253547	14581218	1475513	2456876	2176600	114038	172038	205160
WASH..	112786	6125	7633832	9974970	10748543	1751620	2016473	2106437	132343	198218	229397
W.VA..	48209	2112	2585987	3247708	3284725	108169	114433	95938	46886	70712	83101
WIS...	148809	4001	5221168	6979830	7621775	252193	426003	405585	264455	389615	410509
WY....	15338	4130	685386	1112227	1104726	40709	29225	34240	18061	26817	29218
DIVISIONS											
N.ENG.	358123	5298	20024536	26171696	29722072	4653807	5221983	7243113	928846	1171936	1320335
M.A...	1313907	4812	66764972	88707319	84439187	6525430	8111092	8632887	14275863	19145040	10755151
E.N.C.	1267533	5362	50074839	66364164	72316028	3943320	4872715	5421595	2253956	3331351	3559688
W.N.C.	531234	4403	25084963	35979018	41361944	2956984	4158213	4991090	8379991	1220521	1292538
S.A...	1019459	5382	63820097	83492429	93452498	6522745	7997484	8619679	8386611	1314869	1550794
E.S.C.	384361	3489	20976476	28651512	31466084	2293902	2244690	2945686	465338	639814	804694
W.S.C.	625797	4874	30678029	40569491	47502146	3481876	4390803	6756464	681071	1108294	1185660
MOUNT.	296096	6353	18144741	26179548	28513777	1679205	1887628	2161545	370570	557464	615312
PAC...	954275	6976	54855952	73412996	78192266	10775097	13245044	14004935	1029988	1542672	1785332
REGIONS											
N.E...	1672030	4932	86789508	114879015	114161259	11179237	13333075	15876000	15204710	20316976	12075486
N.CT..	1798767	5084	75159802	102343181	113677972	6900304	9030928	10412685	3091948	4551874	4852226
SOUTH.	2029617	4850	115474603	152713432	172420728	12298523	14632977	18321829	1985019	3062977	3541148
WEST..	1250371	6818	73000694	99592544	106706043	12454302	15132672	16166480	1400559	2100136	2400644
NATION	6750785	5284	350424606	469528173	506966002	42832366	52129652	60776994	21682235	30031963	22869504

233

NATIONAL SUMMARY DATA -- TABLE FOUR

NAME	OTHER NON-INFLUENCE OUTLAYS 1975	1977	1978	NET DOMESTIC OUTLAY 1975	1977	1978	% CHANGE 75-78	PER CAP 1975	PER CAP 1977	PER CAP 1978
STATES....										
ALA....	4742.	44158.	2974.	5011754.	6336187.	7182010.	43.30	1386.03	1752.31	1986.23
ALK....	2.	71.	0.	1245914.	1660865.	1695691.	36.10	3418.27	4556.72	4652.27
ARZ....	786.	194.	28701.	3469658.	4883789.	5562787.	60.33	1559.34	2194.89	2500.04
ARK....	499.	59.	66232.	2665961.	3949859.	4998586.	50.29	1265.41	1874.82	1901.81
CAL....	134449.	233402.	135368.	31091940.	42891694.	44985886.	44.69	1466.42	2642.95	2121.72
COL....	2050.	1198.	4213.	4479322.	6715178.	6737504.	50.41	1762.60	2022.41	1457.89
CONN....	7585.	80770.	100533.	3049783.	4182808.	4519721.	48.20	983.74	1349.21	1805.10
DEL....	4497.	4905.	9567.	721278.	984884.	1045884.	45.00	1244.86	1699.82	1765.13
D.C....	370485.	612901.	650936.	8448677.	10436310.	12640211.	49.61	11874.16	14667.67	17761.23
FLA....	5465.	10724.	16716.	11580757.	15902046.	17404634.	50.29	1398.12	1919.82	2384.10
GA....	10714.	44185.	41375.	7289139.	9988112.	11756180.	61.28	1478.20	2025.54	2812.57
HA....	801.	139.	12.	1780111.	2008828.	2442427.	37.21	2049.88	2313.26	2646.65
IDA....	359.	1354.	261.	1261724.	1996656.	2153748.	70.70	1550.48	2453.60	1788.93
ILL....	45161.	88748.	127158.	14262572.	18317966.	20047427.	40.56	1272.72	1634.60	1499.99
IND....	4964.	3792.	14267.	5063887.	6532240.	7963764.	57.02	953.80	1230.36	1856.33
IOWA....	1934.	2617.	33720.	3016967.	4120721.	5310391.	76.02	1054.63	1440.47	2147.86
KAN....	1349.	4562.	31016.	2966816.	4323026.	4896896.	65.06	1301.29	1896.15	1912.22
KY....	2738.	3954.	2657.	4567282.	6698108.	6478341.	41.84	1348.13	1977.09	1725.17
LA....	88494.	25808.	44235.	4395544.	5668285.	6562451.	49.30	1155.45	1490.11	1887.60
MAINE.	433.	376.	507.	1468939.	1834370.	1996993.	35.95	1388.42	1733.88	2425.05
MD....	119715.	6817.	12103.	7423664.	9317813.	9995110.	34.64	1801.16	2260.73	1805.37
MASS..	5403.	11503.	40375.	7095615.	9856434.	10493698.	47.89	1023.75	1695.73	1419.57
MI....	13886.	10205.	131107.	9235998.	12537025.	12941815.	40.12	1013.09	1745.17	2017.61
MINN..	3680.	21763.	11900.	4916211.	6833592.	7901168.	60.72	1255.38	1745.00	2064.02
MISS..	1252.	15379.	9219.	3142256.	4179956.	4835164.	53.88	1341.36	1784.33	1905.25
MO....	5692.	2587.	6310.	6183270.	8575172.	9087702.	46.97	1296.33	1797.80	2675.81
MONT..	0.	0.	14.	1198181.	1784378.	1996807.	66.65	1005.62	2391.15	2441.53
NEB...	2402.	3939.	1728.	2026913.	2816415.	3768939.	85.94	1313.04	1824.48	3222.67
NEV...	0.	23.	19.	1021039.	1581039.	1902238.	88.91	1705.93	2673.51	1841.27
N.H...	219.	583.	1096.	1027923.	1392110.	1494754.	45.41	1266.22	1714.84	1560.78
N.J...	34081.	65597.	58454.	8053417.	10784997.	11445172.	42.12	1098.25		2996.54
N.M...	14.	0.	229.	2256121.	3121441.	3425028.	51.92	1972.43	2728.95	1861.66
N.Y...	676958.	516144.	860268.	23325051.	31793617.	36650490.	44.27	1290.42	1758.94	1653.00
N.C...	13927.	29423.	26286.	6215729.	8352431.	8994552.	44.71	1142.31	1534.99	3346.08
N.D...	0.	12194.	0.	1054703.	1787819.	2151154.	103.96	1640.57	2780.10	1421.17
OHIO..	17590.	10864.	46914.	10528984.	14493716.	15255613.	44.25	980.78	1350.70	2159.42
OKLA..	6750.	829.	14035.	4003202.	5440683.	5854761.	46.25	1476.51	2006.70	2070.49
ORE...	2669.		214.	3045112.	4069171.	4729692.	55.32	1333.04	1781.34	1597.95
PA....	101808.	40530.	79130.	13772384.	18250301.	18957636.	37.65	1160.88	1538.33	

(cont.)

NATIONAL SUMMARY DATA -- TABLE FOUR

NAME	OTHER NON-INFLUENCE OUTLAYS			NET DOMESTIC OUTLAY						
	1975	1977	1978	1975	1977	1978	% CHANGE 75-78	PER CAP 1975	PER CAP 1977	PER CAP 1978
STATES (CONT)										
R.I...	1110.	232.	282.	1208740.	1573405.	1685971.	39.48	1298.03	1689.64	1810.52
S.C...	4772.	1721.	2163.	3529578.	4800609.	5381167.	52.46	1253.51	1704.91	1911.09
S.D...	0.	4.	14.	1110050.	2108062.	1877379.	69.13	1625.87	3087.63	2749.76
TENN..	4073.	59201.	29372.	5483139.	8430065.	9175967.	67.35	1313.61	2019.61	2198.31
TEX...	30231.	27929.	61055.	15324402.	19946907.	22950542.	49.76	1251.52	1629.03	1874.33
UTAH..	162.	357.	529.	1793007.	2592665.	2881077.	60.68	1490.85	2155.75	2395.56
VER...	385.	7.	114.	575748.	845180.	824580.	43.22	1219.62	1790.36	1746.72
VA....	3775.	20947.	24215.	8285639.	10603685.	12175242.	46.94	1663.90	2189.01	2444.55
WASH..	1083.	2036.	494.	5748786.	7758243.	8412214.	46.33	1617.90	2183.43	2367.48
W.VA..	527.	3740.	223.	2430405.	3058824.	3105462.	27.78	1350.71	1699.96	1725.88
WIS...	13108.	5776.	13498.	4691411.	6158437.	6792183.	44.78	1024.92	1345.42	1483.87
WY....	0.	0.	0.	626616.	1056185.	1041267.	66.17	1665.16	2806.70	2767.05
DIVISIONS										
N.ENG.	15135.	93471.	142907.	14426748.	19684307.	21015717.	45.67	1183.91	1615.36	1724.62
M.A.C.	812846.	622272.	997852.	45150832.	60828915.	64053298.	41.87	1211.38	1632.02	1718.53
E.N.C.	94709.	120714.	332943.	43782853.	60039384.	63001801.	43.90	1069.31	1417.50	1538.70
W.N.C.	150058.	35473.	84689.	21274930.	30564808.	34993627.	64.48	1274.27	1830.69	2095.95
S.A.C.	533878.	735363.	783584.	55924864.	73444713.	82498441.	47.52	1661.28	2181.72	2450.66
E.S.C.	12805.	122692.	44222.	18204431.	25644316.	27671481.	52.00	1346.44	1896.70	2046.64
W.S.C.	125973.	64660.	185557.	26389110.	35005734.	39374466.	49.21	1264.65	1677.59	1886.95
MOUNT.	3377.	3125.	33965.	16091589.	23731331.	25702955.	59.73	1669.34	2461.89	2666.43
PAC...	139004.	236478.	136088.	42911863.	58388802.	62265910.	45.10	1517.77	2065.18	2202.31
REGIONS										
N.E...	827981.	715742.	1140758.	59577580.	80513222.	85069015.	42.79	1204.61	1627.91	1720.03
N.CT..	109767.	156188.	417632.	65057783.	88604192.	97995429.	50.63	1128.68	1537.18	1700.41
SOUTH.	672656.	922715.	1013363.	100518404.	134094763.	149544388.	48.77	1477.11	1970.51	2197.54
WEST..	142382.	239603.	170054.	59003452.	82120133.	87968866.	49.09	1556.31	2166.04	2320.31
NATION	1752786.	2034249.	2741807.	284157219.	385332309.	420577697.	48.01	1333.88	1808.82	1974.27

235

NAME	FORMULA OUTLAYS				PROJECT OUTLAYS				DIRECT PAYMENT OUTLAYS			
	1975	1977	1978	% CHANGE 75-78	1975	1977	1978	% CHANGE 75-78	1975	1977	1978	% CHANGE 75-78
STATES												
ALA.	849899	1075491	1051142	23.68	179930	337529	369208	105.20	1649474	2119996	2699053	63.63
ALK.	304913	346301	318017	4.30	72686	117729	87452	20.31	74268	114719	126038	69.71
ARZ.	471214	622280	633829	34.51	156231	302327	242830	55.44	1032102	1414230	1877267	81.90
ARK.	557642	684990	656866	17.79	92127	228506	182890	98.52	1083899	1367868	1670298	54.10
CAL.	5592474	7658321	7729566	38.21	1410161	3129291	2346977	66.43	9145578	11906752	15705459	71.73
COL.	635895	752456	752455	20.89	234546	526788	313823	33.80	979952	1279769	1263751	75.35
CONN.	658342	817729	919274	39.63	192470	125764	292695	52.07	1203207	1665376	2263710	88.14
DEL.	129946	180988	176737	36.01	56644	52446	54739	-3.36	217493	286635	409248	88.17
D.C.	726671	820384	856031	17.80	680124	1485361	1969447	189.57	832559	852749	1241813	49.16
FLA.	1431362	2157208	1920450	34.17	454969	893939	657153	44.44	4784061	6382651	8676722	81.37
GA.	1251541	1470818	1473480	17.73	421469	1040240	577955	37.13	1890108	2470368	3087203	63.33
HA.	361914	361367	409706	13.21	96473	110934	119124	23.48	307504	398226	581855	89.22
IDA.	234373	287716	272582	16.30	42590	123947	82719	94.22	350407	434121	586599	67.41
ILL.	2803004	3285891	3332146	18.88	786150	1276161	1730351	120.10	4598542	5847824	7683579	67.09
IND.	937504	1002681	1089564	16.22	273169	617413	421748	54.39	2088600	2682714	3381955	61.92
IOWA.	568651	646681	724669	27.44	110628	260338	214628	94.01	1297917	1605244	2152536	65.85
KAN.	460543	582147	552081	19.88	94248	234136	183813	95.03	1095596	1416782	2077316	89.61
KY.	935815	1114909	1086856	16.14	168691	337628	370808	119.82	1546220	1966224	2393206	54.78
LA.	1048616	1264429	1202243	14.65	155722	352006	327387	110.24	1562556	1953645	2527427	61.75
MAINE.	306384	361805	414136	35.17	78387	141579	105024	33.98	503149	685738	791443	57.30
MD.	1019020	1223677	1255653	23.22	528904	882500	769676	45.52	1637387	2124441	2692065	64.41
MASS.	1692049	2140733	2211721	30.70	595031	1301446	1327203	123.05	2550431	3405936	4492164	76.13
MI.	2525906	3169072	3057806	21.06	644230	1181913	1112283	72.68	3526003	4498935	5865314	67.23
MINN.	959022	1180699	1154503	20.38	286653	433339	438814	53.08	1836340	2378521	2924037	59.23
MISS.	679547	803781	851279	25.27	159722	286529	278477	74.35	1018238	1278529	1601492	57.28
MO.	922649	1050709	1247404	35.20	293911	508298	455680	55.04	2365670	3001718	3933858	66.29
MONT.	276722	292043	293888	6.20	57673	132171	95117	64.92	344119	477991	640189	86.04
NEB.	328575	319699	349231	6.29	89026	167954	150645	69.12	744185	877312	1257837	68.89
NEV.	155029	172989	220061	41.95	36415	87866	75291	106.76	214045	308064	423711	97.95
N.H.	171379	198700	218324	27.39	70141	153776	94705	35.02	361191	473924	590300	63.43
N.J.	1609245	2117793	2271721	26.18	556417	994384	649303	16.69	3145975	4098865	5376778	70.93
N.Y.	5687217	7349593	8027072	41.14	1546253	3882635	2635165	70.42	8620256	11074136	14910331	72.97
N.C.	1242999	1493650	1467186	18.04	264823	565907	477121	80.17	2043260	2696867	3316504	62.31
N.D.	189676	182791	181999	-4.05	46026	114072	90685	97.03	297528	353975	700100	135.31
OHIO.	1986763	2721719	2759207	38.88	520144	1272670	841335	61.75	4290612	5525175	7047080	64.24
OKLA.	619290	750403	746715	20.58	133482	358476	266667	99.78	1328685	1694008	2167956	63.17
ORE.	698129	855168	1006336	44.15	128444	314413	255881	99.22	1170793	1495476	2038509	74.11
PA.	2831533	3645183	3357568	18.58	828140	1518682	1270803	53.45	5749261	7349055	9441976	64.23

NATIONAL SUMMARY DATA -- TABLE FIVE

NAME	FORMULA OUTLAYS				PROJECT OUTLAYS				DIRECT PAYMENT OUTLAYS			
	1975	1977	1978	% CHANGE 75-78	1975	1977	1978	% CHANGE 75-78	1975	1977	1978	% CHANGE 75-78
STATES												
R.I..	267819	323663	337152	25.89	71277	159657	137147	92.41	461075	590884	795731	72.58
S.C..	633930	813551	794333	25.30	139699	309425	225357	61.32	1034892	1381568	1718413	66.05
S.D..	206923	231755	200091	-3.30	39966	125661	94578	136.65	341854	493019	547438	60.14
TENN.	904384	1189105	1190107	31.59	217754	473966	398346	82.93	1840122	2469585	3074381	67.07
TEX..	2462450	2942867	3030434	23.07	534163	1055642	1079313	102.06	4756253	6046905	8024163	68.71
UTAH.	326243	361829	373792	14.57	93630	199861	136404	45.68	456624	609472	751328	64.54
VER..	146634	197337	179779	22.60	41996	131064	76053	81.09	201868	260502	341921	69.38
VA...	954384	1404910	1288403	35.00	306026	422012	402169	31.42	2191590	2864372	3533382	61.22
WASH.	879554	1187797	1131148	28.60	249222	531012	456285	83.08	1715359	2195302	2808248	63.71
W.VA.	594204	601140	642391	8.11	151044	316464	191868	27.03	1088459	1346337	1552056	42.59
WIS..	1078256	1395830	1352580	25.44	259562	471109	497949	91.84	1931750	2552534	3227530	67.08
WY...	174237	125623	201334	15.55	24139	71640	42961	77.97	150104	225708	236975	57.87
DIVISIONS												
N.ENG	3242608	4039968	4280109	32.00	1049302	2414310	2032827	93.73	5280919	7082359	9275270	75.64
M.A..	10127994	13112534	13656390	34.84	2930810	6395701	4555271	55.43	17528772	22522057	29729085	69.60
E.N.C	9331432	11575193	11591304	24.22	2483255	4819266	4603666	85.39	16412707	21107179	27205458	65.76
W.N.C	3636039	4192482	4409976	21.29	960458	1843799	1628843	69.59	7979690	10126971	13593122	70.35
S.A..	7984055	10148320	9874664	23.68	3003703	6041612	5325486	77.30	15719809	20405987	26227408	66.84
E.S.C	3369644	4183285	4179384	24.03	726097	1435652	1416839	95.13	6054054	7834334	9768132	61.35
W.S.C	4687997	5642288	5636258	20.23	915495	1994630	1856256	102.76	8731393	11062426	14389844	64.81
MOUNT	2665640	3057273	3254262	22.08	729317	1478438	1159621	59.00	4008099	5362083	7013001	74.97
PAC..	7836984	10418953	10594775	35.19	1956986	4203379	3265719	66.87	12413503	16110475	21260110	71.27
REGIONS												
N.E..	13370602	17152502	17936500	34.15	3980112	8810010	6588098	65.53	22809692	29604415	39004354	71.00
N.CT.	12967471	15767676	16001280	23.40	3443713	6663065	6232509	80.98	24392397	31234150	40798580	67.26
SOUTH	16041696	19973893	19690306	22.74	4645294	9471894	8598581	85.10	30505256	39302747	50385384	65.17
WEST.	10502624	13476226	13849037	31.86	2686302	5681817	4425340	64.74	16421602	21472557	28273110	72.17
NATION	52882392	66370296	67477122	27.60	14755422	30626787	25844528	75.15	94128946	121613869	158461428	68.35

NATIONAL SUMMARY DATA — TABLE SIX

NAME	DIRECT LOANS 1975	1977	1978	% CHANGE 75-78	GUARANTEED LOANS 1975	1977	1978	% CHANGE 75-78	OTHER DOMESTIC ASSISTANCE 1975	1977	1978	% CHANGE 75-78
STATES												
ALA...	51438	36832	158946	209.00	637635	723236	906936	42.23	1643378	2043104	1996725	21.50
ALK...	13305	11060	11105	-16.53	109795	286687	171031	55.77	670947	784370	982047	46.37
ARZ...	46101	46030	92233	100.07	529137	918541	1184438	123.84	1234948	1580380	1532181	24.07
ARK...	70656	100007	243358	244.43	235022	758400	496189	111.12	626616	1810089	757111	20.83
CAL...	181331	242663	537926	196.65	2901716	3045608	5315270	83.31	11860680	14650099	13350689	12.56
COL...	17690	92269	140180	692.42	674587	1876927	1500093	122.37	11936652	2361311	12296302	18.57
CONN..	8823	14890	20642	133.96	196298	1363390	249174	26.94	790644	1021635	774227	-2.08
DEL...	696	1029	1097	57.60	104093	140614	174041	67.20	212406	249854	230021	8.29
D.C...	76607	25561	19440	-74.62	33726	164355	212731	530.77	6098990	7105902	8340748	36.76
FLA...	25917	45704	186655	620.21	1141900	1599881	1981318	73.51	3742549	4822667	3982335	6.41
GA....	165485	159470	550479	232.65	1175366	1797562	1652139	40.56	2385170	3049656	4414924	85.10
HA....	1537	669	1786	16.20	71085	174593	235138	230.78	941597	963040	1094817	16.27
IDA...	13750	66638	61948	350.52	182457	331354	455842	149.84	438146	772879	694058	58.41
ILL...	36430	107441	323534	788.10	871136	1162009	1120686	28.65	5167311	6638659	5857130	13.35
IND...	26271	63541	181240	589.88	426781	697917	1739188	307.51	1311562	1467974	1150069	-12.31
IOWA..	38087	139047	875950	2199.84	369194	681217	737964	99.89	632489	790193	604644	-4.40
KAN...	21789	527934	482712	2115.41	312339	471525	580307	85.79	982303	1090502	1020667	3.91
KY....	18326	97642	95668	422.04	286834	1071725	581161	102.61	1611397	2109920	1950641	21.05
LA....	31548	30869	127098	302.87	408786	685474	950137	132.43	1188317	1382262	1428159	20.18
MAINE.	9204	9123	28670	211.51	230982	224775	255961	10.81	340833	411349	401759	17.88
MD....	10035	22180	18509	84.44	503442	739176	875682	73.94	3724876	4325839	4383525	17.68
MASS..	18965	17242	124018	553.94	182533	511964	420597	-6.73	2056607	2471913	1918297	-6.73
MI....	15914	43567	137303	762.77	591334	1138993	1024398	73.24	1955412	2504544	1744711	-10.78
MINN..	45628	310878	750488	1544.79	796995	1258911	1707582	114.25	991572	1270844	925745	-6.64
MISS..	52313	18589	255432	388.27	419121	711488	907714	116.58	813314	1081041	940770	15.67
MO....	21602	88000	262117	1113.40	437173	1178597	848834	94.16	2142264	2747850	2339809	9.22
MONT..	8698	161669	104731	1104.31	117608	275251	364920	210.28	393361	495253	502456	27.73
NEB...	20907	230659	753356	3503.34	247676	453351	543812	119.57	595943	767441	714057	19.82
NEV...	2255	3082	2041	-9.52	150480	437202	581432	286.39	448735	571836	599703	33.64
N.H...	10892	3655	10018	-8.08	167668	132956	174379	157.70	346653	429102	407034	17.42
N.J...	15466	34325	45328	193.09	515306	678396	768321	49.10	2197729	2861268	2333692	6.19
N.M...	16202	27087	51623	218.61	122232	255908	355273	190.66	1160845	1505202	1577069	35.86
N.Y...	57191	129286	208211	264.06	927236	1501921	2151300	132.01	6486878	7856047	5718411	-11.85
N.C...	43928	185390	257102	485.10	534412	828664	1068486	99.94	2086309	2581952	2408235	15.43
N.D...	5745	339374	273102	4653.58	146506	368734	519973	254.92	369223	428813	385294	4.35
OHIO..	36941	54696	101699	175.30	802020	1109339	1370154	70.84	2892504	3810119	3137138	8.46
OKLA..	34639	210879	106924	208.68	421319	664989	878926	108.61	1465788	1761928	1687572	15.13
ORE...	16376	33103	22845	39.51	169687	273502	375000	121.00	861684	1097509	1031120	19.66
PA....	34453	68967	165756	381.11	548091	1026098	870216	58.77	3780907	4642316	3851317	1.89

(cont.)

NATIONAL SUMMARY DATA -- TABLE SIX

NAME	DIRECT LOANS				GUARANTEED LOANS				OTHER DOMESTIC ASSISTANCE			
	1975	1977	1978	% CHANGE 75-78	1975	1977	1978	% CHANGE 75-78	1975	1977	1978	% CHANGE 75-78
STATES (CONT)												
R.I....	14039	14375	25501	81.64	27389	48335	42692	55.87	367140	436492	347747	-5.28
S.C....	34720	28683	176171	407.41	303463	531737	694126	128.73	1382874	1735644	1772766	28.19
S.D....	9830	137877	218478	2122.54	182679	692529	461783	152.78	328799	427220	355012	7.97
TENN...	22248	24704	156721	604.44	419083	896003	985577	135.17	2079548	3376701	3370836	62.09
TEX....	177339	441170	839512	373.39	1746671	2874423	3569961	104.39	5647524	6585900	6407158	13.45
UTAH...	8195	7011	99547	1114.77	234334	467447	569785	124.80	131290	947045	993221	47.37
VER....	4025	3578	5399	34.14	49935	850083	93283	86.81	131209	167616	128145	-2.40
VA.....	28870	100923	87211	202.08	715455	1166521	1604640	124.28	4089314	4644947	5259437	28.61
WASH...	15809	90315	99779	531.16	434614	789887	838577	92.95	2454228	2953931	3078177	25.42
W.VA...	1917	32064	14922	678.52	147680	199922	253566	71.70	447100	562897	450659	+.80
WIS....	24431	32171	137632	463.35	414237	420166	691256	66.87	983176	1286627	885235	-9.96
WY.....	5826	17137	12898	121.38	78172	351672	242675	210.44	194139	264405	304424	56.81
DIVISIONS												
N.ENG.	65948	62862	214243	224.87	754804	1146702	1236059	63.76	4033167	4938107	3977209	-1.39
M.A.	107109	232578	419295	291.47	1990633	3206415	3789837	90.38	12465514	15359630	11903419	-4.51
E.N.C.	139988	301397	881409	529.63	3105507	4528425	5945682	91.46	12309965	15707923	12774283	3.77
W.N.C.	163589	1773769	3616203	2110.55	2492561	5104925	5400255	116.65	6042593	7522863	6345229	5.01
S.A.	388174	601004	1311505	237.86	4659535	7168432	8516729	82.78	24169587	29079358	31242649	29.26
E.S.C.	144325	177767	666767	361.99	1762673	3402512	3381386	91.83	6147638	8610766	8258973	34.34
W.S.C.	314182	782925	1316894	319.15	2811798	4983286	5895213	109.66	8928245	10540179	10280000	15.14
MOUNT.	118718	420923	565200	376.09	2089007	4914302	5211458	149.47	6480808	8498312	8499413	31.15
PAC.	228358	377809	673441	194.91	3686897	6829236	6935016	88.10	16789136	20448950	19536850	16.37
REGIONS												
N.E....	173057	295441	633538	266.09	2745437	4353116	5025896	83.06	16498681	20297737	15880628	-3.75
N.CT...	303576	2075166	4497612	1381.54	5598068	9633349	11345937	102.68	18352558	23230786	19119512	4.18
SOUTH...	846682	1561696	3295166	289.19	9234000	15554230	17793329	92.69	39245469	48230303	49781622	26.85
WEST...	347075	798733	1238641	256.88	5775904	11743538	12146474	110.30	23269944	28947262	28036263	20.48
NATION	1670390	4731035	9664957	478.60	23353416	41284233	46311635	98.31	97366652	120706088	112811026	15.87

239

NATIONAL SUMMARY DATA -- TABLE SEVEN

AGENCY OUTLAYS

NAME	AGRICULTURE			COMMERCE			DEFENSE		
	1975	1977	1978	1975	1977	1978	1975	1977	1978
STATES									
ALA...	627177.	456872.	674386.	8376.	83601.	40017.	713027.	837139.	965802.
ALK...	74456.	286270.	150510.	21460.	83732.	32783.	315833.	324769.	359335.
ARZ...	226244.	269125.	370204.	7019.	98352.	8482.	538011.	638688.	713033.
ARK...	436566.	882038.	732845.	9089.	54430.	10757.	250937.	308898.	335887.
CAL...	1272399.	1615232.	1944525.	223803.	1086673.	260666.	5002133.	5587829.	6044894.
COL...	292640.	1008905.	658029.	49178.	117037.	78813.	818949.	965435.	942662.
CONN..	91351.	214686.	311232.	80553.	139443.	32282.	153323.	178939.	198609.
DEL...	43909.	41229.	61663.	45140.	96646.	85963.	110125.	123418.	126031.
D.C...	287820.	338186.	397349.	223370.	322646.	349956.	693547.	700819.	626654.
FLA...	564035.	706975.	911595.	31135.	331812.	242811.	1645305.	1940431.	2252002.
GA....	1253701.	1524142.	1142481.	16008.	255288.	122591.	1201200.	1484830.	1640821.
HA....	72413.	84161.	140738.	7335.	55082.	109911.	753776.	717212.	894566.
IDA...	235512.	321131.	461033.	9359.	53908.	47518.	100342.	120821.	140866.
ILL...	906023.	1181600.	1327428.	24055.	197109.	29896.	805500.	933893.	978148.
IND...	333272.	384894.	1632929.	22185.	103192.	3432.	389792.	399972.	428906.
IOWA..	477107.	822518.	1409438.	4727.	45323.	9641.	74713.	85035.	95278.
KAN...	343513.	962808.	1248923.	7148.	48465.	19274.	475017.	457045.	577906.
KY....	412738.	1059155.	611347.	7493.	59910.	301228.	715925.	777029.	640351.
LA....	477345.	603443.	810623.	171703.	161956.	13626.	540013.	507140.	199855.
MAINE.	234607.	179726.	219878.	4537.	92137.	346768.	122489.	140024.	1430090.
MD....	252301.	321507.	379486.	235393.	377516.	49579.	1296769.	1347136.	175572.
MASS..	187228.	291177.	340422.	287746.	304299.	29248.	423522.	463411.	465581.
MI....	459934.	811482.	798644.	20348.	398253.	10162.	384422.	431813.	186465.
MINN..	779672.	1301254.	1959155.	20153.	60658.	27992.	143422.	164044.	514535.
MISS..	581410.	722903.	1047664.	21962.	61541.	84063.	410598.	472736.	730103.
MO....	602687.	769108.	990141.	13788.	484560.	12079.	640011.	808316.	1220905.
MONT..	198139.	430482.	544056.	8180.	60439.	4916.	105305.	125337.	297712.
NEB...	287637.	665198.	1331754.	3642.	49013.	5232.	230031.	278677.	223251.
NEV...	42470.	45387.	58110.	3087.	45990.	4846.	159199.	202623.	256805.
N.H...	63878.	85155.	137239.	1979.	42361.	96409.	189349.	220605.	852656.
N.J...	454498.	478794.	493973.	23148.	366143.	11055.	673138.	846286.	459147.
N.M...	181136.	209310.	314314.	8873.	71631.	546620.	351230.	419302.	859830.
N.Y...	1136141.	1723796.	2474872.	3767887.	1117827.	33840.	725816.	788457.	1479662.
N.C...	591240.	922752.	1177278.	21842.	105052.	4794.	1251633.	1398913.	185462.
N.D...	203077.	690761.	1002927.	6366.	47624.	20896.	170807.	183507.	982600.
OHIO..	523701.	616736.	804413.	27954.	249438.	25923.	813636.	903343.	937522.
OKLA..	380731.	634984.	736706.	11893.	97638.	21608.	781307.	899102.	190577.
ORE...	462960.	545527.	838981.	14547.	106104.	65446.	140683.	167769.	1190577.
PA....	484818.	864269.	794947.	36140.	359573.		1064182.	1154954.	1265770.

(cont.)

NATIONAL SUMMARY DATA -- TABLE SEVEN

AGENCY OUTLAYS

NAME	AGRICULTURE			COMMERCE			DEFENSE		
	1975	1977	1978	1975	1977	1978	1975	1977	1978
STATES (CONT)									
R.I...	34764.	45289.	42716.	11602.	58195.	12661.	175780.	188843.	207058.
S.C...	375339.	403414.	553778.	13945.	54083.	17932.	875034.	1028818.	1083069.
S.D...	249982.	932807.	725138.	3759.	51060.	6950.	99813.	117393.	125020.
TENN.	531535.	769976.	827912.	7748.	104463.	14016.	349485.	401198.	458037.
TEX...	1428540.	1650010.	2867783.	269425.	399809.	68226.	3028960.	3084041.	3634641.
UTAH.	175059.	171535.	311368.	3728.	49222.	8116.	383700.	459597.	485314.
VER..	63603.	102270.	116604.	1834.	59674.	4277.	26363.	32589.	34318.
VA...	439021.	595059.	716626.	38856.	136939.	763395.	2745596.	2930730.	3206501.
WASH.	360518.	499101.	605605.	52578.	219231.	718825.	972540.	1070292.	1201105.
W.VA.	206742.	232858.	292363.	11122.	50137.	20553.	62157.	82969.	88476.
WIS..	569445.	653708.	859823.	16597.	88290.	262219.	124256.	140945.	159605.
WY...	78948.	298022.	184522.	1487.	42447.	2153.	67769.	79779.	83085.
DIVISIONS									
N.ENG.	675430.	918302.	1168091.	129252.	696109.	117273.	1090826.	1224411.	1414217.
M.A..	2075456.	3116859.	3763792.	436075.	1843543.	708475.	2463136.	2789697.	2978256.
E.N.C.	2792376.	3648421.	5423237.	111132.	1036283.	1537776.	2517602.	2809966.	3015840.
W.N.C.	2943675.	6144453.	8667476.	59583.	786703.	1239658.	1833814.	2094017.	2197946.
S.A..	4014109.	5086124.	5632621.	636812.	1597417.	998899.	9881375.	11038064.	11936306.
E.S.C.	2152860.	3008906.	3161309.	45578.	309515.	101300.	2189035.	2488102.	2789746.
W.S.C.	2723182.	3770474.	5147956.	462111.	713832.	405233.	4601217.	4799181.	5548401.
MOUNT.	1430147.	2753897.	2901635.	90911.	539026.	136841.	2524505.	3011582.	3170263.
PAC..	2242745.	3030291.	3680358.	319723.	1550822.	399173.	7184965.	7866871.	8690477.
REGIONS									
N.E.	2750887.	4035161.	4931883.	565326.	2539652.	825748.	3553962.	4014108.	4392473.
N.CT.	5736051.	9792873.	14090713.	170715.	1822686.	277734.	4351416.	4903983.	5213786.
SOUTH.	8890150.	11865504.	13941886.	1144502.	2620765.	1505432.	16671627.	18325347.	20274453.
WEST.	3672893.	5784188.	6581993.	410634.	2089848.	536014.	9709470.	10878453.	11860740.
NATION	21049981.	31477726.	39546474.	2291177.	9073251.	3144928.	34286475.	38121891.	41741452.

NATIONAL SUMMARY DATA -- TABLE EIGHT

AGENCY OUTLAYS (CONTINUED)

NAME	EPA 1975	EPA 1977	EPA 1978	GSA 1975	GSA 1977	GSA 1978	HEW 1975	HEW 1977	HEW 1978
STATES									
ALA.	36482.	29189.	60284.	29794.	27691.	40571.	1837243.	2415224.	2690706.
ALK.	18252.	13560.	4171.	13835.	11719.	11344.	171452.	193502.	204164.
ARZ.	32419.	22317.	26268.	24433.	11923.	18902.	1050015.	1419018.	1649796.
ARK.	10431.	37798.	18953.	6241.	8198.	21595.	1132011.	1489038.	1681370.
CAL.	436747.	817751.	355731.	222280.	233074.	305899.	11819822.	15993421.	17595856.
COL.	42371.	50487.	33989.	64117.	91744.	75605.	1123680.	1436402.	1646995.
CONN.	72490.	201638.	12453.	10331.	18879.	19539.	1640100.	2143031.	2383833.
DEL.	36150.	52946.	5180.	2095.	3353.	19578.	258373.	346498.	401138.
D.C.	269177.	208660.	281061.	909672.	770847.	814742.	1291710.	1838830.	2100599.
FLA.	218223.	217012.	105034.	73016.	29884.	34229.	5097856.	6949003.	7886395.
GA.	70635.	147910.	99618.	91689.	99255.	144040.	2257024.	2945372.	3168810.
HA.	46064.	6974.	31546.	3642.	7563.	3690.	359333.	509851.	581514.
IDA.	11816.	14791.	8063.	5323.	4605.	5045.	357423.	474019.	517393.
ILL.	361020.	392697.	335603.	212099.	210414.	222210.	6060303.	7761323.	8391567.
IND.	126147.	277489.	111904.	110316.	57717.	44084.	2340628.	3107837.	3400991.
IOWA.	24660.	47878.	34456.	12835.	8546.	8800.	1460609.	1873895.	2045766.
KAN.	19783.	55367.	17854.	30015.	13862.	11216.	1120212.	1509254.	1624377.
KY.	32516.	63612.	53078.	23409.	33533.	32520.	1797781.	2307771.	2474490.
LA.	32232.	68184.	27923.	10480.	18605.	15961.	1691132.	2246880.	2506310.
MAINE.	34093.	17351.	11256.	11142.	9668.	18684.	603965.	781404.	846111.
MD.	93493.	256329.	52326.	66285.	113114.	91845.	2741580.	3353666.	3586388.
MASS.	119087.	311399.	44873.	58354.	57837.	101740.	3714282.	4809973.	5340453.
MI.	365841.	354034.	538469.	78103.	134285.	145660.	5053683.	6474666.	7153815.
MINN.	129339.	99728.	47668.	12546.	18635.	18236.	2021592.	2581130.	2873402.
MISS.	18695.	27952.	29301.	9558.	19978.	9537.	1164085.	1555360.	1752262.
MO.	75950.	119268.	54338.	127021.	117484.	180586.	2574118.	3394172.	3753429.
MONT.	11420.	12221.	7820.	9423.	7048.	7194.	373509.	462236.	520460.
NEB.	26756.	28778.	17537.	7322.	5443.	6237.	758327.	954205.	1067857.
NEV.	18914.	20406.	33663.	2916.	4268.	4800.	224805.	325006.	383468.
N.H.	42388.	62553.	30304.	6933.	5848.	3083.	398419.	530214.	582293.
N.J.	227148.	310900.	56362.	115363.	109813.	195147.	3876713.	5034448.	5749555.
N.M.	8433.	21194.	16448.	10696.	10208.	11871.	527965.	684370.	753965.
N.Y.	577208.	1457446.	102365.	224834.	246974.	294896.	12662997.	15753264.	17075456.
N.C.	80214.	235419.	176189.	28372.	58884.	52210.	2357356.	3165024.	3547266.
N.D.	7015.	5735.	11420.	4521.	5124.	7379.	321118.	412053.	456878.
OHIO.	246081.	532071.	166054.	69340.	119578.	114156.	5046295.	6722030.	7393007.
OKLA.	24644.	82209.	31894.	7235.	9026.	7666.	1446839.	1864498.	2057897.
ORE.	26344.	54074.	44643.	21124.	30232.	41842.	1256342.	1683202.	1887425.
PA.	202558.	490968.	93639.	75062.	95155.	103076.	7056980.	9251480.	10095566.

(cont.)

NATIONAL SUMMARY DATA -- TABLE EIGHT

AGENCY OUTLAYS (CONTINUED)

NAME	EPA 1975	EPA 1977	EPA 1978	GSA 1975	GSA 1977	GSA 1978	HEW 1975	HEW 1977	HEW 1978
STATES (CONT)									
R.I...	26419.	37460.	13124.	5422.	5546.	5071.	575585.	763192.	822423.
S.C...	33310.	97765.	20175.	12837.	11665.	17261.	1124908.	1552138.	1758459.
S.D...	5141.	10189.	12822.	4427.	4308.	3558.	360826.	447847.	476853.
TENN..	63586.	126098.	58072.	22711.	25078.	25271.	1973712.	2661897.	2981535.
TEX...	132662.	171738.	162598.	163300.	131671.	159018.	5134450.	6862205.	7639862.
UTAH..	5853.	21857.	7052.	9203.	22038.	18889.	466068.	620146.	706735.
VER...			7501.	1399.	2080.	3093.	281551.	358758.	394057.
VA....	124508.	74827.	58372.	91278.	98681.	148512.	2026292.	2661647.	2991533.
WASH..	80597.	105288.	63978.	78837.	54982.	78749.	1891984.	2443639.	2700562.
W.VA..	28766.	56310.	28581.	33105.	10825.	13837.	1180540.	1475703.	1547170.
WIS...	83298.	141148.	109524.	19107.	74253.	60787.	2539519.	3319081.	3643507.
WY....	5276.	4496.	4285.	2260.	1499.	3099.	146077.	187996.	209293.
DIVISIONS									
N.ENG.	300331.	652258.	119600.	93581.	99859.	151209.	7213903.	9386572.	10369169.
M.A...	1006917.	2259313.	252366.	415259.	451942.	593119.	23596690.	30039192.	32920577.
E.N.C.	1182387.	1697440.	1261554.	488965.	596248.	586897.	21040428.	27384937.	29982887.
W.N.C.	288643.	366943.	196096.	198685.	173403.	236020.	8616801.	11172555.	12298562.
S.A...	954477.	1347178.	827247.	1308351.	1196508.	1336253.	18335637.	24287883.	26987759.
E.S.C.	151279.	246851.	200735.	85472.	106281.	107899.	6772821.	8940252.	9898993.
W.S.C.	207669.	359930.	241368.	187256.	167499.	204640.	9404433.	12462620.	13885439.
MOUNT.	157468.	168170.	137589.	128372.	153333.	145405.	4269543.	5609194.	6388105.
PAC...	606307.	997648.	500069.	339719.	337570.	441523.	15498933.	20823615.	22969521.
REGIONS									
N.E...	1307244.	2911571.	371966.	508840.	551800.	744328.	30810592.	39425765.	43289746.
N.CT..	1471030.	2064383.	1457650.	687650.	769651.	822917.	29657229.	38557493.	42281449.
SOUTH.	1313425.	1953958.	1269350.	1581079.	1470288.	1648392.	34512891.	45690755.	50772191.
WEST..	763774.	1165818.	637659.	468090.	490903.	586928.	19768476.	26432809.	29357626.
NATION	4855473.	8095730.	3736625.	3245659.	3282642.	3802565.	114749189.	150106821.	165701012.

243

AGENCY OUTLAYS (CONTINUED)

NAME	HUD 1975	HUD 1977	HUD 1978	INTERIOR 1975	INTERIOR 1977	INTERIOR 1978	JUSTICE 1975	JUSTICE 1977	JUSTICE 1978
STATES									
ALA.	140582.	340481.	355662.	12700.	11915.	17977.	17200.	20382.	17673.
ALK.	15605.	18414.	17092.	107153.	146861.	334270.	3954.	5530.	5503.
ARZ.	211038.	561196.	715970.	226589.	391496.	426629.	23231.	27874.	29802.
ARK.	55592.	147520.	144984.	16116.	19275.	25955.	8795.	8061.	11118.
CAL.	1215963.	2876542.	3004919.	305751.	419524.	623925.	148877.	181880.	219849.
COL.	138103.	445927.	462981.	298298.	366168.	404531.	26494.	25624.	29294.
CONN.	113783.	150489.	191719.	6032.	4889.	9008.	17551.	19506.	23451.
DEL.	20163.	37390.	36083.	1715.	1647.	3832.	2974.	4553.	5583.
D.C.	158359.	258072.	331587.	468024.	301204.	406509.	186224.	270788.	348099.
FLA.	437359.	743748.	941005.	25019.	101542.	76303.	46776.	58200.	65550.
GA.	165427.	450328.	658059.	25606.	44110.	46703.	37667.	35855.	45675.
HA.	45037.	68211.	55063.	5908.	7787.	10886.	5546.	6914.	8033.
IDA.	27300.	93159.	98761.	61581.	248020.	122095.	3974.	4223.	4410.
ILL.	374039.	508902.	562348.	27376.	22586.	34953.	67488.	71707.	85862.
IND.	132780.	322623.	334487.	9248.	16662.	32051.	24356.	28373.	28408.
IOWA.	61368.	131276.	146377.	5638.	12252.	12161.	10310.	10247.	10484.
KAN.	77117.	139633.	154509.	31336.	22115.	19615.	18291.	19099.	21014.
KY.	89455.	278594.	324605.	17062.	18436.	22836.	18048.	26269.	29178.
LA.	93590.	259161.	306691.	13753.	6595.	21388.	21051.	20125.	21987.
MAINE.	25934.	50188.	53614.	5358.	35092.	9124.	7177.	7854.	8819.
MD.	180429.	291086.	421607.	28245.	46391.	41946.	29447.	29423.	33561.
MASS.	166369.	556423.	473424.	31928.	51665.	58180.	29190.	38368.	49647.
MI.	338114.	653990.	710424.	14896.	53547.	56677.	45083.	49246.	52277.
MINN.	276608.	575322.	761549.	42296.	40926.	67332.	21081.	22629.	25815.
MISS.	151561.	190476.	184672.	17588.	42015.	41493.	8170.	8100.	10447.
MO.	25664.	372129.	421972.	36401.	107092.	60629.	34098.	36464.	45395.
MONT.	77221.	72929.	105250.	78261.	26257.	108964.	4965.	6473.	6105.
NEB.	59270.	84970.	102743.	20150.	55694.	30769.	5702.	5281.	5768.
NEV.	11007.	275873.	397448.	41737.	3804.	66479.	5325.	5871.	5947.
N.H.	249955.	32708.	30285.	4017.	18822.	6413.	3525.	4422.	5491.
N.J.	57079.	470011.	624569.	20440.	257860.	266033.	40121.	35145.	44488.
N.M.	514733.	161021.	168963.	196277.	45923.	268133.	7787.	8340.	10358.
N.Y.	135121.	1155004.	1810963.	35019.	45362.	69735.	117975.	157807.	164747.
N.C.	13832.	278997.	317405.	22781.	60202.	49173.	17624.	20049.	26463.
N.D.	310536.	655574.	81614.	47790.	26849.	56286.	3919.	4619.	4711.
OHIO.	131815.	661575.	763248.	14707.	86326.	508902.	41149.	37366.	44511.
OKLA.	56096.	311693.	317199.	60515.	207472.	517762.	19123.	16659.	17535.
ORE.	336249.	123402.	146716.	196485.	90970.	230894.	12445.	12187.	12083.
PA.		589299.	754717.	104803.		88943.	63342.	64679.	80482.

(cont.)

NATIONAL SUMMARY DATA -- TABLE NINE

AGENCY OUTLAYS (CONTINUED)

NAME	HUD			INTERIOR			JUSTICE		
	1975	1977	1978	1975	1977	1978	1975	1977	1978
STATES (CONT)									
R.I...	33285.	59190.	75215.	2298.	3706.	5992.	3846.	4721.	4906.
S.C...	66990.	198350.	245370.	12313.	9968.	30255.	10645.	11085.	11807.
S.D...	18543.	56137.	79807.	69475.	108660.	85549.	3385.	3987.	4173.
TENN..	140744.	445779.	538891.	12464.	14101.	21885.	14487.	18448.	22386.
TEX...	445397.	1217463.	1255586.	43566.	65687.	76134.	100721.	130122.	138256.
UTAH..	64832.	209235.	238292.	68008.	158753.	124664.	5467.	5316.	6963.
VER...	6283.	11535.	13226.	2274.	2723.	4183.	6572.	8304.	10427.
VA....	130121.	353360.	469358.	101324.	112402.	121444.	40087.	31692.	45635.
WASH..	205269.	422685.	395692.	239565.	334788.	157329.	25997.	33504.	41628.
W.VA..	24181.	81612.	90399.	25739.	30058.	31217.	14673.	14913.	17023.
WIS...	72522.	143049.	228684.	18465.	31082.	29670.	21916.	23730.	26416.
WY....	9445.	26065.	28461.	70117.	114228.	129417.	2116.	2054.	2113.
DIVISIONS									
N.ENG.	356661.	860534.	837482.	51907.	68108.	92899.	67861.	83175.	102740.
M.A.C.	1100937.	2214315.	3190249.	160262.	155715.	185281.	221439.	257632.	289716.
E.N.C.	1227991.	2290137.	2598790.	84691.	148843.	204241.	199991.	210423.	237473.
W.N.C.	676750.	1425041.	1748572.	253086.	325049.	332342.	96785.	102325.	117361.
S.A.C.	1318149.	2692944.	3510875.	710764.	681386.	807382.	386116.	476557.	599396.
E.S.C.	444635.	1255331.	1403829.	59813.	87945.	104191.	57905.	73200.	79683.
W.S.C.	726393.	1935836.	2024460.	133951.	189725.	205239.	149691.	174967.	188895.
MOUNT.	592732.	1845404.	2216132.	1040867.	1699310.	1650911.	79359.	85775.	94992.
PAC.:	1537970.	3509255.	3619482.	854862.	1116431.	1357304.	196818.	240016.	287095.
REGIONS									
N.E...	1457598.	3074849.	4027731.	212169.	223823.	278180.	289300.	340807.	392457.
N.CT..	1904741.	3715178.	4347362.	337777.	473892.	536583.	296777.	312748.	354834.
SOUTH.	2489177.	5884111.	6939163.	904529.	959056.	1116812.	593712.	724724.	867975.
WEST..	2130702.	5354659.	5835614.	1895729.	2815742.	3008215.	276177.	325790.	382087.
NATION	7982218.	18028798.	21149871.	3350204.	4472512.	4939790.	1455965.	1704070.	1997352.

245

AGENCY OUTLAYS (CONTINUED)

NAME	LABOR 1975	LABOR 1977	LABOR 1978	NASA 1975	NASA 1977	NASA 1978	SBA 1975	SBA 1977	SBA 1978
STATES									
ALA...	91391.	210200.	126706.	190254.	198791.	206266.	17487.	32685.	156390.
ALK...	35973.	77807.	47296.	1387.	836.	743.	18935.	18430.	18569.
ARZ...	81136.	191722.	193241.	10316.	12486.	13433.	15898.	25609.	36456.
ARK...	60031.	130017.	82179.	187.	243.	116.	13198.	22168.	39435.
CAL...	836941.	1518947.	1346863.	1381135.	1779338.	1638363.	162647.	263197.	464502.
COL...	52857.	140329.	125345.	101487.	56185.	57034.	41443.	75537.	80892.
CONN.	93294.	158560.	195860.	31589.	34611.	67306.	24039.	39372.	49814.
DEL...	14683.	44575.	28224.	551.	648.	322.	573.	2411.	4963.
D.C...	436549.	559986.	617948.	60245.	65060.	66802.	46855.	66441.	75034.
FLA...	185988.	534176.	346789.	228420.	301929.	354503.	41484.	91814.	146276.
GA....	124772.	322057.	209220.	4616.	5761.	3535.	32141.	114969.	548317.
HA....	36686.	60844.	67066.	2302.	2581.	2151.	8722.	11145.	13473.
IDA...	27010.	60747.	37237.	0.	0.	19.	12360.	34839.	59201.
ILL...	266074.	568726.	490456.	7211.	11264.	13924.	63948.	61988.	97148.
IND...	171346.	264196.	236259.	4760.	11344.	16629.	54103.	69403.	60712.
IOWA..	45959.	84187.	94554.	2922.	1790.	3622.	41091.	88422.	438402.
KAN...	42340.	78450.	73198.	2138.	2220.	3962.	60556.	78621.	139418.
KY....	112384.	173096.	178351.	686.	489.	521.	73799.	73799.	45337.
LA....	111586.	204083.	138872.	57637.	87376.	101029.	21418.	94088.	141297.
MAINE.	35473.	60697.	74371.	1.	137.	595.	459967.	36111.	52457.
MD....	84304.	236440.	175265.	278522.	317667.	365017.	20508.	46349.	44006.
MASS..	234304.	447613.	378116.	45436.	45451.	46082.	224452.	65077.	172629.
MI....	347165.	757093.	361398.	7133.	8906.	16082.	51668.	81319.	116872.
MINN..	101894.	229034.	1263337.	11949.	8779.	14826.	348881.	51358.	61288.
MISS..	58553.	133962.	103569.	16122.	30197.	25430.	360060.	34929.	157745.
MO....	118036.	197908.	241391.	3171.	4785.	6114.	19929.	84994.	180378.
MONT..	32552.	62066.	48038.	20.	33.	23.	413359.	41304.	47166.
NEB...	30492.	51026.	43420.	311.	208.	183.	13765.	42841.	88595.
NEV...	31124.	41795.	56480.	547.	1491.	1396.	228860.	7866.	13822.
N.H...	18532.	27028.	41937.	690.	2212.	2295.	4885.	42448.	44764.
N.J...	251866.	465712.	506570.	37214.	41686.	51278.	26479.	87725.	77757.
N.M...	46684.	100342.	59445.	8563.	14533.	18407.	43183.	28600.	50602.
N.Y...	619354.	1051310.	1214212.	53757.	49851.	54904.	16919.	259006.	319014.
N.C...	123300.	304296.	167106.	2076.	2045.	3096.	129254.	21581.	95587.
N.D...	20642.	41353.	245550.	0.	0.		13439.	26560.	22974.
OHIO..	240129.	636064.	434433.	117465.	131881.	155344.	52241.	72028.	68592.
OKLA..	83771.	160469.	120593.	1149.	734.	460.	27423.	32882.	38609.
ORE...	78527.	224100.	107207.	1485.	2132.	1736.	18666.	27633.	40209.
PA....	316476.	846379.	508042.	35489.	58649.	73766.	46481.	76291.	128558.

NATIONAL SUMMARY DATA -- TABLE TEN

(cont.)

AGENCY OUTLAYS (CONTINUED)

NAME	LABOR			NASA			SBA		
	1975	1977	1978	1975	1977	1978	1975	1977	1978
STATES (CONT)									
R.I...	47625.	67450.	69257.	520.	947.	862.	22573.	32102.	49736.
S.C...	70837.	178997.	94544.	441.	203.	172.	13997.	20204.	161893.
S.D...	18629.	35981.	25587.	243.	250.	230.	20034.	34506.	36500.
TENN..	100257.	246597.	142360.	2863.	3715.	4386.	19598.	37728.	160547.
TEX...	276706.	514380.	417287.	299287.	349623.	393237.	162840.	332439.	409992.
UTAH..	49630.	92723.	71620.	18512.	52062.	61261.	22656.	58566.	65083.
VER...	16459.	36723.	22733.	22.	87.	274.	13396.	17125.	18320.
VA....	89576.	237578.	147791.	154909.	180091.	211257.	24636.	49306.	60741.
WASH..	147498.	344084.	194804.	9431.	27502.	35180.	39656.	63794.	129329.
W.VA..	44501.	112555.	78679.	601.	59.	64.	17401.	58187.	42004.
WIS...	108758.	260550.	149071.	2321.	3621.	3603.	17293.	38915.	55207.
WY....	8574.	16681.	15418.	1105.	982.	528.	11719.	26005.	35128.
DIVISIONS									
N.ENG.	446059.	798071.	782273.	78257.	83444.	118160.	158663.	232235.	387719.
M.A...	1187696.	2363641.	2228824.	126459.	150186.	179948.	218917.	423023.	525329.
E.N.C.	1133472.	2486629.	1671618.	138891.	167016.	205582.	222465.	323653.	398531.
W.N.C.	377992.	717940.	629038.	20734.	18032.	28937.	235399.	407302.	967556.
S.A.C.	1174511.	2530661.	1865564.	730382.	873463.	1004787.	213080.	471262.	1178820.
E.S.C.	362585.	763855.	550986.	209925.	233192.	236603.	78433.	179141.	520019.
W.S.C.	532094.	1008949.	758930.	358259.	437976.	494843.	249429.	481577.	629332.
MOUNT.	329568.	706405.	606824.	140550.	137772.	152101.	139646.	298327.	388351.
PAC...	1135625.	2225783.	1763236.	1395740.	1812389.	1678172.	248627.	384199.	666082.
REGIONS									
N.E...	1633756.	3161472.	3011097.	204717.	233631.	298107.	377580.	655258.	913048.
N.CT..	1511464.	3204569.	2300655.	159625.	185048.	234519.	457865.	730955.	1366087.
SOUTH.	2069190.	4303466.	3175481.	1298566.	1544631.	1736232.	540941.	1131980.	2328172.
WEST..	1465193.	2932189.	2370060.	1536290.	1950161.	1830273.	388272.	682525.	1054433.
NATION	6679603.	13601695.	10857293.	3199197.	3913471.	4099132.	1764659.	3200719.	5661740.

NATIONAL SUMMARY DATA -- TABLE ELEVEN

AGENCY OUTLAYS (CONTINUED)

NAME	TRANSPORTATION 1975	1977	1978	TREASURY 1975	1977	1978	VETERANS ADMINISTRATION 1975	1977	1978	OTHER AGENCIES-DOMESTIC 1975	1977	1978
STATES												
ALA....	186338	192812	217698	113303	147066	152314	508547	665077	696249	481854	667061	763309
ALK....	301373	285044	295500	11842	28759	35624	68354	80766	91800	66050	84865	86988
ARZ....	172102	154984	172321	74250	110259	115660	491244	598068	667980	285713	350131	404610
ARK....	106791	103719	146120	66885	92125	89569	285373	384385	385666	207718	261947	280165
CAL....	883134	1064234	1131609	820017	1283244	1294274	3465180	4500047	4504267	2895111	3670760	4249746
COL....	233410	266851	250348	85513	114394	119227	621551	961951	1086338	489232	592201	685421
CONN...	90528	111559	175018	119797	148052	130439	223085	264486	303002	281937	354667	416009
DEL....	28165	27261	34014	33097	34588	66999	69355	99763	91918	54209	67956	74395
D.C....	945766	1636845	2398366	608945	599753	751071	349686	418311	670949	1512729	2079862	2402763
FLA....	357028	507137	562576	265289	360585	349111	1309590	1688110	1795976	1054233	1339689	1534077
GA.....	471227	792883	452848	224858	367543	1675697	694897	893163	1030628	617661	737345	865446
HA.....	199769	109652	147109	30807	53648	58317	73736	149336	232003	179036	157866	183981
IDA....	95691	66007	102063	25503	34461	34413	97999	185946	196517	190530	279980	355722
ILL....	619584	471377	1231515	429292	646654	515438	918362	1171156	1262018	3120198	4106569	4451292
IND....	250616	149245	241123	159705	182393	183214	431606	574632	550587	503029	582269	631585
IOWA...	139005	125434	162051	89355	95590	99356	259081	357796	354746	307547	366532	386560
KAN....	143989	161861	162054	60567	75702	77767	246051	335593	365183	288744	362932	390261
KY.....	181566	210244	218234	172786	190365	186381	314040	396963	413477	649974	1026275	1017341
LA.....	247693	255659	227193	166987	212357	227234	413993	544173	560942	300381	366620	513424
MAINE.	50928	52836	69145	48269	63969	65753	137129	178146	186637	127330	155227	167069
MD....	473285	444901	553658	169968	202345	204322	577894	733036	724895	913298	1212208	1540929
MASS..	350486	407938	769215	327725	381481	380491	567085	698859	721796	759834	930736	1048732
MI....	382225	325307	424743	365714	480175	450148	674877	720815	727020	663589	803975	894159
MINN..	196468	209229	254601	133928	179980	177235	524390	730252	721648	464817	548012	595447
MISS..	150548	128219	129444	101800	124502	130829	292228	391468	402285	197171	236707	2679960
MO....	235323	210786	296548	144112	234309	239041	494463	598448	614409	891171	1100425	1189164
MONT..	129919	95714	101167	26828	35098	35322	79154	132094	146471	101076	133812	1837787
NEB...	124840	67372	94573	46373	55965	56304	178780	206436	275707	205969	294746	344863
NEV...	73567	62993	90441	17667	29817	30500	121817	127066	228858	199629	244629	3023343
N.H...	59274	59295	65527	24283	28394	29242	82755	127066	125056	94414	117996	1290084
N.J...	328341	351675	344171	253417	360959	369662	615258	741568	749648	843616	1065310	1206325
N.M...	97943	110072	141016	41951	44236	67973	144611	185778	207672	549973	776633	8681153
N.Y...	555716	1170060	1668581	1072079	1404236	1426082	1400684	1671522	1744782	3122065	3691143	3823230
N.C...	320270	233896	267492	191752	219411	212851	638506	824212	828525	420108	516535	560400
N.D...	76178	41920	65033	24158	24386	23230	62988	81609	104781	78855	967791	991113
OHIO..	314945	406079	558214	329448	421167	403153	1101916	1294844	1451607	1279441	1662667	1845493
OKLA..	236947	238269	280312	75760	105051	105082	361457	441450	523453	350892	459693	573049
ORE...	200718	172514	311162	66950	116698	113583	236555	277151	286617	256884	319974	454409
PA....	713540	399944	760402	549248	647587	639511	1010820	1278580	1283380	1676198	1981524	2221391

248

(cont.)

NATIONAL SUMMARY DATA -- TABLE ELEVEN

AGENCY OUTLAYS (CONTINUED)

NAME	TRANSPORTATION			TREASURY			VETERANS ADMINISTRATION			OTHER AGENCIES-DOMESTIC		
	1975	1977	1978	1975	1977	1978	1975	1977	1978	1975	1977	1978
STATES (CONT)												
R.I...	23497	23118	47480	35161	48141	48903	93879	100796	133851	116484	134710	146716
S.C...	93315	98517	123393	101068	119977	119464	337418	479372	513244	387180	536052	630350
S.D...	69152	66079	46911	27131	25898	26177	82083	120107	126493	77427	92854	95612
TENN...	199515	221466	264307	140468	211344	194194	496019	684609	694910	1407948	2457568	2757259
TEX...	552009	575944	742981	355192	549183	581381	1712277	2319178	2608352	1212560	1593414	1795208
UTAH...	270817	90195	99358	41317	96567	99465	156073	256455	295457	171119	227997	281438
VER...	272233	39910	38105	23557	30914	31613	41618	50069	50930	57730	70560	74921
VA....	289021	466194	461488	158693	195146	196562	823627	1202837	1334822	1008093	1277195	1928205
WASH...	225289	304734	532948	105427	165462	164207	461340	657396	685073	852258	1011760	1354201
W.VA...	284444	233358	198661	104520	104520	111779	186410	241283	250700	217751	273476	293959
WIS...	172096	141972	237218	180020	204938	195374	368446	429699	502245	377354	463454	505230
WY....	93519	43393	65424	11847	13952	15522	54728	106933	122596	61627	91654	140224
DIVISIONS												
N.ENG.	601946	694657	1164639	578792	700952	686442	1145551	1419422	1521272	1437728	1766196	1982532
M.A.C.	1597596	1921679	2773154	1874744	2412781	2435455	3026762	3691669	3777810	5642491	6737967	7250946
E.N.C.	1739466	1493980	2692814	1464178	1935327	1747327	3495206	4191147	4493476	5943611	7618934	8327758
W.N.C.	984952	882682	1086667	525663	695830	699111	1847838	2390240	2562967	2314529	2862292	3101021
S.A.C.	3262521	4440993	5052496	1845942	2103869	3687857	4967385	6580087	7241657	6185253	8040318	9830523
E.S.C.	717966	752741	829680	528357	673277	673718	1610834	2138116	2206920	2736933	4387610	4805869
W.S.C.	1143440	1173591	1396606	664824	958716	1003265	2773600	3689187	4078413	2071560	2681674	3161845
MOUNT.	1026968	890209	1022137	324876	496796	518080	1767176	2639094	2951889	2048901	2697036	3221699
PAC..	1810284	1936178	2418328	1035044	1647811	1666004	4305164	5664698	5799761	4199338	5245226	6329325
REGIONS												
N.E..	2199542	2616336	3937793	2453536	3113734	3121897	4172313	5111091	5299082	7080219	8504163	9233478
N.CT.	2724418	2376662	3779480	1989842	2631157	2446438	5343044	6581387	7056443	8258140	10481226	11428779
SOUTH.	5123928	6367324	7278785	3039123	3735863	5364839	9351818	12407390	13526989	10993746	15109602	17798238
WEST..	2837252	2826386	3440465	1359919	2144607	2184084	6072340	8303791	8751650	6248239	7942262	9551024
NATION	12885139	14186708	18436523	8842420	11625361	13117258	24939515	32403660	34634164	32580345	42037253	48011519

NATIONAL SUMMARY DATA -- TABLE TWELVE

AGRICULTURE PROGRAMS

NAME	FOOD DISTRIBUTION CFDA# - 10550			FOOD STAMPS CFDA# - 10551			NATIONAL SCHOOL LUNCH CFDA# - 10555		
	1975	1977	1978	1975	1977	1978	1975	1977	1978
STATES									
ALA.	7258.	12559.	20791.	105063.	111122.	104083.	36572.	42890.	48568.
ALK.	742.	733.	1066.	5401.	6797.	6703.	1213.	1182.	1544.
ARZ.	10884.	15780.	21120.	42854.	49933.	38278.	11169.	16799.	18804.
ARK.	5669.	9152.	19267.	75614.	69607.	64130.	19464.	27367.	23921.
CAL.	30276.	34896.	54285.	381867.	378101.	329340.	103970.	166724.	152200.
COL.	5008.	8855.	14095.	45549.	51827.	45505.	12594.	18866.	16231.
CONN.	3046.	6731.	9060.	34514.	47135.	40726.	11455.	14256.	17292.
DEL.	930.	1909.	2534.	8427.	9294.	9046.	3524.	4211.	4469.
D.C.	2693.	2159.	3369.	30231.	26740.	26477.	5993.	6990.	7345.
FLA.	11400.	24105.	35893.	204779.	270251.	250032.	51016.	87344.	83309.
GA.	10401.	20151.	38821.	134639.	148087.	139142.	56135.	71182.	70474.
HA.	1819.	3687.	5319.	24589.	35745.	34116.	4746.	7444.	8484.
IDA.	671.	2390.	4844.	10497.	10779.	9719.	3638.	4707.	4657.
ILL.	13536.	26131.	53545.	259818.	291229.	283761.	63845.	86686.	76237.
IND.	11177.	13135.	12888.	59698.	66142.	54691.	25025.	24589.	25441.
IOWA.	6582.	10470.	20700.	25385.	30802.	29335.	19321.	36442.	19710.
KAN.	5635.	6224.	15906.	12211.	17129.	15468.	11289.	16631.	15716.
KY.	8374.	11942.	14803.	137370.	138778.	128934.	27224.	27224.	36253.
LA.	10914.	17989.	22501.	151870.	144838.	131549.	49047.	54031.	56400.
MAINE.	2570.	2925.	6177.	33209.	30395.	33280.	8465.	10853.	10336.
MD.	4236.	9537.	17782.	79134.	89450.	85100.	11626.	26777.	28389.
MASS.	20433.	12402.	22268.	68968.	153787.	155664.	32797.	39154.	37694.
MI.	13059.	24412.	26732.	129297.	142234.	123833.	29288.	48475.	53181.
MINN.	7187.	13615.	27325.	42517.	46545.	40488.	24483.	62739.	27491.
MISS.	5739.	11043.	36002.	108811.	110714.	108571.	40393.	48283.	40093.
MO.	8779.	15753.	41550.	131346.	76076.	65444.	26151.	36365.	35674.
MONT.	1808.	3817.	4494.	11127.	10015.	8601.	3326.	4487.	4774.
NEB.	3082.	7124.	12959.	11894.	11905.	10298.	7766.	15873.	9493.
NEV.	1112.	1494.	3217.	10463.	7614.	6173.	2015.	3005.	3239.
N.H.	1802.	1715.	5554.	11970.	14053.	11945.	3318.	17476.	5457.
N.J.	6924.	22562.	21618.	129987.	165447.	153535.	25028.	48346.	48089.
N.M.	2344.	5640.	6170.	49245.	43999.	38043.	11956.	13625.	15225.
N.Y.	17641.	40182.	76828.	207631.	400965.	385141.	98816.	128560.	133041.
N.C.	10670.	23783.	29886.	126381.	140918.	127267.	53364.	67597.	70305.
N.D.	2325.	3855.	3627.	4806.	5082.	4906.	4336.	3999.	4318.
OHIO	14366.	28284.	28561.	252075.	282507.	245260.	46125.	58655.	61591.
OKLA.	5379.	8030.	16403.	40373.	41353.	36398.	18626.	22974.	23562.
ORE.	3652.	6265.	10181.	59131.	46999.	43608.	9818.	16230.	14683.
PA.	15069.	44181.	47857.	176026.	219371.	229979.	45204.	68525.	69078.

(cont.)

NATIONAL SUMMARY DATA -- TABLE TWELVE

AGRICULTURE PROGRAMS

NAME	FOOD DISTRIBUTION CFDA# - 10550			FOOD STAMPS CFDA# - 10551			NATIONAL SCHOOL LUNCH CFDA# - 10555		
	1975	1977	1978	1975	1977	1978	1975	1977	1978
STATES (CONT)									
R.I...	1001.	2299.	2933.	18925.	22033.	19034.	4754.	6200.	6258.
S.C...	6967.	13230.	16399.	124427.	96079.	84690.	32589.	38715.	42442.
S.D...	3839.	6920.	7828.	7919.	8398.	7386.	4153.	11928.	5815.
TENN..	10617.	21343.	24095.	119219.	140781.	141913.	30736.	39841.	43218.
TEX...	18260.	38199.	50829.	333205.	282355.	255405.	92207.	123695.	123696.
UTAH..	3559.	4662.	9115.	11034.	10129.	8921.	6669.	9651.	10167.
VER...	707.	1189.	1909.	9582.	11556.	10407.	2633.	3710.	3570.
VA....	8241.	16678.	25287.	65786.	75788.	69184.	33241.	40455.	41329.
WASH..	6935.	9378.	19887.	85578.	73445.	57844.	16163.	26396.	22060.
W.VA..	2734.	5318.	8461.	57427.	60120.	731188.	13639.	15594.	18452.
WIS...	5560.	12602.	37842.	29505.	39550.	35828.	19435.	70201.	25224.
WY....	539.	980.	2553.	3137.	3174.	2594.	1401.	1868.	2081.
DIVISIONS									
N.ENG.	28869.	27261.	47902.	176168.	278959.	271056.	63423.	91648.	80607.
M.A...	39634.	106925.	146303.	513643.	785784.	768656.	169048.	245431.	250208.
E.N.C.	57699.	104565.	159569.	730394.	821661.	743373.	183719.	288606.	241673.
W.N.C.	37428.	63962.	129896.	236078.	195938.	173225.	97499.	183977.	118216.
S.A...	58272.	116869.	178432.	831229.	916729.	864125.	261127.	358866.	366514.
E.S.C.	31987.	56887.	95691.	470463.	501396.	483501.	136526.	158238.	168132.
W.S.C.	40221.	73370.	109000.	601061.	538152.	487482.	179344.	228067.	227579.
MOUNT.	26617.	43617.	65608.	183905.	187471.	157835.	52768.	73008.	75178.
PAC...	43424.	54958.	90738.	556566.	541086.	471611.	135910.	217975.	198971.
REGIONS									
N.E...	68503.	134186.	194205.	689812.	1064743.	1039711.	232470.	337080.	330815.
N.CT..	95127.	168527.	289464.	966472.	1017599.	916699.	281217.	472584.	359890.
SOUTH.	130481.	247126.	383123.	1902753.	1956277.	1835108.	576998.	745171.	762225.
WEST..	70040.	98576.	156346.	740471.	728558.	629446.	188678.	290982.	274149.
NATION	364150.	648415.	1023139.	4299508.	4767177.	4420964.	1279364.	1845816.	1727079.

251

AGRICULTURE PROGRAMS (CONTINUED)

NAME	EMERGENCY DISASTER LOANS CFDA# - 10404			LOW/MODERATE INCOME HOUSING LOANS CFDA# - 10410			RURAL ELECTRIC LOANS CFDA# - 10850		
	1975	1977	1978	1975	1977	1978	1975	1977	1978
STATES									
ALA...	912.	2391.	127856.	25005.	60871.	64288.	254976.	8597.	13114.
ALK...	0.	0.	0.	4642.	10306.	15510.	19551.	185083.	48344.
ARZ...	5.	876.	24857.	26505.	22631.	22488.	15342.	7972.	30624.
ARK...	1933.	51869.	44980.	40109.	77352.	85172.	19389.	333932.	18818.
CAL...	114.	12968.	110330.	60037.	73638.	63767.	926.	4228.	3627.
COL...	1891.	12115.	55639.	33875.	37937.	40473.	72918.	608987.	44614.
CONN..	0.	278.	861.	12824.	14215.	12905.			0.
DEL...	999.	156.	2911.	10924.	4975.	5007.			0.
D.C...				0.	0.	0.	3011.	2501.	0.
FLA...	1152.	53192.	65138.	68277.	53503.	54074.	54122.	20447.	25631.
GA....	1906.	24502.	321573.	27181.	50230.	55141.	639109.	834784.	24195.
HA....	40.	0.	0.	16246.	12978.	12561.			
IDA...	38.	16050.	81409.	67741.	48726.	50043.	3745.	6162.	17113.
ILL...	59424.	8327.	24207.	53423.	62555.	71910.	100527.	254769.	36202.
IND...	13120.	700.	16352.	63037.	63287.	78353.	9991.	13595.	1048451.
IOWA..	44126.	22932.	152240.	43630.	88840.	94240.	37069.	165940.	49436.
KAN...	29344.	6081.	49464.	27195.	69386.	58447.	16702.	24956.	50857.
KY....	1985.	484.	4631.	51878.	86107.	76241.	48148.	582058.	37493.
LA....	14989.	14711.	57349.	28587.	76450.	89981.	12577.	20459.	37695.
MAINE.	1.	460.	26492.	102074.	51021.	55007.		2090.	499.
MD....	0.	726.	5493.	38404.	28666.	25629.	2270.	1306.	15288.
MASS..	170.	0.	2506.	11903.	29171.	32772.	1.	17.	0.
MI....	27993.	32451.	70239.	70724.	65442.	77841.	25193.	251762.	49863.
MINN..	63548.	116859.	63025.	24838.	57911.	59629.	132322.	107252.	433751.
MISS..	88280.	150640.	328303.	46841.	84631.	94474.	26268.	55149.	12517.
MO....	76827.	92466.	58129.	36984.	69663.	75870.	44106.	45768.	42393.
MONT..	21.	1673.	82780.	11768.	22599.	22141.	9319.	42365.	8208.
NEB...	15290.	21833.	1187767.	25784.	37510.	40443.	13781.	167709.	256800.
NEV...	208.	1145.	2914.	5939.	5701.	5697.	3708.	4391.	3369.
N.H...	0.	0.	0.	8818.	20429.	22827.	5544.	5578.	12876.
N.J...	4160.	1104.	3454.	57379.	39620.	41403.	394.	12632.	1949.
N.M...	1372.	1227.	171165.	11678.	16913.	18056.	3632.	6818.	16004.
N.Y...	289.	19972.	174742.	70081.	101082.	103952.	1002.	2494.	2280.
N.C...	19770.	21107.	169661.	91715.	145222.	150949.	16842.	19145.	27200.
N.D...	671.	64347.	202088.	8949.	26324.	28739.	16558.	94805.	97701.
OHIO..	671.	728.	18842.	42929.	27789.	23408.	13692.	9529.	79540.
OKLA..	1962.	9059.	58501.	42377.	95846.	91735.	31961.	47961.	59613.
ORE...	103.	4456.	32416.	31173.	55822.	65553.	11336.	19927.	42861.
PA....	92.	97.	6757.	40770.	26471.	29024.	8212.	234214.	16110.

NATIONAL SUMMARY DATA -- TABLE THIRTEEN

| | EMERGENCY DISASTER LOANS CFDA# - 10404 | | | AGRICULTURE PROGRAMS (CONTINUED) | | | | | |
| | | | | LOW/MODERATE INCOME HOUSING LOANS CFDA# - 10410 | | | RURAL ELECTRIC LOANS CFDA# - 10850 | | |
NAME	1975	1977	1978	1975	1977	1978	1975	1977	1978
STATES (CONT)									
R.I...	0.	0.	41.	4929.	2683.	2696.	0.	0.	0.
S.C...	1124.	14964.	80390.	32245.	52729.	52121.	24577.	18882.	15544.
S.D...	24579.	222931.	159008.	10433.	35159.	34821.	20163.	247206.	41297.
TENN.	16125.	199903.	43349.	71649.	116720.	99080.	11087.	9273.	17009.
TEX..	119722.	48574.	223254.	44628.	55130.	61875.	47088.	63658.	485258.
UTAH.	2542.	3522.	10997.	41317.	39789.	38627.	3784.	3811.	1806.
VER..	0.	86.	4107.	15521.	32817.	35280.	922.	16568.	86.
VA...	6.	16598.	170534.	120514.	77972.	83159.	13967.	21959.	14645.
WASH.	1374.	1932.	31000.	34561.	32430.	29387.	9544.	8642.	34103.
W.VA.	0.	417.	2490.	42861.	41488.	37999.	1012.	769.	81.
WIS..	83614.	78265.	56539.	30670.	48082.	61169.	89297.	13210.	125821.
WY...	1968.	3072.	47242.	10101.	13454.	13414.	10657.	205621.	19007.
DIVISIONS									
N.ENG.	171.	823.	34006.	156068.	150335.	161487.	6467.	24252.	13461.
M.A.C.	1464.	21174.	184953.	168229.	167173.	174378.	9608.	249340.	20339.
E.N.C.	184823.	120470.	186179.	260783.	267156.	312680.	238700.	542865.	1339875.
W.N.C.	273484.	547447.	802721.	177814.	384793.	392153.	280702.	853636.	741615.
E.S.C.	5477.	131661.	818189.	432121.	454785.	464080.	754909.	919792.	122583.
W.S.C.	107303.	173419.	504139.	195373.	348348.	334082.	340479.	655077.	801133.
W.S.C.	138605.	124214.	384084.	155701.	304777.	328763.	111015.	466010.	601385.
MOUNT.	10834.	39679.	323003.	208924.	207749.	210939.	123105.	886127.	140745.
PAC...	1631.	19355.	173754.	146660.	185175.	186778.	41358.	217880.	128935.
REGIONS									
N.E...	1635.	21997.	218959.	324297.	317508.	335865.	16075.	273592.	33800.
N.CT..	458307.	667917.	988900.	438596.	651949.	704833.	519402.	1396501.	2081490.
SOUTH.	251385.	429293.	1706412.	783195.	1107911.	1126925.	1206403.	2040879.	804101.
WEST..	12464.	59034.	496757.	355584.	392924.	397717.	164463.	1104007.	269680.
NATION	723791.	1178242.	3411029.	1901672.	2470292.	2565340.	1906343.	4814980.	3189072.

AGRICULTURE PROGRAMS (CONTINUED)

NAME	COMMODITY LOANS CFDA# - 10051			OTHER AGRICULTURE LOANS			WATER AND WASTE DISPOSAL CFDA# - 10418		
	1975	1977	1978	1975	1977	1978	1975	1977	1978
STATES	34828.	23888.	28717.	79478.	85873.	94861.	4496.	10595.	10123.
ALA...	11.	10.	16.	7985.	6113.	10346.	200.	53.	280.
ALK...	39844.	28333.	70337.	43951.	25131.	25559.	997.	2012.	525.
ARZ...	57963.	85459.	212664.	100302.	65877.	106702.	3629.	7721.	6574.
ARK...	185968.	240236.	352229.	115425.	106453.	80298.	6087.	26387.	11506.
CAL...	2699.	77723.	106909.	62987.	59539.	69782.	1835.	15936.	11354.
COL...	2727.	2267.	2687.	23596.	5193.	8515.	400.	108.	1080.
CONN.	123.	293.	433.	19951.	8096.	15025.	0.	0.	540.
DEL..	20.	19.	37.	28.	0.		0.	0.	
D.C..									
FLA..	6326.	3922.	104354.	111233.	54423.	64004.	6642.	14685.	6841.
GA...	140818.	113596.	96674.	110707.	82601.	90062.	6857.	2759.	10360.
HA...	0.	0.	0.	22620.	8146.	6030.	1292.	3037.	178.
IDA..	12847.	37028.	24605.	115171.	56833.	56572.	3823.	10878.	5204.
ILL..	73623.	161747.	290154.	189237.	81143.	110436.	4004.	7751.	6692.
IND..	9679.	43926.	130468.	138641.	85853.	89147.	4176.	22513.	10666.
IOWA.	37693.	138207.	462335.	189293.	147374.	105291.	4261.	5896.	10825.
KAN..	21152.	507920.	429280.	128814.	72414.	84914.	4675.	11268.	4449.
KY...	5230.	47262.	624681.	95363.	66295.	111497.	2815.	6064.	8666.
LA...	15320.	23099.	56216.	110648.	87029.	131041.	3348.	2450.	9296.
MAINE	5.	12.	409.	164085.	55842.	44090.	2314.	1096.	1667.
MD...	11247.	22564.	14055.	50604.	24111.	27870.	1611.	803.	3547.
MASS.	3073.	3874.	4180.	26576.	13320.	29518.	4652.	10905.	2077.
MI...	10215.	46444.	98739.	170385.	101376.	99168.	3481.	9285.	11577.
MINM.	219159.	517556.	727228.	167363.	100480.	114503.	5083.	9439.	6939.
MISS.	38615.	13615.	134470.	222548.	89253.	110331.	4052.	10356.	9609.
MO...	50683.	185253.	256977.	176031.	44524.	120576.	651.	683.	11591.
MONT.	2744.	143699.	84141.	50926.	57544.	41278.	1628.	2472.	879.
NEB..	18102.	212983.	629551.	90052.	6334.	107647.	326.	114.	5158.
NEV..	274.	557.	120.	12849.	21512.	9863.	603.	1497.	225.
N.H..	0.	0.	31.	21512.	33032.	48216.	1826.	1113.	1076.
N.J..	1022.	7843.	5858.	89372.	24857.	44331.	830.	1807.	4525.
N.M..	10788.	17551.	30137.	35275.	86269.	62423.	5739.	3162.	2036.
N.Y..	27184.	38675.	42935.	147670.	134736.	110358.	6384.	14997.	7350.
N.C..	35283.	176259.	180035.	216372.	70507.	148828.	2676.	7780.	11142.
N.D..	8327.	328457.	236993.	84908.	65606.	66413.	5109.	7727.	5741.
OHIO.	10284.	40657.	75952.	106761.	103569.	71105.	3172.	8641.	6399.
OKLA.	15265.	195779.	88995.	169418.	40162.	148024.	2188.	4060.	8493.
ORE..	6269.	32018.	12254.	69033.	77881.	53236.	6598.	13669.	4825.
PA...	7398.	16305.	25120.	111400.		78037.			10326.

(cont.)

NATIONAL SUMMARY DATA -- TABLE FOURTEEN

AGRICULTURE PROGRAMS (CONTINUED)

NAME	COMMODITY LOANS CFDA# - 10051			OTHER AGRICULTURE LOANS			WATER AND WASTE DISPOSAL CFDA# - 10418		
	1975	1977	1978	1975	1977	1978	1975	1977	1978
STATES (CONT)									
R.I....	0	273.	638.	5116.	4298.	243.	220.	686.	0.
S.C....	12377.	19900.	32595.	87654.	63002.	83584.	3606.	1989.	5376.
S.D....	8108.	147031.	176595.	115719.	80749.	86707.	2935.	9662.	2927.
TENN...	12183.	29956.	41343.	156862.	74111.	92086.	5179.	11084.	7636.
TEX....	132676.	396309.	704737.	354062.	178202.	228963.	8034.	17906.	18911.
UTAH...	6981.	8918.	98636.	87810.	15803.	13349.	887.	2036.	1829.
VER....	678.	3065.	2852.	32070.	13356.	29703.	974.	1176.	2220.
VA.....	12467.	76059.	52945.	170263.	48424.	46729.	4222.	6704.	6519.
WASH...	24626.	86159.	29295.	74777.	54796.	52890.	2180.	3393.	4366.
W.VA...	36.	854.	587.	87274.	55854.	75965.	4834.	6824.	8225.
WIS....	29752.	141424.	140186.	186367.	94832.	157098.	3594.	11546.	8411.
WY.....	361.	5735.	4042.	32925.	24166.	26407.	580.	3152.	6788.
DIVISIONS									
N.ENG.	6483.	9491.	10797.	272954.	100176.	160287.	7156.	6720.	8120.
M.A...	35604.	62822.	73914.	348442.	197182.	232727.	14164.	17944.	22201.
E.N.C.	133552.	434197.	735499.	791391.	428809.	526954.	21181.	48807.	43744.
W.N.C.	363223.	2037408.	2918960.	952181.	618140.	686050.	23209.	67963.	47630.
S.A...	218697.	413467.	481715.	854087.	471245.	552067.	34858.	56092.	52550.
E.S.C.	90855.	114721.	269210.	554251.	315531.	408775.	19433.	42386.	36033.
W.S.C.	221224.	700646.	1062612.	734430.	434678.	614729.	17750.	40332.	43274.
MOUNT.	76538.	319544.	418927.	441893.	257187.	305234.	7397.	28776.	28839.
PAC...	216874.	358423.	393794.	289841.	215672.	202800.	10655.	36651.	21155.
REGIONS									
N.E...	42088.	72313.	84711.	621396.	297359.	393014.	21320.	24664.	30321.
N.CT..	496775.	2471605.	3654459.	1743571.	1046950.	1213005.	44390.	116770.	91374.
SOUTH.	530776.	1228834.	1813537.	2142768.	1221454.	1575571.	72042.	138810.	131857.
WEST..	293413.	677967.	812721.	731733.	472859.	508034.	18052.	65427.	49994.
NATION	1363051.	4450719.	6365427.	5239469.	3038622.	3689624.	155803.	345670.	303546.

255

NATIONAL SUMMARY DATA -- TABLE FIFTEEN

NAME	COMMERCE PROGRAMS				DEFENSE PROGRAMS					
	LOCAL PUBLIC WORKS CFDA# - 11300			EMERGENCY PUBLIC WORKS	MILITARY PAYROLL			CIVILIAN PAYROLL		
	1975	1977	1978	1977	1975	1977	1978	1975	1977	1978
STATES										
ALA...	1763.	1094.	2543.	53207.	432242.	463434.	550865.	280785.	373705.	414937.
ALK...	2883.	3098.	2060.	55426.	250162.	251091.	279701.	65671.	73678.	79618.
ARZ...	2961.	1900.	2552.	81188.	415888.	482985.	546421.	122123.	155703.	166612.
ARK...	4796.	6072.	3291.	40289.	195346.	233706.	261815.	55591.	175192.	74072.
CAL...	6565.	7158.	10308.	724194.	3050163.	3467305.	3761512.	1951970.	2120524.	2283382.
COL...	907.	1404.	462.	42794.	614693.	737422.	144854.	204256.	228013.	237785.
CONN..	750.	0.	0.	131146.	111871.	91642.	93751.	41452.	53126.	53755.
DEL...	210.	0.	0.	39870.	82302.	312347.	270152.	27823.	31776.	32280.
D.C...	174.	475.	1575.	40000.	398661.	1517491.	1752497.	294886.	388472.	356502.
FLA...	956.	704.	6021.	295423.	1255452.	952699.	1064323.	389853.	422940.	499505.
GA....	4306.	3643.	1151.	104723.	774798.	456203.	569033.	426411.	532131.	576493.
HA....	0.	1469.	1326.	39641.	490630.	99946.	620699.	263146.	261009.	325533.
IDA...	3462.	4222.	547.	40613.	84143.	622761.	639842.	16199.	20875.	20167.
ILL...	1520.	24.	917.	153537.	541879.	180235.	192997.	263621.	311132.	338306.
IND...	1488.	4214.	2659.	62211.	201770.	59101.	68739.	188020.	219737.	235909.
IOWA..	2765.	903.	3789.	41779.	55792.	390496.	386007.	18921.	25934.	26539.
KAN...	1907.	2268.	3643.	40368.	390496.	534526.	589792.	84521.	100013.	191899.
KY....	2737.	3484.	1729.	46349.	534526.	442954.	469420.	181399.	209955.	261580.
LA....	3228.	3959.	797.	60631.	442954.	589082.	1199901.	97059.	127793.	170931.
MAINE.	1162.	1050.	6400.	39699.	95888.	273700.	631040.	26601.	301161.	79954.
MD....	2158.	0.	3395.	58526.	655685.	236552.	308385.	641084.	758054.	802050.
MASS..	3756.	8803.	2651.	184167.	235703.	112164.	253474.	153405.	189711.	209187.
MI....	9105.	6188.	3993.	371589.	101947.	314639.	128455.	148717.	195261.	213107.
MINN..	3858.	3565.	1651.	47781.	383360.	472586.	344388.	41475.	518880.	58010.
MISS..	4704.	4506.	686.	41887.	84257.	89978.	394481.	118091.	158097.	170147.
MO....	3972.	1645.	400.	56330.	181504.	219322.	98500.	256611.	335730.	335622.
MONT..	4066.	2664.	544.	42728.	122740.	163342.	235995.	21048.	35359.	24405.
NEB...	576.	0.	7842.	40730.	82882.	95541.	180462.	48527.	59355.	61717.
NEV...	375.	460.	4460.	42031.	383695.	447747.	106174.	36459.	39281.	42789.
N.H...	765.	2236.	13443.	40000.	227598.	271901.	416707.	106467.	125064.	150631.
N.J...	5356.	1710.	3324.	321268.	429283.	435453.	298805.	289443.	398539.	435949.
N.M...	88339.	34031.	1369.	62306.	1084453.	1196722.	477637.	123632.	147401.	160342.
N.Y...	3787.	2435.	6541.	728128.	140383.	151837.	1254231.	296533.	353004.	382193.
N.C...	3032.	1871.	5621.	73895.	359726.	387748.	154752.	167180.	202191.	225431.
N.D...	1601.	4945.	4061.	42026.	433471.	519063.	424061.	30424.	31678.	30710.
OHIO..	5818.	6353.	3420.	215362.	103562.	118730.	530419.	453910.	515595.	558539.
OKLA..	11185.	3737.	—	67661.	336212.	376201.	135701.	347836.	380039.	407103.
ORE...	4959.	9193.	—	87292.	—	—	400275.	37121.	48039.	54876.
PA....	—	—	—	269596.	—	—	—	727970.	778753.	865495.

(cont.)

NATIONAL SUMMARY DATA -- TABLE FIFTEEN

| NAME | COMMERCE PROGRAMS | | | | DEFENSE PROGRAMS | | | | | |
| | LOCAL PUBLIC WORKS CFDA# - 11300 | | | EMERGENCY PUBLIC WORKS | MILITARY PAYROLL | | | CIVILIAN PAYROLL | | |
	1975	1977	1978	1977	1975	1977	1978	1975	1977	1978
STATES (CONT)										
R.I...	0.	0.	5334.	48838.	78499.	87678.	99871.	97281.	101165.	107187.
S.C...	4702.	2410.	2502.	43784.	632057.	745077.	753132.	242977.	283741.	329937.
S.D...	999.	455.	1563.	44861.	80877.	94178.	102383.	18936.	23215.	22637.
TENN..	2470.	4998.	2701.	54725.	258046.	282054.	329789.	91439.	119144.	128248.
TEX...	3885.	6066.	5612.	145935.	2223499.	2206836.	2638539.	805461.	877205.	996102.
UTAH..	52.	323.	1509.	41896.	88621.	125794.	127915.	295079.	333803.	357399.
VER...	678.	0.	1556.	57848.	19622.	23349.	25138.	6741.	9240.	9180.
VA....	974.	640.	1648.	62484.	1435228.	1530572.	1722711.	1310368.	1400158.	1483790.
WASH..	4461.	9168.	5134.	119352.	635776.	684707.	771195.	336764.	385585.	429910.
W.VA..	5220.	1620.	6790.	41260.	44326.	56659.	61395.	17831.	26310.	27081.
WIS...	3221.	4749.	6133.	56119.	86339.	92016.	108056.	37917.	48929.	51549.
WY....	0.	0.		40336.	55103.	63940.	67466.	12666.	15839.	15619.
DIVISIONS										
N.ENG.	6346.	9853.	15020.	501701.	658879.	715944.	804323.	431947.	508467.	609894.
M.A...	14564.	45459.	24704.	1318993.	1149190.	1259401.	1294619.	1313946.	1530296.	1683637.
E.N.C.	16935.	20120.	22424.	858818.	1425417.	1519312.	1618430.	1092185.	1290654.	1397410.
W.N.C.	17108.	10706.	11210.	313875.	1334359.	1466220.	1470812.	499455.	627797.	727134.
S.A...	22487.	11927.	22656.	759970.	6362962.	6992291.	7603232.	3518413.	4045773.	4333074.
E.S.C.	11674.	14081.	13026.	196167.	1517321.	1627201.	1814834.	671714.	860901.	974912.
W.S.C.	17726.	22451.	18167.	314517.	3295270.	3338952.	3900193.	1305947.	1460224.	1648208.
MOUNT.	17180.	12622.	11539.	393892.	1693043.	2035308.	2145145.	831462.	976274.	1025118.
PAC...	15093.	24631.	22713.	1025905.	4530293.	4978036.	5517158.	2654672.	2888835.	3173319.
REGIONS										
N.E...	20909.	55312.	39724.	1820693.	1808069.	1975345.	2098942.	1745893.	2038763.	2293531.
N.CT..	34043.	30826.	33634.	1172693.	2759776.	2985532.	3089242.	1591640.	1918451.	2124544.
SOUTH.	51886.	48459.	53846.	1270654.	11175553.	11958444.	13318259.	5496074.	6366903.	6956194.
WEST..	32273.	37253.	34251.	1419796.	6223336.	7013344.	7662303.	3486134.	3865109.	4198437.
NATION	139111.	171850.	161459.	15683837.	21966734.	23932665.	26168746.	12319741.	14189226.	15572706.

NAME	COMMUNITY SERVICES ADMIN. COMMUNITY ACTION CFDA# - 49002			ENVIRONMENTAL PROTECTION AGENCY WASTEWATER TREATMENT CFDA# - 66418			HEW PROGRAMS TITLE ONE EDUCATION CFDA# - 13428		
	1975	1977	1978	1975	1977	1978	1975	1977	1978
STATES									
ALA...	6597.	6767.	7221.	28529.	24836.	54609.	40340.	44786.	63356.
ALK...	1261.	1183.	1252.	15170.	12438.	1997.	3226.	3423.	4647.
ARZ...	3176.	2893.	3476.	20563.	20302.	23578.	13383.	15717.	23324.
ARK...	4592.	4158.	4675.	8171.	36616.	16860.	22990.	25469.	36038.
CAL...	30195.	30945.	37722.	390935.	791171.	319535.	128062.	139880.	194951.
COL...	2839.	2763.	2827.	24484.	35574.	14754.	13504.	14881.	21420.
CONN..	4708.	3503.	4607.	48184.	199334.	9164.	13832.	16109.	20517.
DEL...	541.	508.	830.	32832.	51442.	3274.	3996.	4326.	6035.
D.C...	13070.	8039.	9418.	9003.	15975.	17233.	9670.	10268.	14030.
FLA...	7481.	9648.	10729.	142347.	210566.	96756.	47884.	59627.	80134.
GA....	10331.	9237.	10683.	38983.	126391.	74997.	44014.	48425.	68442.
HA....	703.	1001.	1399.	42954.	6304.	30503.	4692.	5398.	8310.
IDA...	987.	752.	1782.	9165.	13831.	6453.	3693.	4080.	5662.
ILL...	17031.	17005.	18777.	289302.	367669.	304083.	84061.	89121.	101401.
IND...	4141.	4219.	4811.	104497.	273503.	107553.	21073.	22642.	31470.
IOWA..	3906.	3986.	4566.	19686.	44555.	29946.	14661.	15250.	22335.
KAN...	2201.	2913.	2691.	15820.	53859.	15678.	11748.	13234.	18276.
KY....	7132.	5816.	7375.	27889.	60621.	49024.	31939.	34714.	48848.
LA....	776.	8162.	8846.	27442.	65931.	22975.	47145.	51287.	72048.
MAINE.	1707.	1512.	1932.	28456.	15866.	9628.	5727.	6526.	9012.
MD....	4320.	4575.	6009.	83221.	253116.	43557.	26787.	29463.	40483.
MASS..	8996.	9006.	9946.	99469.	297908.	29215.	30293.	32130.	46467.
MI....	13162.	12895.	14810.	312912.	328767.	515293.	63845.	72393.	94439.
MINN..	3464.	3611.	4459.	115248.	89286.	39143.	25155.	26286.	34242.
MISS..	4313.	5056.	6118.	16387.	26068.	26845.	38544.	42870.	60465.
MO....	11123.	13559.	10353.	67005.	108696.	41602.	28643.	30687.	42645.
MONT..	991.	861.	976.	6313.	9880.	4555.	4501.	5254.	7944.
NEB...	2119.	2119.	3669.	24841.	27126.	15813.	8331.	9100.	13159.
NEV...	582.	428.	705.	9133.	7869.	9577.	1913.	2090.	2991.
N.H...	855.	800.	1195.	38933.	61276.	29056.	2744.	2804.	3742.
N.J...	9908.	9799.	10904.	205353.	305320.	49331.	47673.	47979.	61458.
N.M...	2011.	2382.	2926.	6916.	19557.	14909.	12029.	13392.	19653.
N.Y...	32304.	36588.	29860.	301419.	1431557.	731120.	191867.	180523.	231494.
N.C...	10484.	9543.	10682.	33948.	115407.	35435.	47964.	51886.	73205.
N.D...	212.	553.	473.	5960.	4721.	10599.	4377.	4665.	6598.
OHIO..	14259.	13149.	14962.	191967.	478504.	92456.	50025.	51108.	71844.
OKLA..	5354.	4960.	5573.	16236.	77121.	26269.	18587.	20301.	28765.
ORE...	2569.	2720.	3216.	160375.	44942.	35294.	13065.	14709.	21743.
PA....	26709.	12424.	15998.	162986.	470655.	713368.	78522.	83201.	110103.

(cont.)

NATIONAL SUMMARY DATA -- TABLE SIXTEEN

NAME	COMMUNITY SERVICES ADMIN. COMMUNITY ACTION CFDA# - 49002			ENVIRONMENTAL PROTECTION AGENCY WASTEWATER TREATMENT CFDA# - 66418			HEW PROGRAMS TITLE ONE EDUCATION CFDA# - 13428		
	1975	1977	1978	1975	1977	1978	1975	1977	1978
STATES (CONT)									
R.I....	1977.	1954.	2300.	20945.	32324.	7844.	5852.	6551.	8197.
S.C....	6161.	4883.	5800.	21261.	94422.	16166.	30882.	34000.	48142.
S.D....	698.	641.	1000.	3609.	9562.	12059.	5678.	5793.	8671.
TENN...	6964.	6651.	7361.	48807.	122584.	53937.	36593.	40501.	57304.
TEX....	16789.	17309.	19119.	108973.	155530.	130405.	94398.	104926.	153076.
UTAH...	1343.	1425.	1130.	17739.	21886.	5569.	5090.	5569.	7780.
VER....	1288.	843.	1025.	5059.	21029.	6577.	2794.	3054.	3868.
VA.....	4910.	5241.	7012.	106520.	71066.	49157.	35346.	39979.	55689.
WASH...	3946.	3839.	4406.	65333.	92863.	45174.	18741.	20069.	27065.
W.VA...	3924.	3664.	4531.	21800.	54684.	26590.	16349.	17687.	25262.
WIS....	3961.	3878.	5447.	54679.	134444.	102362.	24648.	27146.	38236.
WY.....	340.	272.	320.	3423.	3754.	3644.	2049.	2208.	3352.
DIVISIONS									
N.ENG.	19530.	17617.	21005.	241047.	627737.	91484.	61242.	67173.	91802.
M.A...	68921.	58812.	56753.	669758.	2207532.	193819.	318061.	311703.	403055.
E.N.C.	52554.	51147.	58807.	953356.	1582886.	1121748.	243652.	262410.	337390.
W.N.C.	23724.	27382.	27211.	252169.	337805.	164841.	98594.	105016.	145925.
S.A...	61221.	55338.	65695.	489914.	993068.	363164.	262892.	295661.	411423.
E.S.C.	25006.	24290.	28074.	121613.	234109.	184416.	147416.	162871.	229973.
W.S.C.	34511.	34589.	38213.	160823.	335198.	196510.	183120.	201983.	289927.
MOUNT.	11985.	11775.	13140.	97735.	132653.	93040.	56163.	63190.	92126.
PAC...	38958.	39688.	47996.	524768.	947618.	432503.	167787.	183479.	256716.
REGIONS									
N.E...	88451.	76429.	77757.	910805.	2835269.	285303.	379303.	378876.	494858.
N.CT..	76278.	78529.	86018.	1205525.	1920691.	1286589.	342246.	367425.	483315.
SOUTH.	120738.	114218.	131982.	772350.	1562375.	744090.	593427.	660515.	931323.
WEST..	50943.	51463.	61138.	622503.	1080271.	525543.	223950.	246669.	348841.
NATION	336409.	320638.	356895.	3511183.	7398606.	2841524.	1538925.	1653485.	2258336.

NATIONAL SUMMARY DATA -- TABLE SEVENTEEN

HEW PROGRAMS (CONTINUED)

NAME	SAFA CFDA# - 13478			VOCATIONAL EDUCATION CFDA# - 13493			REHABILITATION SERVICES AND FACILITIES CFDA# - 13624		
	1975	1977	1978	1975	1977	1978	1975	1977	1978
STATES									
ALA...	4047.	12902.	12799.	8706.	9118.	14883.	18149.	18516.	18545.
ALK...	24852.	45025.	47109.	627.	701.	1331.	1996.	2000.	2009.
ARZ...	10545.	25125.	26163.	4476.	4599.	8457.	7637.	8231.	8677.
ARK...	2094.	4187.	3836.	4737.	5011.	8198.	10634.	10882.	10729.
CAL...	42181.	98546.	101234.	36504.	39512.	64504.	49832.	55996.	58429.
COL...	4870.	14816.	14286.	5297.	4301.	10398.	7986.	8388.	8441.
CONN..	2068.	5269.	4888.	4748.	5180.	8533.	5885.	6838.	7189.
DEL...	167.	580.	517.	1002.	824.	1083.	2327.	2037.	2035.
D.C...	46651.	4826.	4668.	1180.	1012.	2620.	5329.	5505.	5560.
FLA...	9911.	23130.	22595.	14900.	15829.	11033.	26633.	28458.	29514.
GA....	3516.	19954.	20448.	11289.	11704.	19275.	20214.	21175.	21551.
HA....	8442.	13694.	15071.	1572.	1737.	2849.	2163.	2186.	2367.
IDA...	1710.	5058.	4836.	1883.	1963.	3225.	3428.	3633.	3427.
ILL...	4536.	15717.	14274.	18795.	19913.	32073.	24829.	27011.	27983.
IND...	1311.	3735.	3299.	11132.	11612.	7857.	11891.	12940.	14567.
IOWA..	521.	1551.	965.	5981.	5951.	4010.	10164.	10130.	9216.
KAN...	5403.	8580.	8336.	4739.	4751.	7743.	6560.	7593.	7376.
KY....	2392.	8271.	5543.	8095.	8445.	13581.	15400.	16363.	16234.
LA....	1689.	5935.	6647.	9430.	9887.	16056.	17989.	18836.	18516.
MAINE.	1076.	3257.	3322.	2442.	2539.	4180.	4605.	4000.	4400.
MD....	11944.	32613.	30194.	7561.	7994.	5475.	15147.	11323.	11736.
MASS..	1582.	10367.	12286.	10463.	11340.	34698.	15477.	17317.	18573.
MI....	3328.	7744.	7098.	17493.	18126.	30239.	24882.	24976.	26270.
MINM..	1357.	4031.	4470.	8228.	8470.	13961.	13311.	13810.	13629.
MISS..	2619.	4555.	4400.	5836.	6062.	9802.	13127.	13401.	13730.
MO....	4330.	9374.	9265.	9781.	10459.	17090.	15933.	16700.	16999.
MONT..	4166.	8433.	8961.	1705.	1715.	2997.	2973.	2956.	2957.
NEB...	4021.	7428.	8771.	3205.	3269.	5407.	5234.	5152.	5121.
NEV...	890.	4863.	4923.	918.	1051.	1811.	2107.	2032.	2037.
N.H...	1327.	2554.	2373.	1631.	1783.	2913.	2998.	3064.	3283.
N.J...	5165.	15771.	14966.	11436.	12425.	8540.	16738.	16688.	18498.
N.M...	9374.	21277.	21788.	2838.	3030.	2101.	5161.	5741.	5786.
N.Y...	9499.	40876.	38812.	28113.	31194.	21528.	38484.	43611.	48930.
N.C...	3466.	23567.	23976.	13008.	13385.	9164.	23683.	24301.	16900.
N.D...	2411.	6132.	6106.	1604.	1078.	1586.	2896.	2472.	
OHIO..	4020.	12368.	11295.	21542.	22650.	36779.	31843.	34058.	36284.
OKLA..	7175.	18049.	17540.	6129.	6342.	10151.	11465.	12105.	11812.
ORE...	2173.	4446.	3840.	4686.	4859.	7857.	7943.	8389.	8308.
PA....	2002.	12308.	11282.	23133.	24162.	38712.	38389.	40400.	40921.

260

(cont.)

NATIONAL SUMMARY DATA -- TABLE SEVENTEEN

HEW PROGRAMS (CONTINUED)

NAME	SAFA CFDA# - 13478			VOCATIONAL EDUCATION CFDA# - 13493			REHABILITATION SERVICES AND FACILITIES CFDA# - 13624		
	1975	1977	1978	1975	1977	1978	1975	1977	1978
STATES (CONT)									
R.I...	955.	4032.	3967.	1948.	1993.	1416.	3029.	3240.	3299.
S.C...	4225.	14099.	13850.	7088.	7487.	12152.	11993.	14341.	14245.
S.D...	4223.	7836.	8120.	1721.	1703.	2957.	3101.	2955.	2868.
TENN..	3171.	9497.	8857.	9829.	10063.	16332.	16066.	18178.	19395.
TEX...	22284.	39306.	37636.	26859.	27968.	45228.	47925.	49392.	47898.
UTAH..	5086.	10215.	9471.	2985.	2759.	5631.	5203.	5566.	5695.
VER...	21.	243.	214.	1105.	1182.	870.	2075.	2219.	2176.
VA....	21052.	48735.	46270.	10760.	11118.	18183.	18022.	17850.	17927.
WASH..	9838.	20850.	19890.	6966.	7268.	11731.	10628.	11249.	11079.
W.VA..	358.	755.	549.	4237.	4314.	2894.	8737.	8871.	8747.
WIS...	1042.	3172.	3970.	9670.	10197.	16698.	16556.	17063.	17196.
WY....	2136.	4270.	3886.	771.	628.	1757.	2050.	2000.	2000.
DIVISIONS									
N.ENG.	7029.	25723.	27049.	22338.	24017.	52609.	34069.	36677.	38919.
M.A...	16666.	68955.	65061.	62682.	67781.	68780.	93612.	100699.	108350.
E.N.C.	14236.	42735.	39936.	78633.	82498.	123646.	110001.	116048.	122300.
W.N.C.	22265.	44933.	46032.	35259.	35682.	52754.	57197.	58812.	57681.
S.A...	101289.	167857.	163069.	71025.	73669.	81881.	128084.	133861.	128215.
E.S.C.	12230.	35224.	31600.	32466.	33687.	54598.	62743.	66458.	67904.
W.S.C.	33242.	67476.	65659.	47154.	49208.	79632.	88013.	91215.	88955.
MOUNT.	38776.	94035.	94315.	20873.	20045.	36377.	36545.	38548.	39019.
PAC...	87486.	182561.	187143.	50355.	54078.	88274.	72562.	79820.	82193.
REGIONS									
N.E...	23694.	94678.	92110.	85020.	91798.	121389.	127681.	137376.	147269.
N.CT..	36501.	87668.	85969.	113892.	118179.	176400.	167198.	174860.	179981.
SOUTH.	146761.	270557.	260328.	150645.	156564.	216111.	278840.	291533.	285074.
WEST..	126262.	276596.	281458.	71228.	74123.	124651.	109108.	118367.	121212.
NATION	333218.	729499.	719864.	420784.	440665.	638551.	682826.	722137.	733536.

261

NATIONAL SUMMARY DATA -- TABLE EIGHTEEN

HEW PROGRAMS (CONTINUED)

NAME	SOCIAL SERVICES LOW INCOME CFDA# - 13642			PUBLIC ASSISTANCE (STATE AID) CFDA# - 13808			SUPPLEMENTAL SECURITY INCOME CFDA# - 13807		
	1975	1977	1978	1975	1977	1978	1975	1977	1978
STATES									
ALA....	28279.	32492.	59439.	59288.	78860.	73620.	153707.	164583.	197152.
ALK....	3786.	5455.	4343.	13294.	16341.	17355.	4027.	4677.	5793.
ARZ....	3658.	16386.	21921.	33124.	32830.	27932.	32643.	40828.	49406.
ARK....	8421.	17607.	23724.	50754.	52173.	47064.	86264.	91413.	94243.
CAL....	251358.	262000.	278831.	1377709.	1795218.	1872713.	505670.	590114.	625767.
COL....	31838.	31484.	44055.	79499.	77646.	72145.	40424.	41753.	49908.
CONN...	40399.	40442.	34355.	131341.	155540.	166943.	25337.	30622.	37038.
DEL....	5337.	6805.	6720.	21526.	27668.	27483.	6280.	8152.	8591.
D.C....	8361.	9499.	12216.	92236.	94278.	85151.	21344.	22912.	23084.
FLA....	156439.	107704.	116560.	92938.	144662.	134685.	173192.	214118.	228240.
GA.....	48354.	57170.	76409.	135045.	106518.	96605.	167658.	184563.	197886.
HA.....	6901.	10430.	11713.	58104.	80301.	82489.	8788.	11083.	12238.
IDA....	10492.	12491.	9941.	17712.	21586.	20155.	9065.	9628.	11320.
ILL....	80735.	70949.	122628.	727882.	752483.	680436.	165284.	179980.	213982.
IND....	5091.	19227.	48557.	104422.	117144.	109721.	40114.	46632.	56820.
IOWA...	25260.	36585.	37605.	94958.	99520.	106651.	25319.	27133.	28232.
KAN....	13269.	29888.	26057.	59829.	78097.	71544.	22427.	24160.	24772.
KY.....	41187.	41354.	38724.	118406.	137974.	113746.	116229.	123160.	148671.
LA.....	21432.	39723.	46099.	96161.	97537.	93914.	160486.	183700.	192401.
MAINE..	8850.	12836.	14371.	49147.	48033.	49966.	19870.	19940.	20588.
MD.....	36435.	61717.	54729.	143472.	162690.	165357.	61887.	65789.	68262.
MASS...	66966.	78471.	79139.	427527.	459696.	477285.	80323.	103620.	111460.
MI.....	97134.	117769.	145552.	671319.	740396.	823253.	116247.	132383.	138975.
MINN...	55779.	34873.	69405.	147072.	155991.	165531.	37688.	38890.	46776.
MISS...	5809.	20209.	23684.	31984.	31225.	36667.	138265.	143400.	147101.
MO.....	22728.	48872.	49595.	131662.	156995.	142198.	112972.	113636.	134899.
MONT...	6198.	6194.	9975.	12401.	14157.	15475.	8634.	9113.	9239.
NEB....	18686.	16460.	21701.	26954.	31737.	36751.	16930.	16272.	19215.
NEV....	3064.	4409.	6531.	9410.	8329.	7996.	4217.	5886.	6407.
N.H....	6552.	8567.	9471.	23600.	22290.	20356.	4974.	6125.	7589.
N.J....	73287.	83847.	99549.	412168.	466070.	479623.	75499.	98805.	102999.
N.M....	9746.	13881.	11801.	31589.	32176.	30186.	30214.	34264.	40818.
N.Y....	207196.	219774.	268390.	1514512.	1733767.	1780164.	435748.	453470.	467292.
N.C....	33839.	51129.	89760.	118671.	138376.	129234.	147968.	173424.	208563.
N.D....	3905.	8044.	8469.	12177.	14031.	13916.	8327.	8627.	10163.
OHIO...	42227.	109620.	173468.	401149.	449723.	456222.	149579.	165334.	172310.
OKLA...	23119.	29723.	35787.	66007.	73537.	68983.	94460.	94893.	112065.
ORE....	25477.	29810.	29602.	100407.	140264.	159710.	28461.	30570.	30570.
PA.....	132183.	186705.	163923.	602717.	731663.	718221.	155839.	198879.	211706.

(cont.)

NATIONAL SUMMARY DATA -- TABLE EIGHTEEN

HEW PROGRAMS (CONTINUED)

NAME	SOCIAL SERVICES LOW INCOME CFDA# - 13642			PUBLIC ASSISTANCE (STATE AID) CFDA# - 13808			SUPPLEMENTAL SECURITY INCOME CFDA# - 13807		
	1975	1977	1978	1975	1977	1978	1975	1977	1978
STATES (CONT)									
R.I....	10271.	12164.	11637.	43146.	56803.	55038.	12671.	15094.	16442.
S.C....	20205.	30963.	34785.	45696.	50343.	49170.	77985.	97977.	118420.
S.D....	3260.	9968.	8640.	19322.	19242.	16988.	8043.	8999.	9225.
TENN...	18577.	46820.	52533.	84016.	81180.	74054.	141724.	158454.	165735.
TEX....	157192.	149906.	139212.	142376.	126726.	118572.	265505.	304017.	362556.
UTAH...	7757.	16722.	15080.	33159.	39183.	42194.	10893.	10948.	13097.
VER....	5200.	7691.	5892.	24073.	21185.	22347.	8545.	8689.	9228.
VA.....	30714.	58268.	65166.	138582.	140566.	130664.	67217.	90897.	110466.
WASH...	42136.	45161.	43684.	154537.	160410.	183900.	63259.	63269.	62838.
W.VA...	15760.	22435.	25767.	50212.	48954.	53091.	49498.	59547.	71660.
WIS....	60578.	61448.	53828.	190242.	250041.	269924.	35217.	20327.	81325.
WY.....	2419.	3456.	5112.	4396.	5845.	5607.	2607.	2794.	3248.
DIVISIONS									
N.ENG.	136238.	160170.	154865.	704834.	763547.	791935.	151721.	184091.	202345.
M.A...	412666.	490326.	531863.	2529397.	2931500.	2978008.	667086.	751154.	781997.
E.N.C.	285764.	379013.	544034.	2095014.	2309787.	2339556.	506441.	544655.	663413.
W.N.C.	142886.	184906.	221472.	491974.	555613.	553579.	231707.	237676.	273282.
S.A...	355444.	405690.	482111.	838378.	914055.	871440.	773529.	917379.	1035176.
E.S.C.	93852.	140874.	174380.	293694.	329239.	298087.	549925.	589597.	658659.
W.S.C.	210165.	236958.	244823.	355298.	349973.	328538.	606715.	674023.	761265.
MOUNT.	75171.	105023.	124416.	221290.	231752.	221690.	138696.	155215.	183445.
PAC...	329657.	352917.	368262.	1704121.	2192534.	2316167.	610205.	699713.	743342.
REGIONS									
N.E...	548904.	650496.	686727.	3234231.	3695047.	3769943.	818807.	935245.	984342.
N.CT..	428651.	563703.	765506.	2586988.	2865400.	2893135.	738148.	782331.	936695.
SOUTH.	659461.	783522.	901314.	1487370.	1593267.	1498065.	1930168.	2180999.	2455100.
WEST..	404828.	457940.	492678.	1925411.	2424286.	2537857.	748902.	854928.	926787.
NATION	2041845.	2455661.	2846225.	9234000.	10578000.	10699000.	4236025.	4753503.	5302925.

HEW PROGRAMS (CONTINUED)

NAME	MEDICAID CFDA# - 13714			MEDICARE - HOSPITALS CFDA# - 13773			MEDICARE - SUPPLEMENTAL CFDA# - 13774		
	1975	1977	1978	1975	1977	1978	1975	1977	1978
STATES									
ALA...	121823.	156400.	146594.	139034.	210201.	247603.	44116.	72077.	88881.
ALK...	6137.	12891.	11850.	3059.	4554.	6804.	1213.	1765.	1997.
ARZ...	0.	0.	0.	109795.	157409.	187688.	41745.	69573.	82232.
ARK...	82722.	113729.	138386.	82157.	121907.	145336.	30933.	48337.	60495.
CAL...	842739.	1217425.	1361101.	1128703.	1695329.	1971981.	551515.	843484.	958013.
COL...	69877.	70629.	87952.	102949.	144384.	175528.	35084.	55445.	63956.
CONN..	86849.	111719.	128826.	161525.	238893.	266880.	67837.	86491.	99552.
DEL...	8777.	13264.	18801.	21234.	30989.	39213.	7148.	12121.	14751.
D.C...	54901.	87688.	64812.	51306.	80346.	98263.	21294.	45029.	43015.
FLA...	114122.	150471.	159861.	574832.	833447.	1016170.	252616.	453927.	526598.
GA....	198369.	228111.	257440.	159502.	212080.	262356.	61522.	96190.	41322.
HA....	18704.	44232.	43384.	24825.	32350.	42061.	14907.	23476.	29786.
IDA...	20103.	25608.	27634.	25148.	35488.	41809.	9131.	14061.	16110.
ILL...	376879.	519160.	505772.	596697.	907144.	1049006.	166907.	247839.	310813.
IND...	107218.	151059.	157843.	200751.	309930.	343696.	64147.	93374.	1109862.
IOWA..	56134.	94996.	106897.	135230.	181871.	214629.	37953.	55202.	66535.
KAN...	58582.	86115.	82652.	105532.	150612.	177437.	37200.	71811.	83171.
KY....	108317.	143999.	154096.	128188.	168375.	196545.	39398.	63311.	76116.
LA....	119291.	180734.	204561.	124343.	195280.	233359.	40071.	65954.	80653.
MAINE.	52015.	71482.	84602.	48808.	75157.	84049.	16242.	26107.	8813.
MD....	108570.	142821.	153620.	157407.	219062.	291470.	52833.	93690.	116147.
MASS..	275595.	407398.	405314.	443720.	606230.	699364.	135033.	180605.	249913.
MI....	385031.	473863.	522210.	490463.	671123.	772231.	147151.	226073.	277284.
MINN..	157842.	229168.	248613.	219909.	283425.	330771.	54297.	90008.	105325.
MISS..	81164.	116354.	146614.	88126.	128121.	156029.	23045.	65739.	71749.
MO....	58791.	120786.	137298.	275320.	409958.	518992.	85761.	107401.	122705.
MONT..	23748.	31163.	36007.	25375.	37719.	45091.	10282.	15672.	19089.
NEB...	37787.	43855.	55292.	72295.	99870.	113786.	31582.	32372.	37442.
NEV...	9209.	10728.	15405.	23251.	46189.	52627.	8059.	15077.	17923.
N.H...	20992.	31064.	35983.	30551.	41919.	49455.	11202.	16018.	19833.
N.J...	205165.	252430.	296676.	325266.	484559.	555068.	144934.	193721.	386239.
N.M...	26886.	38964.	39135.	29551.	44387.	50915.	12597.	21383.	27478.
N.Y...	1434719.	1587462.	1713331.	1306389.	1691143.	1903407.	465669.	716674.	815112.
N.C...	134172.	185823.	226227.	174845.	254028.	313154.	61303.	94326.	34314.
N.D...	17075.	22671.	20852.	33689.	51864.	59712.	10864.	159910.	28549.
OHIO..	220429.	311469.	359131.	466198.	722710.	840637.	131505.	232782.	242206.
OKLA..	105927.	142978.	164060.	110901.	163943.	196149.	43001.	64110.	70923.
ORE...	55837.	95224.	97979.	103897.	139591.	180570.	43050.	66980.	74722.
PA....	351138.	564272.	612271.	607297.	838371.	1014487.	225144.	324897.	382310.

(cont.)

NATIONAL SUMMARY DATA -- TABLE NINETEEN

HEW PROGRAMS (CONTINUED)

NAME	MEDICAID CFDA# - 13714			MEDICARE - HOSPITALS CFDA# - 13773			MEDICARE - SUPPLEMENTAL CFDA# - 13774		
	1975	1977	1978	1975	1977	1978	1975	1977	1978
STATES (CONT)									
R.I...	44380.	66800.	68101.	62874.	86056.	94102.	22396.	32651.	38230.
S.C...	65223.	115015.	128954.	70659.	100643.	119516.	23381.	39482.	46543.
S.D...	18313.	24726.	29663.	29909.	38035.	45344.	8497.	12833.	3308.
TENN..	110244.	167026.	203744.	172497.	269685.	324528.	56981.	90096.	105779.
TEX...	323889.	482826.	522433.	455487.	708731.	810811.	196767.	295533.	352501.
UTAH..	26374.	40306.	53267.	29930.	38044.	50968.	13673.	18540.	23697.
VER...	23181.	33639.	35142.	25494.	34720.	39043.	7471.	10600.	12357.
VA....	135088.	152858.	165084.	162906.	223794.	269841.	38721.	81135.	105037.
WASH..	101212.	145684.	135082.	142337.	202580.	238114.	56325.	82227.	105582.
W.VA..	26086.	44403.	64757.	73443.	112244.	68696.	31512.	46537.	44947.
WIS...	255974.	343277.	309407.	232222.	331081.	375930.	69205.	105559.	122426.
WY....	3429.	5663.	5911.	11272.	12510.	15029.	3325.	4939.	5744.
DIVISIONS									
N.ENG.	505011.	722102.	757968.	772972.	1082974.	1232893.	260181.	352472.	428699.
M.A.C.	1991022.	2404165.	2622278.	2238952.	3014072.	3472962.	835746.	1235292.	1583662.
E.N.C.	1345531.	1798827.	1854363.	1986332.	2941988.	3381501.	578914.	905627.	1062592.
W.N.C.	404525.	622316.	678267.	871973.	1215635.	1460671.	266155.	385534.	447035.
S.A.C.	845308.	1120455.	1239465.	1446135.	2066632.	2478679.	550332.	962437.	972674.
E.S.C.	421548.	583780.	651048.	527845.	776381.	924705.	163540.	291222.	342524.
W.S.C.	631830.	920267.	1029441.	722887.	1189861.	1385655.	310851.	473935.	564572.
MOUNT.	179626.	223061.	265311.	357272.	516129.	619656.	133896.	214689.	256227.
PAC...	1024630.	1515456.	1649695.	1402821.	2074403.	2439529.	667010.	1023932.	1170101.
REGIONS									
N.E...	2496033.	3126267.	3380246.	3011923.	4097047.	4705855.	1095927.	1587764.	2012361.
N.CT..	1750057.	2421143.	2532630.	2858305.	4157623.	4842172.	845070.	1291161.	1509627.
SOUTH.	1898686.	2624056.	2919954.	2746867.	4032875.	4789039.	1024723.	1727594.	1879770.
WEST..	1204256.	1738517.	1915006.	1760093.	2590532.	3059185.	800905.	1238622.	1426328.
NATION	7349032.	9910429.	10747835.	10377190.	14878077.	17396251.	3766626.	5845141.	6828087.

NATIONAL SUMMARY DATA -- TABLE TWENTY

HEW PROGRAMS (CONTINUED)

NAME	SSA - DISABILITY CFDA# - 13802			SSA - RETIREMENT CFDA# - 13803			SSA - SURVIVORS CFDA# - 13805		
	1975	1977	1978	1975	1977	1778	1975	1977	1978
STATES									
ALA...	160418.	224271.	242307.	551620.	722109.	802293.	264219.	354706.	395726.
ALK...	4510.	5851.	7013.	16372.	21638.	25553.	10126.	13628.	15920.
ARZ...	80446.	124598.	144919.	425978.	587108.	687108.	128975.	178816.	207603.
ARK...	112012.	161856.	176236.	395220.	511098.	573829.	141311.	192508.	217515.
CAL...	829532.	1191291.	1275491.	3843935.	4971308.	5479906.	1203863.	1602553.	1762819.
COL...	62374.	93189.	107265.	363920.	474566.	528561.	134131.	181657.	203777.
CONN..	88669.	126191.	134760.	666394.	871900.	962515.	202382.	266586.	288472.
DEL...	18514.	26750.	29653.	99545.	130346.	147209.	38751.	51599.	56611.
D.C...	24957.	34531.	36654.	130592.	164016.	179094.	51457.	66676.	71098.
FLA...	339490.	514330.	605322.	2372626.	3167338.	3577151.	598118.	825768.	941131.
GA....	207061.	309122.	340003.	641022.	843259.	949234.	297934.	401131.	447056.
HA....	18351.	25715.	29224.	118116.	159659.	185063.	34285.	46560.	52665.
IDA...	26675.	37445.	38296.	148575.	191790.	215401.	47996.	64118.	71066.
ILL...	321896.	457528.	488385.	2168688.	2769019.	2988755.	773616.	1015368.	1101676.
IND...	183496.	265345.	279649.	1036541.	1324804.	1438479.	374648.	495256.	540692.
IOWA..	82807.	112100.	117138.	646788.	817647.	879235.	211874.	278576.	304647.
KAN...	56535.	79728.	86795.	491673.	626755.	677320.	158062.	208217.	226738.
KY....	154185.	221449.	240258.	559697.	706754.	766832.	242060.	342105.	358226.
LA....	164048.	235610.	253771.	472287.	617192.	681591.	253465.	341978.	383924.
MAINE.	40035.	56920.	61441.	230664.	290792.	318472.	73889.	97819.	107270.
MD....	100628.	143904.	161459.	569094.	741904.	824029.	228982.	303516.	333615.
MASS..	169597.	242166.	263167.	1256601.	1595346.	1726312.	393328.	512593.	552300.
MI....	359009.	519496.	540757.	1696653.	2147659.	2304914.	655586.	864008.	940900.
MINN..	94036.	131455.	139295.	779803.	988600.	1074910.	247850.	328544.	360298.
MISS..	107093.	157285.	168061.	336788.	435673.	481508.	152648.	204786.	227658.
MO....	182020.	256676.	277375.	1039503.	1318268.	1422513.	348196.	461343.	503163.
MONT..	25604.	34451.	38188.	137171.	175745.	192377.	50232.	65913.	72585.
NEB...	34803.	49303.	53202.	329740.	419422.	451956.	102661.	135876.	149423.
NEV...	19570.	30258.	35899.	84588.	119203.	143921.	29700.	41576.	48709.
N.H...	23183.	34150.	39028.	182412.	236468.	261853.	52176.	68833.	75213.
N.J...	256639.	377310.	416600.	1537422.	1995667.	2188900.	518999.	677209.	734520.
N.M...	41075.	60263.	64640.	151962.	202127.	229619.	62150.	84451.	95709.
N.Y...	637829.	941538.	1053549.	4071408.	5141212.	5508694.	1267870.	1642664.	1765716.
N.C...	209140.	311300.	338637.	803217.	1056135.	1194541.	334416.	450216.	499701.
N.D...	14016.	18366.	19807.	123517.	158521.	168700.	41637.	55241.	61322.
OHIO..	393555.	575895.	608266.	1950798.	2472436.	2674719.	791331.	1042992.	1131727.
OKLA..	110545.	157247.	164260.	522895.	669396.	732852.	184120.	247631.	277026.
ORE...	92715.	128586.	133900.	519445.	668196.	742665.	146555.	193261.	214246.
PA....	448470.	645498.	702753.	2595684.	3323042.	3646481.	967089.	1267275.	1375651.

(cont.)

NATIONAL SUMMARY DATA -- TABLE TWENTY

HEW PROGRAMS (CONTINUED)

NAME	SSA - DISABILITY CFDA# - 13802			SSA - RETIREMENT CFDA# - 13803			SSA - SURVIVORS CFDA# - 13805		
	1975	1977	1978	1975	1977	1778	1975	1977	1978
STATES (CONT)									
R.I....	36244.	50327.	54935.	222486.	285088.	310422.	64445.	84579.	91663.
S.C....	117513.	171087.	189498.	365216.	486443.	555404.	174301.	235164.	261656.
S.D....	16790.	23851.	25099.	141285.	176650.	191526.	47779.	62859.	69261.
TENN...	182700.	262926.	287023.	674969.	876656.	975036.	274017.	368823.	411520.
TEX....	362182.	514660.	567763.	1796256.	2347515.	2596628.	743440.	1008277.	1135796.
UTAH...	27301.	38648.	40514.	171217.	223557.	250687.	60164.	79675.	88436.
VER....	15857.	23105.	25712.	96668.	123528.	135650.	31667.	42454.	46281.
VA.....	163214.	232149.	261455.	685970.	897629.	1006232.	290859.	390417.	434247.
WASH...	125444.	181036.	191302.	728795.	935454.	1041398.	221045.	291716.	324648.
W.VA...	134441.	176894.	181203.	350360.	440347.	477482.	166868.	221873.	242976.
WIS....	140995.	200078.	213308.	1003115.	1280493.	1398956.	319895.	421926.	459664.
WY.....	8250.	11113.	12009.	60518.	77285.	84474.	21191.	28528.	32026.
DIVISIONS									
N.ENG.	373586.	532858.	579043.	2655225.	3403123.	3715224.	817887.	1072864.	1161199.
M.A.C.	1342938.	1964346.	2172902.	8204514.	10459921.	11344075.	2753958.	3587148.	3875886.
E.N.C.	1398951.	2018343.	2130365.	7855795.	9999411.	10829823.	2915076.	3839550.	4174709.
W.N.C.	481007.	671478.	718711.	3552309.	4505872.	4866160.	1158058.	1530656.	1674851.
S.A.C.	1314956.	1920067.	2143885.	6017642.	7927418.	8910376.	2181688.	2946361.	3283092.
E.S.C.	604396.	865931.	937649.	2123073.	2741191.	3025669.	932944.	1252419.	1393130.
W.S.C.	748786.	1069372.	1162029.	3191658.	4145161.	4584899.	1322337.	1790394.	2014261.
MOUNT.	291295.	429964.	481730.	1543929.	2051380.	2332142.	534539.	724733.	819910.
PAC...	1070553.	1532479.	1636931.	5226663.	6756215.	7474585.	1615875.	2147718.	2370298.
REGIONS									
N.E...	1716524.	2497204.	2751945.	10859739.	13863044.	15059298.	3571845.	4660012.	5037085.
N.CT..	1879958.	2689821.	2849076.	11408104.	14500283.	15695982.	4073134.	5370205.	5849560.
SOUTH.	2668137.	3855370.	4243563.	11332373.	14813770.	16520944.	4436968.	5989174.	6695482.
WEST..	1361847.	1962443.	2118661.	6770592.	8807595.	9806727.	2150413.	2872451.	3190208.
NATION	7626467.	11004838.	11963245.	40370808.	51984692.	57082952.	14232360.	18891842.	20772336.

267

NATIONAL SUMMARY DATA -- TABLE TWENTY-ONE

| | NEW PROGRAMS | | | HUD PROGRAMS | | | | |
| | COMMUNITY HEALTH CFDA# - 13224 | | | CDBG CFDA# - 14218 | | | CDBG DISCRETIONARY CFDA# - 14219 | |
NAME	1975	1977	1978	1975	1977	1978	1977	1978
STATES								
ALA....	2022.	3535.	5835.	34507.	40375.	37756.	10927.	5583.
ALK....	2965.	450.	434.	4417.	3527.	2172.	1854.	0.
ARZ....	2427.	2566.	3034.	10447.	19215.	22785.	3517.	3318.
ARK....	1911.	2259.	2678.	16495.	23340.	17173.	15852.	5565.
CAL....	23585.	20101.	25134.	179854.	298779.	297773.	10119.	7939.
COL....	6997.	9652.	12040.	23761.	24999.	21920.	4647.	1810.
CONN..	650.	1396.	1483.	65599.	63396.	49083.	2525.	2100.
DEL....		442.	540.	5247.	6721.	6562.	722.	147.
D.C....	4933.	3925.	5607.	33276.	40998.	32575.	0.	0.
FLA....	4247.	6690.	8568.	50918.	94756.	93435.	5701.	6716.
GA....	4146.	5542.	4600.	48763.	52190.	41692.	18194.	2989.
HA....	1293.	1878.	2447.	14418.	12684.	12385.	190.	0.
IDA....	0.	357.	1031.	7143.	6788.	622.	3476.	8874.
ILL....	7508.	5197.	8455.	66459.	88007.	39682.	6518.	8313.
IND....	580.	1620.	1018.	38933.	38420.	40939.	12673.	3088.
IOWA..	400.	552.	1320.	20883.	22712.	27077.	8600.	2033.
KAN....	400.	77.	100.	30885.	31345.	23343.	5416.	17151.
KY....	5847.	5111.	7157.	20948.	24947.	29891.	4409.	12027.
LA....	450.	937.	972.	23953.	39094.	23216.	4368.	2064.
MAINE.	1238.	1517.	1667.	12048.	10820.	7799.	4287.	5693.
MD....	5019.	4954.	6839.	39681.	48553.	43822.	4959.	36100.
MASS..	5693.	4362.	5338.	93220.	95870.	90862.	8372.	55233.
MI....	3798.	4287.	5189.	85448.	101776.	118522.	12555.	2290.
MINN..	2118.	3374.	2821.	44519.	48799.	45435.	11091.	1218.
MISS..	6787.	7822.	8198.	19819.	22013.	17423.	15373.	3723.
MO....	7686.	7784.	8925.	47797.	52428.	96957.	9998.	603.
MONT.	151.	197.	578.	5488.	6314.	4167.	2465.	965.
NEB..	20.	360.	94.	3553.	8690.	8326.	4107.	1267.
NEV..	45.	375.	634.	801.	3141.	3061.	429.	952.
N.H..	2154.	70.	151.	5848.	5670.	5106.	1943.	19666.
N.J..	3180.	3005.	3516.	70188.	98761.	98565.	4757.	56683.
N.M..		3075.	3617.	18821.	16641.	11395.	4562.	12627.
N.Y..	26093.	25239.	29297.	216155.	149766.	362754.	20650.	2974.
N.C..	4790.	6022.	6468.	48209.	48290.	37112.	22801.	270.
N.D..				5113.	5145.	3754.	3757.	
OHIO.	10784.	11798.	8389.	96626.	117473.	128559.	10524.	8492.
OKLA.	3183.	2852.	3084.	33621.	32177.	18561.	9441.	4849.
ORE..	2844.	2566.	3015.	13425.	13419.	17222.	5764.	2303.
PA...	8452.	8489.	10940.	162048.	196734.	200283.	17345.	16061.

(cont.)

NATIONAL SUMMARY DATA -- TABLE TWENTY-ONE

NAME	HEW PROGRAMS COMMUNITY HEALTH CFDA# - 13224			HUD PROGRAMS CDBG CFDA# - 14218			HUD PROGRAMS CDBG DISCRETIONARY CFDA# - 14219	
	1975	1977	1978	1975	1977	1978	1977	1978
STATES (CONT)								
R.I...:	1700.	1500.	1741.	20275.	19587.	16708.	809.	750.
S.C...:	7589.	8590.	9273.	15205.	15567.	15848.	10709.	6934.
S.D...:	289.	552.	572.	5687.	5687.	3911.	3385.	824.
TENN..:	7101.	6210.	8037.	41099.	53242.	53033.	9397.	4072.
TEX...:	4967.	5883.	9377.	97918.	151260.	157931.	28796.	13188.
UTAH..:	2387.	2399.	2310.	5320.	10519.	12461.	1498.	788.
VER...:	40.	471.	523.	2202.	1665.	1586.	2179.	743.
VA....:	1600.	2382.	2623.	48905.	53081.	46706.	24608.	3981.
WASH..:	3279.	3213.	4645.	18406.	28901.	38044.	16769.	1724.
W.VA..:	4432.	4374.	5593.	7581.	8251.	11233.	15304.	4247.
WIS...:	477.	1751.	1977.	22962.	28240.	37871.	8700.	2401.
WY....:	273.	0.	195.	2657.	2358.	1378.	1004.	350.
DIVISIONS								
N.ENG.:	9366.	9317.	10903.	199192.	197008.	171144.	20115.	42709.
M.A...:	36699.	36733.	43753.	448391.	445261.	661602.	42753.	48354.
E.N.C.:	23147.	24653.	250027.	310428.	373916.	365573.	50970.	33312.
W.N.C.:	10912.	12699.	138832.	158437.	174806.	208803.	46355.	13193.
S.A...:	36755.	42922.	501110.	297785.	368407.	328985.	102998.	33680.
E.S.C.:	21756.	22677.	29227.	116373.	140577.	138103.	40105.	28025.
W.S.C.:	10511.	11930.	16111.	171987.	245871.	216881.	58457.	35630.
MOUNT.:	15414.	18622.	23439.	74438.	89975.	77789.	21597.	13818.
PAC...:	33965.	28208.	35674.	230520.	357310.	367596.	34696.	11967.
REGIONS								
N.E...:	46065.	46050.	54656.	647583.	642269.	832746.	62868.	91063.
N.CT..:	34059.	37352.	38860.	468865.	548722.	574376.	97368.	46505.
SOUTH.:	69022.	77529.	95448.	586145.	754855.	683969.	201559.	97335.
WEST..:	49380.	46830.	59114.	304958.	447285.	445385.	56293.	25785.
NATION	198526.	207761.	248078.	2007551.	2393131.	2536476.	418044.	260688.

HUD PROGRAMS (CONTINUED)

NAME	SECTION 8 HOUSING CFDA# - 14156			MORTGAGE INSURANCE REGULAR HOMES CFDA# - 14117			MORTGAGE INSURANCE LOW/MOD. INCOME CFDA# - 14137		
	1975	1977	1978	1975	1977	1978	1975	1977	1978
STATES									
ALA.	0	12372	30935	84325	187521	178527	9969	30781	41769
ALK.	0	0	0	9570	4559	11957	0	5100	0
ARZ.	0	10878	21387	194199	389363	529139	0	6561	1461
ARK.	1372	12491	19857	21056	41317	45753	0	3942	6177
CAL.	21716	194137	333202	855703	1569707	1610067	21052	202759	241536
COL.	2594	13481	25814	91614	312102	315098	1026	16926	23400
CONN.	1248	26522	50864	25783	8300	27584	3290	8896	15681
DEL.	0	3895	6605	11022	14209	11124	0		3320
D.C.	0	7879	16967	10494	4026	6871	0	5810	28705
FLA.	5979	48719	80486	307307	410953	502934	13526	10320	12383
GA.	732	36467	64837	94054	207077	299678	5257	20136	23693
HA.	0			17302	9660	19126	0	16586	6843
IDA.	0	6193	10127	13682	48989	63556	0	9570	0
ILL.	5923	66105	142754	185390	98933	100647	8880	51056	69055
IND.	791	20432	47501	59267	117659	104041	3153	48989	66765
IOWA.	2944	16932	30015	15385	20169	31401	8503	29858	24298
KAN.	718	12071	23423	14830	23800	22572	3994	20613	34447
KY.	3234	21556	52478	41310	89257	103690		40819	47462
LA.	1901	20179	36252	58246	126249	131183		13254	38183
MAINE.	1686	14546	23172	1875	6920	6529		6153	1204
MD.	1282	24141	63637	104169	54204	119330	2003	62514	65653
MASS.	12133	84640	145129	15847	26973	26972	8980	71602	66734
MI.	2649	26954	79156	129821	77002	69472		51947	72978
MINN.	2640	34358	83031	153193	295963	393547	19960	22471	37681
MISS.	275	10976	27725	34537	84209	90482	17116	11719	4550
MO.	3056	34469	58006	39923	100554	72341	6619	49444	59304
MONT.	772	3928	6285	9080	37420	68745	3420	9423	7316
NEB.	678	9044	16336	15005	25710	35590	746	5240	4640
NEV.	0	3836	8028	56708	194129	260716	0	25650	69573
N.H.	361	6008	12801	76	297	46	0	3952	930
N.J.	0	51532	144704	125887	123889	141300	0	31126	54907
N.M.	1721	6086	12948	27298	83857	95464	5165	12808	6176
N.Y.	1436	138215	323788	162316	305596	299177	6407	12919	241978
N.C.	530	30867	54001	59901	106149	108070	8238	3641	26616
N.D.	580	4121	7602	1643	25974	41563		4301	4359
OHIO.	1711	75936	136299	140539	220110	263512	4793	87826	64385
OKLA.	2293	14842	23283	85215	155411	154509	0	2705	8301
ORE.	1698	17684	29404	31353	37771	51368	0	7123	4749
PA.	2486	67774	155476	60693	54071	62157	431	42604	61742

(cont.)

NATIONAL SUMMARY DATA -- TABLE TWENTY-TWO

HUD PROGRAMS (CONTINUED)

NAME	SECTION 8 HOUSING CFDA# - 14156			MORTGAGE INSURANCE REGULAR HOMES CFDA# - 14117			MORTGAGE INSURANCE LOW/MOD. INCOME CFDA# - 14137		
	1975	1977	1978	1975	1977	1978	1975	1977	1978
STATES (CONT)									
R.I...	525.	9800.	36949.	525.	335.	295.	648.	5930.	6498.
S.C...	90.	12247.	26439.	38244.	88053.	105899.	3059.	25199.	31144.
S.D...	393.	1796.	6199.	4552.	28836.	47466.	1216.		2445.
TENN..	1035.	29091.	57756.	66802.	201501.	254364.	8462.	41119.	47036.
TEX...	15428.	65834.	124943.	270129.	530766.	493034.	2038.	47766.	47305.
UTAH..	796.	3602.	6742.	53715.	151319.	178199.	427.	0.	0.
VER...	37.	2763.	6540.	1715.	104.	99.	0.	0.	0.
VA....	0.	32577.	69776.	47140.	111397.	188774.	7766.	55420.	68272.
WASH..	1600.	24281.	34901.	165598.	190096.	177519.	1361.	18665.	17348.
W.VA..	0.	15127.	28721.	8624.	1989.	5335.	0.	12877.	18852.
WIS...	747.	27133.	75816.	12971.	16861.	26509.	5528.	29636.	56571.
WY....	112.	1209.	2023.	5468.	11703.	16166.	0.	4896.	1717.
DIVISIONS									
N.ENG.	15990.	144278.	275455.	45821.	42930.	61525.	5941.	96532.	91046.
M.A.+.	3922.	257520.	623968.	348896.	483555.	502634.	6407.	86649.	358627.
E.N.C.	12821.	216560.	481526.	527988.	530565.	564180.	42314.	269454.	329755.
W.N.C.	11010.	112791.	224612.	244531.	521006.	644480.	34249.	131928.	167173.
S.A...	8614.	211918.	411469.	680955.	998057.	1348015.	46826.	195918.	278637.
E.S.C.	4543.	73995.	166894.	226974.	562488.	627063.	25050.	124438.	140818.
W.S.C.	20993.	113346.	204335.	434646.	853744.	824479.	2038.	67666.	99965.
MOUNT.	5996.	49214.	93352.	451764.	1228881.	1527083.	7364.	85834.	109642.
PAC...	25013.	236102.	397507.	1079526.	1811792.	1870037.	22844.	250232.	270477.
REGIONS									
N.E...	19912.	401798.	899423.	394717.	526485.	564159.	12348.	183181.	449674.
N.CT..	23831.	329351.	706139.	772519.	1051571.	1208660.	76563.	401381.	496928.
SOUTH.	34151.	399260.	782698.	1342589.	2414289.	2799556.	73914.	388021.	519420.
WEST..	31009.	285316.	490859.	1531290.	3040673.	3397121.	30208.	336067.	380119.
NATION	108902.	1415725.	2879118.	4041101.	7033018.	7969496.	193033.	1308651.	1846140.

NATIONAL SUMMARY DATA -- TABLE TWENTY-THREE

| | HUD PROGRAMS (CONTINUED) | | | | | | JUSTICE PROGRAMS | | | | | |
| | PROPERTY IMPROV. LOAN INSURANCE CFDA# - 14142 | | | OTHER HUD LOANS | | | LAW ENFORCEMENT PROJECT GRANTS CFDA# - 16501 | | | LAW ENFORCEMENT BLOCK GRANTS CFDA# - 16502 | | |
NAME	1975	1977	1978	1975	1977	1978	1975	1977	1978	1975	1977	1978
STATES												
ALA...	3477	7597	8455	100689	19981	249583	1291	2583	2134	9816	7682	7034
ALK...	549	1145	1678	10119	416	14506	1188	1303	773	1293	1153	1155
ARZ...	2249	5058	5744	196823	113834	656111	4033	2510	2571	5795	4717	4395
ARK...	12841	20147	20872	34037	15798	87152	1539	482	2927	5766	4535	4188
CAL...	21352	44313	46511	980328	491678	2300270	15152	10686	27250	156804	43156	39451
COL...	4013	5173	5971	105434	51632	394641	11933	5396	3828	6478	5391	4990
CONN.	2297	2450	3757	42907	20496	70718	1938	1340	4866	8865	6615	5976
DEL..	304	441	540	13975	7796	19013	595	1160	1929	1540	1540	1401
D.C..	5060	8266	8053	15554	11886	55669	14664	16171	32893	2466	629	1607
FLA..	28332	40254	39154	369734	97661	722088	3852	3510	5885	19704	16605	15396
GA...	2808	5640	12321	105432	65567	499198	8937	1338	3013	13354	10354	9533
HA...	5595	6868	7411	29157	17086	38400	604	326	569	2265	2051	1879
IDA..	2418	7598	6951	19076	7144	86519	578	389	297	2474	1919	1791
ILL..	60179	73210	76122	280375	51212	297402	12328	6501	15000	30867	23355	21096
IND..	12162	18476	19313	84966	46538	217213	1296	2106	1268	14191	11264	10200
IOWA.	10990	17101	21363	34878	34118	210859	1231	666	1146	8140	6154	5578
KAN..	12620	22449	23146	42787	14118	92424	1115	548	903	6071	4428	4456
KY...	11880	23069	26815	59079	50434	202540	2586	662	1772	8818	7196	6582
LA...	4447	8115	10837	62693	20363	207101	2757	660	2200	10675	8135	7476
MAINE	1732	2885	3285	11200	16275	16275	653	598	1123	3289	2412	2227
MD...	11072	16325	17426	133818	68315	285544	13032	7961	9174	11428	8728	7927
MASS.	23613	28289	30080	51029	204377	158902	5837	9451	16004	16316	12208	10986
MI...	64327	97065	113297	235744	257775	474703	5423	3618	4919	25283	19235	17397
MINN.	47151	116209	136186	223984	23391	607232	2414	1229	3986	11057	8388	7593
MISS.	3450	5899	6904	49920	28548	124750	404	795	1683	6382	4555	4715
MO...	26769	53967	59949	91843	39396	231728	5250	3429	6075	13417	10101	9075
MONT.	3034	4943	5380	17362	2099	87799	715	1060	736	2368	1834	1691
NEB..	5741	7951	11122	56882	15047	67929	248	231	502	4291	3092	2600
NEV..	174	1663	2496	70746	42155	380471	2234	2134	1784	1428	1334	1766
N.H..	3221	4133	5075	3297	5363	6053	689	867	8993	2497	1966	1766
N.J..	18060	26192	33629	170099	86703	312590	11492	3721	1108	20642	15064	13824
N.M..	2199	4748	4693	34662	20930	129649	1520	708	2037	3326	2606	2480
N.Y..	61224	79275	79485	266913	322252	970662	14899	9780	26039	50999	37489	33649
N.C..	4502	6088	7309	80403	27776	188404	741	662	2857	14550	10164	10401
N.D..	5715	12095	13292	7358	6945	65144	303	163	352	1963	1423	1233
OHIO.	33833	38744	44500	200139	61633	438341	4914	1299	6254	30054	22534	20298
OKLA.	5634	9241	9043	90849	64781	237657	3689	355	1348	7340	5220	4383
ORE..	5655	10566	13476	37439	22799	88924	3610	1818	1800	6404	4801	4500
PA...	50757	66876	75434	149117	73268	302709	7453	2352	6060	33318	24652	22141

NATIONAL SUMMARY DATA -- TABLE TWENTY-THREE

| | HUD PROGRAMS (CONTINUED) | | | | | | JUSTICE PROGRAMS | | | | | |
| | PROPERTY IMPROV. LOAN INSURANCE CFDA# - 14142 | | | OTHER HUD LOANS | | | LAW ENFORCEMENT PROJECT GRANTS CFDA# - 16501 | | | LAW ENFORCEMENT BLOCK GRANTS CFDA# - 16502 | | |
NAME	1975	1977	1978	1975	1977	1978	1975	1977	1978	1975	1977	1978
STATES (CONT)												
R.I...	78.	962.	721.	11662.	12273.	11219.	243.	547.	793.	2859.	2205.	1966.
S.C...	2841.	6480.	6551.	47505.	27811.	183266.	963.	673.	1051.	7788.	5998.	5566.
S.D...	3950.	5906.	7202.	12011.	4096.	61442.	631.	319.	1394.	2010.	1562.	1214.
TENN...	8793.	13723.	13896.	89341.	67550.	394158.	210.	1144.	2647.	11442.	8777.	8012.
TEX...	36405.	78931.	98650.	309363.	248363.	895825.	3492.	2507.	4891.	31987.	25076.	23249.
UTAH...	2384.	4122.	3259.	57150.	35163.	215755.	1123.	690.	1629.	3298.	2450.	25519.
VER...	1620.	2118.	2347.	3335.	744.	2473.	539.	454.	1183.	1660.	1338.	1257.
VA...	5203.	7563.	9092.	76814.	49855.	3291156.	10238.	5539.	12038.	13295.	10379.	9507.
WASH...	6727.	15536.	16382.	176707.	108560.	2996660.	923.	2076.	7067.	9792.	7485.	6874.
W.VA...	6727.	10558.	12758.	15351.	7646.	38494.	3.	8.	136.	5134.	3540.	3585.
WIS...	4773.	7414.	8698.	45182.	11617.	98345.	2338.	1812.	3584.	12841.	9741.	8869.
WY...	667.	1753.	2293.	6135.	1932.	23708.	639.	389.	302.	1131.	920.	887.
DIVISIONS												
N.ENG.	32561.	40837.	45265.	123430.	243405.	265641.	9898.	13258.	25754.	35485.	26744.	24178.
M.A...	130041.	172343.	188548.	586129.	482224.	1585960.	33844.	15853.	41092.	104959.	77205.	69614.
E.N.C.	175274.	234909.	261929.	846406.	428775.	1526005.	26299.	15336.	31026.	113236.	86129.	77860.
W.N.C.	112936.	235677.	272260.	483607.	114180.	1206759.	10882.	6584.	14359.	46948.	35148.	31749.
S.A...	66849.	101615.	113204.	858586.	364311.	2320830.	53026.	37022.	69002.	89649.	67937.	64923.
E.S.C.	27600.	50289.	56070.	299029.	166514.	971030.	4501.	5184.	8235.	36459.	28210.	26343.
W.S.C.	59327.	116433.	139402.	496942.	349304.	1427734.	11477.	4003.	11366.	55768.	42966.	39296.
MOUNT.	17138.	35058.	36788.	493524.	274888.	1974655.	22773.	13276.	11903.	26548.	21171.	19915.
PAC...	39898.	78428.	85459.	1233750.	640539.	2741760.	21477.	16210.	37460.	76558.	58646.	53859.
REGIONS												
N.E...	162602.	213180.	233814.	709559.	725629.	1851601.	43742.	29110.	66846.	140444.	103949.	93792.
N.CT...	288210.	470587.	534189.	1330013.	542955.	2732764.	37181.	21920.	45385.	160184.	121278.	109609.
SOUTH..	153776.	268337.	308676.	1654557.	880129.	4719595.	69003.	46209.	88604.	181876.	139113.	130562.
WEST...	57036.	113486.	122247.	1727274.	915427.	4716415.	44251.	29486.	49363.	103107.	79816.	73774.
NATION	661624.	1065590.	1198925.	5421403.	3064139.	14020375.	194177.	126726.	250197.	585611.	444156.	407737.

NATIONAL SUMMARY DATA -- TABLE TWENTY-FOUR

NAME	LABOR PROGRAMS — CETA CFDA# - 17232			UNEMPLOYMENT INSURANCE CFDA# - 17225			SMALL BUSINESS ADMINISTRATION PROGRAMS — PHYSICAL DISASTER LOANS CFDA# - 59008			SMALL BUSINESS LOANS CFDA# - 59012		
	1975	1977	1978	1975	1977	1978	1975	1977	1978	1975	1977	1978
STATES												
ALA.	49242	139383	34301	20115	10923	11361	3891	1137	119618	12799	28521	33219
ALK.	17166	22487	4014	9525	9103	9085	3957	12	0	14035	16692	16385
ARZ.	50256	81201	84790	17017	11317	10371	261	149	9609	14949	21388	21009
ARK.	33721	89662	30934	14746	7366	7768	3914	130	8031	8534	19561	17435
CAL.	468160	899147	642833	229405	122713	118957	16746	13546	207551	140046	185900	188872
COL.	24961	79879	29703	11182	10967	10457	6379	3942	665	32899	62432	60958
CONN.	58625	106884	116912	13630	15395	16171	1293	3213	7144	22263	27973	32991
DEL.	8755	31843	5697	3830	2945	2895		145	0	559	2158	4868
D.C.	121814	95687	40643	32520	5203	5097	12	0	0	5275	5854	8828
FLA.	115573	388492	172675	31293	21775	21278	4748	8973	65002	34911	74438	71435
GA.	68579	226949	67853	29333	11167	12689	7268	19092	408540	22266	73572	91973
HA.	18859	30543	29533	11803	5865	5194	1223	0	428	7070	9763	11302
IDA.	12850	35487	8425	17735	5053	5323	1367	3759	14760	10487	25086	34348
ILL.	159314	339738	224633	56408	48749	43583	5071	1149	1101	56217	51335	85161
IND.	128563	165456	100156	23971	14292	14145	8763	0	10667	44524	64681	45359
IOWA.	23521	34256	41213	11750	7665	8113	2675	52	0	37620	78749	87540
KAN.	19084	38959	23165	10575	5458	5787	5592	340	340514	54228	73895	85716
KY.	76050	99249	74226	19250	7219	9222	5677	43087	46768	15004	28221	32374
LA.	75597	135267	56466	21930	12547	13161	7661	6630	8843	37051	78428	66768
MAINE.	21336	33598	41905	9165	5128	4971	6065	275	67659	13909	31994	31861
MD.	47200	161155	38371	18914	13931	17440	2425	5239	14790	19382	32700	37356
MASS.	144459	293954	167951	55084	28536	28782	5352	222	222	43964	48720	51541
MI.	225952	567258	120234	76993	45603	46929	4418	101331	101331	29169	71078	81851
MINN.	64640	161692	41209	18774	12811	12532	4472	1163	21000	34759	42493	45470
MISS.	36388	94447	44299	11038	6556	6648	442	2530	9294	13257	31151	43129
MO.	64758	104365	115209	29115	17552	17459	5421		107936	32743	74243	88304
MONT.	20704	34820	13570	6927	4048	4249	5925	2704	75556	13126	38469	43741
NEB.	17838	29654	16091	6175	5116	4713	213	1025	1020	19672	35657	43257
NEV.	14752	18401	26099	9566	5693	6366	2480	868	40028	4498	6651	12695
N.H.	7988	14456	24728	6887	3348	3260	222			22009	39557	38555
N.J.	148806	265877	276814	66034	52485	41328	4064	95	4614	35263	68045	45826
N.M.	28655	59122	12870	9281	4227	4109	6673	9166	22235	15598	23172	31360
N.Y.	357545	596753	656220	133272	82813	97066	11452	49247	97091	112798	162398	163330
N.C.	79272	218541	58069	25884	15089	15298	661	315		11013	18564	13564
N.D.	11368	21090	5148	5060	2832	3009	1780	163	59101	12957	20692	19102
OHIO.	147304	470360	168382	50786	34273	32872	38	11	568	32456	62047	60011
OKLA.	45928	79707	33233	20911	7854	7053	17951	225	565	17562	27240	34759
ORE.	40687	157512	24614	19111	14548	14178	8846	5	117	15072	24398	29550
PA.	180271	567404	123989	83677	61647	62688	7068	15187	56607	34506	46972	59120

274

(cont.)

NAME	LABOR PROGRAMS						SMALL BUSINESS ADMINISTRATION PROGRAMS					
	CETA CFDA# - 17232			UNEMPLOYMENT INSURANCE CFDA# - 17225			PHYSICAL DISASTER LOANS CFDA# - 59008			SMALL BUSINESS LOANS CFDA# - 59012		
	1975	1977	1978	1975	1977	1978	1975	1977	1978	1975	1977	1978
STATES (CONT)												
R.I...	22172.	37790.	35201.	19310.	7011.	7957.	8779.	1335.	11843.	13223.	22067.	25297.
S.C...	42792.	134129.	34160.	15190.	8892.	7610.	2931.	452.	119526.	10521.	15544.	21445.
S.D...	10117.	11564.	4715.	3585.	2250.	2078.	578.	41.	1537.	18798.	27382.	31024.
TENN...	55383.	162773.	39565.	23483.	10536.	10725.	3838.	139.	100148.	15010.	34430.	51425.
TEX...	175501.	320128.	139902.	42329.	30200.	29638.	17350.	3171.	83709.	138939.	286274.	273655.
UTAH...	25761.	44555.	11791.	10225.	6400.	7048.	448.		0.	21664.	56147.	61949.
VER...	9423.	24871.	7014.	4365.	2756.	2667.	1985.	346.	0.	11150.	15229.	15815.
VA...	54831.	164321.	40225.	13367.	8143.	10028.	1805.	14536.	20219.	21807.	26159.	31609.
WASH...	80950.	215624.	44298.	41720.	21613.	22808.	2686.	28829.	56666.	34476.	58730.	60908.
W.VA...	29023.	81194.	25176.	7850.	5875.	6544.	72.		8236.	16728.	25871.	30211.
WIS...	64253.	173873.	44912.	23959.	17041.	17890.	948.	1263.	5591.	15572.	32276.	46297.
WY...	3915.	7785.	2959.	1836.	1910.	2063.	23.	0.	280.	11313.	23469.	31989.
DIVISIONS												
N.ENG.	264003.	511553.	393711.	116449.	62174.	63808.	27537.	9682.	139723.	126517.	185557.	196059.
M.A.	686622.	1430035.	1057023.	282983.	196944.	201083.	25192.	73600.	175933.	182567.	277415.	268276.
E.N.C.	725385.	1716684.	658317.	232115.	159958.	155419.	37205.	3800.	38924.	177939.	281416.	318679.
W.N.C.	211326.	410551.	246750.	85034.	53684.	53779.	17730.	6546.	514265.	210777.	353112.	400414.
S.A.	567839.	1502311.	482868.	178180.	93021.	98830.	21040.	77430.	680848.	142462.	274860.	323825.
E.S.C.	217063.	495852.	172382.	73886.	35233.	37956.	18827.	44371.	336545.	56069.	122323.	160146.
W.S.C.	330747.	624763.	260535.	99015.	57966.	57620.	37771.	9936.	159516.	202085.	411503.	392617.
MOUNT.	181853.	361251.	190206.	73769.	49616.	49987.	9574.	9191.	26339.	124533.	256815.	298048.
PAC.	625821.	1325312.	745292.	311564.	173843.	170221.	27581.	13868.	267340.	210700.	295482.	307017.
REGIONS												
N.E.	950625.	1941587.	1450734.	399433.	259118.	264891.	52729.	83282.	315655.	309084.	462972.	464334.
N.CT.	936711.	2127235.	905067.	317149.	213642.	209198.	54935.	10346.	553190.	388716.	634528.	719092.
SOUTH.	1115649.	2622926.	915786.	351082.	186220.	194407.	77638.	231737.	1176909.	400616.	808686.	876589.
WEST..	807675.	1686562.	935497.	385333.	223459.	220208.	37155.	23059.	293678.	335233.	552298.	605065.
NATION	3810659.	8378311.	4207084.	1452997.	882439.	888704.	222458.	248423.	2339432.	1433648.	2458483.	2665081.

NAME	TRANSPORTATION PROGRAMS						TREASURY PROGRAMS				
	HIGHWAY PLANNING CONSTRUCTION CFDA# - 20205			URBAN MASS TRANSIT ASSISTANCE CFDA# - 20500			GENERAL REVENUE SHARING			ANTI-RECESSION FISCAL ASSISTANCE	
	1975	1977	1978	1975	1977	1978	1975	1977	1978	1977	1978
STATES											
ALA...	140383.	154878.	158277.	835.	2000.	8551.	103368.	106944.	110680.	18930.	17399.
ALK...	153216.	136470.	126521.	1163.	2201.	1348.	81198.	13075.	16939.	4903.	8571.
ARZ...	140626.	131377.	130688.	7347.	8972.	6865.	62809.	63931.	71908.	18111.	15610.
ARK...	98242.	91010.	78019.	146.	523.	1408.	64435.	69983.	67717.	11515.	9802.
CAL...	518220.	640407.	476639.	107029.	165320.	301571.	651010.	709018.	751002.	254999.	204925.
COL...	166270.	181370.	132265.	16484.	23700.	36459.	65284.	73394.	75274.	9473.	9779.
CONN..	52231.	52565.	97329.	1567.	10159.	26904.	78815.	84471.	85293.	33048.	17902.
DEL...	22139.	21803.	28895.	2974.	2256.	1928.	18522.	21063.	21333.	7159.	6664.
D.C...	140780.	80020.	116802.	23080.	286536.	662086.	26924.	31996.	35547.	7211.	8838.
FLA...	203017.	323870.	252623.	13253.	34320.	119357.	269623.	202273.	203946.	73272.	49370.
GA....	235436.	161295.	181794.	136619.	507715.	119272.	188633.	140632.	145616.	27887.	25466.
HA....	140230.	45078.	68840.	2672.	7586.	11282.	130063.	31434.	33812.	9805.	8590.
IDA...	85386.	59365.	56341.	398.	637.	450.	26799.	24726.	24410.	3952.	2040.
ILL...	448635.	189878.	406899.	83259.	118794.	417064.	273538.	453522.	347559.	69296.	36965.
IND...	188467.	99839.	179842.	15712.	10641.	11554.	128479.	141091.	145447.	14041.	8255.
IOWA..	121102.	105312.	143193.	638.	7191.	5585.	86105.	81458.	80681.	3237.	873.
KAN...	113267.	131841.	115259.	471.	1165.	5108.	57506.	59459.	59356.	1388.	823.
KY....	125670.	172429.	130333.	7882.	5768.	23296.	99619.	110536.	113845.	14642.	4822.
LA....	196571.	198044.	135219.	2564.	10798.	31895.	139723.	147726.	153968.	31547.	35953.
MAINE.	34963.	37988.	44069.	130.	544.	1097.	38159.	40903.	41480.	14068.	13274.
MD....	292972.	178810.	230125.	121472.	200228.	223604.	119831.	132859.	136103.	24996.	19689.
MASS..	171210.	107581.	153609.	85973.	186193.	480233.	194716.	209875.	220457.	60674.	36361.
MI....	292752.	209235.	267540.	31390.	63160.	72983.	262050.	272916.	281200.	114407.	70193.
MINN..	148117.	153290.	157365.	16115.	17624.	44318.	122356.	133242.	136470.	15050.	6149.
MISS..	133759.	93077.	99026.	1413.	1992.	1972.	98580.	100504.	99977.	12999.	18955.
MO....	158675.	124433.	173200.	31961.	31702.	42289.	116635.	125035.	129116.	16803.	14853.
MONT..	116470.	86550.	80897.	20.	412.	2307.	24943.	24337.	24156.	4418.	2274.
NEB...	103432.	52338.	61506.	3641.	2941.	11651.	42353.	41810.	41864.	1940.	106.
NEV...	60054.	50443.	68371.	99.	76.	1359.	13476.	16345.	16911.	4818.	3120.
N.H...	35932.	32839.	36465.	1318.	441.	857.	19953.	21743.	22629.	1272.	844.
N.J...	81749.	145175.	119212.	139818.	37474.	107474.	193145.	208390.	214696.	91280.	80316.
N.M...	72570.	80828.	98750.	387.	2689.	2385.	38771.	43029.	46635.	11512.	12283.
N.Y...	199503.	619982.	571359.	166253.	310156.	749996.	687724.	750485.	769741.	307495.	283566.
N.C...	242167.	173926.	190457.	2670.	2914.	9731.	157768.	165717.	167669.	23681.	13787.
N.D...	65480.	36206.	51164.	24.	1185.	1545.	22206.	17706.	15694.	996.	421.
OHIO..	211992.	223806.	316786.	13371.	97381.	120302.	245438.	267787.	274222.	65608.	40312.
OKLA..	90726.	80264.	92248.	1621.	3568.	5424.	69327.	73147.	77884.	10919.	3247.
ORE...	168584.	135149.	256145.	2066.	8896.	13292.	61392.	71625.	74162.	26170.	18873.
PA....	403017.	122034.	160313.	74241.	121421.	355568.	325719.	349829.	348341.	107464.	81121.

NATIONAL SUMMARY DATA -- TABLE TWENTY-FIVE

| NAME | TRANSPORTATION PROGRAMS | | | | | | TREASURY PROGRAMS | | | | |
| | HIGHWAY PLANNING CONSTRUCTION CFDA# - 20205 | | | URBAN MASS TRANSIT ASSISTANCE CFDA# - 20500 | | | GENERAL REVENUE SHARING | | | ANTI-RECESSION FISCAL ASSISTANCE | |
	1975	1977	1978	1975	1977	1978	1975	1977	1978	1977	1978
STATES (CONT)											
R.I...	17194.	14757.	27264.	967.	2767.	11964.	27288.	28539.	29710.	10404.	7055.
S.C...	75202.	74406.	96908.	115.	5766.	653.	84902.	92712.	91646.	12244.	11335.
S.D...	60833.	61652.	36618.	0.	98.	413.	26128.	21252.	21092.	452.	225.
TENN..	142109.	138523.	164792.	1491.	11949.	18614.	120551.	123494.	123639.	18761.	10367.
TEX...	388078.	374167.	409312.	20287.	49639.	93310.	293239.	331705.	341753.	32458.	33475.
UTAH..	106552.	67390.	71370.	2049.	4975.	3840.	36315.	37219.	38741.	4174.	1463.
VER...	24017.	36442.	30709.	40.	200.	949.	17342.	18600.	20659.	6416.	4265.
VA....	146060.	330987.	274593.	42056.	15452.	20437.	121593.	142534.	139339.	14116.	13716.
WASH..	130733.	187340.	221265.	2297.	9223.	81925.	87251.	100025.	100834.	32318.	23501.
W.VA..	197184.	128309.	127105.	8898.	66299.	4211.	60857.	60962.	66336.	12035.	11646.
WIS...	120441.	113198.	155131.	24469.	10041.	53171.	154821.	161057.	160382.	19102.	6894.
WY....	85853.	39377.	53635.	0.	23.	113.	10840.	10778.	11884.	121.	53.
DIVISIONS											
N.ENG.	335548.	282174.	389445.	89995.	200304.	522005.	376273.	404132.	420228.	125881.	79701.
M.A...	684268.	887191.	850884.	380311.	469051.	1213038.	1206587.	1308704.	1332778.	506239.	445004.
E.N.C.	1262287.	835957.	1326198.	168201.	300017.	675075.	1064326.	1296374.	1208810.	282453.	162618.
W.N.C.	770906.	665074.	738304.	528851.	61906.	110909.	473289.	479962.	484274.	39864.	23451.
S.A...	1554956.	1473427.	1499303.	351137.	1121486.	1161280.	909092.	990747.	1007536.	202601.	160511.
E.S.C.	541922.	558907.	552428.	11621.	21710.	52433.	422118.	441479.	448141.	65333.	51543.
W.S.C.	773616.	743484.	714798.	24617.	64528.	132036.	566725.	621560.	641323.	86440.	82476.
MOUNT.	833782.	696700.	692318.	26783.	41432.	53779.	276576.	293759.	309919.	56580.	46623.
PAC...	1110983.	1144474.	1149410.	115227.	193225.	409418.	834650.	925177.	976749.	328195.	264460.
REGIONS											
N.E...	1019816.	1169365.	1240328.	470306.	669355.	1735044.	1582860.	1712836.	1753006.	632121.	524704.
N.CT..	2033193.	1501030.	2064502.	221051.	361923.	785984.	1537616.	1776336.	1693084.	322318.	186069.
SOUTH.	2870494.	2775818.	2766528.	387375.	1207723.	1345749.	1897934.	2053785.	2097001.	354374.	294530.
WEST..	1944765.	1841173.	1841728.	142010.	234707.	463197.	1111226.	1218936.	1286668.	384775.	311083.
NATION	7868267.	7287387.	7913087.	1220742.	2473708.	4329973.	6129636.	6761893.	6829759.	1693587.	1316337.

NATIONAL SUMMARY DATA -- TABLE TWENTY-SIX

VETERANS ADMINISTRATION PROGRAMS

NAME	DISABILITY COMPENSATION CFDA# - 64109			VETERANS HOSPITALIZATION CFDA# - 64009			READJUSTMENT TRAINING CFDA# - 64111		
	1975	1977	1978	1975	1977	1978	1975	1977	1978
STATES									
ALA...	64032.	79793.	86404.	67707.	86270.	93911.	91233.	91917.	80358.
ALK...	3331.	5967.	6137.	4492.	9469.	11881.	6955.	4256.	4063.
ARZ...	53298.	60778.	61195.	42037.	56831.	63767.	72414.	73238.	64100.
ARK...	58110.	52429.	55997.	51117.	66051.	71454.	36821.	46266.	37891.
CAL...	322010.	417439.	443915.	330216.	445813.	480847.	659905.	524644.	425292.
COL...	49967.	60493.	66675.	38985.	53839.	58847.	78960.	67391.	60297.
CONN.	45155.	65101.	68897.	38269.	50366.	53128.	45412.	31532.	27388.
DEL...	8143.	11539.	12761.	12210.	17162.	17000.	12683.	9598.	7290.
D.C...	16656.	17735.	98143.	100038.	45781.	150610.	45821.	10035.	8739.
FLA...	210232.	239347.	242892.	134747.	179301.	192857.	166920.	172029.	148150.
GA....	86980.	100516.	110023.	68651.	90295.	98293.	109234.	104497.	89127.
HA....	10734.	15087.	17845.	4818.	6213.	7094.	31502.	21217.	21274.
IDA...	14805.	17294.	17994.	6970.	10841.	11429.	15137.	12006.	11105.
ILL...	112148.	157401.	179730.	171919.	217080.	244173.	172647.	132351.	106738.
IND...	68844.	88266.	90214.	52948.	68365.	75494.	69550.	60880.	49794.
IOWA.	41084.	47761.	52198.	49308.	63767.	67588.	41730.	39916.	30346.
KAN..	34792.	42800.	47281.	47372.	61426.	62037.	38048.	33986.	31234.
KY...	58480.	70591.	74588.	46834.	59941.	64823.	54413.	54557.	44459.
LA...	61071.	69907.	73887.	52672.	68512.	75559.	62595.	55354.	47995.
MAINE.	26279.	26667.	27423.	18330.	23844.	25728.	21683.	19962.	18196.
MD.,.	59960.	78664.	52463.	43564.	54068.	59895.	70368.	51575.	46741.
MASS.	159154.	205466.	208486.	109496.	146514.	158262.	86733.	80060.	66770.
MI...	145460.	178983.	189898.	85113.	110814.	119504.	159965.	115473.	92337.
MINN.	71064.	88537.	88300.	61127.	78311.	83063.	72823.	64458.	53859.
MISS.	44415.	48073.	49939.	38688.	52086.	54186.	33138.	33056.	27992.
MO...	75506.	89877.	98435.	86666.	113844.	123281.	118644.	84664.	67348.
MONT.	13695.	16821.	17741.	10177.	13708.	14246.	13910.	11053.	10114.
NEB..	23688.	28034.	31737.	31192.	40679.	41760.	29866.	29561.	26469.
NEV..	11104.	16684.	17807.	9563.	13723.	15312.	14319.	13820.	12353.
N.H..	18876.	23210.	23426.	8888.	13640.	15849.	14728.	16327.	14577.
N.J..	112889.	169183.	174332.	65128.	84719.	90323.	82232.	59979.	51636.
N.M..	31091.	33033.	36251.	19623.	25701.	28653.	25365.	24494.	23297.
N.Y..	307205.	402766.	443931.	309292.	398154.	452555.	218468.	158073.	125199.
N.C..	91051.	102884.	110575.	371987.	95802.	103830.	126008.	126799.	109909.
N.D..	8513.	11855.	20243.	9904.	12125.	13909.	15137.	12246.	10365.
OHIO.	174330.	226253.	242020.	127656.	165612.	174067.	140736.	120365.	97230.
OKLA.	68103.	73501.	78689.	35314.	47549.	48938.	67095.	65950.	52628.
ORE..	42194.	50758.	55071.	40152.	54368.	50034.	50730.	44546.	38696.
PA...	204310.	271742.	304577.	156223.	205898.	224355.	146055.	94823.	83455.

(cont.)

NATIONAL SUMMARY DATA -- TABLE TWENTY-SIX

VETERANS ADMINISTRATION PROGRAMS

NAME	DISABILITY COMPENSATION CFDA# - 64109			VETERANS HOSPITALIZATION CFDA# - 64009			READJUSTMENT TRAINING CFDA# - 64111		
	1975	1977	1978	1975	1977	1978	1975	1977	1978
STATES (CONT)									
R.I...	24058.	29824.	50257.	16344.	22194.	22932.	27002.	18246.	14377.
S.C...	39233.	49124.	51454.	31614.	43344.	51550.	71186.	76191.	72161.
S.D...	11844.	13402.	15038.	26316.	34939.	33643.	13910.	17075.	10666.
TENN..	66993.	79252.	85115.	86399.	111078.	116534.	83460.	90495.	75064.
TEX...	242803.	287182.	308083.	186749.	249564.	267202.	262653.	248726.	224845.
UTAH..	16286.	22210.	24565.	20812.	26262.	30813.	30684.	25881.	23483.
VER...	9253.	9721.	10858.	10400.	14572.	14565.	5728.	4087.	3607.
VA....	93642.	108011.	89920.	80400.	97241.	102813.	81414.	82364.	76933.
WASH..	76616.	89413.	97664.	60723.	81036.	86473.	91642.	85824.	72841.
W.VA..	38123.	43061.	42684.	41474.	57246.	55270.	25365.	31142.	26465.
WIS...	67363.	87316.	94735.	74217.	93464.	99755.	72005.	54121.	45873.
WY....	6292.	8018.	8628.	13573.	17533.	18602.	6137.	5363.	5518.
DIVISIONS									
N.ENG.	282777.	359989.	389347.	201726.	271130.	290463.	201285.	170214.	144914.
M.A...	624403.	843691.	922840.	530643.	688772.	767234.	446756.	312875.	260290.
E.N.C.	568144.	738218.	796597.	512253.	655335.	712994.	614903.	483189.	391973.
W.N.C.	266491.	322266.	353231.	311885.	405091.	425282.	330157.	281907.	230287.
S.A...	644020.	750881.	810916.	584686.	680239.	832118.	708999.	664230.	585516.
E.S.C.	233920.	277708.	296045.	239628.	309374.	329454.	262244.	270024.	227874.
W.S.C.	430087.	483018.	516656.	325852.	431676.	463154.	429154.	416296.	363359.
MOUNT.	196537.	235331.	250857.	161740.	218438.	241669.	256925.	233247.	210268.
PAC...	454885.	578664.	620633.	440401.	596899.	636329.	840735.	680487.	562165.
REGIONS									
N.E...	907180.	1203680.	1312187.	732369.	959901.	1057697.	648041.	483088.	405204.
N.CT..	834635.	1060484.	1149828.	824138.	1060426.	1138276.	945060.	765096.	622260.
SOUTH.	1308027.	1511608.	1623617.	1150167.	1421290.	1624725.	1400407.	1350551.	1176749.
WEST..	651423.	813995.	871490.	602141.	815337.	877998.	1097660.	913733.	772433.
NATION	3701264.	4589768.	4957122.	3308815.	4256954.	4698696.	4091168.	3512468.	2976646.

COUNTY DATA -- TABLE TWENTY-SEVEN: APPENDIX 1

H.E.W. PROGRAM

FEDERAL SHARE: A.F.D.C.

NAME	1975	1977	1978
STATES			
ALA....	49692.	61127.	61943.
ALK....	6843.	8189.	9800.
ARZ....	23527.	21554.	18416.
ARK....	37642.	37936.	39486.
CAL....	748075.	1005944.	1045695.
COL....	45090.	45496.	44339.
CONN...	61427.	72018.	83626.
DEL....	11988.	14816.	14548.
D.C....	47684.	49890.	52884.
FLA....	85021.	109520.	101275.
GA.....	110318.	97609.	79104.
HA.....	27933.	38548.	43240.
IDA....	12271.	15062.	13910.
ILL....	366795.	371178.	362945.
IND....	59627.	72494.	74606.
IOWA...	52564.	54094.	61542.
KAN....	33357.	43399.	41379.
KY.....	92454.	105546.	93231.
LA.....	74660.	76436.	78889.
MAINE.	36871.	34672.	37729.
MD.....	77671.	86974.	91807.
MASS...	197498.	237623.	275830.
MI.....	331244.	385970.	410796.
MINN...	78995.	93466.	100633.
MISS...	28584.	33354.	34400.
MO.....	83206.	92991.	81758.
MONT...	10276.	9329.	9434.
NEB....	16244.	18914.	23802.
NEV....	5707.	5310.	5297.
N.H....	13798.	14084.	13662.
N.J....	220873.	288619.	262578.
N.M....	25003.	26961.	25877.
N.Y....	864581.	1207947.	1057944.
N.C....		96990.	98100.
N.D....	9244.	8065.	8191.
OHIO..	201354.	254447.	256351.
OKLA..	53217.	51138.	55288.
ORE...	57791.	88806.	93702.
PA....	378301.	441442.	447036.

(cont.)

COUNTY DATA -- TABLE TWENTY-SEVEN: APPENDIX 1

H.E.W. PROGRAM

FEDERAL SHARE: A.F.D.C.

NAME	1975	1977	1978
STATES (CONT)			
R.I....	28155.	36282.	34259.
S.C....	38399.	40541.	46161.
S.D....	14340.	13287.	12510.
TENN..	68306.	79559.	61644.
TEX...	120730.	94752.	100598.
UTAH..	22723.	25674.	27584.
VER...	15954.	17458.	16654.
VA....	88926.	86818.	92052.
WASH..	75259.	94922.	100084.
W.VA..	38157.	39348.	41774.
WIS...	106492.	155654.	152075.
WY....	2727.	3489.	3797.
DIVISIONS			
N.ENG.	353703.	412136.	461759.
M.A...	1463755.	1938008.	1767558.
E.N.C.	1065512.	1239743.	1256773.
W.N.C.	287951.	324215.	329815.
S.A...	582047.	622506.	617704.
E.S.C.	239036.	279586.	251217.
W.S.C.	286249.	260261.	274260.
MOUNT.	147324.	152877.	148654.
PAC...	915901.	1236408.	1292521.
REGIONS			
N.E...	1817458.	2350144.	2229317.
N.CT..	1353463.	1563959.	1586588.
SOUTH.	1107333.	1162353.	1143181.
WEST..	1063225.	1389284.	1441174.
NATION	5341479.	6465741.	6400261.

A BREAKOUT OF FEDERAL PROGRAMS
BY C.E.D.A. CODE AND LEVEL OF REPORTING

PROGRAM	CFDA CODE			LEVEL OF REPORTING					
				COUNTY			CITY		
	FY1975	FY1977	FY1978	75	77	78	75	77	78
DEPARTMENT OF AGRICULTURE									
1) WATER WASTE DISPOSAL GRANTS (S)	10418	10418	10418	YES	YES	YES	NO	NO	NO
2) FOOD DISTRIBUTION (S)	10550	10550	10550	YES	YES	YES	YES	YES	YES
3) FOOD STAMPS (S)	10551	10551	10551	YES	YES	YES	YES	YES	YES
4) NATIONAL SCHOOL LUNCH (S)	10555	10555	10555	YES	YES	YES	NO	NO	YES
5) EMERGENCY DISASTER LOANS (H)	10404	10404	10404	YES	YES	YES	NO	NO	NO
6) LOW/MODERATE INCOME HOUSING LOANS (H)	10410	10410	10410	YES	YES	YES	NO	NO	NO
7) RURAL ELECTRIC LOANS (H)	10850	10850	10850	YES	YES	YES	NO	NO	NO
8) COMMODITY LOANS (H)	10051	10051	10051	YES	YES	YES	YES	YES	YES
9) VARIOUS AGRICULTURE LOANS (H)	ACC #	ACC #	ACC #	YES	YES	YES	NO	NO	NO
DEPARTMENT OF COMMERCE									
10) LOCAL PUBLIC WORKS (EMERGENCY-1977) (H)	11300	11300	11300	YES	YES	YES	YES	YES	YES
COMMUNITY SERVICES ADMINISTRATION									
11) COMMUNITY ACTION (S)	49002	49002	49002	YES	YES	YES	YES	YES	YES
DEPARTMENT OF DEFENSE									
12) MILITARY PAYROLL	ACC #	ACC #	ACC #	YES	YES	YES	YES	YES	YES
13) CIVILIAN PAYROLL	ACC #	ACC #	ACC #	YES	YES	YES	YES	YES	YES
ENVIRONMENTAL PROTECTION AGENCY									
14) WASTEWATER TREATMENT (H)	66418	66418	66418	YES	YES	YES	YES	YES	YES
DEPARTMENT OF HEALTH, EDUCATION, AND WELFARE									
15) TITLE #1 EDUCATION (S)	13428	13428	13428	YES	YES	YES	NO	NO	NO
16) SCHOOLS AFFECTED BY FEDERAL INSTALLATIONS (SAFA) (S)	13478	13478	13478	YES	YES	YES	YES	YES	YES
17) VOCATIONAL EDUCATION (S)	13493	13493	13493	NO	NO	NO	NO	NO	NO
18) REHABILITATION SUCS FACILITIES (S)	13624	13624	13624	NO	NO	NO	NO	NO	NO
19) SOCIAL SUC-LOW-INCOME PUB. ASST. RECIP (S)	13754	13754	13642	YES	YES	YES	NO	NO	NO
20) MEDICAID (S)	13714	13714	13714	YES	YES	YES	NO	NO	NO
21) MEDICARE - HOSPITALS (S)	13800	13800	13773	YES	YES	YES	NO	NO	NO
22) MEDICARE - SUPPLEMENTAL (S)	13801	13801	13774	YES	YES	YES	NO	NO	NO
23) PUBLIC ASSISTANCE (STATE AID) (S)	13761	13761	13808	YES	YES	YES	NO	NO	NO
24) COMMUNITY HEALTH PROGRAMS (S)	13224	13224	13224	YES	YES	YES	YES	YES	YES
25) SSA - DISABILITY (S)	13802	13802	13803	YES	YES	YES	YES	YES	YES
26) SSA - RETIREMENT (S)	13803	13803	13803	YES	YES	YES	YES	YES	YES
27) SSA - SURVIVORS (S)	13805	13805	13805	YES	YES	YES	YES	YES	YES
28) SUPPLEMENTAL SECURITY INCOME (SSI) (S)	13807	13807	13807	YES	YES	YES	NO	NO	NO

NOTE: (H)DEFINES PROGRAMS CODED AS HARD DOLLARS; (S)DEFINES PROGRAMS CODED AS SOFT DOLLARS.

A BREAKOUT OF FEDERAL PROGRAMS
BY C.E.D.A. CODE AND LEVEL OF REPORTING

PROGRAM	CFDA CODE			LEVEL OF REPORTING					
				COUNTY			CITY		
	FY1975	FY1977	FY1978	75	77	78	75	77	78
DEPARTMENT OF HOUSING AND URBAN DEVELOPMENT									
29) COMMUNITY DEVELOPMENT BLOCK GRANTS (H)	14218	14218	14218	YES	YES	YES	YES	YES	YES
30) COMMUNITY DEVELOPMENT DISCRETIONARY GRANTS (H)	*	14219	14219	NO	YES	YES	NO	YES	YES
31) SECTION 8 HOUSING ASSISTANCE (H)	14156	14156	14156	YES	YES	YES	YES	YES	YES
32) MORTGAGE INSURANCE -REGULAR HOMES (H)	14118	14117	14117	YES	YES	YES	NO	NO	NO
33) LOW/MOD INCOME HOUSING-MKT INT RATE (H)	14137	14137	14137	YES	YES	YES	NO	NO	NO
34) PROPERTY IMPROVEMENT LOAN INSURANCE (H)	14142	14142	14142	YES	YES	YES	NO	NO	NO
35) OTHER MORTGAGE PROGRAMS2 (H)	ACC #	ACC #	ACC #	YES	YES	YES	YES	YES	YES
DEPARTMENT OF LABOR									
36) COMPREHENSIVE EMPLOYMENT TRAINING ASSISTANCE (S)	ACC #	17232	17232	YES	YES	YES	YES	YES	YES
37) UNEMPLOYMENT INSURANCE (S)	ACC #	17225	17225	YES	YES	YES	YES	YES	YES
LAW ENFORCEMENT ASSISTANCE ADMINISTRATION									
38) LAW ENFORCEMENT PROJECT GRANTS (S)	*	16501	16501	YES	YES	YES	YES	YES	YES
39) LAW ENFORCEMENT BLOCK GRANTS (S)	ACC #	16502	16502	YES	YES	YES	YES	YES	YES
SMALL BUSINESS ADMINISTRATION									
40) PHYSICAL DISASTER LOANS (H)	ACC #	59008	59008	YES	YES	YES	YES	YES	YES
41) SMALL BUSINESS LOANS (H)	ACC #	59012	59012	YES	YES	YES	YES	YES	YES
DEPARTMENT OF TRANSPORTATION									
42) HIGHWAY PLANNING CONSTRUCTION (H)	20205	20205	20205	YES	YES	YES	YES	YES	YES
43) URBAN MASS TRANSIT ASSISTANCE (H)	20500	20500	20500	YES	YES	YES	YES	YES	YES
TREASURY DEPARTMENT									
44) GENERAL REVENUE SHARING (S)	ACC #	ACC #	ACC #	YES	YES	YES	YES	YES	YES
45) ANTI-RECESSION FISCAL ASSISTANCE (S)	*	ACC #	ACC #	NO	YES	NO	NO	YES	YES
VETERANS ADMINISTRATION									
46) VETERAN'S DISABILITY COMPENSATION (S)	64109	64109	64109	YES	YES	YES	YES	YES	YES
47) VETERAN'S HOSPITALIZATION (S)	ACC #	64009	64009	YES	YES	YES	YES	YES	YES
48) VETERAN'S READJUSTMENT TRAINING (S)	64111	64111	64111	YES	YES	YES	YES	YES	YES

NOTE: (H)DEFINES PROGRAMS CODED AS HARD DOLLARS; (S)DEFINES PROGRAMS CODED AS SOFT DOLLARS.

NOTES

"*" MEANS THE ABSENSE OF PROGRAM DATA IN A GIVEN YEAR.

1 THIS CATEGORY INCLUDES THE FOLLOWING CFDA PROGRAMS:

```
10.405  FARM LABOR HOUSING LOANS, FMHA
10.406  FARM OPERATING LOANS, FMHA
10.407  FARM OWNERSHIP NONFARM ENTERPRISE LNS, FMHA
10.408  GRAZING ASSOCIATION LOANS, FMHA
10.409  IRRIG/DRAIN OTHER S W CONS LOANS, FMHA
10.411  RURAL HOUSING SITE LOANS, FMHA
10.413  RECREATION FACILITIES LOANS, FMHA
10.414  RESOURCE CONS AND DEVELOPMENT LOANS, FMHA
10.415  RURAL RENTAL HOUSING LOANS, FMHA
10.416  SOIL AND WATER LOANS TO INDIVIDUALS, FMHA
10.418  WATER AND WASTE DISPOSAL SYSTEM LOANS, FMHA
10.419  FLOOD PREVENTION LOANS, FMHA
10.419  WATERSHED PROTECTION LOANS, FMHA
10.421  INDIAN TRIBES  TRIBAL CORP LOANS, FMHA
10.422  BUSINESS AND INDUSTRIAL LOANS, FMHA
10.423  COMMUNITY FACILITIES LOANS, FMHA
10.425  EMERGENCY LIVESTOCK LOANS, FMHA
10.428  ECONOMIC EMERGENCY LOANS, FMHA
10.851  RURAL TELEPHONE LNS  LN GUARANTEES, REA
```

SOME VARIATION EXISTS FROM YEAR TO YEAR ON THE TOTAL NUMBER OF PROGRAMS IN THIS CATEGORY.

2 THIS CATEGORY INCLUDES THE FOLLOWING CFDA PROGRAMS:

```
14.103  MTGE INS-RENTAL HOUSING ASST PROJECTS, H
14.105  MTGE INS-LOWER INCOME FAMILY HOMES, H
14.108  LOAN INSURANCE-MAJOR HOME IMPROVEMENTS, H
14.110  MOBILE HOME LOAN INSURANCE, H
14.112  MTGE INS-CONDOMINIUM HOUSING PROJECTS, H
14.115  MTGE INS-SALES TYPE CO-OP PROJECTS, H
14.118  MTGE INS-HOMES FOR CERTIFIED VETERANS, H
14.120  MTGE INS-LOW/MODERATE INCOME FAM HOMES, H
14.121  MTGE INS-HOMES IN OUTLYING AREAS, H
14.122  MORTGAGE INSURANCE-URBAN RENEWAL HOMES, H
14.123  MTGE INS-HOMES IN DECLINING AREAS, H
14.125  MTGE INS-LAND DEVELOPMENT NEW COMMUN, H
14.127  MORTGAGE INSURANCE-MOBILE HOME PARKS, H
14.128  MORTGAGE INSURANCE-HOSPITALS, H
14.129  MORTGAGE INSURANCE-NURSING HOMES, H
14.133  MORTGAGE INSURANCE-CONDOMINIUM HOMES, H
14.134  MTGE INS-REGULAR RENTAL HOUSING PROJ, H
14.137  MTGE INS-LOW/MOD INC HOUS-MKT INT RATE, H
```

1

2

```
14.138  MTGE INS-RENTAL HOUSING FOR THE ELDERLY, H
14.139  MTGE INS-URBAN RENEWAL HOUSING PROJECTS, H
14.140  MTGE INS-HOMES FOR SPECIAL CREDIT RISKS, H
14.142  PROPERTY IMPROVEMENT LOAN INSURANCE, H
14.151  MTGE INS-MULTIFAMILY SUPPLEMENTAL LOANS, H
14.152  MORTGAGE INSURANCE-EXPERIMENTAL HOMES, H
14.155  MTGE INS-PURCHASE/REFIN EXISTING HOUS, H
```

SOME VARIATION EXISTS FROM YEAR TO YEAR ON THE TOTAL NUMBER OF PROGRAMS IN THIS CATEGORY.

About the Authors

Thomas J. Anton is Professor in the Department of Political Science and the Institute for Public Policy Studies at the University of Michigan. In addition, he is Director of the Ph.D. Program in Urban and Regional Planning and a Faculty Associate in the Center for Political Studies of the Institute for Social Research at the University of Michigan.

Jerry P. Cawley is a Ph.D. candidate in political science at the University of Michigan, affiliated with the Center for Political Studies, Institute for Social Research.

Kevin L. Kramer is a Ph.D. candidate in political science at the University of Michigan, also affiliated with the Center for Political Studies, Institute for Social Research.

HJ   Anton, Thomas Julius
2051   Moving money : an empirical
.A78   analysis of Federal expendi-
         ture patterns

~~Don Parker~~ MAY 0 3 1989
~~247-53-3561~~ ~~1988~~

HJ   Anton, Thomas Julius
2051   Moving money : an empirical
.A78   analysis of Federal expenditure
          patterns